It Pays to Get Certified

In a digital world, digital literacy is an essential survival skill. Certification proves you have the knowledge and skill to solve business problems in virtually any business environment. Certifications are highly-valued credentials that qualify you for jobs, increased compensation, and promotion.

CompTIA Network+ certification held by many IT Staff in organizations: - 21% of IT staff within a random sampling of U.S. organizations within a cross section of industry verticals hold Network+ certification.

- **The CompTIA Network+ credential –** proves knowledge of networking features and functions and is the leading vendor-neutral certification for networking professionals.
- **Starting Salary** - The average starting salary of network engineers can be up to $70,000.
- **Career Pathway –** CompTIA Network+ is the first step in starting a networking career, and is recognized by Microsoft as part of their MS program. Other corporations, such as Novell, Cisco and HP also recognize CompTIA Network+ as part of their certification tracks.
- **More than 260,000** – individuals worldwide are CompTIA Network+ certified.
- **Mandated/Recommended by organizations worldwide -** such as Cisco, HP, Ricoh, the U.S. State Department, and U.S. government contractors such as EDS, General Dynamics, and Northrop Grumman.

How Certification Helps Your Career

IT Knowledge and Skills Gets Jobs

Certifications are essential credentials that qualify you for jobs, increased compensation, and promotion.

Retain your Job and Salary

Make your expertise stand above the rest. Competence is usually retained during times of change.

Want to Change Jobs

Certifications qualify you for new opportunities, whether locked into a current job, see limited advancement, or need to change careers.

Stick Out from the Resume Pile

Hiring managers can demand the strongest skill set.

Steps to Getting Certified and Staying Certified	
Review Exam Objectives	Review the certification objectives to make sure you know what is covered in the exam. http://certification.comptia.org/Training/testingcenters/examobjectives.aspx
Practice for the Exam	After you have studied for the certification, take a free assessment and sample test to get an idea of what type of questions might be on the exam. http://certification.comptia.org/Training/testingcenters/samplequestions.aspx **Error! Hyperlink reference not valid.**
Purchase an Exam Voucher	Purchase your exam voucher on the CompTIA Marketplace, which is located at: http://www.comptiastore.com/
Take the Test!	Select a certification exam provider and schedule a time to take your exam. You can find exam providers at the following link: http://certification.comptia.org/Training/testingcenters.aspx
Stay Certified! **Continuing Education**	Effective January 1, 2011, CompTIA Network+ certifications are valid for three years from the date of certification. There are a number of ways the certification can be renewed. For more information go to: http://certification.comptia.org/getCertified/steps_to_certification/stayCertified.aspx

How to obtain more information

- **Visit CompTIA online** - www.comptia.org to learn more about getting CompTIA certified.
- **Contact CompTIA** - call 866-835-8020 ext. 5 or email questions@comptia.org
- **Join the IT Pro Community** – http://itpro.comptia.org to join the IT community to get relevant career information.
- **Connect with us :**    

CompTIA® Network+® (Exam N10-005)

Part Number: 085708
Course Edition: 1.1

NOTICES

How to Become CompTIA Certified: This training material can help you prepare for and pass the related CompTIA certification exam or exams. In order to achieve CompTIA certification, you must register for and pass a CompTIA certification exam or exams. In order to become CompTIA certified, you must:

1. Select a certification exam provider. For more information, visit **www.comptia.org/certifications/testprep.aspx**.
2. Register for and schedule a time to take the CompTIA certification exam(s) at a convenient location.
3. Read and sign the Candidate Agreement, which will be presented at the time of the exam(s). The text of the Candidate Agreement can be found at **www.comptia.org/certifications/policies/agreement.aspx**.

HELP US IMPROVE OUR COURSEWARE

Your comments are important to us. Please contact us at Element K Press LLC, 1-800-478-7788, 500 Canal View Boulevard, Rochester, NY 14623, Attention: Product Planning, or through our Web site at **http://support.elementkcourseware.com.**

CompTIA® Network+®
(Exam N10-005)

Lesson 1: Network Theory

Lesson 2: Network Communications Methods

Lesson 3: Network Media and Hardware

Lesson 4: Network Implementations

Lesson 5: Networking Models

Lesson 6: TCP/IP Addressing and Data Delivery

Lesson 7: TCP/IP Services

Lesson 8: LAN Infrastructure

Lesson 9: WAN Infrastructure

Lesson 10: Remote Networking

Lesson 11: System Security

About This Course

The *CompTIA Network+® (Exam N10-005)* course builds on your existing user-level knowledge and experience with personal computer operating systems and networks to present the fundamental skills and concepts that you will need to use on the job in any type of networking career. If you are pursuing a CompTIA technical certification path, the CompTIA A+ certification is an excellent first step to take before preparing for the CompTIA Network+ certification.

The *CompTIA Network+® (Exam N10-005)* course can benefit you in two ways. It can assist you if you are preparing to take the CompTIA Network+ examination (Exam N10-005). Also, if your job duties include network troubleshooting, installation, or maintenance, or if you are preparing for any type of network-related career, it provides the background knowledge and skills you will require to be successful.

Course Description

Target Student

This course is intended for entry-level computer support professionals with a basic knowledge of computer hardware, software, and operating systems to prepare for the CompTIA® Network+® (Exam N10-005), or who wish to increase their knowledge and understanding of networking concepts and acquire the required skills to prepare for a career in network support or administration. A typical student taking up the CompTIA® Network+® (Exam N10-005) course should have a minimum of nine months or more of professional computer support experience as a PC or help desk technician. Networking experience is helpful but not mandatory; A+ certification or equivalent skills and knowledge is helpful but not mandatory.

Course Prerequisites

To ensure your success, you will need basic Windows end-user computer skills. To meet this prerequisite, you can take any one or more of the following Element K courses, or have equivalent experience:

- *Introduction to Personal Computers: Using Windows XP*
- *Windows XP Professional: An Introduction*
- *Introduction to Personal Computers: Using Windows 7*
- *Microsoft® Windows® 7: Level 1*
- *Microsoft® Windows® 7: Level 2*

In addition, we highly recommend that you hold the CompTIA A+ certification, or have equivalent skills and knowledge. You may want to take the following Element K course: *CompTIA® A+® Certification: A Comprehensive Approach for All 2009 Exam Objectives (Windows® 7)*

Course Objectives

In this course, you will describe the major networking technologies, systems, skills, and tools in use in modern networks.

You will:

- Identify the basic network theory concepts.
- Identify the major network communications methods.
- Describe network media and hardware components.
- Identify the major types of network implementations.
- Identify the components of a TCP/IP network implementation.
- Identify TCP/IP addressing and data delivery methods.
- Identify the major services deployed on TCP/IP networks.
- Identify the components of a LAN implementation.
- Identify the infrastructure of a WAN implementation.
- Identify the components of a remote network implementation.
- Identify the major issues and methods to secure systems on a network.
- Identify the major issues and technologies in network security.
- Identify network security threats and attacks.
- Identify the tools, methods, and techniques used in managing a network.
- Describe troubleshooting of issues on a network.

Certification

This course is designed to help you prepare for the following certification.

Certification Path: The CompTIA® Network+® (Exam N10-005) course is designed to help you prepare for the N10-005 exam. Taking this course and using this student guide will help you prepare for the certification. You should also refer to the exam objectives to see how they map to the course content.

How to Use This Book

As a Learning Guide

This book is divided into lessons and topics, covering a subject or a set of related subjects. In most cases, lessons are arranged in order of increasing proficiency.

The results-oriented topics include relevant and supporting information you need to master the content. Each topic has various types of activities designed to enable you to practice the guidelines and procedures as well as to solidify your understanding of the informational material presented in the course.

At the back of the book, you will find a glossary of the definitions of the terms and concepts used throughout the course. You will also find an index to assist in locating information within the instructional components of the book.

In the Classroom

This book is intended to enhance and support the in-class experience. Procedures and guidelines are presented in a concise fashion along with activities and discussions. Information is provided for reference and reflection in such a way as to facilitate understanding and practice.

Each lesson may also include a Lesson Lab or various types of simulated activities. You will find the files for the simulated activities along with the other course files on the enclosed CD-ROM. If your course manual did not come with a CD-ROM, please go to **www.elementk.com/courseware-file-downloads** to download the files. If included, these interactive activities enable you to practice your skills in an immersive business environment, or to use hardware and software resources not available in the classroom. The course files that are available on the CD-ROM or by download may also contain sample files, support files, and additional reference materials for use both during and after the course.

As a Teaching Guide

Effective presentation of the information and skills contained in this book requires adequate preparation. As such, as an instructor, you should familiarize yourself with the content of the entire course, including its organization and approaches. You should review each of the student activities and exercises so you can facilitate them in the classroom.

Throughout the book, you may see Instructor Notes that provide suggestions, answers to problems, and supplemental information for you, the instructor. You may also see references to "Additional Instructor Notes" that contain expanded instructional information; these notes appear in a separate section at the back of the book. PowerPoint slides may be provided on the included course files, which are available on the enclosed CD-ROM or by download from **www.elementk.com/courseware-file-downloads**. The slides are also referred to in the text. If you plan to use the slides, it is recommended to display them during the corresponding content as indicated in the instructor notes in the margin.

The course files may also include assessments for the course, which can be administered diagnostically before the class, or as a review after the course is completed. These exam-type questions can be used to gauge the students' understanding and assimilation of course content.

As a Review Tool

Any method of instruction is only as effective as the time and effort you, the student, are willing to invest in it. In addition, some of the information that you learn in class may not be important to you immediately, but it may become important later. For this reason, we encourage you to spend some time reviewing the content of the course after your time in the classroom.

As a Reference

The organization and layout of this book make it an easy-to-use resource for future reference. Taking advantage of the glossary, index, and table of contents, you can use this book as a first source of definitions, background information, and summaries.

Course Icons

Icon	Description
	A **Caution Note** makes students aware of potential negative consequences of an action, setting, or decision that are not easily known.
	Display Slide provides a prompt to the instructor to display a specific slide. Display Slides are included in the Instructor Guide only.
	An **Instructor Note** is a comment to the instructor regarding delivery, classroom strategy, classroom tools, exceptions, and other special considerations. Instructor Notes are included in the Instructor Guide only.
	Notes Page indicates a page that has been left intentionally blank for students to write on.
	A **Student Note** provides additional information, guidance, or hints about a topic or task.
	A **Version Note** indicates information necessary for a specific version of software.

Course Requirements

Hardware

This course requires one computer for each student, one computer for the instructor, and one computer to function as a classroom server. Each computer will need:

- 1.4 gigahertz (GHz) (single 64–bit) processor or 1.3 GHz (dual core) processor or above.
- 4 GB of RAM or greater.
- 320 GB of hard disk or larger.
- Super VGA (SVGA) or higher resolution monitor capable of a screen resolution of at least 1024 x 768 pixels, at least 256-color display, and a video adapter with at least 64 MB of memory.
- A mouse or other pointing device.
- A CD/DVD-ROM drive.
- Network adapter and cabling connecting each classroom computer.
- Network interface card and network cabling.
- A projection system for the instructor.
- Internet access.
- To support the activities in Lesson 3, the instructor should provide as many physical examples of different types of network media and connectors as possible.
- For the data backup activity in Appendix D, the instructor needs to provide an alternative backup location (such as a removable USB drive or a folder on the hard disk).
- To support the activities in Lessons 3 and 15, the instructor should provide as many physical examples of hardware tools as possible.

- For the optional cable assembly activity in Lesson 15, the instructor will need to provide students with raw cable, the appropriate connectors, the appropriate crimping tool, a cable tester, and an optional eye loupe.

Software

The setup instructions and the classroom activities were designed and tested for systems running Windows Server 2008 R2 (Standard Edition). It is very possible that the activities will work properly or with little alteration if the classroom systems are running Windows Server 2008 instead, but Element K has not tested this configuration.

- Microsoft Windows Server 2008 R2, Standard Edition, with sufficient licenses.
- The Microsoft Network Monitor should be installed on the Instructor and Student machines. It is available at **www.microsoft.com/downloads/en/details.aspx?FamilyID=983b941d-06cb-4658-b7f6-3088333d062f&displaylang=en**. Copy the NM34_x64.exe file into the **Tools** folder that is created during the extraction of the course data files.
- Third-party security tool: SuperScan. It is available at **www.mcafee.com/us/downloads/free-tools/superscan.aspx**. Copy the file into the **Tools** folder that is created during the extraction of the course data files.

Class Setup

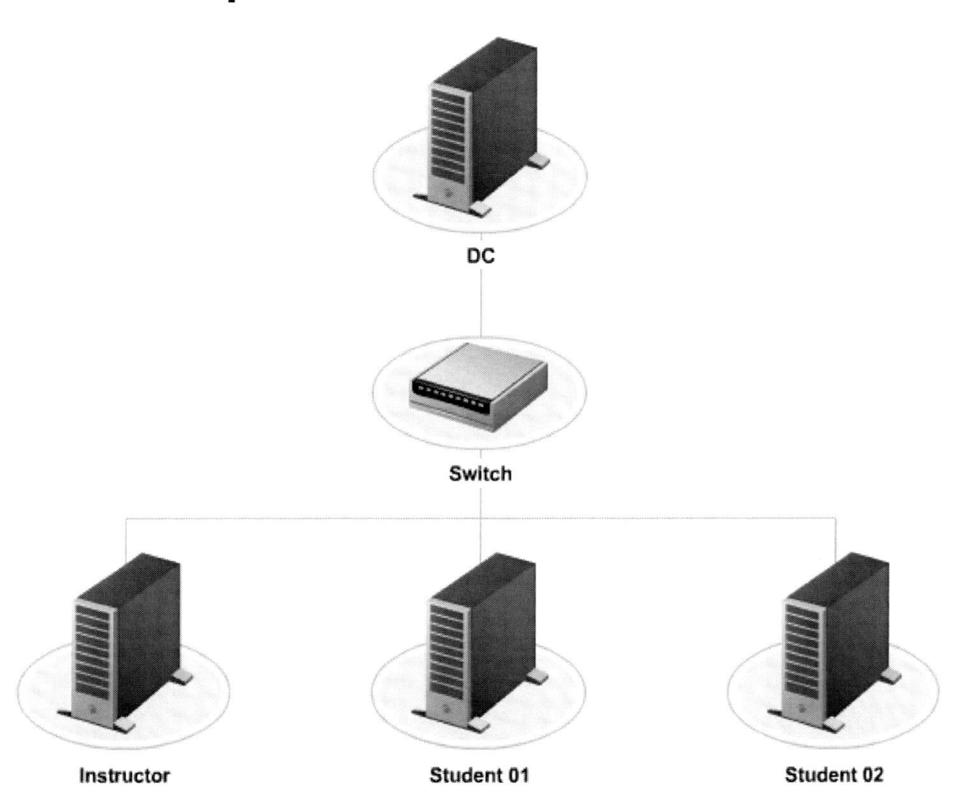

Figure 0-1: *A network diagram of the class setup. The number of student computers will differ.*

On the Domain Controller:

See your manufacturer's reference manual for hardware considerations that apply to your specific hardware setup.

Approximate initial setup time: 3 to 4 hours for the domain controller. It will take about 45 minutes to set up each student computer if you install them individually, but you can save a great deal of time by either performing the operating system installation simultaneously on all systems by sharing the installation source files rather than running all directly from the installation DVD, or by installing one system and then imaging it to the other computers.

Once you have created the basic installation for the instructor and student computers, imaging the systems is highly recommended, as this will make it easier to set up class or lab activities repeatedly. You may wish to run the image within a virtual machine environment.

The system designated as Domain Controller needs to be a dedicated server. This system will remain idle throughout the course. Activities should not be performed on this computer.

1. Boot the computer with the Windows Server 2008 R2 installation DVD. Press a key when prompted to boot from DVD or CD to start the Windows Server 2008 R2 setup program.
2. Install a new copy of Windows Server 2008 R2 using the following parameters:
    a. In the Install Windows window, accept the default values to set **Language to install** to **English, Time and currency format** to **English (United States), Keyboard or input method** to **US.** Click **Next.**
    b. Click **Install now.**
    c. On the **Type your product key for activation** page, type your product key and click **Next.**
    d. On the **Select the operating system you want to install** page, verify that **Windows Server 2008 R2 Standard (Full Installation)** is selected and click **Next.**
    e. On the **Please read the license terms** page, read the terms, check **I accept the license terms,** and click **Next.**
    f. On the **Which type of installation do you want** page, click **Custom (advanced).**
    g. Delete the existing partitions.
        1. Click **Drive options (advanced),**
        2. Select the drives one at a time and click **Delete.** In the **Install Windows** dialog box, click **OK.** Repeat the step till all the drives are deleted.
    h. Select the **Disk 0 Unallocated Space** and click **New.** In the **Size** text box, double-click and type ***41060*** and click **Apply** to allocate 40 GB to the C drive.
    i. In the **Install Windows** message box, click **OK** to allows Windows to create additional partitions for system files.
    j. Select the **Disk 0 Unallocated Space** and click **New.** In the **Size** text box, double-click and type ***61440*** and click **Apply** to allocate 60 GB.

k. Select the **Disk 0 Unallocated Space** and click **New.** In the **Size** text box, double-click and type ***61440*** and click **Apply** to allocate 60 GB.
l. Select the **Disk 0 Partition 2** and click **Next.**
m. On the **Installing Windows** page, observe the progress of the installation. Wait for the installation to complete. The system will automatically reboot.
n. Wait approximately 15 minutes for Windows to set up your computer. When prompted to press a key to boot from DVD or CD, ignore the message. At this point, it will be safe for you to remove the disc from the DVD drive.
o. The **Installing Windows** page will be displayed with the updated installation details. The system will automatically reboot.

3. On rebooting, the system will display a message "The user's password must be changed before logging on the first time." Click **OK** to change the password.
4. For the **Administrator** user, in the **New password** and the **Confirm password** text boxes, type ***!Pass1234*** as the password and click the right arrow button.
5. The message "Your password has been changed." is displayed. Click **OK.**
6. For the domain controller, change the computer name to DC.
   a. In the Initial Configuration Tasks window, in the **Provide Computer Information** section, click the **Provide computer name and domain** link.
   b. In the **System Properties** dialog box, click **Change.**
   c. In the **Computer Name/Domain Changes** dialog box, in the **Computer name** text box, select the existing computer name and type ***DC*** and click **OK.**
   d. In the **Computer Name/Domain Changes** message box, click **OK** to restart the computer.
   e. In the **System Properties** dialog box, click **Close.**
   f. In the **Microsoft Windows** dialog box, click **Restart Later.**
7. Configure the IP address.
   a. In the **Provide Computer Information** section, click the **Configure networking** link.
   b. In the Network Connections window, select the **Local Area Connection** icon, right-click, and choose **Properties.**
   c. In the **Local Area Connection Properties** dialog box, in the **This connection uses the following items** section, select **Internet Protocol Version 4 (TCP/IPv4).** Click **Properties.**
   d. In the **Internet Protocol Version 4 (TCP/IPv4) Properties** dialog box, select the **Use the following IP address** option. Configure it with a static IP address of **192.168.1.200** and press **Tab** to automatically populate the subnet mask of **255.255.255.0.** Enter this same IP address as the **Preferred DNS server** address. (You will install and configure DNS later.) If necessary, specify the default Gateway as appropriate for your environment.
   e. In the **Internet Protocol Version 4 (TCP/IPv4) Properties** dialog box, click **OK.**
   f. If necessary, to disable the IPv6 protocol, in the **Local Area Connection Properties** dialog box, in the **This connection uses the following items** section, uncheck the **Internet Protocol Version 6 (TCP/IPv6)** check box. Click **Close.**
   g. In the **Local Area Connection Properties** dialog box, click **Close.**

   h. Close the Network Connections window.

8. In the Initial Configuration Tasks window, click **Close.**
9. In the **Initial Configuration Tasks** dialog box, click **Yes** to restart the computer.
10. If you were not able to perform the previous step, in the Server Manager window, at the bottom of the window, click **Restart,** and then click **Yes** to restart the computer.
11. When installation is complete, log on as **Administrator** with the password ***!Pass1234***
12. If necessary, set the Date and Time Zone.
    a. In the Initial Configuration Tasks window, under **Provide Computer Information**, click **Set time zone.**
    b. In the **Date and Time** dialog box, in the **Time zone** section, click **Change time zone.**
    c. In the **Time zone** drop-down list, select your time zone, and click **OK.**
    d. In the **Date and Time** dialog box, click **OK.**
13. Change your display settings so that the screen area is at least 1024 x 768 pixels.
    a. Choose **Start→Control Panel.**
    b. In the Control Panel window, in the **Appearance** section, click the **Adjust screen resolution** link.
    c. In the Screen Resolution window, in the **Change the appearance of your display** section, in the **Resolution** drop-down list, drag the slider from **Low, 800 by 600 pixels,** to the resolution at **1024 by 768 pixels.** Click outside the slider to collapse the drop-down list. Click **OK.**
    d. In the **Display Settings** dialog box, click **Keep changes** to apply the new display settings.
    e. Close the Control Panel window.
14. Change drive letter of **E:** as **S:** and format the drives **S:** and **D:** as NTFS.
    a. Choose **Start→Administrative Tools→Computer Management.**
    b. In the Computer Management window, in the left pane, with **Storage** expanded, select **Disk Management.**
    c. In the **Disk Management** section, select the **E:** drive. Choose **Action→All Tasks→ Change Drive Letter and Paths.** In the **Change Drive Letter and Paths for E:** () dialog box, click **Change.**
    d. In the **Change Drive Letter or Path** dialog box, from the **Assign the following drive letter** drop-down list, select **S** and click **OK.**
    e. In the **Disk Management** dialog box, click **Yes.**
    f. On the task bar, click the blinking Folder icon. In the **Microsoft Windows** dialog box, click **Format disk.**
    g. In the **Format Local Disk (S:)** dialog box, click **Start.**
    h. In the **Format Local Disk (S:)** message box, click **OK** to start formatting the drive.
    i. In the **Format Local Disk (S:)** message box, click **OK.**
    j. In the **Format Local Disk (S:)** dialog box, click **Close.**
    k. In the **Disk Management** section, select the **D:** drive. Choose **Action→All Tasks→ Format.** In the **Format D:** dialog box with the **Perform a quick format** check box checked, click **OK.** In the **Format D:** dialog box, click **OK.**

l. Close the Computer Management window.

15. Install the **Active Directory Domain Services** role and promote the computer to a domain controller.
    a. In the Initial Configuration Tasks window, in the **Customize This Server** section, click the **Add roles** link.
    b. In the **Add Roles Wizard,** on the **Before You Begin** page, click **Next.**
    c. On the **Select Server Roles** page, check the **Active Directory Domain Services** check box.
    d. In the **Add Roles Wizard** dialog box, click **Add Required Features** to add all the suggested features.
    e. On the **Select Server Roles** page, click **Next.**
    f. On the **Active Directory Domain Services** page, click **Next.**
    g. On the **Confirm Installation Selections** page, click **Install.**
    h. On the **Installation Results** page, click the **Close this wizard and launch the Active Directory Domain Services Installation Wizard (dcpromo.exe)** link.
    i. In the **Active Directory Domain Services Installation Wizard,** on the **Welcome to the Active Directory Domain Services Installation Wizard** page, click **Next.**
    j. On the **Operating System Compatibility** page, click **Next.**
    k. On the **Choose a Deployment Configuration** page, select the **Create a new domain in a new forest** option, and click **Next.**
    l. On the **Name the Forest Root Domain** page, in the **FQDN of the forest root domain** text box, type ***Classnet.com*** and click **Next.**
    m. On the **Set Forest Functional Level** page, in the **Forest functional level** section, from the **Forest functional level** drop-down list, select **Windows Server 2008 R2,** and click **Next.**
    n. On the **Additional Domain Controller Options** page, with the **DNS server** check box checked, click **Next.**
    o. In the **Active Directory Domain Services Installation Wizard** dialog box, click **Yes.**
    p. On the **Location for Database, Log Files, and SYSVOL** page, in the **SYSVOL folder** text box, change the path to **D:\Windows\SYSVOL**. Accept the default path for Database and Log files folders and click **Next.**
    q. On the **Directory Services Restore Mode Administrator Password** page, in the **Password** and **Confirm password** text boxes, type ***p@ssw0rd*** and click **Next.**
    r. On the **Summary** page, click **Next.**
    s. In the **Active Directory Domain Services Installation Wizard** message box, observe the progressive installation messages. Wait for the installation to complete, and on the **Completing the Active Directory Domain Services Installation Wizard** page, click **Finish.**
    t. In the **Active Directory Domain Services Installation Wizard** dialog box, click **Restart Now** to restart the computer.
    u. Log on to Classnet.com domain as **Administrator** with the password ***!Pass1234***

16. Create user accounts in Active Directory.
    a. Choose **Start→Administrative Tools→Active Directory Users and Computers.**

b. Expand the **Classnet.com** object.
c. Right-click the **Users** folder and choose **New→User.**
d. Enter ***User##*** in the **Last Name** and **User logon Name** fields, and click **Next.**
e. In the **Password** and **Confirm Password** fields, type ***!Pass1234*** and uncheck **User must change password at next login.** Check the **User cannot change password** and **Password never expires** check boxes and click **Next.**
f. Click **Finish**. Repeat these steps for each student in the classroom, where User## corresponds to the number of students. Be sure to create an instructor account using User100.
g. Close the Active Directory Users and Computers window.

17. Install the DHCP server.
    a. In the Initial Configuration Tasks window, in the **Customize This Server** section, click the **Add roles** link.
    b. In the **Add Roles Wizard,** on the **Before You Begin** page, click **Next.**
    c. On the **Select Server Roles** page, check **DHCP Server** check box and click **Next.**
    d. On the **DHCP Server** page, click **Next.**
    e. On the **Select Network Connection Bindings** page, click **Next.**
    f. On the **Specify IPv4 DNS Server Settings** page, click **Next.**
    g. On the **Specify IPv4 WINS Server Settings** page, click **Next** to proceed without a WINS server.
18. On the **Add or Edit DHCP Scopes** page, click **Add.** In the **Add Scope** dialog box, create a DHCP scope using the following parameters:
    a. In the **Scope name** text box, type ***Classnet scope***
    b. In the **Starting IP address** and **Ending IP address** text boxes, enter *192.168.1.25* and *192.168.1.95,* respectively.
    c. In the **Subnet mask** text box, verify that the address is **255.255.255.0.**
    d. Verify that the **Activate this scope** check box is checked and click **OK.**
    e. On the **Add or Edit DHCP Scopes** page, verify that the Classnet scope is listed and click **Next.**
    f. On the **Configure DHCPv6 Stateless Mode** page, in the **Select the DHCPv6 stateless mode configuration for this server** section, select the **Disable DHCPv6 stateless mode for this server** option and click **Next.**
    g. On the **Authorize DHCP Server** page, in the **Specify credentials to use for authorizing this DHCP server in AD DS** section, with the **Use current credentials** option selected, click **Next.**
    h. On the **Confirm Installation Selections** page, click **Install.**
    i. Wait for the installation to complete the process and display the results.
    j. On the **Installation Results** page, click **Close.**
19. Create a Reverse Lookup Zone and add a Pointer record.
    a. Choose **Start→Administrative Tools→DNS.**
    b. Expand the DC object, and select **Reverse Lookup Zones.**
    c. Choose **Action→New Zone.**

d. In the **New Zone Wizard** dialog box, click **Next.**

e. Verify that **Primary zone** is selected and click **Next.**

f. Verify that **To all DNS servers running on domain controllers in this domain: Classnet.com** is selected and click **Next.**

g. Verify that **IPv4 Reverse Lookup Zone** is selected and click **Next.**

h. With the Network ID radio button selected, type ***192.168.1*** and click **Next.**

i. Verify that **Allow only secure dynamic updates (recommended for Active Directory)** is selected, and click **Next.**

j. Click **Finish.**

k. Under **Reverse Lookup Zones,** expand and right-click the **1.168.192.in-addr.arpa** folder and choose **New Pointer (PTR).**

l. In the **New Resource Record** dialog box, in the **Host IP Address** text box, type ***200*** onto the end of the incomplete IP address.

m. In the **Host name** text box, click and type ***DC*** and click **OK.**

n. Close the DNS Manager window.

20. Install the Microsoft Loopback Adapter.

a. Choose **Start→Administrative Tools→Server Manager.**

b. In the Server Manager window, in the left pane, expand **Diagnostics** and select **Device Manager.**

c. In the middle pane, select the DC server object, and choose **Action→Add legacy hardware.**

d. In the **Add Hardware wizard,** on the **Welcome to the Add Hardware Wizard** page, click **Next.**

e. On the **The wizard can help you install other hardware** page, in the **What do you want the wizard to do** section, select the **Install the hardware that I manually select from a list (Advanced)** option and click **Next.**

f. In the **Common hardware types** list, scroll down and select **Network adapters.** Click **Next.**

g. In the **Manufacturer** list, select **Microsoft.** In the **Network Adapter** list, scroll down and select **Microsoft Loopback Adapter**. Click **Next.**

h. On the **The wizard is ready to install your hardware** page, click **Next.**

i. On the **Completing the Add Hardware Wizard** page, click **Finish.** The adapter will obtain an APIPA address (169.254.x.x).

j. Choose **Start→Network.** Click **Network and Sharing Center.**

k. In the left pane, click the **Change adapter settings** link.

l. In the Network Connections window, right-click **Local Area Connection 2** (the loopback adapter) and choose **Rename.**

m. Enter ***Loopback Adapter***.

n. Close the Network Connections window.

21. Add the **Routing and Remote Access Services** role.

a. In the Server Manager window, in the left pane, select **Roles.** In the right pane, click the **Add Roles** link.

b. In the **Add Roles Wizard,** on the **Before You Begin** page, click **Next.**

c. On the **Select Server Roles** page, check the **Network Policy and Access Services** check box and click **Next.**
d. On the **Network Policy and Access Services** page, click **Next.**
e. On the **Select Role Services** page, check the **Routing and Remote Access Services** check box and click **Next.**
f. On the **Confirm Installation Selections** page, click **Install.**
g. Wait for the installation to complete the process and display the results.
h. On the **Installation Results** page, click **Close.**
i. Close the Server Manager window.

22. Allow authenticated users to log on to the domain controller.
    a. Choose **Start→Administrative Tools→Group Policy Management.**
    b. Expand the tree (Forest: Classnet.com→Domains→Classnet.com→Domain Controllers) and click **Default Domain Controllers Policy.**
    c. In the **Group Policy Management Console** message box, click **OK.**
    d. Choose **Action→Edit.**
    e. In the Group Policy Management Editor window, if necessary, expand **Computer Configuration.** Expand **Policies, Windows Settings, Security Settings, Local Policies.**
    f. Select **User Rights Assignment.**
    g. In the details pane, double-click **Allow log on locally.**
    h. In the **Allow log on locally Properties** dialog box, click **Add User or Group.**
    i. In the **Add User or Group** dialog box, in the **User and group names** text box, click **Browse.**
    j. In the **Select Users, Computers, Service Accounts, or Groups** dialog box, click **Advanced.**
    k. In the **Select Users, Computers, Service Accounts, or Groups** dialog box, click **Find Now.**
    l. In the **Search results** section, select **Authenticated Users** and click **OK.**
    m. In the **Select Users, Computers, Service Accounts, or Groups** dialog box, click **OK.** In the **Add User or Group** dialog box, click **OK.** In the **Allow log on locally Properties** dialog box, click **OK** to close it.
    n. Close the Group Policy Management Editor and Group Policy Management windows.

23. Configure and enable Routing and Remote Access Services.
    a. Choose **Start→Administrative Tools→Routing and Remote Access.**
    b. Select the server object (DC (local)) and choose **Action→Configure and Enable Routing and Remote Access.**
        1. In the **Routing and Remote Access Server Setup Wizard** dialog box, on the **Welcome to the Routing and Remote Access Server Setup Wizard** page, click **Next.**
        2. On the **Configuration** page, verify that **Remote access (dial-up or VPN)** option is selected and click **Next.**
        3. On the **Remote Access** page, check the **VPN** check box and click **Next.**

4. On the **VPN Connection** page, in the **Network interfaces** section, select **Loopback Adapter** and click **Next.**
5. On the **IP Address Assignment** page, verify that the **Automatically** option is selected and click **Next.**
6. On the **Managing Multiple Remote Access Servers** page, verify that the **No, use Routing and Remote Access to authenticate connection requests** option is selected and click **Next.**
7. On the **Completing the Routing and Remote Access Server Setup Wizard** page, click **Finish.**

c. After you finish the **Routing and Remote Access Server Setup Wizard,** click **OK** to close the **Routing and Remote Access** dialog box.

d. After the RRAS service starts, in the Routing and Remote Access window, configure the agent with the server's IP address (192.168.y.#).

1. Expand **IPv4,** and select the **DHCP Relay Agent.**
2. Choose **Action→Properties** and in the **DHCP Relay Agent Properties** dialog box, in the **Server address** text box, type the server's IP address (**192.168.1.200**). Click **Add** and then click **OK.**
3. Right-click **DHCP Relay Agent** and choose **New Interface.** Select the **Loopback Adapter** and click **OK.** Click **OK** to accept the default relay agent properties.

e. Collapse all the expanded nodes of the tree and close the Routing and Remote Access window.

24. Configure and enable the Remote Procedure Call (RPC) Locator service.

a. Choose **Start→Administrative Tools→Computer Management.**

b. Expand **Services and Applications.** Select **Services.**

c. Enable the **Remote Procedure Call (RPC) Locator** service.

1. In the middle pane, double-click **Remote Procedure Call (RPC) Locator.**
2. In the **Remote Procedure Call (RPC) Locator Properties (Local Computer)** dialog box, from the **Startup type** drop-down list, select **Automatic.** Click **Apply.** Click **Start.** Wait for the service to start and then click **OK** to close the **Properties** dialog box.

d. Close the Computer Management window.

25. Configure Internet Explorer.

a. Choose **Start→Internet Explorer.**

b. In the **Set Up Windows Internet Explorer 8** dialog box, on the **Welcome to Internet Explorer 8** page, click **Next.**

c. On the **Turn on Suggested Sites** page, select the **Yes, turn on Suggested Sites** option and click **Next.**

d. On the **Choose your settings** page, select the **Use express settings** option and click **Finish.**

e. Close the Windows Internet Explorer window.

26. Turn on Network Discovery.

a. Choose **Start→Network** and click **Network and Sharing Center.**

b. Click the **Change advanced sharing settings** link. In the Advanced sharing settings window, in the **Network Discovery** section, select the **Turn on network discovery** option.

c. Click **Save changes.**

d. Close the Network and Sharing Center window.

27. Turn off the Windows Firewall.

a. In the Initial Configuration Tasks window, in the **Customize This Server** section, click the **Configure Windows Firewall** link.

b. In the Windows Firewall window, in the left pane, click the **Turn Windows Firewall on or off** link.

c. In the Customize Settings window, on the **Customize settings for each type of network** page, in the each of the three sections—**Domain network location settings, Home or work (private) network location settings,** and **Public network location settings,—** select the **Turn off Windows Firewall (not recommended)** option and click **OK.**

d. Close the Windows Firewall window.

e. In the Initial Configuration Tasks window, check the **Do not show this window at logon** check box and click **Close** to close the Initial Configuration Tasks window.

28. Disable the Windows Firewall service.

a. Choose **Start →Administrative Tools→Services.**

b. In the Services window, in the right pane, scroll down and double-click **Windows Firewall**.

c. In the **Windows Firewall Properties (Local Computer)** dialog box, click **Stop.**

d. From the **Startup type** drop-down list, select **Disabled.**

e. Click **Apply.**

f. Click **OK** to close the Properties dialog box.

g. Close the Services window.

29. Complete the setup.

a. Eject the DVD from the DVD-ROM drive.

b. Choose **Start→Log off.**

On the Instructor and Student Computers:

1. Boot the computer with the Windows Server 2008 R2 installation DVD. Press a key when prompted to boot from DVD or CD to start the Windows Server 2008 R2 setup program.
2. Install a new copy of Windows Server 2008 R2 using the following parameters:

a. In the Install Windows window, accept the default values to set **Language to install** to **English, Time and currency format** to **English (United States), Keyboard or input method** to **US.** Click **Next.**

b. Click **Install now.**

c. On the **Type your product key for activation** page, type your product key and click **Next.**

d. On the **Select the operating system you want to install** page, verify that **Windows Server 2008 R2 Standard (Full Installation)** is selected and click **Next.**

   e. On the **Please read the license terms** page, read the terms, check **I accept the license terms,** and click **Next.**
   f. On the **Which type of installation do you want** page, click **Custom (advanced).**
   g. Delete the existing partitions.
      1. Click **Drive options (advanced),**
      2. Select the drives one at a time and click **Delete.** In the **Install Windows** dialog box, click **OK.** Repeat the step till all the drives are deleted.
   h. Select the **Disk 0 Unallocated Space** and click **New.** In the **Size** text box, double-click and type ***41060*** and click **Apply** to allocate 40 GB to the C drive.
   i. In the **Install Windows** message box, click **OK** to allows Windows to create additional partitions for system files.
   j. Select the **Disk 0 Unallocated Space** and click **New.** In the **Size** text box, double-click and type ***61440*** and click **Apply** to allocate 60 GB.
   k. Select the **Disk 0 Unallocated Space** and click **New.** In the **Size** text box, double-click and type ***61440*** and click **Apply** to allocate 60 GB.
   l. Select the **Disk 0 Partition 2** and click **Next.**
   m. On the **Installing Windows** page, observe the progress of the installation. Wait for the installation to complete. The system will automatically reboot.
   n. Wait approximately 15 minutes for Windows to set up your computer. When prompted to press a key to boot from DVD or CD, ignore the message. At this point, it will be safe for you to remove the disc from the DVD drive.
   o. The **Installing Windows** page will be displayed with the updated installation details. The system will automatically reboot.
3. On rebooting, the system will display a message "The user's password must be changed before logging on the first time." Click **OK** to change the password.
4. For the **Administrator** user, in the **New password** and the **Confirm password** text boxes, type ***!Pass1234*** as the password and click the right arrow button.
5. The message "Your password has been changed." is displayed. Click **OK.**
6. Verify the automatically assigned IP address of the computer and configure the preferred DNS server.
   a. In the Initial Configuration Tasks window, in the **Provide Computer Information** section, click the **Configure networking** link.
   b. In the Network Connections window, select the **Local Area Connection** icon, right-click, and choose **Status.** In the **Local Area Connection Status** dialog box, click **Details.**
   c. In the **Network Connection Details** dialog box, verify that the IPv4 address is within the range of 192.168.1.25 to 192.168.1.95 which is the range of the DHCP scope. Click **Close.**
   d. In the **Local Area Connection Status** dialog box, click **Properties.**
   e. In the **Local Area Connection Properties** dialog box, in the **This connection uses the following items** section, select **Internet Protocol Version 4 (TCP/IPv4).** Click **Properties.**

   f. In the **Internet Protocol Version 4 (TCP/IPv4) Properties** dialog box, select the **Use the following DNS server addresses** option. In the **Preferred DNS server** text box, type ***192.168.1.200*** and click **OK.**
   g. If necessary, to disable the IPv6 protocol, in the **Local Area Connection Properties** dialog box, in thc **This connection uses the following items** section, uncheck the **Internet Protocol Version 6 (TCP/IPv6)** check box.
   h. Click **Close.**
   i. In the **Local Area Connection Status** dialog box, click **Close.**
   j. Close the Network Connections window.
7. Change the computer name.
   a. In the Initial Configuration Tasks window, in the **Provide Computer Information** section, click the **Provide computer name and domain** link.
   b. In the **System Properties** dialog box, click **Change.**
   c. In the **Computer Name/Domain Changes** dialog box, in the **Computer name** text box, select the existing computer name and type ***Computer100*** for the Instructor machine, and ***Computer##*** for the student machine, where ## is the number assigned to each student.
   d. In the **Member of** section, select **Domain.** In the **Domain** text box, type ***Classnet*** and click **OK.**
   e. In the **Windows Security** dialog box, in the **User name** text box, type **Administrator.** In the **Password** text box, click and type ***!Pass1234*** and click **OK.**
   f. In the **Computer Name/Domain Changes** message box, verify that the message "Welcome to the Classnet domain." is displayed and click **OK.**
   g. In the **Computer Name/Domain Changes** message box, click **OK** to restart the computer.
   h. In the **System Properties** dialog box, click **Close.**
   i. In the **Microsoft Windows** dialog box, click **Restart Now.**
8. When the system restarts, in the log on screen, click **Switch User** and then click **Other User.** In the **User name** text box, type ***Classnet\Administrator*** and in the **Password** text box, type ***!Pass1234*** and press **Enter.**
9. If necessary, set the Date and Time Zone.
   a. In the Initial Configuration Tasks window, under **Provide Computer Information**, click **Set time zone.**
   b. In the **Date and Time** dialog box, in the **Time zone** section, click **Change time zone.**
   c. In the **Time zone** drop-down list, select your time zone, and click **OK.**
   d. In the **Date and Time** dialog box, click **OK.**
10. Change your display settings so that the screen area is at least 1024 x 768 pixels.
   a. Choose **Start→Control Panel.**
   b. In the Control Panel window, in the **Appearance** section, click the **Adjust screen resolution** link.

c. In the Screen Resolution window, in the **Change the appearance of your display** section, in the **Resolution** drop-down list, drag the slider from **Low, 800 by 600 pixels,** to the resolution at **1024 by 768 pixels.** Click outside the slider to collapse the drop-down list. Click **OK.**

d. In the **Display Settings** dialog box, click **Keep changes** to apply the new display settings.

e. Close the Control Panel window.

11. Change drive letter of **E:** as **S:** and format the drives **S:** and **D:** as NTFS.

a. Choose **Start→Administrative Tools→Computer Management.**

b. In the Computer Management window, in the left pane, with **Storage** expanded, select **Disk Management.**

c. In the **Disk Management** section, select the **E:** drive. Choose **Action→All Tasks→Change Drive Letter and Paths.** In the **Change Drive Letter and Paths for E: ()** dialog box, click **Change.**

d. In the **Change Drive Letter or Path** dialog box, from the **Assign the following drive letter** drop-down list, select **S** and click **OK.**

e. In the **Disk Management** dialog box, click **Yes.**

f. On the task bar, click the blinking Folder icon. In the **Microsoft Windows** dialog box, click **Format disk.**

g. In the **Format Local Disk (S:)** dialog box, click **Start.**

h. In the **Format Local Disk (S:)** message box, click **OK** to start formatting the drive.

i. In the **Format Local Disk (S:)** message box, click **OK.**

j. In the **Format Local Disk (S:)** dialog box, click **Close.**

k. In the **Disk Management** section, select the **D:** drive. Choose **Action→All Tasks→Format.** In the **Format D:** dialog box with the **Perform a quick format** check box checked, click **OK.** In the **Format D:** dialog box, click **OK.**

l. Close the Computer Management window.

12. Install the **Active Directory Domain Services** role and promote the computer to a domain controller.

a. In the Initial Configuration Tasks window, in the **Customize This Server** section, click the **Add roles** link.

b. In the **Add Roles Wizard,** on the **Before You Begin** page, click **Next.**

c. On the **Select Server Roles** page, check the **Active Directory Domain Services** check box.

d. In the **Add Roles Wizard** dialog box, click **Add Required Features** to add all the suggested features.

e. On the **Select Server Roles** page, click **Next.**

f. On the **Active Directory Domain Services** page, click **Next.**

g. On the **Confirm Installation Selections** page, click **Install.**

h. On the **Installation Results** page, click the **Close this wizard and launch the Active Directory Domain Services Installation Wizard (dcpromo.exe)** link.

i. In the **Active Directory Domain Services Installation Wizard,** on the **Welcome to the Active Directory Domain Services Installation Wizard** page, click **Next.**

j. On the **Operating System Compatibility** page, click **Next.**

k. On the **Choose a Deployment Configuration** page, select the **Existing forest** option, and click **Create a new domain in an existing forest** option. Click **Next.**

l. On the **Network Credentials** page, in the **Type the name of any domain in the forest where you plan to install this domain controller** section, verify that Classnet.com is the listed domain name. In the **Specify the account credentials to use to perform the installation** section, verify that **My current logged on credentials (CLASSNET\Administrator)** is selected and click **Next.**

m. On the **Name the New Domain** page, in the **FQDN of the parent domain** text box, verify that **Classnet.com** is listed. In the **Single-label DNS name of the child domain** text box, type ***Child##***, where ## corresponds to the number of the student's computer. For the instructor's computer, it is **Child100.** In the **FQDN of the new child domain** section, observe that **Child##.Classnet.com** is listed, where ## corresponds to the number of student's computer. Click **Next.**

n. On the **Select a Site** page, click **Next.**

o. On the **Additional Domain Controller Options** page, with the **DNS server** check box checked, click **Next.**

p. In the **Static IP assignment** dialog box, click **Yes, the computer will use an IP address automatically assigned by a DHCP server (not recommended).**

q. On the **Location for Database, Log Files, and SYSVOL** page, in the **SYSVOL folder** text box, change the path to **D:\Windows\SYSVOL**. Accept the default path for Database and Log files folders and click **Next.**

r. On the **Directory Services Restore Mode Administrator Password** page, in the **Password** and **Confirm password** text boxes, type ***p@ssw0rd*** and click **Next.**

s. On the **Summary** page, click **Next.**

t. In the **Active Directory Domain Services Installation Wizard** message box, observe the progressive installation messages. Wait for the installation to complete, and on the **Completing the Active Directory Domain Services Installation Wizard** page, click **Finish.**

u. In the **Active Directory Domain Services Installation Wizard** message box, click **Restart Now** to restart the computer.

v. Log on to Classnet.com domain as **Administrator** with the password ***!Pass1234***

13. Create user accounts in Active Directory.

a. Choose **Start→Administrative Tools→Active Directory Users and Computers.**

b. Expand the **Child##.Classnet.com** object, where ## corresponds to the computer number.

c. Right-click the **Users** folder and choose **New→User.**

d. Enter ***Test##*** in the **Last Name** and **User logon name** fields, and click **Next.**

e. In the **Password** and **Confirm Password** fields, type ***!Pass1234*** and uncheck **User must change password at next login.** Check the **User cannot change password** and **Password never expires** check boxes and click **Next.**

f. Click **Finish**.

g. Right-click the **Users** folder and choose **New→User.**

h. Enter ***User##*** in the **Last Name** and **User logon name** fields, and click **Next.**

i. In the **Password** and **Confirm Password** fields, type ***!Pass1234*** and uncheck **User must change password at next login.**

j. Check the **User cannot change password** and **Password never expires** check boxes and click **Next.**

k. Click **Finish**.

l. Close the Active Directory Users and Computers window.

14. Allow authenticated users to log on locally.

a. Choose **Start→Administrative Tools→Group Policy Management.**

b. Expand the tree (Forest: Classnet.com).

c. Select **Domains.**

d. Choose **Action→Show Domains.**

e. In the **Show Domains** dialog box, check the **Child##.Classnet.com** for your student number and click **OK.**

f. Expand the tree (Domains→Child##.Classnet.com→Domain Controllers) and click **Default Domain Controllers Policy.**

g. In the **Group Policy Management Console** message box, click **OK.**

h. Choose **Action→Edit.**

i. In the Group Policy Management Editor window, if necessary, expand **Computer Configuration.** Expand **Policies, Windows Settings, Security Settings, Local Policies.**

j. Select **User Rights Assignment.**

k. In the details pane, double-click **Allow log on locally.**

l. In the **Allow log on locally Properties** dialog box, click **Add User or Group.**

m. In the **Add User or Group** dialog box, in the **User and group names** text box, click **Browse.**

n. In the **Select Users, Computers, Service Accounts, or Groups** dialog box, click **Advanced.**

o. In the **Select Users, Computers, Service Accounts, or Groups** dialog box, click **Find Now.**

p. In the **Search results** section, select **Authenticated Users** and click **OK.**

q. In the **Select Users, Computers, Service Accounts, or Groups** dialog box, click **OK.** In the **Add User or Group** dialog box, click **OK.** In the **Allow log on locally Properties** dialog box, click **OK** to close it.

r. Close the Group Policy Management Editor and Group Policy Management windows.

15. Force the Policy update.

a. Choose **Start→Command Prompt**.

b. In the Command Prompt window, enter **`gpupdate /force`**

c. Verify that the User Policy update and Computer Policy update are completed successfully.

d. Close the Command Prompt window.

16. Configure and enable the Remote Procedure Call (RPC) Locator service.

a. Choose **Start→Administrative Tools→Computer Management.**
b. Expand **Services and Applications.** Select **Services.**
c. Enable the **Remote Procedure Call (RPC) Locator** service.
   1. In the middle pane, double-click **Remote Procedure Call (RPC) Locator.**
   2. In the **Remote Procedure Call (RPC) Locator Properties (Local Computer)** dialog box, from the **Startup type** drop-down list, select **Automatic.** Click **Apply.** Click **Start.** Wait for the service to start and then click **OK** to close the **Properties** dialog box.
d. Close the Computer Management window.

17. Configure Internet Explorer.
   a. Choose **Start→Internet Explorer.**
   b. In the **Set Up Windows Internet Explorer 8** dialog box, on the **Welcome to Internet Explorer 8** page, click **Next.**
   c. On the **Turn on Suggested Sites** page, select the **Yes, turn on Suggested Sites** option and click **Next.**
   d. On the **Choose your settings** page, select the **Use express settings** option and click **Finish.**
   e. Close the Windows Internet Explorer window.
18. Turn on Network Discovery.
   a. Choose **Start→Network** and click **Network and Sharing Center.**
   b. Click the **Change advanced sharing settings** link. In the Advanced sharing settings window, in the **Network Discovery** section, select the **Turn on network discovery** option.
   c. Click **Save changes.**
   d. Close the Network and Sharing Center window.
19. Create a Reverse Lookup Zone.
   a. Choose **Start→Administrative Tools→DNS.**
   b. Expand the Computer## object, and select **Reverse Lookup Zones.**
   c. Choose **Action→New Zone.**
   d. In the **New Zone Wizard** dialog box, click **Next.**
   e. Verify that **Primary zone** is selected and click **Next.**
   f. Verify that **To all DNS servers running on domain controllers in this domain: Child##.Classnet.com** is selected and click **Next.**
   g. Verify that **IPv4 Reverse Lookup Zone** is selected and click **Next.**
   h. With the Network ID radio button selected, type ***192.168.1*** and click **Next.**
   i. Verify that **Allow only secure dynamic updates (recommended for Active Directory)** is selected, and click **Next.**
   j. Click **Finish.**
   k. Close the DNS Manager window.
20. Install the Microsoft Loopback Adapter.
   a. Choose **Start→Administrative Tools→Server Manager.**

b. In the Server Manager window, in the left pane, expand **Diagnostics** and select **Device Manager.**

c. In the middle pane, select the **Computer##** object, and choose **Action→Add legacy hardware.**

d. In the **Add Hardware wizard,** on the **Welcome to the Add Hardware Wizard** page, click **Next.**

e. On the **The wizard can help you install other hardware** page, in the **What do you want the wizard to do** section, select the **Install the hardware that I manually select from a list (Advanced)** option and click **Next.**

f. In the **Common hardware types** list, scroll down and select **Network adapters.** Click **Next.**

g. In the **Manufacturer** list, select **Microsoft.** In the **Network Adapter** list, scroll down and select **Microsoft Loopback Adapter**. Click **Next.**

h. On the **The wizard is ready to install your hardware** page, click **Next.**

i. On the **Completing the Add Hardware Wizard** page, click **Finish.** The adapter will obtain an APIPA address (169.254.x.x).

j. Close the Server Manager window.

k. Choose **Start→Network.** Click **Network and Sharing Center.**

l. In the left pane, click the **Change adapter settings** link.

m. In the Network Connections window, right-click **Local Area Connection 2** (the loopback adapter) and choose **Rename.**

n. Enter ***Loopback Adapter***.

o. Close the Network Connections window.

21. Turn off the Windows Firewall.

a. In the Initial Configuration Tasks window, in the **Customize This Server** section, click the **Configure Windows Firewall** link.

b. In the Windows Firewall window, in the left pane, click the **Turn Windows Firewall on or off** link.

c. In the Customize Settings window, on the **Customize settings for each type of network** page, in the each of the three sections—**Domain network location settings, Home or work (private) network location settings,** and **Public network location settings,—** select the **Turn off Windows Firewall (not recommended)** option and click **OK.**

d. Close the Windows Firewall window.

e. In the Initial Configuration Tasks window, check the **Do not show this window at logon** check box and click **Close** to close the Initial Configuration Tasks window.

22. Disable the Windows Firewall service.

a. Choose **Start →Administrative Tools→Services.**

b. In the Services window, in the right pane, scroll down and double-click **Windows Firewall**.

c. In the **Windows Firewall Properties (Local Computer)** dialog box, click **Stop.**

d. From the **Startup type** drop-down list, select **Disabled.**

e. Click **Apply.**

  f. Click **OK** to close the Properties dialog box.
  g. Close the Services window.

23. Complete the setup.
  a. To install the course data files, insert the course CD-ROM and click the **Data Files** button. This will install a folder named **Data** on your C drive. This folder contains all the data files that you will use to complete this course. It also includes several simulated activities that can be used in lieu of the hands-on activities in the course.
  b. Close any other open windows.
  c. Eject all media.
  d. Choose **Start→Log off.**

Lesson Lab Setup Instructions

In the back of the book, there is an optional Lesson Lab for each lesson in this course. Lesson Labs are meant to be self-guided high-level activities for students to reinforce what they learned in class, and are completely separate from the activities you will present in the main flow of instruction. Some labs can be completed in the classroom following their respective lessons, either because they are discussion-only or because they use a similar environment as the classroom configuration. Other labs use different computer and network configurations and must be set up independently outside the classroom if you choose to have students complete them. If specific setup instructions are needed, they are included in the back of the book with each lab activity.

List of Additional Files

Printed with each activity is a list of files students open to complete that activity. Many activities also require additional files that students do not open, but are needed to support the file(s) students are working with. These supporting files are included with the student data files on the course CD-ROM or data disk. Do not delete these files.

1 Network Theory

Lesson Time: 1 hour(s), 10 minutes

Lesson Objectives:

In this lesson, you will identify the basic network theory concepts.

You will:

- Describe common terminology used in computer networking.
- Describe the primary categories of networks.
- Describe the standard networking models.
- Describe the primary physical network topologies.
- Describe the primary logical network topologies.

Introduction

The CompTIA Network+ certification covers a wide range of knowledge and skills that apply to different networking job roles. Any networking job role requires a fundamental knowledge of network terminology, components, models, and topologies. In this lesson, you will identify the basic concepts of the current networking theory.

With a background in CompTIA Network+ information and skills, your networking career can move in many directions. Whether you are a network support technician, installer, or administrator, knowledge of the basic networking theory provides the necessary foundation needed for learning more advanced networking concepts. A good grasp of the fundamental networking theory will help you succeed in any network-related job role.

This lesson covers all or part of the following CompTIA® Network+® (Exam N10-005) certification objectives:

- Topic A:
  - 1.2 Classify how applications, devices, and protocols relate to the OSI model layers.
- Topic B:
  - 1.2 Classify how applications, devices, and protocols relate to the OSI model layers.
- Topic C:
  - 3.5 Describe different network topologies.
- Topic D:
  - 1.2 Classify how applications, devices, and protocols relate to the OSI model layers.
  - 3.5 Describe different network topologies.
  - 3.7 Compare and contrast different LAN technologies.
- Topic E:
  - 3.5 Describe different network topologies.

TOPIC A

Networking Terminology

This lesson introduces the primary elements of the network theory. In the computer industry, there is a set of common terminology used to discuss the network theory. In this topic, you will define common terms used in computer networking.

Networking, like any other technical discipline, has a language of its own. Part of mastering the technology involves familiarity with the language you use to describe that technology. With too many technical terms involved in the field of networking, the information and definitions in this topic will help you get familiar with these terms and the context in which they are used in networking.

Computer Networks

Definition:

A *computer network* is a group of computers that are connected together to communicate and share network resources such as files and peripheral devices. No two computer networks are alike in size or in configuration. Each network, however, includes common components that provide the resources and communications channels necessary for the network to operate.

Example:

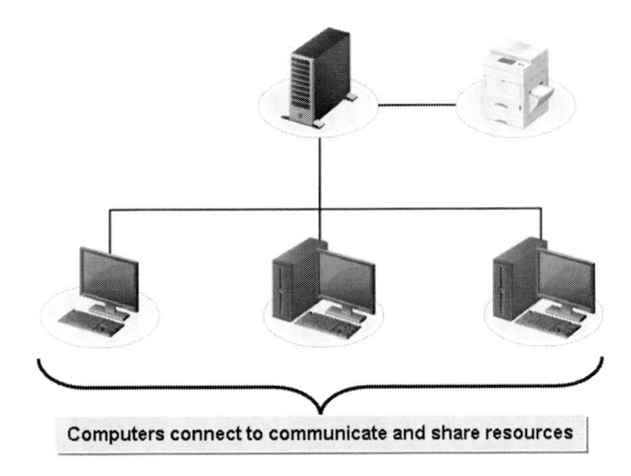

Figure 1-1: *A simple computer network.*

Network Components

There are several common components that make up a computer network, each of which performs a specific task.

Network Component	Description
Device	Hardware such as computers, servers, printers, fax machines, switches, and routers.
Physical media	Media that connects devices to a network and transmits data between the devices.
Network adapter	Hardware that translates data between the network and a device.
Network operating system	Software that controls network traffic and access to common network resources.

Nodes

Definition:

A *node,* commonly referred to as a workstation or a client, is any device that can connect to a network and generate, process, or transfer data. Every node has addressing information to enable other devices to communicate with it. Network nodes can either be endpoints or redistribution points. *Endpoints* are nodes that function as a source or destination for data transfer. *Redistribution points* are nodes that transfer data, such as a network switch or a router.

Example:

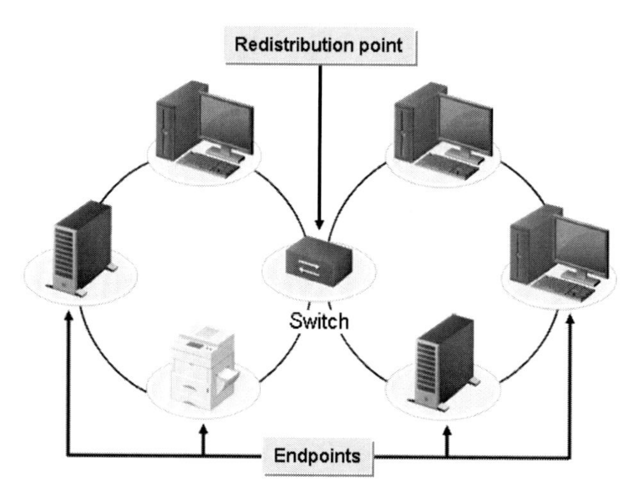

Figure 1-2: *Nodes on a network.*

The Network Backbone

Definition:

The *network backbone* is a very-high-speed transmission path that carries the majority of network data. It connects either small networks into a larger structure, or server nodes to a network where the majority of client computers are attached. The technology in use on a backbone network can be different from that used on client network sections. Since the backbone cabling connects switches and routers on a network, it can carry more traffic than other types of cabling on the network.

Example:

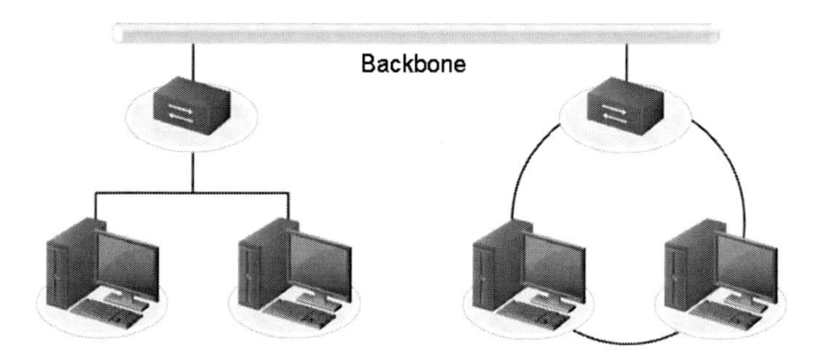

Figure 1-3: *A network backbone is the highest-speed transmission path.*

Types of Network Backbones

There are several types of network backbones that you may encounter.

Network Backbone	*Description*
Serial	Consists of multiple switches connected by one backbone cable. Typically not scaled for enterprise-wide use.
Distributed/hierarchical	Consists of multiple switches connected serially to hubs or routers. Due to their hierarchical structure, these networks can be easily expanded without a significant cost impact. Serves well as one-site enterprise-wide networks; their switch layers can be configured by geography (a floor in a building) or function (a workgroup). Distributed backbone networks enable an administrator to segregate workgroups, simplifying their management.
Collapsed	Uses a router or switch as the nexus for several subnetworks. The router or switch must have multiprocessors to bear the frequently high level of network traffic. Router or switch failures in a collapsed backbone can bring down the entire network. Depending on the routers' processing capabilities, data transmission can also be slow.

Network Backbone	Description
Parallel	Suits enterprise-wide applications. Like the collapsed backbone network, the parallel backbone network uses a central router or switch but augments the dependent switches with multiple cable connections. These multiple links ensure connectivity to the whole enterprise.

Servers

Definition:

A *server* is a network computer that shares resources with and responds to requests from computers, devices, and other servers on the network. Servers provide centralized access and storage for resources that can include applications, files, printers or other hardware, and services such as email. A server can be optimized and dedicated to one specific function, or it can serve general needs. Multiple servers of various types can coexist on the same network.

Example:

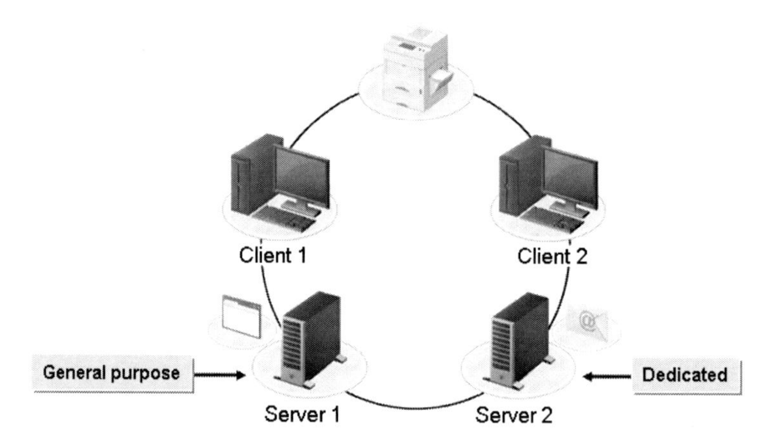

Figure 1-4: *Servers performing generic and dedicated tasks.*

Microsoft Windows Server 2008 R2

Microsoft Windows Server 2008 R2 is the latest version of Microsoft's server-oriented Windows operating system. Windows Server 2008 R2 provides:

- The Active Directory service (ADS).
- Integrated network services such as the *Domain Name System (DNS)* and the *Dynamic Host Configuration Protocol (DHCP).*
- Advanced services such as clustering, a public-key infrastructure, routing, and web services.
- User and group security on the file- and object- levels.

- Advanced security features such as a built-in firewall, file encryption, and Internet Protocol Security (IPSec).

SUSE Linux Enterprise Server

SUSE is an open source server operating system that uses the Linux platform. The latest version is SUSE Linux Enterprise Server 11 SP1.

Clients

Definition:

A *client* is a network computer that utilizes the resources of other network computers, including other clients. The client computer has its own processor, memory, and storage, and can maintain its own resources and perform its own tasks and processing. Any type of computer on a network can function as a client of another computer when needed.

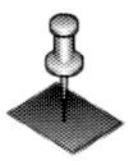

The term "client" most often refers to workstation or desktop computers employed by end users. Any computer on the network can function as a client, when it uses other computers' resources, such as a Windows Server 2008 R2 computer accessing resources on another server.

Example:

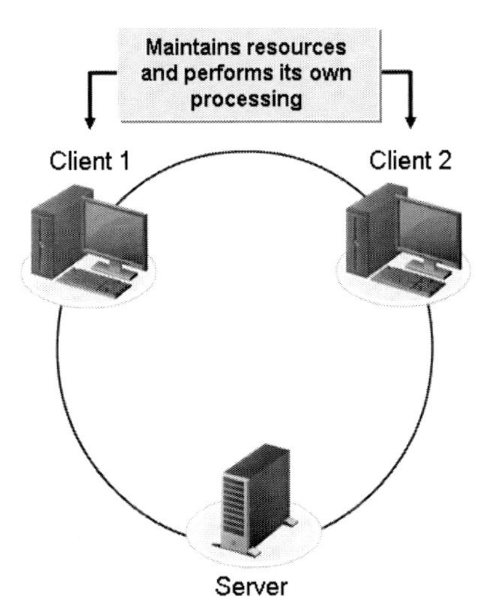

Figure 1-5: *Clients connected to a server.*

Microsoft Windows 7

Microsoft® Windows 7® is a popular and widely deployed operating system on client computers. Windows 7 features an enhanced Graphical User Interface (GUI), support for a wide range of applications and devices, a minimum of 32-bit processing, native networking support, and a large suite of built-in applications and accessories such as the Internet Explorer® browser. Windows 7 currently comes preinstalled on many personal computers sold commercially.

Peer Computers

Definition:

A *peer* is a self-sufficient computer that acts as both a server and a client to other computers on a network. Peer computing is most often used in smaller networks with no dedicated central server, but both clients and servers in other types of networks can share resources with peer computers.

Example:

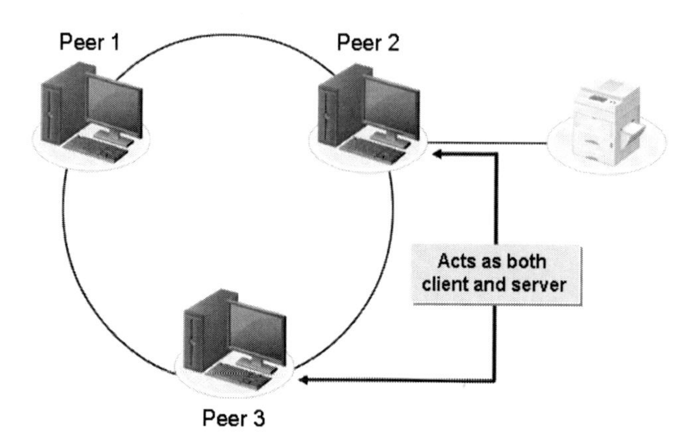

Figure 1-6: *Peer computers in a network.*

Host Computers

Definition:

A *host computer* is a powerful, centralized computer system, such as a mainframe computer, that performs data storage and processing tasks on behalf of clients and other network devices. On a host-based network, the host computer does all computing tasks and returns the resultant data to the end user's computer.

Example:

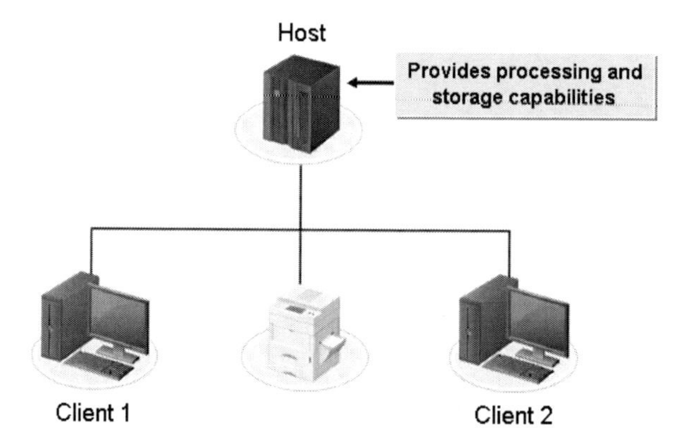

Figure 1-7: *A host computer connected to several network devices.*

TCP/IP Hosts

In the early days of computer networking, all computers were host computers that controlled the activities of network terminal devices. The hosts were joined together to communicate in the early research networks that laid the foundation for the Internet.

As the TCP/IP protocol was adopted and became ubiquitous, and personal computers joined the networks, the term *host* was generalized and is now used to refer to virtually any independent system on a TCP/IP network.

Terminals

Definition:

A *terminal* is a specialized device on a host-based network that transmits data a user enters to a host for processing and displays the results. Terminals are often called "dumb" because they have no processor or memory of their own. Terminals usually consist of just a keyboard and a monitor. Standard client computers that need to interact with host computers can run software called a *terminal emulator* so that they appear as dedicated terminals to the host.

Example:

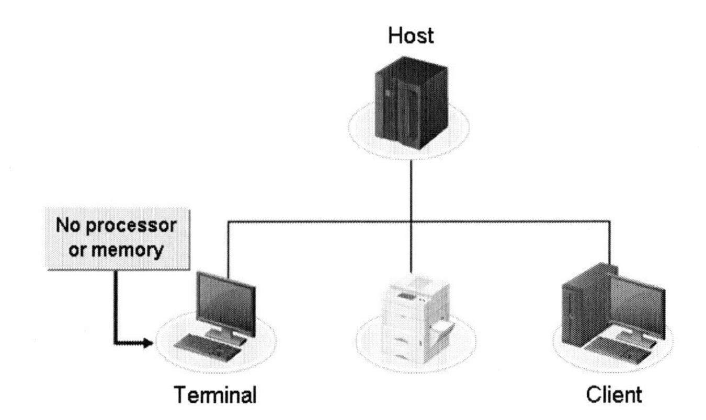

Figure 1-8: *A terminal on a network.*

ACTIVITY 1-1

Defining Networking Terminology

Scenario:

In this activity, you will define common terms used in computer networking.

1. **What is a network computer that shares resources with and responds to requests from other computers called?**
   a) Client
   b) Server
   c) Terminal
   d) Host

2. **Match the network term to its definition.**

	Term		Definition
___	Server	a.	A computer that shares its resources with other computers on a network.
___	Client	b.	A device that transmits data from a user to a host for processing.
___	Host	c.	A computer that uses the resources of other computers on the network.
___	Terminal	d.	A centralized computer that performs storage and processing tasks for other network devices.

3. **What is a network computer that transmits data a user enters to a host for processing and displays the results?**
   a) Server
   b) Host
   c) Terminal
   d) Client

4. **What is a computer that acts as both a server and a client?**
   a) Host
   b) Client
   c) Server
   d) Peer

5. True or False? A host computer transmits data to another computer for processing and displays the result to a user.

__ True

__ False

6. In which type of network are multiple switches connected by a single backbone cable?

a) Distributed

b) Serial

c) Collapsed

d) Parallel

TOPIC B

Network Categories

So far, you have learned about various network components that constitute a network. You will now describe how you can replicate these basic network structures on a larger scale. In this topic, you will identify the primary network categories.

The area covered by present day networks may be small enough to fit a building or large enough to span continents. Networks of different sizes have different requirements and features, and may use completely different technologies. Companies can deploy a network depending on their size and communications needs. As a network professional, you may work with a network of any possible size or type. A thorough knowledge of the size-based classification of networks and their related technologies will help you choose the network type that is best suited for your needs.

LANs

Definition:

A *Local Area Network (LAN)* is a self-contained network that spans a small area, such as a single building, floor, or room. In a LAN, all nodes and segments are directly connected with cables or short-range wireless technologies. It does not require a leased telecommunication system to function. Due to their smaller size and fewer number of nodes, LANs provide faster data transfer than other network types. Different technologies can be implemented on a LAN depending on configuration needs and working of the network. Ethernet is the most commonly implemented LAN technology. Other LAN technologies such as the token ring, the token bus, and the Fiber Distributed Data Interface (FDDI) can also be used on LANs.

Example:

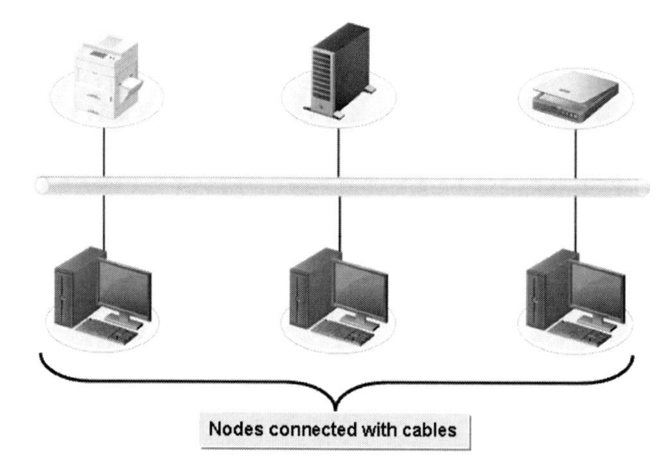

Figure 1-9: *Devices connected to form a LAN.*

LAN Administrator Duties

LAN administrators are responsible for managing and maintaining the local network. The administrator's responsibilities not only include maintaining machines and cabling but also network software. LAN administrators may also be required to perform installation and deployment, upgrades, and troubleshooting for different applications. LAN administrators need to be versatile and adaptable with a broad range of skills and knowledge about network applications and hardware.

WANs

Definition:

A *Wide Area Network (WAN)* is a network that spans a large area, often across multiple geographical locations. WANs typically connect multiple LANs and other networks using long-range transmission media. Such a network scheme facilitates communication among users and computers in different locations. WANs can be private, such as those built and maintained by large, multinational corporations, or they can be public, such as the Internet.

Example:

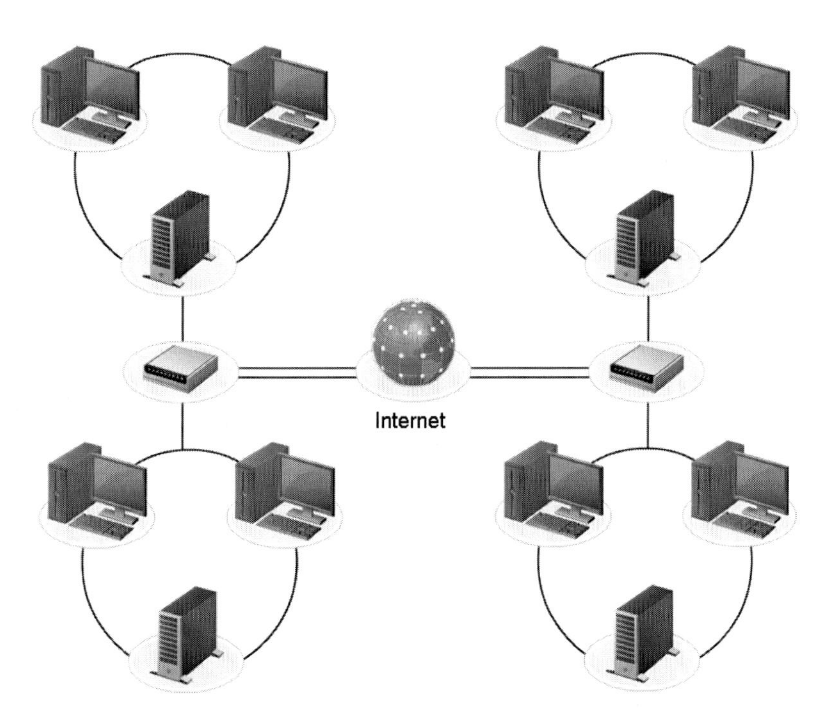

Figure 1-10: *A WAN composed of several LANs.*

WAN Administrator Duties

WAN administrators typically handle more complex technical issues than LAN administrators, and focus on resolving network issues rather than user issues. A WAN administrator performs the following duties:

- Designs and maintains the connection scheme between remote segments of a network.
- Develops and troubleshoots routing structures.
- Works with both voice and data systems.
- Develops scripts to automate complex network administrative tasks.
- Works on security issues and helps implement recovery schemes.
- Plans, tests, and implements hardware and software upgrades.

Network Coverage Areas

There are other network categories based on the geographical area they cover.

Network Category	Description
MAN	A *Metropolitan Area Network (MAN)* covers an area equivalent to a city or a municipality.
CAN	A *Campus Area Network (CAN)* covers an area equivalent to an academic campus or business park. A CAN is typically owned or used exclusively by an entity.
PAN	A *Personal Area Network (PAN)* connects two to three computers with cables and is most often seen in small or home offices. A *Wireless Personal Area Network (WPAN)* is a variation of PAN that connects wireless devices in close proximity but not through a *Wireless Access Point (WAP)*. Infrared and Bluetooth are technologies used for connecting devices in a WPAN.

The Internet

The *Internet* is the single largest global WAN, linking virtually every country in the world. Publicly owned and operated, the Internet is widely used for sending email, transferring files, and carrying out online commercial transactions. All information on the Internet is stored as web pages, which can be accessed through software known as a web browser. Most of the processes related to the Internet are specified by the *Internet Protocol (IP)*, and all the nodes connected to the Internet are identified by a unique address, known as an *IP address.*

The *Internet Corporation for Assigned Names and Numbers (ICANN)* coordinates the assignments of unique identifications on the Internet, such as domain names, IP addresses, and extension names, while the *Internet Society (ISOC)* coordinates and oversees standards and practices for the Internet.

You can get more information on the ISOC at its website **www.isoc.org.**

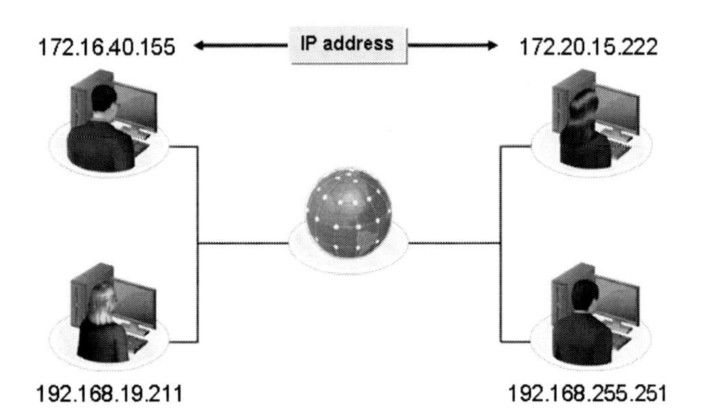

Figure 1-11: *The Internet consists of computers connected across the world.*

Intranets

Definition:

An *intranet* is a private network that uses Internet protocols and services to share a company's information with its employees. As with the Internet, the employees can access an intranet via a web browser and navigate a company's web pages. However, an intranet is not very useful if it is not connected with the Internet. An intranet contains information that is segregated from the Internet for confidentiality and security reasons.

Example:

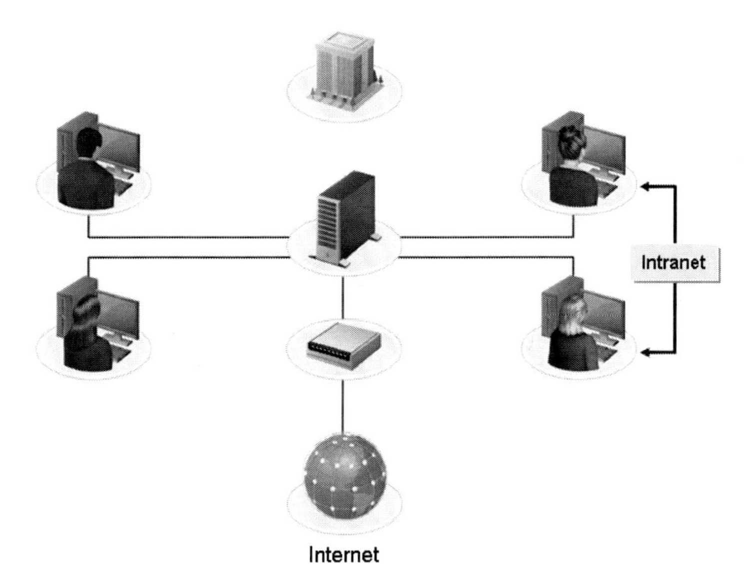

Figure 1-12: *An intranet connecting users in a private network.*

Extranets

Definition:

An *extranet* is a private network that grants controlled access to users outside of the network. It is an extension of an organization's intranet. With the help of an extranet, organizations can grant access to users such as vendors, suppliers, and clients to connect to resources on the network.

Example:

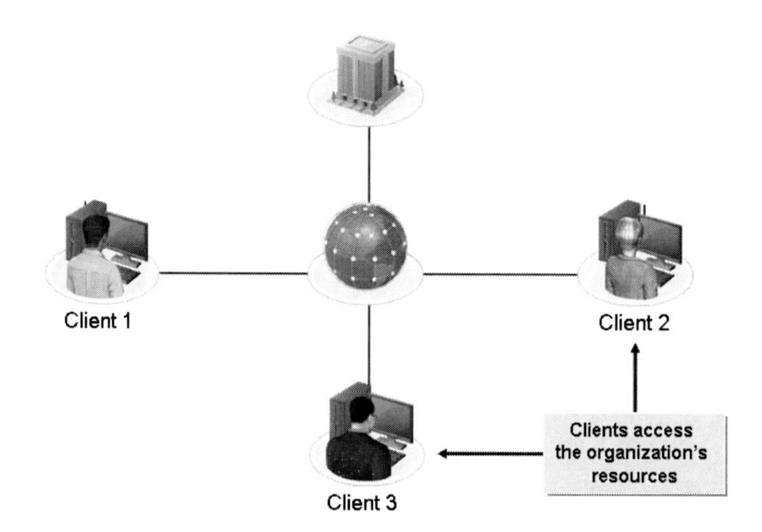

Figure 1-13: *An extranet connecting a user outside of the network.*

Enterprise Networks

Definition:

An *enterprise network* is a network that includes elements of both local and wide area networks. Owned and operated by a single organization to interlink its computers and resources, it employs technologies and software designed for fast data access, email exchange, and collaboration. Enterprise networks are scalable and include high-end equipment, strong security systems, and mission-critical applications.

Example:

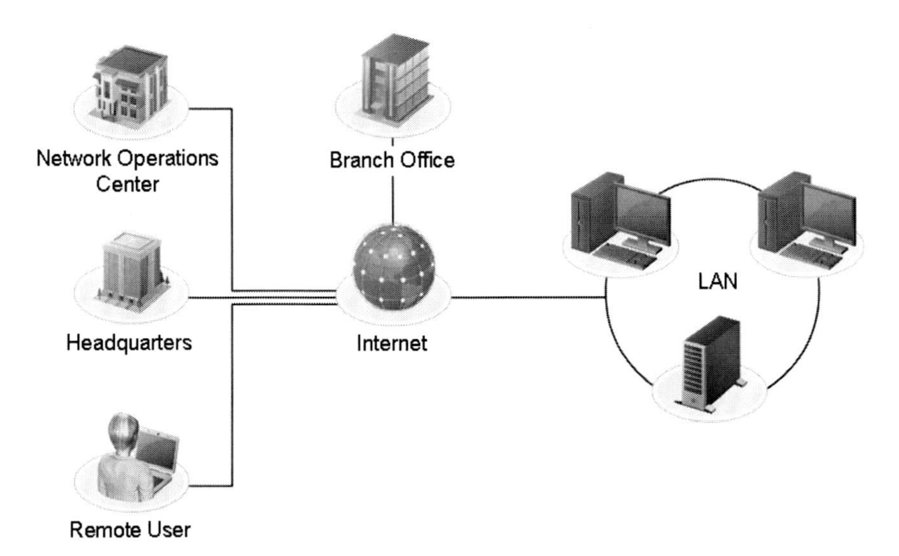

Figure 1-14: *An enterprise network.*

ACTIVITY 1-2

Identifying Network Categories

Scenario:

In this activity, you will identify the primary categories of networks.

---

1. **Ristell & Sons Publishing has a remote office that accesses its corporate office with relatively high bandwidth. Which network category does it use?**

   a) LAN

   b) WAN

   c) CAN

   d) MAN

---

2. **InfiniTrain occupies four floors in the East building of the River View Business Complex. What category does this network fit into?**

   a) LAN

   b) WAN

   c) CAN

   d) MAN

---

3. **This figure represents a company with a central office, an attached warehouse, and a remote supplier. Which portions of the network are LANs?**

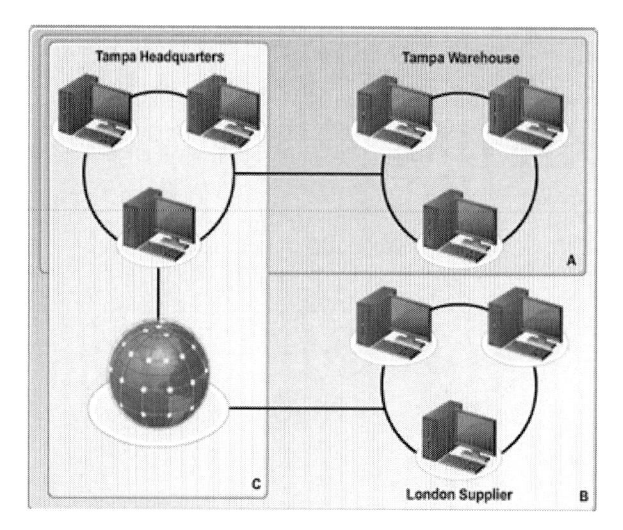

   a) Section C—Tampa Headquarters

   b) Section A—Tampa Headquarters and Tampa Warehouse

   c) Section B—Tampa Warehouse and London Supplier

---

4. This figure represents the same small company with a central office, an attached warehouse, and a remote sales office. Which portion of the network is a WAN?

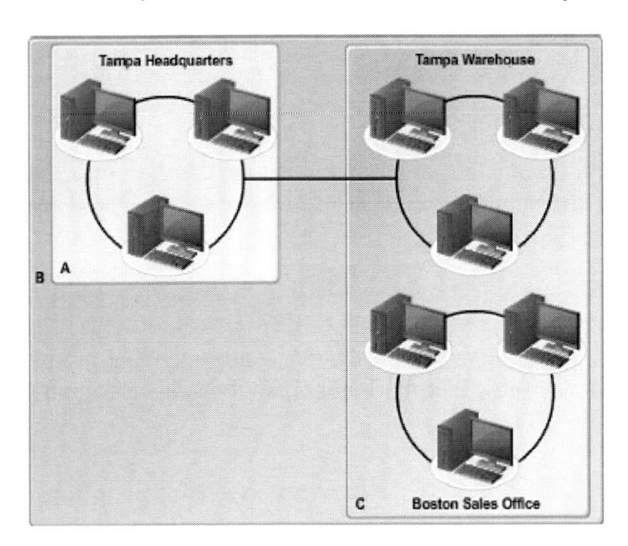

a) Section A—Tampa Headquarters
b) Section B—Tampa Headquarters and Tampa Warehouse
c) Section C—Tampa Warehouse and Boston Sales Office

5. Which network employs elements of both local and wide area networks?

a) Metropolitan area network
b) Personal area network
c) Campus area network
d) Enterprise network

TOPIC C

Standard Network Models

Up to this point, you have identified the primary categories that describe the size and extent of a network. For every network deployed, the actual model of the network will depend on the individual network's requirements that the network is designed to cater. In this topic, you will identify the standard networking models currently in use.

As a networking professional, you will need to work in a variety of network environments that use different technologies, implementation designs, and models. The model to be used is a result of an analysis of requirements, connectivity methods, and technologies that are being used. Some of these models might be more prevalent than others, and you need to understand the different network models you might encounter.

Network Models

Definition:

A *network model* is a design specification for how the nodes on a network are constructed to interact and communicate. A network model determines the degree to which communications and processing are centralized or distributed.

There are three primary network models:

- Centralized or hierarchical
- Client/server
- Peer-to-peer

Example:

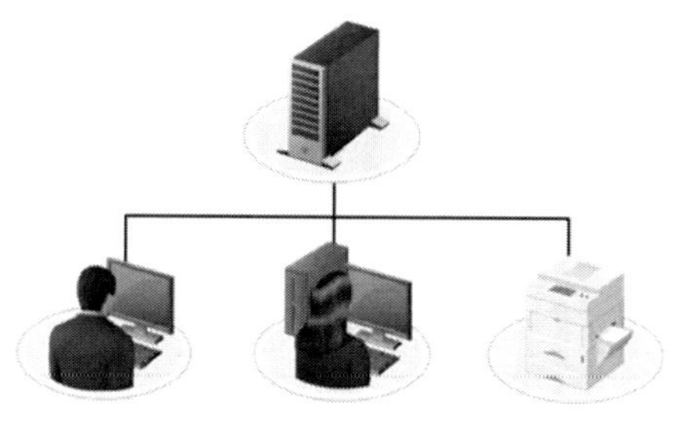

Figure 1-15: *A centralized network.*

Segments

Definition:

A *segment* is a physical subdivision of a network that links a number of devices, or serves as a connection between two nodes. A segment is bounded by physical internetworking devices such as switches and routers. All nodes attached to a segment have common access to that portion of the network.

Example:

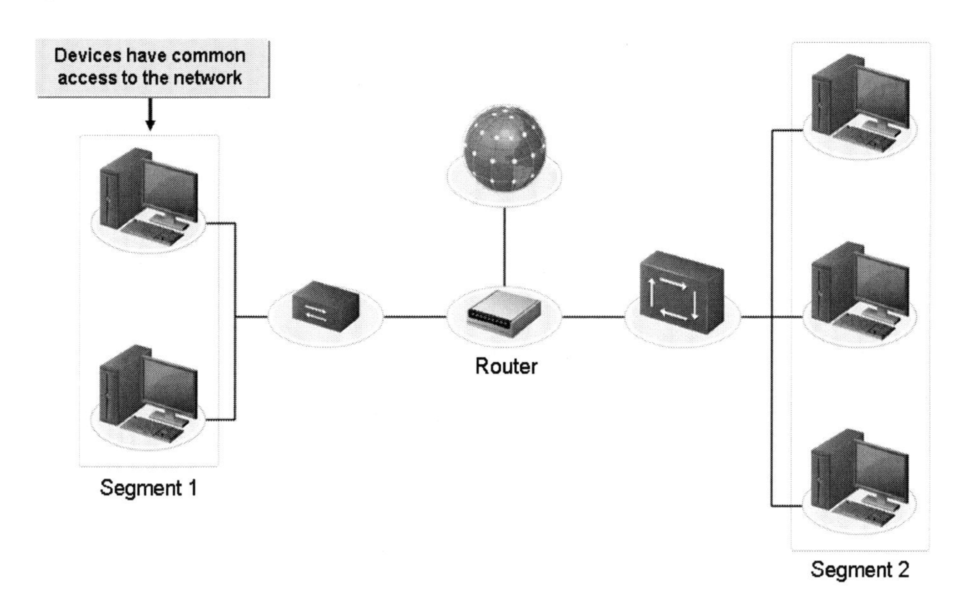

Figure 1-16: *Segments of a network.*

Segmenting for Performance

Dividing a network into segments can improve network performance. With segments, traffic is confined to a portion of the network containing nodes that communicate with each other most often. However, performance can suffer if nodes must regularly communicate with nodes on other segments. Devices such as switches and routers that link segments can lead to slower transmission between segments.

Centralized Networks

Definition:

A *centralized network* is a computer network in which a central host computer controls all network communication, and performs data processing and storage on behalf of clients. Users connect to the host via dedicated terminals or terminal emulators. Centralized networks provide high performance and centralized management, but they are expensive to implement.

The terms “hierarchical network” and “host-based network” can also be used to describe centralized networks.

Example:

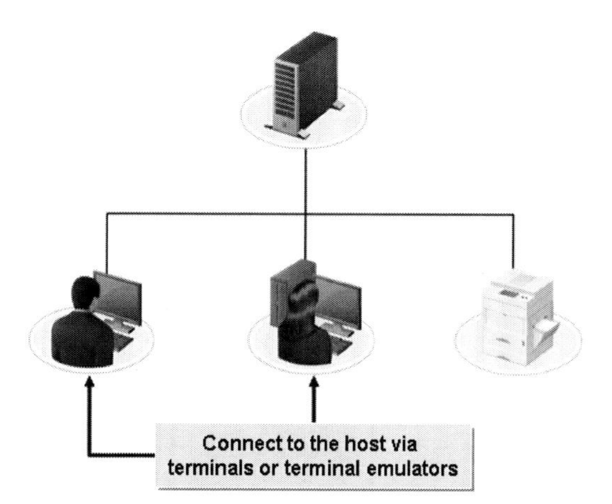

Figure 1-17: *A centralized computer network.*

Decentralized Networks

A pure centralized network is rare in today's environment. Most of the network types you encounter will be decentralized to some extent, with the client/server architecture having some degree of centralization, and the peer-to-peer architecture being almost purely decentralized. In a decentralized network, each peer can connect directly with other peers without being managed by a central server. A server provides services to the nodes upon a request from them. A peer-to-peer network is an example of a decentralized network.

Client/Server Networks

Definition:

A *client/server network* is a network in which servers provide resources to clients. Typically, there is at least one server providing central *authentication* services. Servers also provide access to shared files, printers, hardware storage, and applications. In client/server networks, processing power, management services, and administrative functions can be concentrated where needed, while clients can still perform many basic end-user tasks on their own.

Example:

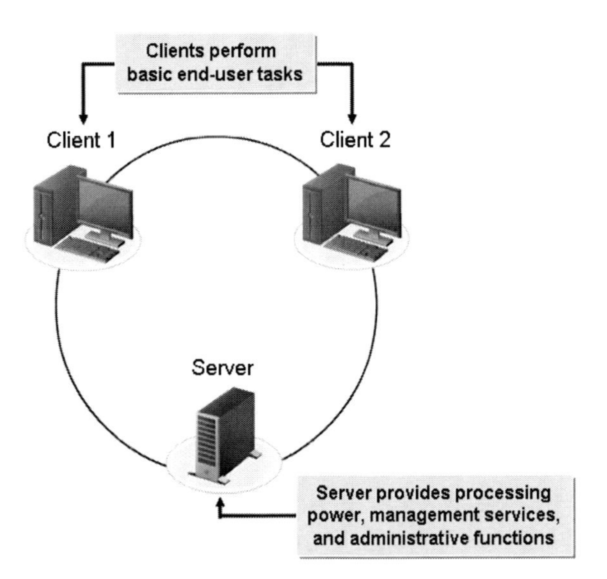

Figure 1-18: *Clients and a server in a client/server network.*

Peer-to-Peer Networks

Definition:

A *peer-to-peer network* is a network in which resource sharing, processing, and communications control are completely decentralized. All clients on the network are equal in terms of providing and using resources, and each individual workstation authenticates its users. Peer-to-peer networks are easy and inexpensive to implement. However, they are only practical in very small organizations, due to the lack of centralized data storage and administration. A peer-to-peer network is more commonly referred to as a *workgroup*. In a peer-to-peer network, user accounts must be duplicated on every workstation from which a user accesses resources. Such distribution of user information makes maintaining a peer-to-peer network difficult, especially as the network grows.

Example:

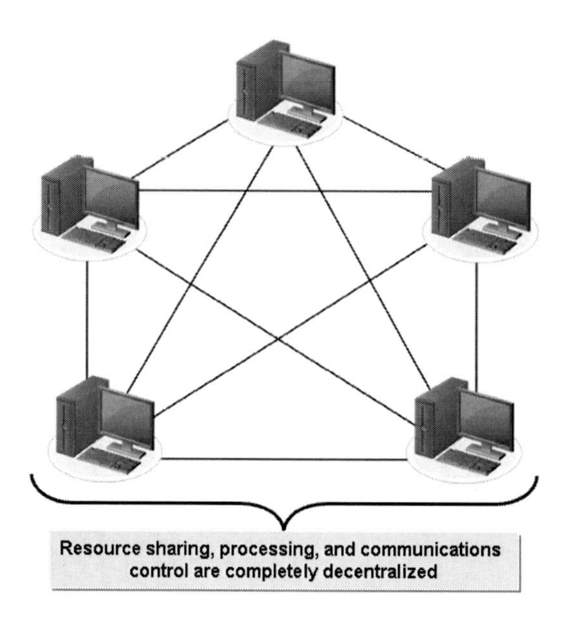

Figure 1-19: *Computers in a peer-to-peer network.*

Mixed Mode Networks

Definition:

A *mixed mode network* incorporates elements from more than one of the three standard network models. Some mixed mode networks consist of a client/server network combined with a centralized mainframe. An end user's workstation functions as a client to the network directory server, and employs terminal emulation software to authenticate to the host system.

Example:

A common example of a mixed mode network is a workgroup created to share local resources within a client/server network. For example, you might share one client's local printer with just a few other users. The client sharing the printer on the network does not use the client/server network's directory structure to authenticate and authorize access to the printer.

Example:

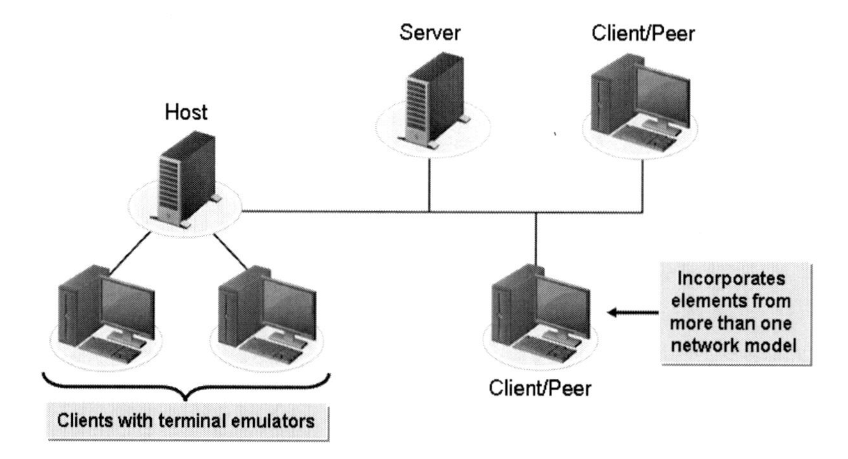

Figure 1-20: *A mixed mode network.*

ACTIVITY 1-3

Identifying the Standard Network Models

Scenario:

In this activity, you will identify the standard network models.

---

1. On your network, users access a single host computer via a terminal for all of their data processing and storage. Which network model does your network use?

a) Peer-to-peer
b) Mixed mode
c) Client/server
d) Centralized

---

2. On your network, users directly share files stored on their computers with other users. Additionally, they access shared storage, printing, and fax resources, which are connected to a department-wide server. Which network model does your network use?

a) Peer-to-peer
b) Client/server
c) Centralized
d) Mixed mode

---

3. Match the network model with its description.

___	Centralized	a. Nodes can perform basic end-user tasks on their own, but depend on another network resource for advanced processing tasks.
___	Client/server	b. Resource sharing, processing, and communications control are completely decentralized.
___	Peer-to-peer	c. A host computer performs data processing and storage on behalf of clients.
___	Mixed mode	d. Displays characteristics of more than one of the three standard network models.

4. **Rudison Technologies Ltd. has four employees who need to share information and hardware such as a scanner and printer. They also need Internet access. None of the users have advanced computing skills. Which type of network would best suit their needs?**

    a) Client/server

    b) Peer-to-peer

    c) Centralized

    d) Mixed mode

TOPIC D

Physical Network Topologies

In the previous topic, you identified the various network models. Now you are ready to see how these components can combine to create large structural units called network topologies. In this topic, you will identify the primary physical network topologies.

Network topologies influence the flow of data through a network and the design of communication protocols to a large extent. Getting to know the different topologies is essential to design or troubleshoot a network. Knowledge of the physical topology of a network is critical for you to be able to successfully execute many network management tasks including fault monitoring and problem isolation. No matter what your role, you will need to understand the characteristics of the network topology you are working with, and identify how the topology affects the network performance and troubleshooting.

Topology

Definition:

A *topology* is a network specification that determines the network's overall layout, signaling, and data-flow patterns. A *physical topology* describes a network's physical wiring layout or shape, while a *logical topology* describes the paths through which data moves. The physical and logical topologies can be different for a network. Common physical topologies include a star, ring, mesh, tree, and bus.

Example:

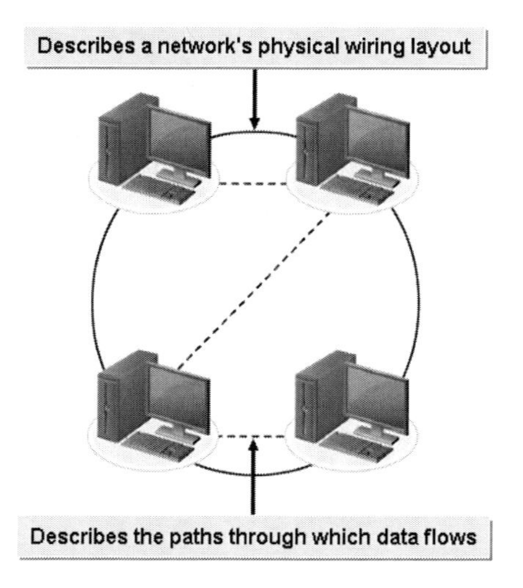

Figure 1-21: *Physical and logical topologies on the same network can differ.*

Point-to-Point Connections

Definition:

A *point-to-point connection* is a direct connection between two nodes on a network. One node transmits data directly to the other. Modern point-to-point connections implementations are present for both wired and wireless connections, including microwave and laser links, as well as Ethernet and coaxial cables. Wireless point-to-point connections often do not work if there are any obstacles in the path between endpoints to establish a good connection.

Example: Direct Connection Between Two Computers

Connecting one host's Network Interface Card (NIC) directly to another host's NIC with a Cat5 crossover cable is an example of a point-to-point connection.

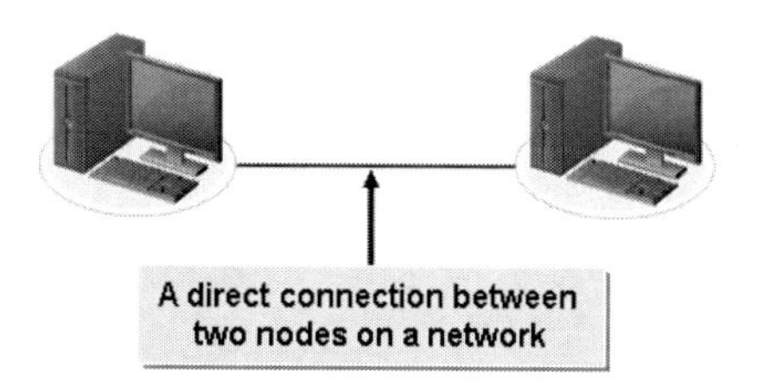

Figure 1-22: *A point-to-point connection between two computers.*

Multipoint Connections

Definition:

Multipoint connections are connections between multiple nodes. Each multipoint connection has more than two endpoints. A signal transmitted by any device on the medium is not private. All devices that share the medium can detect the signal but they do not receive it unless they are the recipients.

Example:

Multipoint connections are the most common way to physically connect a network. Physical bus and star networks are examples of multipoint connections.

Radiated Connections

Definition:

A *radiated,* or *broadcast connection* is a wireless point-to-point or multipoint connection between devices. Wireless LAN, infrared, and Wi-Fi™ networks are all radiated connections.

Example: Wi-Fi

Wi-Fi is a brand name promoted by the Wi-Fi Alliance for WLANs. Wireless radio communications following the IEEE 802.11, or Wi-Fi, standard are the most common choice for ordinary wireless LAN connectivity for portable computers inside homes, offices, and increasingly, public buildings. Choose Wi-Fi when you need to connect portable computer systems to a wired or wireless LAN. Wi-Fi enables users to move from place to place freely without a line of sight connection to the access point. Wi-Fi provides good performance within the wireless access point coverage area, barring any signal interference.

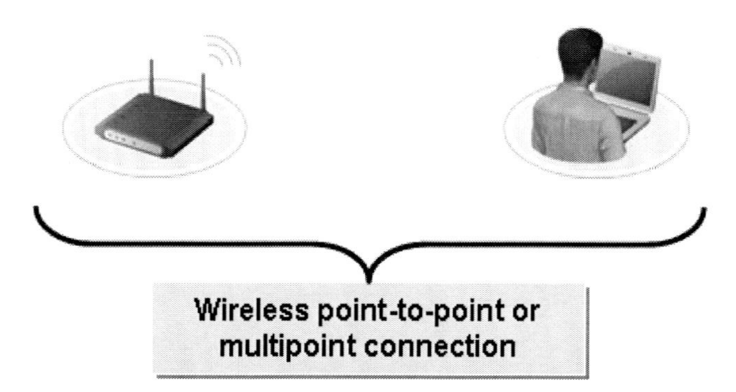

Figure 1-23: *A radiated connection with a wireless router.*

The Physical Bus Topology

Definition:

A *physical bus topology* is a network topology in which the nodes are arranged in a linear format, and a T-connector connects each node directly to the network cable. The cable is called the bus and serves as a single communication channel. Signals can reflect off the ends of the cable, so you must install 50 ohm *terminators* to prevent this reflection. Attaching a terminator at both ends of the network cable prevents a condition called *signal bounce*, in which signals endlessly move from one end of the wire to the other. Terminators impede or absorb signals so they cannot reflect onto the wire.

You must ground a bus network on one end to reduce static electricity.

Disadvantages of the Bus Topology

The bus topology has a few disadvantages. A bus network:

- Is easy to implement but can be unreliable, because the entire bus fails if there is a break in the network cable.
- Cannot support multiple pairs of terminals at the same time.
- Transmits data slower than the other topologies as only two nodes can communicate at any time.

Example:

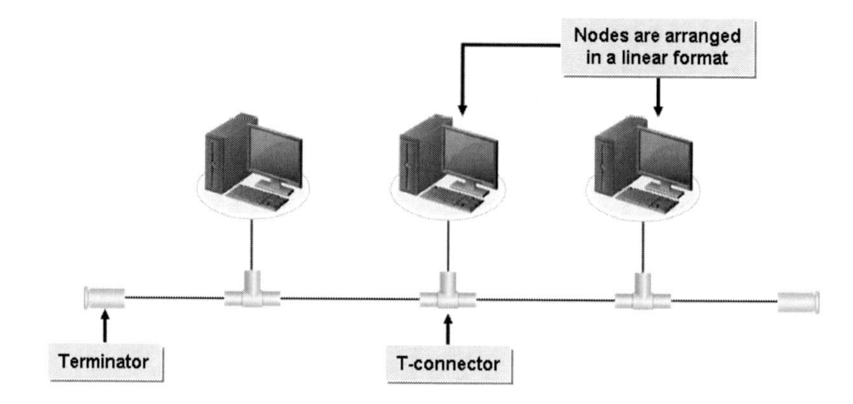

Figure 1-24: *A physical bus topology.*

Data Transmission on a Bus

On a bus, as all communication takes place through the same path, only a single pair of terminals can communicate at a time. Data is transmitted on a bus in a sequence of steps:

1. Each node on a bus listens passively to the channel until it receives a signal. The data signal passes by every node, but not through the node.
2. The node transmits data when the bus is free, and the allocation of the channel to nodes is done on a first-come, first-serve basis.
3. When a node is ready to transmit data to another node, it sends out a broadcast alert to inform all other nodes that a transmission is being done. This is to avoid a collision of data packets from multiple users on the bus.
4. If two nodes try to transmit data at exactly the same time, a collision occurs on the wire. Each node waits a random period of time before retransmission.
5. The destination node picks up the transmission.
6. If none of the nodes accept the transmitted data, such as in the case of the destination node being switched off, the data packet is terminated by the bus itself.

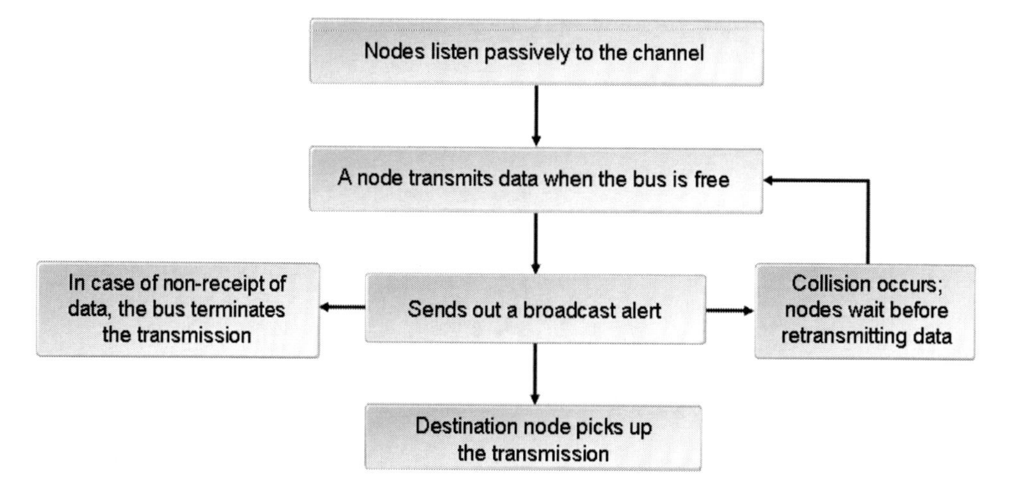

Figure 1-25: *Data transmission on a bus.*

The Physical Star Topology

Definition:

A *physical star topology* is a network topology that uses a central connectivity device, such as a switch, with individual physical connections to each node. The individual nodes send data to the connectivity device, and the device then either forwards data to the appropriate destination node, as in the case of a switch, or simply passes it through to all attached nodes, as in the case of a hub. Star topologies are reliable and easy to maintain as a single failed node does not bring down the whole network. However, if the central connectivity device fails, the entire network fails.

Example:

Although star topologies are extremely common in client/server networks, a host-based computing system is a classic example of a physical star topology. Each node has a connection to the host computer and is not aware of other nodes on the network.

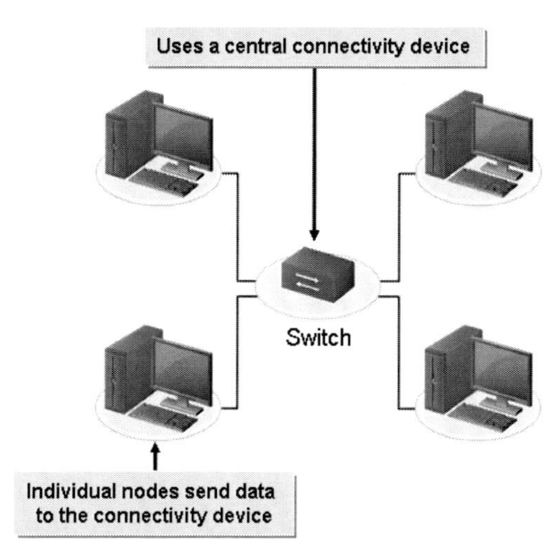

Figure 1-26: *A physical star topology.*

The Physical Ring Topology

Definition:

A *physical ring topology* is a network topology in which each node is connected to the two nearest nodes: the upstream and downstream neighbors. The flow of data in a ring network is unidirectional to avoid collisions. All nodes in the network are connected to form a circle. There is no central connecting device to control network traffic, and each node handles all data packets that pass through it. Data moves in one direction through each node that scans data packets, accepts packets destined for it, and forwards packets destined for another node.

Each node in the ring topology acts as a repeater and boosts the signal when it retransmits the data packet. This boost in the signal ensures that the signal quality is high. Ring topologies are potentially unreliable as the failure of a single node can bring down the entire network.

Example:

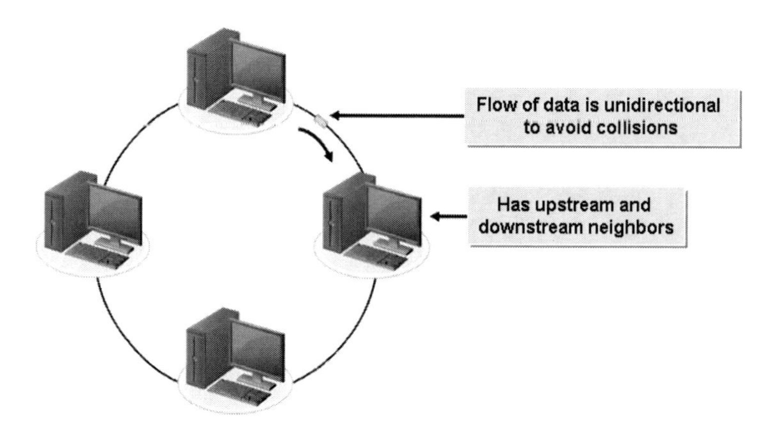

Figure 1-27: *A physical ring topology.*

Example: The Dual Ring Topology

A variant of the ring topology is the *dual ring topology,* which allows the use of two rings with each ring carrying data in opposite directions. Dual ring configurations are faster as data can be sent through the shortest path between a sender and the receiver. It is a more reliable topology because in case of a breakage in the inner or outer ring, the topology automatically reconfigures to a single ring data flow, thus reducing down time on the network.

The Physical Mesh Topology

Definition:

A *physical mesh topology* is a network topology in which each node is directly connected to every other node, similar to the physical point-to-point topology. This configuration allows each node to communicate with multiple nodes at the same time. Since all nodes have dedicated links with other nodes, there is no congestion on the network and data travels very fast. Because no node can be isolated from the network, this topology is extremely reliable. It is also difficult to implement and maintain because the number of connections increases exponentially with the number of nodes. Mesh topologies typically provide reliable communications between independent networks.

The Partial Mesh Topology

The *partial mesh* topology is a variation of the mesh topology in which only a few nodes have direct links with all the other nodes. This differentiates it from the full mesh topology in which all nodes have direct links with others. It is less complex, less expensive, and contains less redundancies than a full mesh topology. A partial mesh topology is commonly used in subnetworks of large networks where the number of users is low and lower data transfer rates can be used.

Example: Mesh Topology on the Internet

The connections between major divisions of the Internet use a mesh topology.

Example:

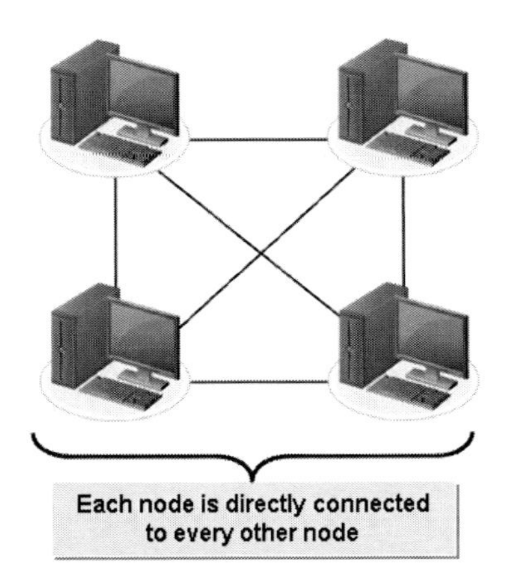

Figure 1-28: *A representation of the physical mesh topology.*

The Physical Tree Topology

Definition:

A *physical tree topology* is a network topology in which a central, or root node is hierarchically connected to one or more second-level nodes, which are one level lower in the hierarchy. The root node has a point-to-point link with each of the second-level nodes, while each of the second-level nodes is connected to one or more third-level nodes via a point-to-point link. The root node is the only node that has no other node above it in the hierarchy. Each node in the network has the same number of lower-level nodes connected to it; this number is referred to as the *branching factor* of the hierarchical tree.

Example:

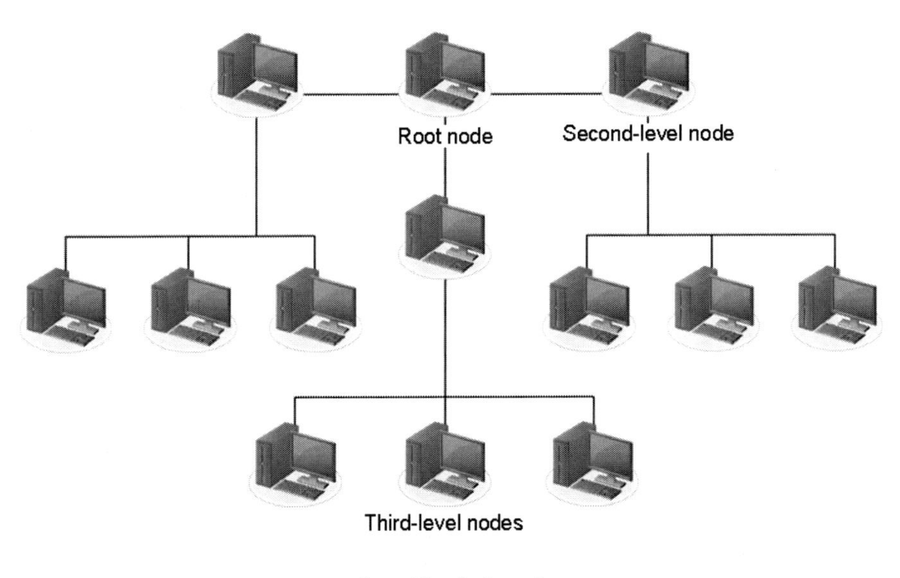

Figure 1-29: *A physical tree topology with a branching factor of 3.*

Hybrid Topologies

Definition:

A *hybrid topology* is any topology that exhibits the characteristics of more than one standard topology. Each section of the network follows the rules of its own topology. Hybrid topologies can be complex to maintain because they typically incorporate a wide range of technologies. Most of the large networks consist of several smaller subnetworks, and each subnetwork may have a different topology.

Example: Common Hybrid Topologies

Two common hybrid topologies are the star bus and the star ring. The star bus topology connects several star networks to a network backbone in a bus layout. The star ring connects several ring networks to a central device in a star configuration. Data is sent in a circular pattern around the star configuration.

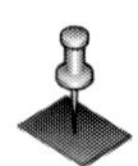

Hybrid topologies are typically not designed as such. They usually arise when administrators connect existing network implementations independently using different topologies.

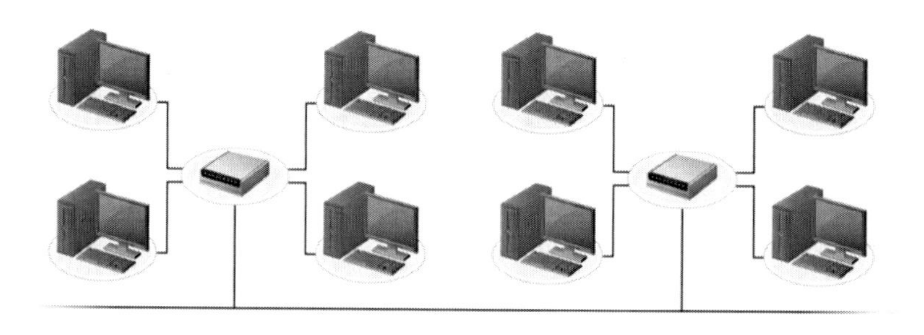

Star-bus topology

Figure 1-30: *The star bus topology connects star networks to a bus.*

Types of Hybrid Topologies

There are other types of hybrid topologies on a network.

Hybrid Topology	*Formed By*
Star-bus	Linking the central nodes of some star networks using a common bus. Inside each subnetwork, data will flow similar to a star network and each of these star networks will be treated as a node on the larger bus network. To move data from one subnetwork to another, it has to be placed on the common bus.
Star-of-stars	Connecting the central nodes of two or more star networks with a new common node. To move data from one subnetwork to another, it must be routed through the new common node.
Star-ring	Connecting the central nodes of multiple star networks in a ring. The data flow between different subnetworks is through this ring.

ACTIVITY 1-4

Identifying Physical Network Topologies

Scenario:

In this activity, you will identify the different physical network topologies.

---

1. **True or False? A physical topology describes the data flow patterns on a network.**

   __ True

   __ False

---

2. **Match the physical network topology with its description.**

___	Bus	a.	Network nodes have a direct connection to every other node.
___	Star	b.	Network nodes connect in a circle.
___	Ring	c.	Network nodes are arranged in a linear format.
___	Mesh	d.	Network nodes connect to a central connectivity device.
___	Hybrid	e.	Exhibits the characteristics of more than one standard topology.

---

3. **Which physical network topology connects each node to both its upstream and downstream neighbors?**

   a) Star

   b) Bus

   c) Tree

   d) Ring

---

4. **Which of these statements are valid with respect to the bus topology?**

   a) All nodes in the network are connected to a common transmission path.

   b) Multiple pairs of nodes can communicate at a time.

   c) It requires less cabling than other topologies.

   d) Data transmission is slower than other topologies.

---

5. **In which network connection type can all the devices detect the signal transmitted on the medium?**

   a) Point-to-point

   b) Radiated

   c) Multipoint

TOPIC E

Logical Network Topologies

In the previous topic, you identified the physical network topologies. Because the path of data flow does not always correspond to the physical wiring layout of the network, you also need to consider how logical data paths work. In this topic, you will identify logical network topologies.

You may be faced with a situation where you need to troubleshoot a logical segment of your network and ensure the flow of data between two links when the physical topology seems just fine. Logical network topologies provide information that physical topologies do not provide such as the data transmission path between a sender and a receiver and the different places in which this path converges or diverges. This information will also help you plan the transmission links and resource sharing capabilities and identify network routes apart from troubleshooting.

The Logical Bus Topology

Definition:

A *logical bus topology* is a network topology in which nodes receive the data transmitted all at the same time, regardless of the physical wiring layout of the network. In a logical bus with the physical star topology, even though nodes connect to a central switch and resemble a star, data appears to flow in a single, continuous stream, from the sending node to all other nodes through the switch. As the transmission medium is shared, only one node can transmit at a time.

Example:

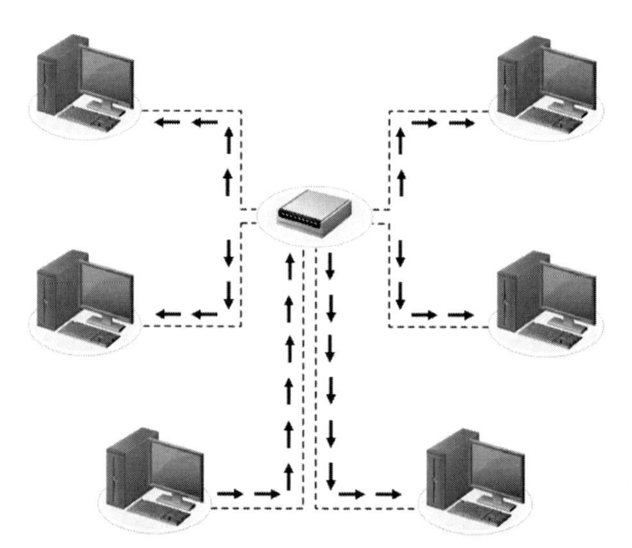

Figure 1-31: *A logical bus topology.*

The Logical Ring Topology

Definition:

A *logical ring topology* is a network topology in which each node receives data only from its upstream neighbor and retransmits data only to its downstream neighbor, regardless of the physical layout of the network. However, a logical ring must be used with a pure or hybrid physical ring topology such as star-ring. Although nodes might be connected to a central device in a star layout, data moves through the network in a circle until it reaches the original transmitting node, which then removes the data from the ring.

Example:

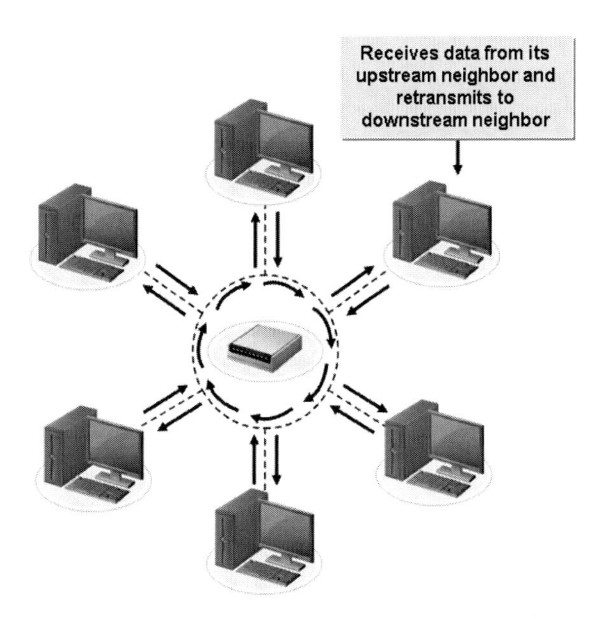

Figure 1-32: *A logical ring topology.*

The Logical Star Topology

Definition:

A *logical star topology* implementation is less common than a logical ring or a logical bus. In a logical star topology, although all nodes are wired onto the same bus cable, a central device polls each node to check to see if it needs to transmit data. The central device also controls how long a node has access to the cable. A *multiplexer (mux)* manages individual signals and enables them to share the media.

Example:

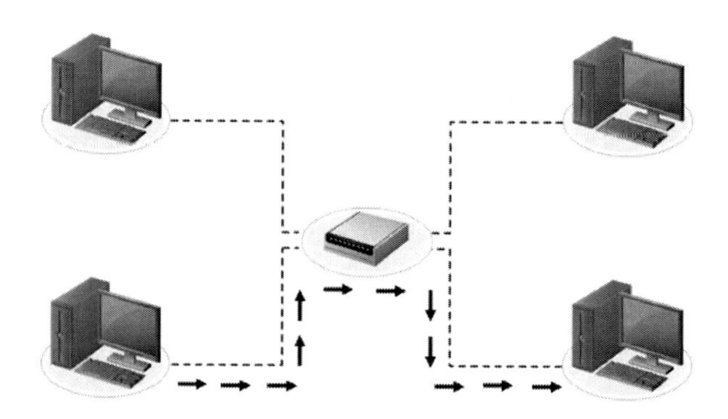

Figure 1-33: *A multiplexer managing signaling between nodes in a logical star topology.*

ACTIVITY 1-5

Identifying Logical Network Topologies

Scenario:

In this activity, you will identify logical network topologies.

---

1. **In which logical network topology do nodes receive the data transmitted simultaneously, regardless of the physical wiring of the network?**
    a) Bus
    b) Star
    c) Ring

---

2. **In which of the logical topologies does a node receive data only from its upstream neighbor and retransmit the data only to its downstream neighbor?**
    a) Star
    b) Bus
    c) Ring

---

3. **In which logical network topology does a central device poll nodes and control access to the channel?**
    a) Bus
    b) Ring
    c) Star

Lesson 1 Follow-up

In this lesson, you identified the basic components of the current networking theory. Any network you encounter will utilize some of these basic networking components and concepts. You need to understand these fundamentals in order to succeed in your professional networking career.

1. **In your opinion, what are the considerations for choosing between the different topologies to implement in your network?**

2. **Describe any background experience you have working with LANs, WANs, or other types of networks.**

2 Network Communications Methods

Lesson Time: 1 hour(s), 25 minutes

Lesson Objectives:

In this lesson, you will identify the major network communications methods.

You will:

- Identify the primary data transmission methods on a network.
- Identify media access methods and their characteristics.
- Identify the major network signaling methods.

Introduction

In the previous lesson, you learned about the basic network components and topologies. All of these network types employ a set of communications methods to transmit data. In this lesson, you will identify the primary transmission, media access, and signaling methods that networks use to communicate.

The essence of networking is communication—sending data from node to node for sharing between users and systems. The methods a network uses to communicate are vital to its proper functioning. Just like humans use different languages for communication, networks often use different communication methods to talk to one another. Understanding the language you need to use for communication is essential to be able to communicate. By the same token, understanding these basic communication methods will be critical to your success as a networking professional.

This lesson covers all or part of the following CompTIA® Network+® (Exam N10-005) certification objectives:

- Topic A:
    - 1.3 Explain the purpose and properties of IP addressing.
    - 3.7 Compare and contrast different LAN technologies.
- Topic B:
    - 3.7 Compare and contrast different LAN technologies.

TOPIC A
Data Transmission Methods

With the network in place, the next step is to identify methods to transmit data. In this topic, you will identify the primary data transmission methods.

As a network professional, you will probably be expected to monitor network performance and response time. The manner in which data is transmitted between nodes on a network can significantly impact network traffic and performance. You will need to understand the characteristics and potential effects of the transmission methods, which are implemented on the networks you support to understand their impact on the network.

Data Transmission

Definition:

Data transmission is the exchange of data among different computers or other electronic devices through a network. Unlike telephony, which involves only transmission of voice, data transmission sends non-voice information such as graphics, animations, audio, text, and video over the network. Most of the data transmission takes place through computer networks and the term data networks is synonymous with computer networks.

Example:

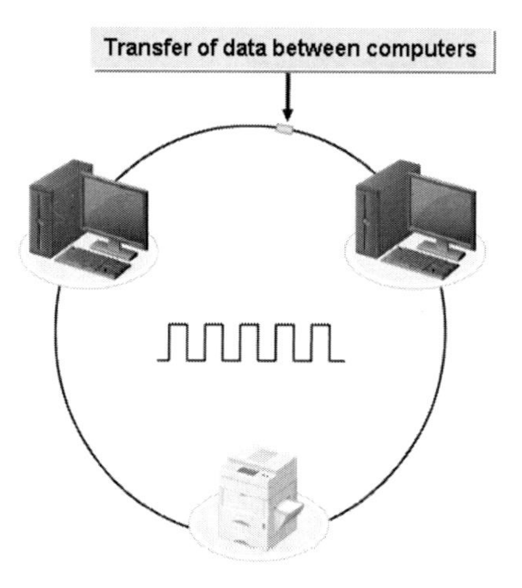

Figure 2-1: *Data communication on a computer network.*

Instantaneous Data Transfer

Though data is typically stored as files before being transmitted, there are exceptions to this process. In some forms of data communication, such as online chat or video conferencing, data needs to be transmitted as soon as it is generated. In such cases, data is immediately converted into a network-compatible format and transmitted without being stored either in main memory or on a disk.

Digital Data Transmission

Digital data transmissions use voltage differences to represent the 1s and 0s in data. Unlike analog signal transmission, they are not modulated over a carrier. On-off keying or Manchester encoding converts data into a digital waveform. Each bit takes a predefined time to transmit, and the sender and receiver synchronize their clocks either by transmitting a bit pattern or by monitoring for the reception of the first bit.

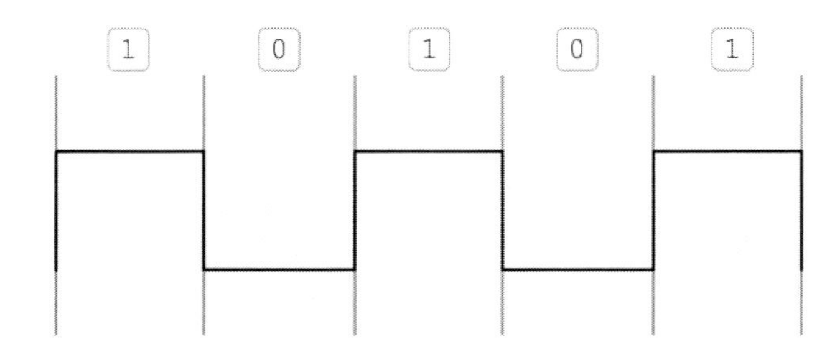

Figure 2-2: *Digital data transmission using on-off keying.*

On-Off Keying

On-off keying is a digital data transmission encoding scheme in which a change in voltage from one state to another within a predetermined interval is symbolized by a 1. No voltage transition is symbolized by a 0. The receiver synchronizes its clock with the sender by watching for 1s.

Variations of this scheme are called *Non-Return to Zero (NRZ)* and *Non-Return to Zero Inverted (NRZI)* encoding. On-off keying is used over serial ports and other relatively low-speed digital data connections.

Because the receiver synchronizes its clock by watching for 1s, problems can arise when long sequences of 1s or 0s must be sent. The receiver may not be able to synchronize its clock for a long interval. With its clock out of sync, the receiver could incorrectly decipher how many 1s or 0s have been transmitted, leading to data corruption.

Manchester Encoding

Manchester encoding was developed as a way to overcome the limitations of on-off keying. The transition from positive to ground represents a binary 0 and a negative to positive voltage transition in the middle of the bit period designates a binary 1. Thus, every bit involves a voltage transition and the problem of transmitting a long string of 1s or 0s is eliminated. Manchester encoding is used over Ethernet and other high-speed digital data connections.

Unicast Transmission

Definition:

Unicast transmission is a method for data transfer from a source address to a destination address. Network nodes not involved in the transfer ignore the transmission. Unicast transmission is the predominant mode of transmission on LANs and the Internet. Some familiar unicast applications are *Hyper-Text Transfer Protocol (HTTP)*, *Simple Mail Transfer Protocol (SMTP)*, and *File Transfer Protocol (FTP)*.

Example:

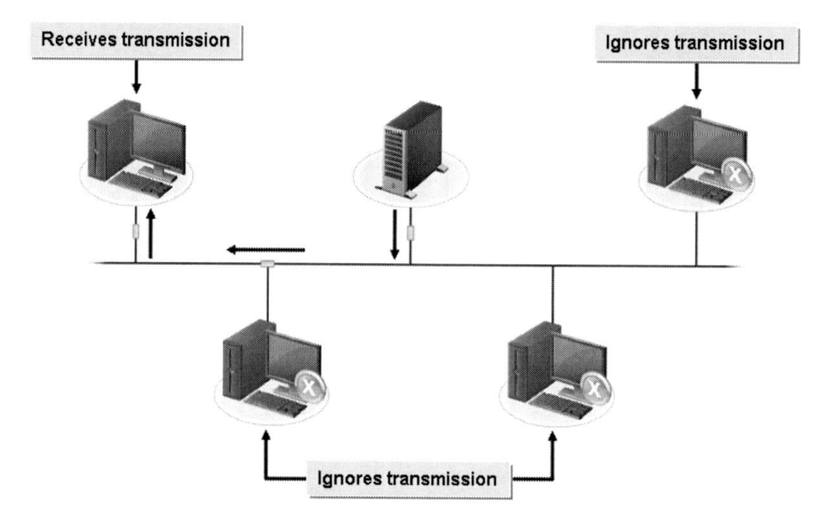

Figure 2-3: *Data transfer in a unicast transmission.*

Broadcast Transmission

Definition:

Broadcast transmission is a transmission method in which data is sent from a source node to all other nodes on a network. Network services that rely on broadcast transmissions generate a great deal of traffic. Occasionally, nodes use broadcast transmissions to check for the availability of a particular service on the network. If the service is not available, the nodes broadcast a request for the service. If a server is present, it responds to the request.

Example:

Some servers periodically advertise their presence to the network by sending a broadcast message.

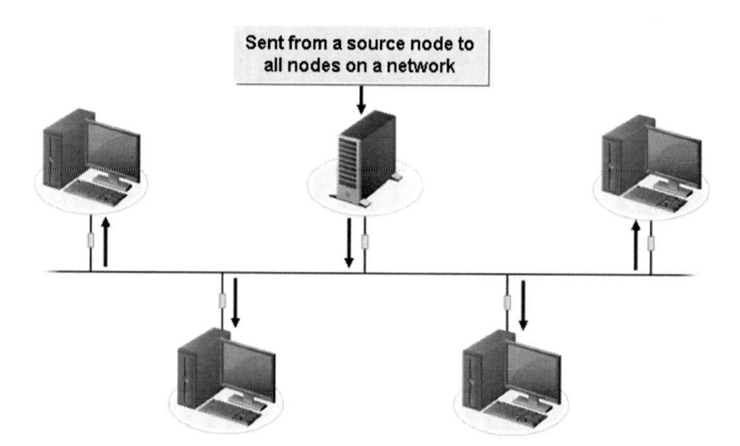

Figure 2-4: *Data transfer in a broadcast transmission.*

Multicast Transmission

Definition:

Multicast transmission is a transmission method in which data is sent from a server to specific nodes that are predefined as members of a multicast group. Network nodes not in the group ignore the data. Communication with nodes outside of a multicast group must be done through unicast or broadcast transmissions.

Example: Television Signal Transmissions

A video server transmitting TV signals is an example of multicast transmission.

Example:

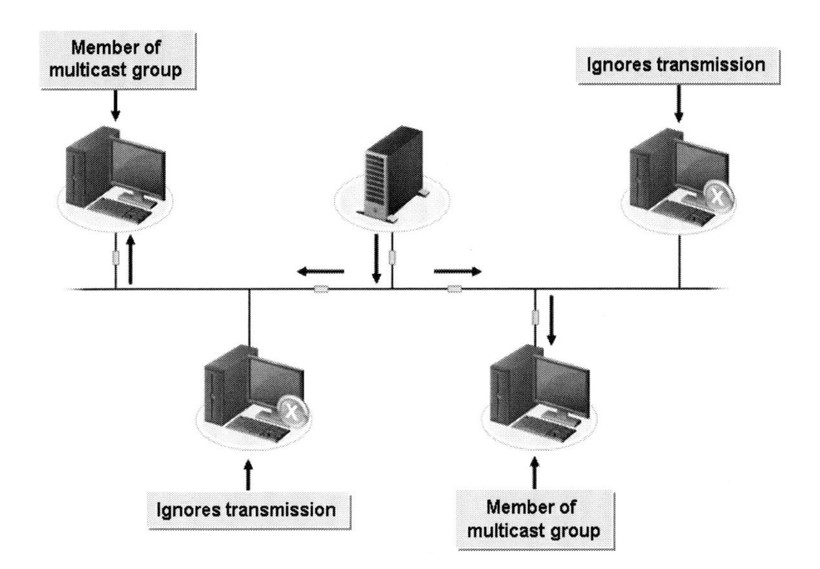

Figure 2-5: *Data transfer in a multicast transmission.*

Serial Data Transmission

With *serial data transmission,* the transmission of bits occurs as one per clock cycle, across a single transmission medium. Transmission of synchronization, start/stop, and error correction bits occurs along with data bits, thus limiting the overall throughput of data. Serial data transmission does not use DC pulses for transmission. Serial transmission can delineate bytes by using either synchronous or asynchronous techniques. Many common networking systems, such as Ethernet, use serial data transmission. Keyboards, mice, modems, and other devices can connect to your PC over a serial transmission port.

A clock cycle refers to the processing speed of a CPU.

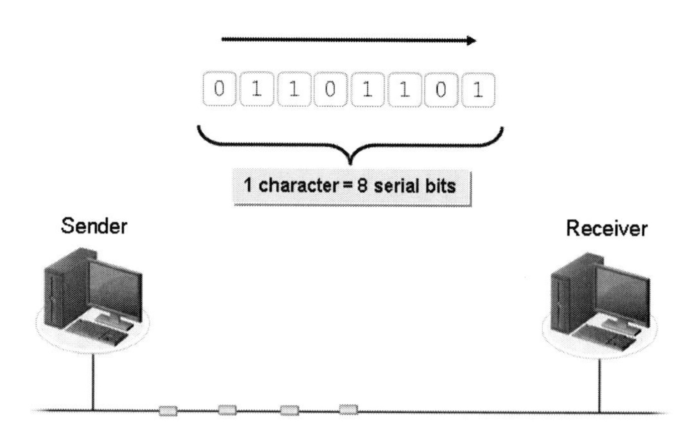

Figure 2-6: *Serial transmission being sent in sequence bitwise.*

Synchronous vs. Asynchronous Communications

The receiver of an analog signal must have a way of delineating between bytes in a stream of data. This can be done using either asynchronous or synchronous techniques.

With *asynchronous communications,* a sender inserts special start and stop bit patterns between each byte of data. By watching for these bit patterns, the receiver can distinguish between the bytes in the data stream.

With *synchronous communications,* a byte is sent after a standardized time interval. The receiver assumes that one byte is transmitted every interval. However, the two devices must start and stop their reckoning of these intervals at precisely the same time. Synchronous devices include a clock chip. A special bit pattern is inserted at specific intervals in the data stream, enabling the receiving device to synchronize its clock with the sender. After synchronizing the clocks, a receiver can use the predetermined time interval as a means to distinguish between bytes in the data stream.

Parallel Data Transmission

With *parallel data transmission,* transmission of multiple bits takes place by using multiple transmission lines. Many bits—even multiple bytes—can be transferred per clock cycle. Transmission of synchronization, start/stop, and error correction bits does not occur along with data bits. They are often sent over additional transmission lines, thus improving the overall throughput of data. Parallel transmission is commonly used on the parallel port on your computer, to which you can connect printers or scanners. Other uses include the system bus inside your PC, the *Small Computer System Interface (SCSI)* data bus, and the PC Card bus.

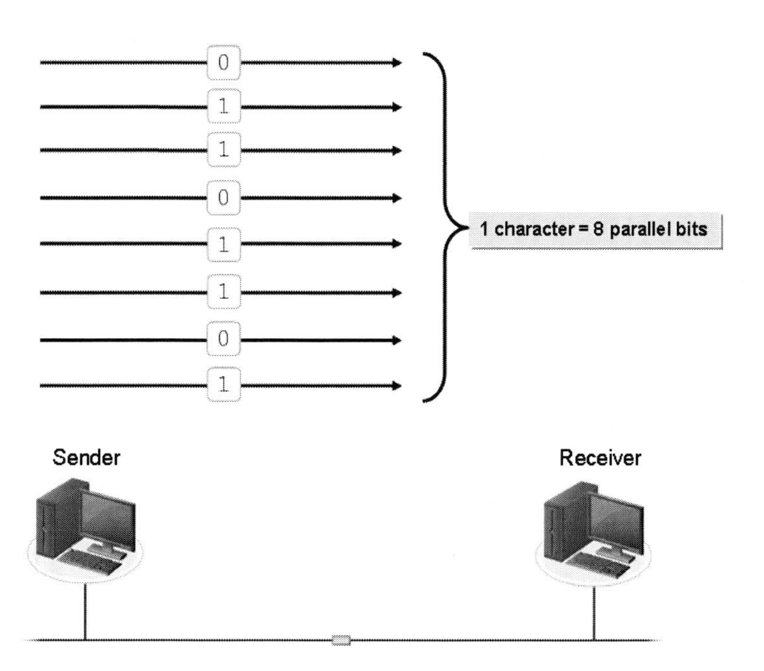

Figure 2-7: *Parallel transmission occurs simultaneously across separate channels.*

Baseband Transmission

In *baseband transmissions,* digital signals are sent via *direct current (DC)* pulses over a single, unmultiplexed signal channel. As all devices share a common transmission channel, they can send and receive over the same baseband medium, but they cannot send and receive simultaneously. Multiple baseband signals can be combined and sent over a single medium using a communication channel that is divided into discrete time slots.

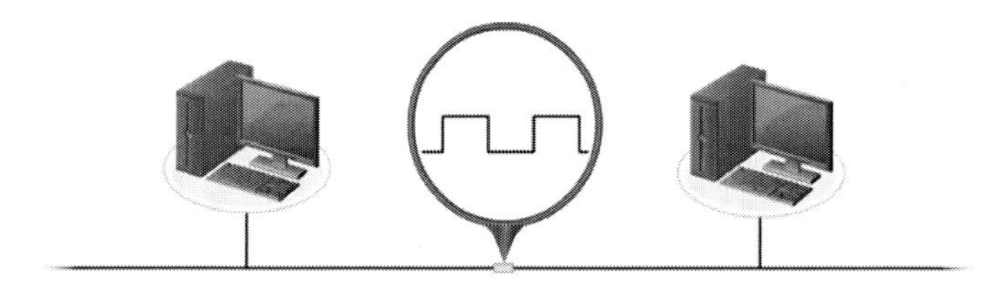

Figure 2-8: *Data transfer in baseband transmission.*

Broadband Transmission

Broadband transmission uses analog signaling to send data over a transmission medium using the complete bandwidth of the medium. Devices cannot send and receive over the same broadband channel; thus signals travel unidirectionally. Multiple broadband signals can be combined and sent over multiple frequencies, or channels, over a single network medium.

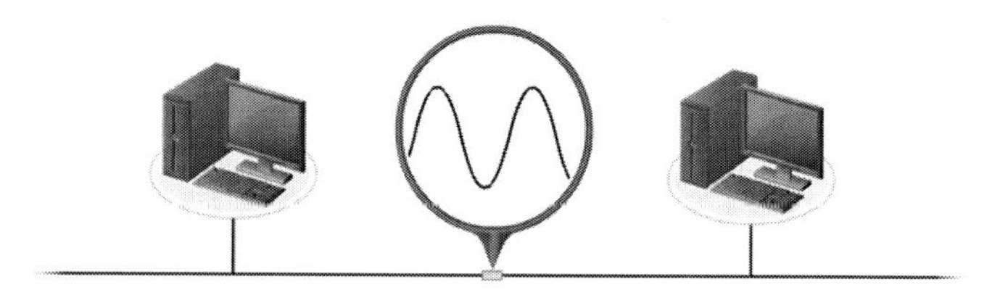

Figure 2-9: *Data transfer in broadband transmission.*

Broadband over Powerlines

Broadband over Powerlines (BPL) is a technology that allows broadband transmission over domestic power lines. This technology aims to use the existing power infrastructure to deliver Internet access to remote areas at a rapid pace. BPL is yet to gain widespread acceptance because of the potential signal interference with other data signals such as wireless transmission and radio waves.

The interference of BPL signals with radio waves affects radio operations, which are the main source of communication during times of natural disaster. In addition, there are concerns about the security of data when it is transmitted as plaintext using BPL, because it is easy to detect and intercept data when the signal travels using a common power source. Accepting and implementing BPL will require enhanced encryption and other security measures.

ACTIVITY 2-1

Identifying Data Transmission Methods

Scenario:

In this activity, you will identify the primary data transmission methods.

---

1. **Identify the transmission method depicted in the graphic.**

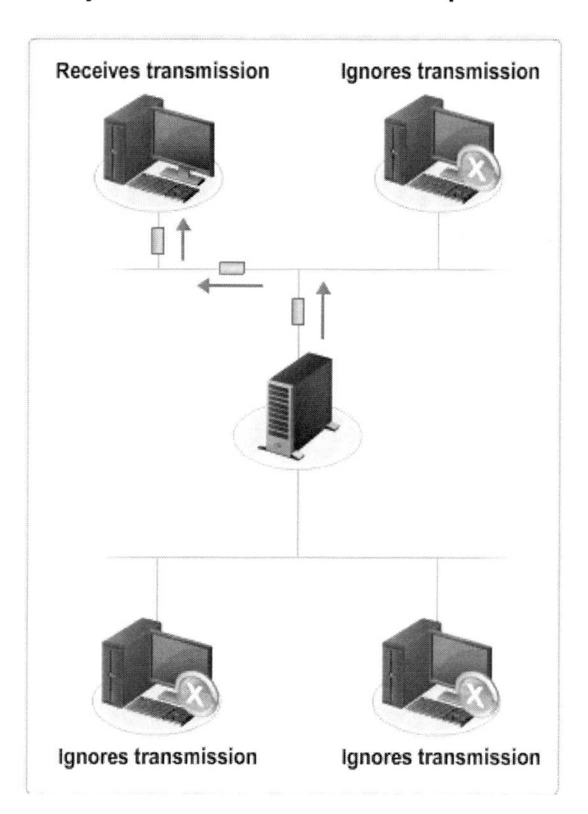

a) Unicast
b) Broadcast
c) Multicast

---

2. **True or False? Multicasting is more efficient in the use of network media than unicast transmission when many clients need to receive communications from a server.**

__ True
__ False

---

3. Match the transmission method to its description.

___	Unicast	a.	Transmission of data to all nodes.
___	Broadcast	b.	Transmission of data to the intended receiving device.
___	Multicast	c.	Transmission of data to a subset of nodes.

4. Which transmission method allows digital signals to be sent as DC pulses over a single, unmultiplexed signal channel?

a) Broadband

b) Parallel

c) Baseband

d) Serial

5. Which of these devices use serial data transmission?

a) Keyboard

b) Mouse

c) USB hard drive

d) Internal bus

6. Match the data transmission method with its description.

___	Serial	a.	Utilizes additional transmission lines to improve the overall data throughput.
___	Parallel	b.	Combines multiple digital signals to be sent over a single medium using a time slot divided communication channel.
___	Baseband	c.	Delineates bytes by using either synchronous or asynchronous techniques.
___	Broadband	d.	Uses voltage differences to directly represent the data as 1s and 0s.
___	Digital	e.	Uses analog signaling to send data using the medium's entire bandwidth.

TOPIC B

Media Access Methods

In the previous topic, you identified the primary data transmission methods. The next component of network communication is media access. In this topic, you will identify common media access methods.

Human communications follow unwritten rules that help everyone involved to hear and be heard. Computers on a network must also follow rules so that every node has a fair chance to communicate. As a network technician, you need to understand these media access methods so you can choose the best one for your network, and also ensure that every node follows the same access method.

Types of Media Access

Depending upon the traffic on the network media, a node can transmit data on a network. The *media access method* determines whether or not a particular node can transmit data on the network at a given time. Media access methods fall into two categories—contention-based and controlled. With *contention-based* or *competitive* media access, the nodes themselves negotiate for media access time. With *controlled* or *deterministic* media access, a central device or system controls when and for how long each node can transmit.

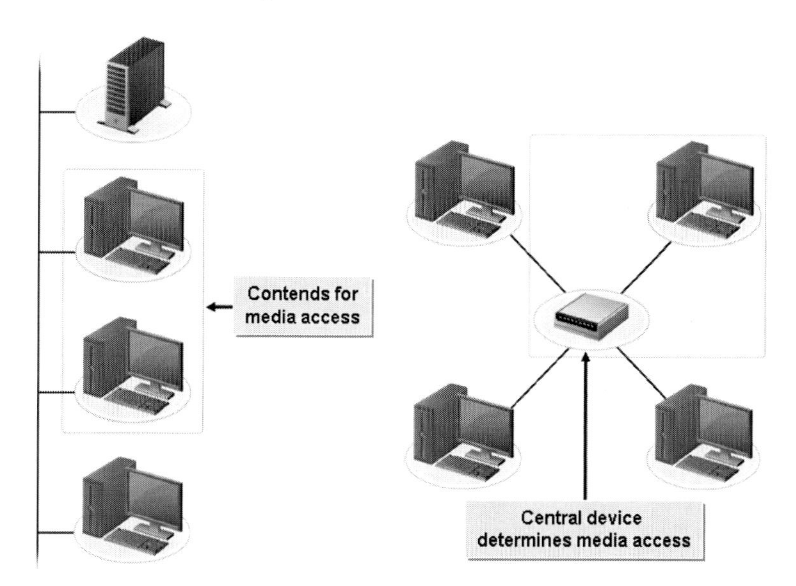

Figure 2-10: *Contention-based and controlled media access deployed on networks.*

Comparing Media Access Categories

Deterministic access methods are beneficial when network access is time critical. For example, in an industrial setting, key control and safety equipment, such as flow-shutoff sensors in chemical storage facilities, must have guaranteed transmission time. Deterministic systems ensure that a single node cannot saturate the media; all nodes get a chance to transmit data. However, they require additional hardware and administration to configure and maintain. Contention-based systems are simpler to set up and administer, but timely media access is not guaranteed for any node.

Multiplexing

Definition:

Multiplexing is a controlled media access method in which a central device combines signals from multiple nodes and transmits the combined signal across a medium. To carry multiple signals, the medium or channel is separated logically into multiple, smaller channels. Signals can be multiplexed using *Time-Division Multiplexing (TDM)* or *Frequency-Division Multiplexing (FDM)*. Both multiplexing techniques rely on a central device, called a *multiplexer,* or *mux*, to manage multiplexing from the sending end. At the receiving end, a *demultiplexer,* or *demux,* separates the signals.

TDM

In TDM, a communication channel is divided into discrete time slots. Each node on a network is assigned a time slot, and each sender is given exclusive access to the medium for a specific period of time. Nodes have exclusive access to the connection between themselves and a mux for that period of time. The mux combines each node's signal, and in turn, sends the resulting combined signal over the primary network medium. Using TDM, multiple baseband signals can be combined and sent over a single medium.

FDM

In FDM, data from multiple nodes is sent over multiple frequencies, or channels, using a network medium. Nodes have exclusive access to the connection between themselves and a mux. The mux includes each node's signal onto its own channel, sending the resulting combined signal over the primary network medium. Using FDM, multiple broadband signals can be combined and sent over a single medium.

Example:

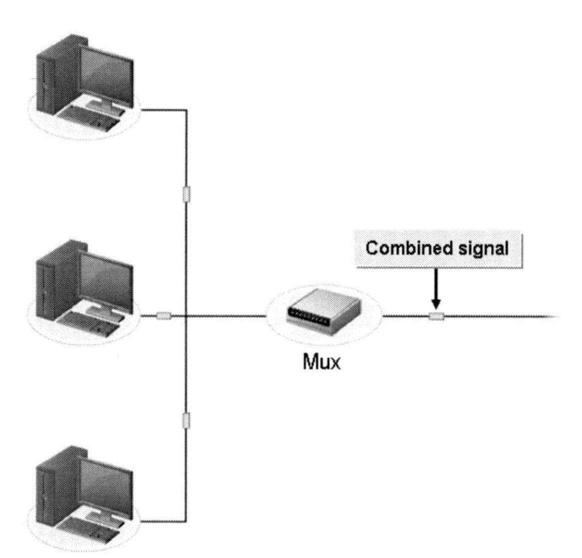

Figure 2-11: *The multiplexed media access method.*

Polling

Definition:

Polling is a controlled media access method in which a central device contacts each node to check whether it has data to transmit. Each node is guaranteed access to the media, but network time can be wasted if polling nodes have no data to transmit. The polling process is repeated by giving each node access to the media until the media reaches the node that needs to transmit data.

Example: Demand Priority

Demand priority is a polling technique in which nodes signal their state—either ready to transmit or idle—to an intelligent hub. The hub polls the state of each node and grants permission to transmit. Additionally, a node can signal that its data is high priority. The hub will favor high-priority transmission requests. Safeguards in the protocol prevent nodes from assigning every transmission request as high priority. This is done by ensuring that each node has an equal opportunity to transmit and a node is not allowed second normal transmission unless all nodes have completed their first normal transmission.

The Institute of Electronic and Electronics Engineers (*IEEE*), which is an organization dedicated to advancing theory and technology in the electrical sciences, has not standardized polling in general. However, the IEEE 802.12 standard defines 100VG-AnyLAN, which uses a specific polling technique called demand priority to control media access.

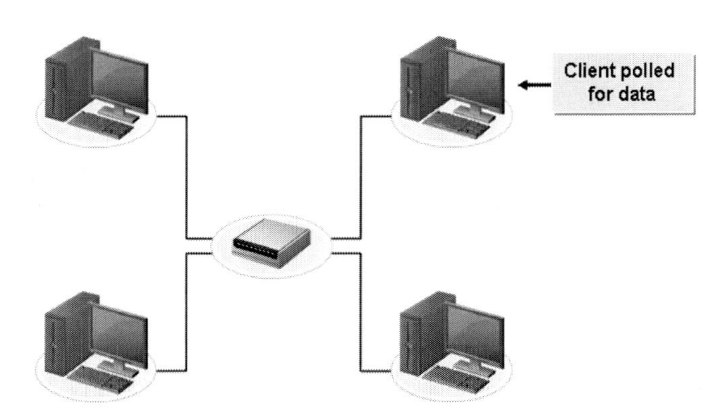

Figure 2-12: *The polling media access method.*

Managed Hubs

A *managed hub* is a type of hub that includes functions that enable you to monitor and configure its operation. Typically, you connect to the hub using special software or via a dedicated management port. Managed hubs are also called intelligent hubs.

CSMA/CD

CSMA/CD is the access method for Ethernet formalized in the 802.3 standard, a specification issued by IEEE to standardize Ethernet and expand it to include a wide range of cable media.

Carrier Sense Multiple Access/Collision Detection (CSMA/CD) is a contention-based media access method used in Ethernet LANs to provide collision free data transfer over a medium. Nodes can transmit whenever they have data to send. However, they must take steps to detect and manage the inevitable collisions that occur when multiple nodes transmit simultaneously. The busier a network becomes, the greater the probability of collisions, and the lower the CSMA/CD efficiency.

There are five steps involved in the CSMA/CD process.

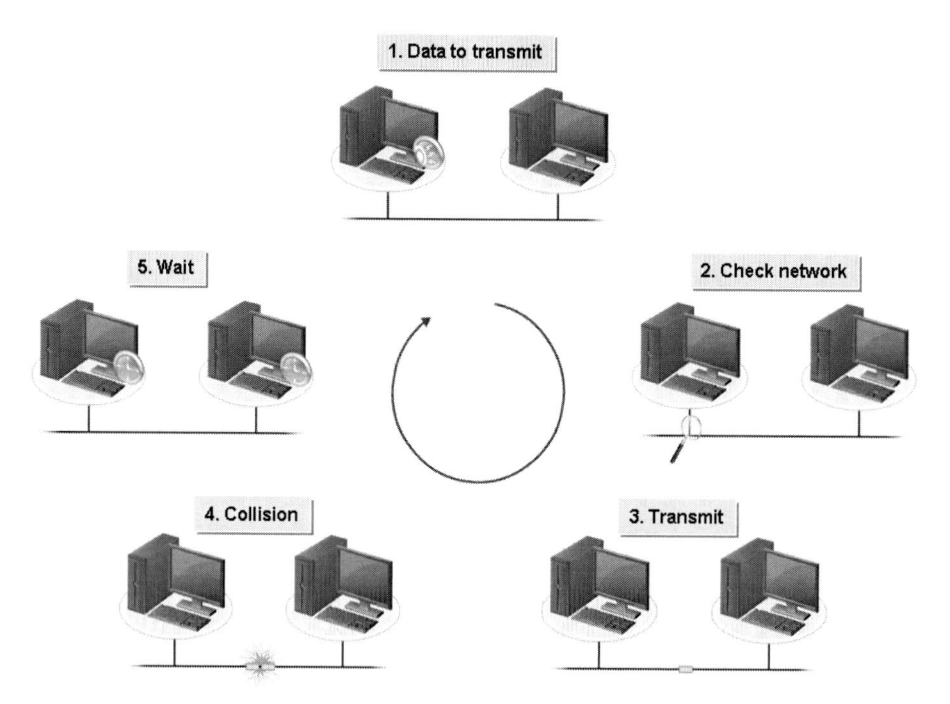

Figure 2-13: *The CSMA/CD media access method.*

Step	Description
Step 1: Data to transmit	A node has data to transmit.
Step 2: Check network	The node determines if the media is available by polling.
Step 3: Transmit	If available, the node transmits data. After transmission, it waits for an acknowledgement from the receiving node, which indicates whether or not the transmission was successful.
Step 4: Collision	The node checks the packet size to detect data fragments that indicate the occurrence of a collision.
Step 5: Wait	If a collision occurs, both transmitting devices wait for a random *backoff* period (in milliseconds), before retransmitting data. The nodes then repeat the process until successful.

Power Over Ethernet (PoE)

Power over Ethernet (PoE) has been finalized as the 802.3af standard. The PoE standard specifies a method for supplying electrical power over Ethernet connections. PoE specifies two device types: power sourcing equipment (PSE) and PDs (powered devices). PSEs provide the power and PDs are those devices that receive the power from the PSE. PoE requires CAT 5 or higher copper cable.

CSMA/CA

Carrier Sense Multiple Access/Collision Avoidance (CSMA/CA) is a contention-based media access method that is primarily used in 802.11–based *wireless LANs (WLANs)*. In CSMA/CA, nodes can transmit whenever they have data to send. However, they take steps before they transmit data to ensure that the media is not in use.

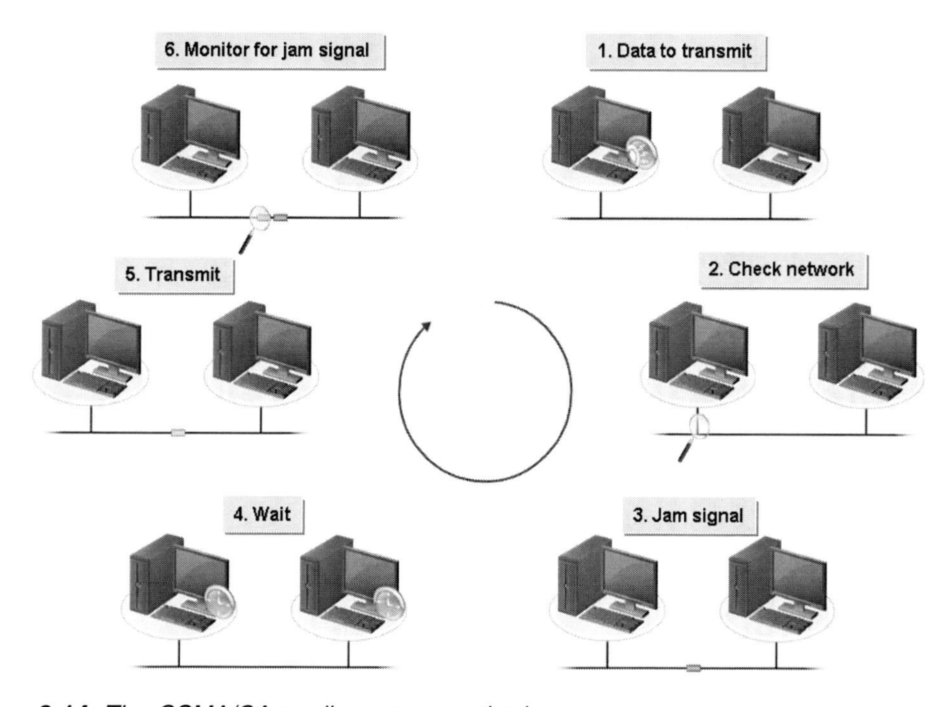

Figure 2-14: *The CSMA/CA media access method.*

The 802.11 standard is a family of specifications developed by the IEEE for wireless LAN technology.

Step	***Description***
Step 1: Data to transmit	A node has data to transmit.
Step 2: Check network	The node determines if the media is available by polling.
Step 3: Jam signal	If available, the node transmits a jam signal, advertising its intent to transmit data.

Step	Description
Step 4: Wait	The node waits until all nodes have had time to receive the jam signal.
Step 5: Transmit	The node transmits data.
Step 6: Monitor for jam signal	During transmission, the node monitors the media for a jam signal from any other node that may already be transmitting data. If a jam signal is received, it stops transmitting and retries after a random delay.

The IEEE 802.11 Standard

CSMA/CA is a contention-based media access method that is primarily used in 802.11–based wireless LANs. The 802.11 standard is a family of specifications developed by the IEEE for wireless LAN technology.

Contention Domains

Definition:

A *contention domain*, also called a *collision domain*, is a contention-based network on which a group of nodes are allowed to compete with each other for media access. This competition results in collisions caused by frames that are transmitted simultaneously by two or more nodes. Networking devices such as switches define the size of the contention domain. Dividing a large network of many nodes into smaller contention domains reduces collisions, thus improving network performance.

Example:

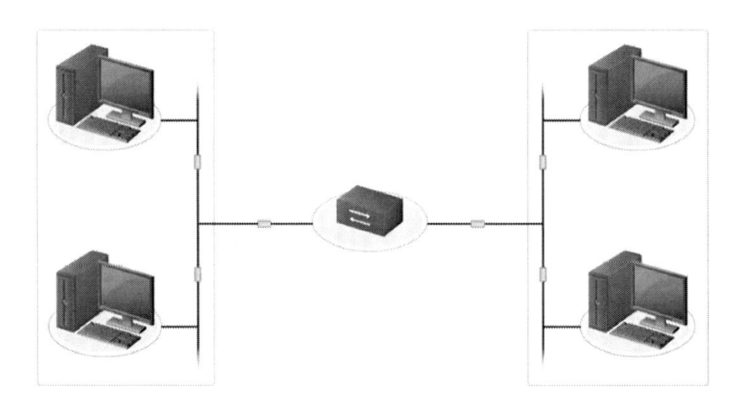

Figure 2-15: *Contention domains on a network.*

Broadcast Domain

A *broadcast domain* is a logical area in a computer network where any node connected to the network can directly transmit to any other node in the domain without having to go through a central routing device. A broadcast domain refers to the set of devices that receive a broadcast data frame originating from any device within a LAN segment or subnet. Switches cannot determine the size of the broadcast domain. Routers can determine the size of the broadcast domain.

Broadcast Domain vs. Collision Domain

Collision and broadcast domains primarily differ from the perspective of the size of the domains. Multiple collision domains can make up a broadcast domain, but a broadcast domain associates itself only with a single collision domain. Broadcast and collision domains also differ in the way they affect performance on a network. All devices in a broadcast domain receive broadcasts sent on the network. On a collision domain, an increase in traffic results in a higher probability of collisions on the network. As broadcast domains generate a lot of network traffic, they work best in smaller domains.

ACTIVITY 2-2

Identifying Media Access Methods

Scenario:

In this activity, you will identify the main types of media access methods.

---

1. Match the media access method with its description.

___	Polling	a.	Devices check if the media is available and transmit; collisions are detected.
___	Multiplexing	b.	Devices that possess a special packet transmit, while all other devices wait their turn.
___	CSMA/CD	c.	Devices check media availability and transmit a blocking signal before transmitting data.
___	CSMA/CA	d.	A central device asks each node, in turn, if it has data to transmit.
___	Token-based	e.	Combines data from multiple devices into a single signal.

---

2. Which of these statements describe contention-based media access?

a) Controls when a node can place data on a network.

b) Negotiates with devices for network access.

c) Performs better in smaller segments.

d) Performs predictable access of the network.

---

3. What is the correct sequence of data transmission in the CSMA/CD media access method?

Transmits the data.

Waits for a random backoff period.

Determines occurrence of a collision.

Determines if the media is available.

---

4. Which statements are true of a contention domain?

a) Reduces the number of nodes that contend for media access.

b) Defines a group of nodes to be polled by a hub.

c) Groups nodes logically.

d) Eliminates collisions within the domain.

---

5. **Which statements are true of multiplexing?**

    a) Both TDM and FDM rely on a demux, to manage multiplexing from the sending node.

    b) A central device combines signals from multiple nodes.

    c) The medium or channel is separated logically into multiple, smaller channels.

    d) Signals can be multiplexed using TDM or FDM.

    e) At the receiving node, a mux separates signals.

---

6. **True or False? CSMA/CA is a contention-based media access method primarily used in 802.11-based wireless LANs.**

    __ True

    __ False

TOPIC C
Signaling Methods

In the previous topic, you identified common media access methods used in networks. Now that you are aware of the media to be used, you need to investigate the different types of signaling. In this topic, you will identify the different signaling methods used in networks.

As a network professional, you will encounter different types of signals on the network. The different signaling methods used have various advantages and limitations that will affect the signaling on your network. You can choose the correct signal type for your requirements only if you are aware of the characteristics of each signal type that you can use on networks. This will ensure that you get the optimum result when using the signal type that you select.

Analog Signals

Definition:

A *signal* is data transmitted as electromagnetic pulses across a network medium. An *analog signal* carries information as continuous waves of electromagnetic or optical energy. In computer networking, electrical current commonly generates analog signals, the intensity of which is measured in volts. An analog signal oscillates between maximum and minimum values over time and can take any value between those limits. The size, shape, and other characteristics of the *waveform* describe the analog signal and the information it carries.

Example:

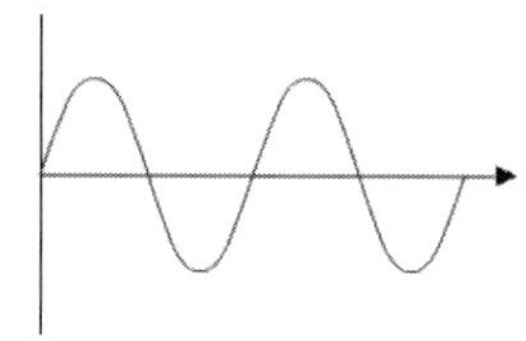

Figure 2-16: *An analog signal.*

Analog Signal Characteristics

The characteristics of an analog signal can be described or categorized using some specific terms.

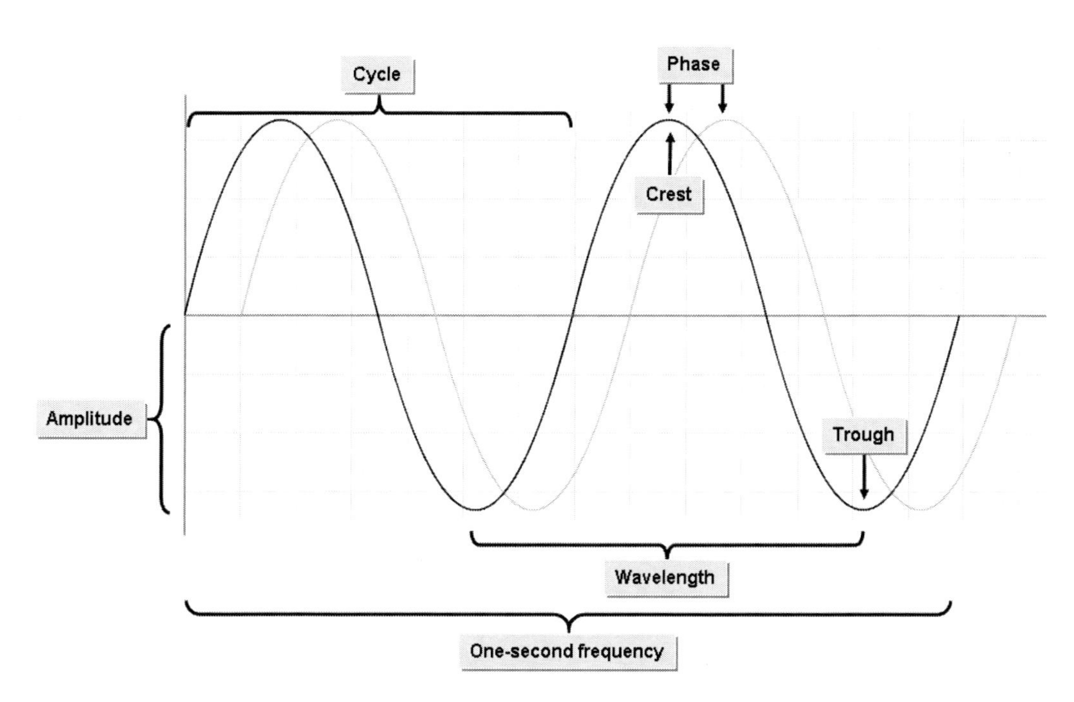

Figure 2-17: *Characteristics of an analog signal.*

Term	***Description***
Amplitude	The distance of the crest or trough of a wave from the midpoint of the waveform to its top or bottom. The *amplitude* is one half of the overall distance from the peak to the trough of the wave.
Cycle	One complete oscillation of an analog signal.
Frequency	The number of complete cycles per second in a wave. It is measured in *hertz*, which is one cycle per second. *Frequency* is also called the period of the wave.
Phase	Is where a wave's cycle begins in relationship to a fixed point. Thus, two waves of the same frequency that begin at the same time are said to be *in phase*. Two waves that either start at an offset from each other or have different frequencies are *out of phase*.
Wavelength	The distance between two successive crests or troughs in a waveform.

Oscilloscope

An *oscilloscope* is a device that plots the amplitude of an analog signal as a function of time. Oscilloscopes display analog signals as sine wave-shaped plots. Typically, it displays the output on a monitor, letting you view the shape of the signal in real time. Originally, oscilloscopes used Cathode Ray Tube (CRT) monitors, but modern oscilloscopes use Liquid Crystal Display (LCD) and Light Emitting Diode (LED) monitors.

Sine Waves

A *sine wave* is a smoothly oscillating curve that is the result of calculating the sine of the angles between zero and 360 and plotting the results. A sine wave can vary in *amplitude*, *phase*, or *frequency*. A wave that follows a sine curve is said to be sinusoidal.

Digital Signals

Definition:

A *digital signal*, unlike an analog signal that can have many possible values, can have combinations of only two values—one and zero. These values represent the presence and the absence of a signal, respectively. Digital data, which is a sequence of ones and zeroes, can be translated into a digital waveform. In computer systems and other digital devices, a waveform can switch between two voltage levels: zero at the ground, or a zero voltage state, and one at a positive or negative voltage level.

Example:

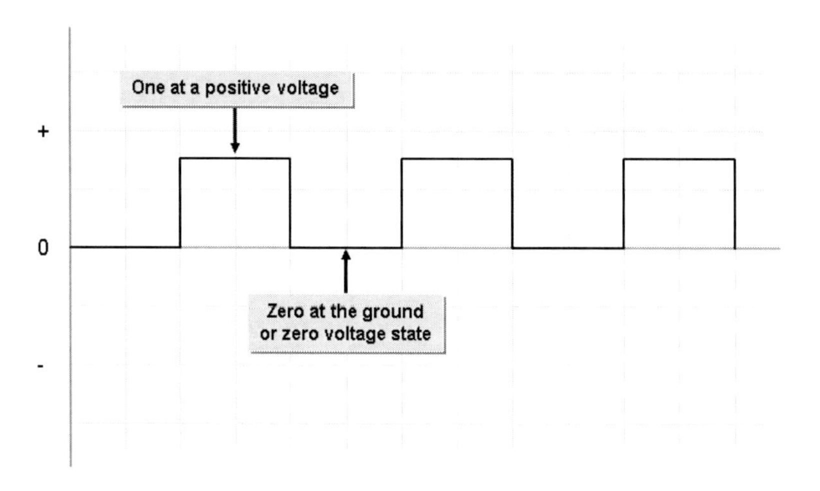

Figure 2-18: *Waveform of a digital signal.*

Binary Data and Digital Signals

Digital signals can hold just two values, and they are well-suited for *encoding* digital data, which is simply a sequence of ones and zeros. Every pulse in a digital signal represents one binary digit, or bit. Eight bits constitute one byte.

Logical State

Digital data is transmitted as electrical pulses, which have either a high or low power voltage levels. To represent the different voltage levels for mathematical reasons and to describe the working of digital devices, digital data is represented as binary 1s and 0s, also known as logical states.

Digital Data Units

Units of digital data are given specific names, as described in this table.

Unit	*Description*
Bit	A single 1 or 0
Nibble	Four bits
Byte	Eight bits

Unit	***Description***
Word	Depends on the processor. • For a 16-bit processor, a word is 16 bits • For a 32-bit processor, a word is 32 bits • For a 64-bit processor, a word is 64 bits

Data Measurement Units

Exponential prefixes are commonly used when measuring data in bits and bytes.

Prefix	***Value***
kilo (k)	1000
mega (M)	1000000 ($1000^{\wedge 2}$)
giga (G)	1000000000 ($1000^{\wedge 3}$)
tera (T)	1000000000000 ($1000^{\wedge 4}$)
peta (P)	1000000000000000 ($1000^{\wedge 5}$)

Analog Signal Modulation and Demodulation

Analog signals generally transmit voice at low frequencies. Transmitting low frequency signals directly may lead to information loss and interference from other signals. To overcome these problems, analog signals are superimposed by a high frequency signal known as a base or *carrier signal* using a *modulator.* The lower frequency analog signal is superimposed over the carrier signal's waveform.

In *modulation,* upon adding a data signal, it modifies one of the properties of the carrier signal—either the amplitude, frequency, or phase. The carrier signal is constant, but after its superimposition, it is shaped to represent the analog signal, resulting in a new signal that includes properties of both the carrier and data signals. When the modulated signal reaches its destination, the receiver decodes the signal by removing data from the carrier, using a process called *demodulation.*

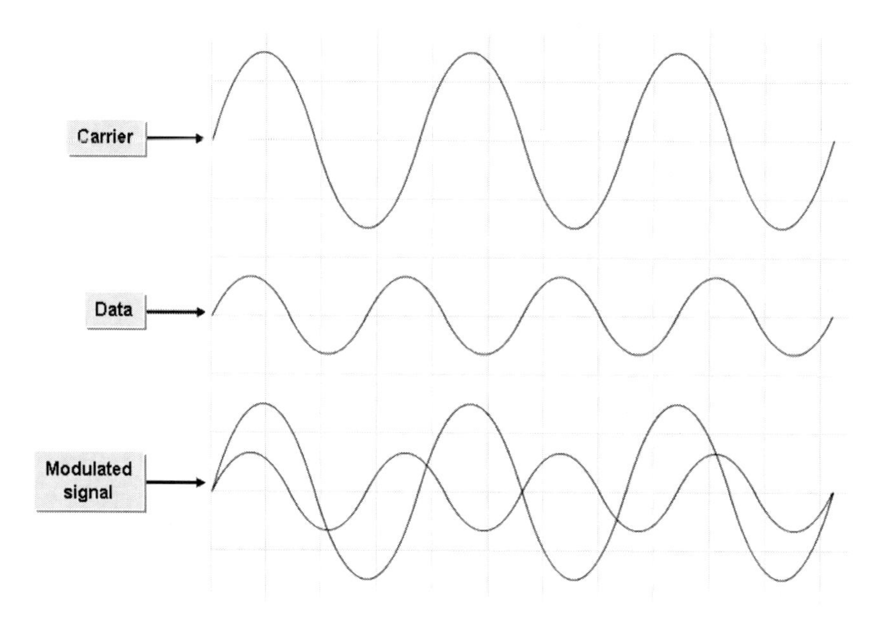

Figure 2-19: *Analog data signal modulation.*

Advantages of Modulation

High frequency signals transmit well over long distances. In contrast, low frequency signals degrade quickly with distance. By combining a low frequency data signal with a high frequency carrier signal, data can be sent over longer distances with minimal signal degradation.

Codecs and DACs/ADCs

A *codec* is software or hardware that encodes and decodes digital data to and from the analog format. A modem is a type of codec; the specific chips that perform the digital-to-analog and analog-to-digital conversion are called Digital-to-Analog Codecs (DACs) and Analog-to-Digital Codecs (ADCs), respectively.

Digital Signal Modulation and Demodulation

Digital data cannot be directly transmitted through a medium over a long distance. *Digital signal modulation* or encoding is the process of representing digital data in the form of an analog signal for transmission of data between different digital devices. Digital data has only two states represented as either 0 or 1. For example, a characteristic of the signal, such as frequency, is set to represent both 0 and 1. More frequency could be set for 1 and less for 0 or vice versa.

For demodulation, the receiving digital device compares the modulated analog signal it received with the preset frequency or amplitude of the signal and uses the comparison results to reconstruct digital data. For example, if the receiving digital device encounters a high frequency and a low frequency signal, it reconstructs the signal as 1 and 0 in the digital format.

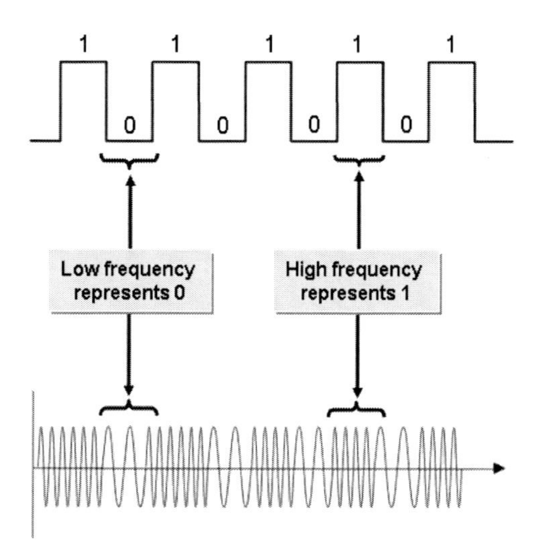

Figure 2-20: A reconstructed Digital Signal.

Modems

A *modem* is a device that modulates and demodulates digital data to an analog signal that can be sent over a telephone line. Its name is a combination of *mo*dulate and *dem*odulate.

Digital Signal Modulation Techniques

There are various techniques to modulate digital data, and each of these techniques is described in the following table.

Modulation Technique	Description
Amplitude Shift Key (ASK) modulation	Changes the amplitude of the analog signal depending on the *logical state* of digital data. The logical state of data can be either 0 or 1.
Frequency Shift Key (FSK) modulation	Changes the frequency of the analog signal depending on the logical state of digital data.
Binary-Phase Shift Key (BPSK) modulation	Changes the phase of the analog signal depending on the logical state of digital data.
Quadrature-Phase Shift (QPSK) Key modulation	Changes the phase of the analog signal to represent two logical states at a time. The logical states can be 00, 01, 10, and 11.
Quadrature Amplitude Modulation (QAM)	Combines both amplitude and phase shift key modulations. This helps represent more than two logical states at a time.

Digital Signal Reference Methods

To demodulate a digital signal, you must have a reference to determine the condition of the signal. This demodulation can be done using one of two methods. In the first method, called *differential,* a modem compares the modulated and demodulated digital signals; and the difference in output becomes the resulting data. With the second method, called *single-ended,* the modem compares the signal on one line to ground. The difference from ground then becomes the data output.

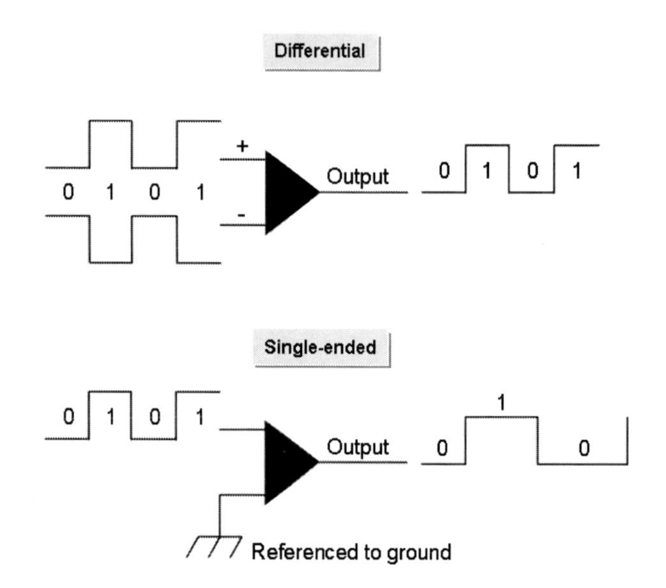

Figure 2-21: *Differential and single-ended demodulation.*

ACTIVITY 2-3

Identifying Signaling Methods

Scenario:

In this activity, you will identify the major signaling methods used in data communication.

---

1. **Which numbering system are digital signals based on?**
   a) Hexadecimal
   b) Binary
   c) Decimal
   d) Alphanumeric

---

2. **Which statements are true of digital signal modulation?**
   a) Digital data can be transmitted through over a long distance.
   b) Digital data can have only two logical states.
   c) Represents digital data in the form of analog signals.
   d) Modifies a characteristic of the signal.

---

3. **True or False? In the single-ended reference method for demodulating a digital signal, the demodulated signal is compared to ground and the difference becomes the output data.**

   __ True

   __ False

---

4. **What are the characteristics of analog signal modulation and demodulation?**
   a) Enables long distance data transmission.
   b) Leads to information loss and interference from other signals.
   c) Superimposes an analog signal and removes it from a high frequency analog carrier.
   d) Modifies all properties of the data signal.

---

5. **Match the characteristic of an analog signal with its description.**

___	Amplitude	a.	One complete analog signal oscillation.
___	Cycle	b.	The period of the wave.
___	Frequency	c.	The distance between two successive crests or troughs in a waveform.
___	Phase	d.	The distance from the crest or trough of a wave to its top or bottom.
___	Wavelength	e.	The beginning of a wave's cycle in relationship to a fixed point.

Lesson 2 Follow-up

In this lesson, you learned about the methods networking devices use to communicate to ensure the proper functioning of your network. Now that you are cognizant of the methods nodes use to transmit data to each other, you are well-positioned to choose the correct communication method for your network.

1. **What are the factors to consider when you need to use unicast, broadcast, or multicast transmissions in your networking environment?**

2. **In your opinion, what is the importance of knowing different signal types?**

3 Network Media and Hardware

Lesson Time: 3 hour(s), 15 minutes

Lesson Objectives:

In this lesson, you will describe network media and hardware components.

You will:

- Identify the common types of bounded network media.
- Identify the common types of unbounded network media.
- Identify noise control methods used in network transmissions.
- Identify different network connectivity devices.

Introduction

In the previous lesson, you identified network data delivery methods. The network media and hardware carry data packets from a source to a destination, and they need to function without interruptions for data to travel reliably across the network. In this lesson, you will identify the different types of media and networking devices that transmit data.

Networking media are like the highways and subways of a city. Without roads and rails, people cannot move through a city to work or home. Without networking media and the devices that support them, you cannot transmit data from one computer to another. For data to travel successfully across your network, you must verify that the network media and devices are compatible with one another and set up correctly for your particular network implementation.

This lesson covers all or part of the following CompTIA® Network+® (Exam N10-005) certification objectives:

- Topic A:
  - 1.2 Classify how applications, devices, and protocols relate to the OSI model layers.
  - 3.1 Categorize standard media types and associated properties.
  - 3.2 Categorize standard connector types based on network media.
  - 3.4 Categorize WAN technology types and properties.
  - 3.8 Identify components of wiring distribution.

- Topic B:
  - 2.2 Given a scenario, install and configure a wireless network.
  - 2.4 Given a scenario, troubleshoot common wireless problems.
  - 3.4 Categorize WAN technology types and properties.
  - 5.1 Given a scenario, implement appropriate wireless security measures.
- Topic C:
  - 2.2 Given a scenario, install and configure a wireless network.
- Topic D:
  - 1.2 Classify how applications, devices, and protocols relate to the OSI model layers.
  - 1.4 Explain the purpose and properties of routing and switching.
  - 1.9 Identify virtual network components.
  - 2.1 Given a scenario, install and configure routers and switches.
  - 2.5 Given a scenario, troubleshoot common router and switch problems.
  - 3.2 Categorize standard connector types based on network media.

TOPIC A

Bounded Network Media

In this lesson, you will identify various types of network media and devices. The network media that carry data across your network can be bounded or unbounded. In this topic, you will identify the most widely implemented network media—bounded.

Bounded media are the most basic networking media type and consist of different types that can be chosen to suit the needs of your network. You are likely to work with bounded media on a daily basis as part of your duties as a network professional. Understanding the characteristics of bounded media and the equipment used will enable you to properly install and service your networks.

Network Media

Network media, the conduit through which signals flow, can be either bounded or unbounded. *Bounded media* use a physical conductor. This conductor can be a metal wire through which electricity flows, or a glass or plastic strand through which pulses of light flow. *Unbounded media* do not need a physical connection between devices, and can transmit electromagnetic signals through air using *radio waves*, *microwaves*, or *infrared radiation*.

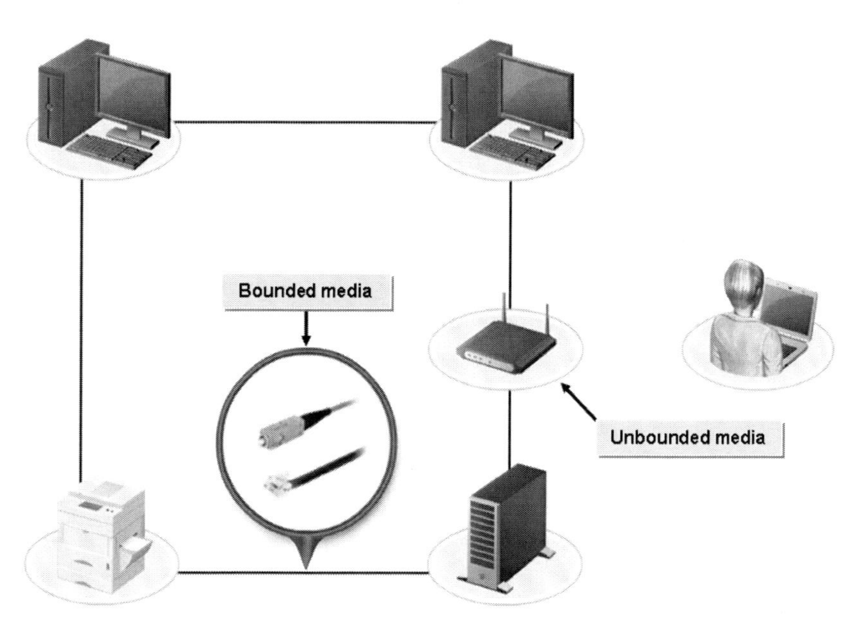

Figure 3-1: *Types of network media.*

Copper Media

Definition:

Copper media is a type of bounded media that uses one or more copper conductors surrounded by an insulated coating. The conductors can be made from a solid wire or from braided strands of wire. Sometimes *shielding*, in the form of a braided wire or foil, is wrapped around one or more conductors to reduce signal interference from nearby sources of electromagnetic radiation.

Example: Types of Copper Media

Two of the most prevalent types of copper media used in networks are *twisted pair* and *coaxial cable.*

Twisted Pair Cables

Definition:

A *twisted pair* cable is a type of cable in which two conductors or pairs of copper wires are twisted around each other and clad in a color-coded, protective insulating plastic sheath or jacket to form a pair. All pairs are encased in a plastic sheath or jacket. The number of pairs within a cable will vary depending on the type of twisted pair cable. Twisted pair cables typically use shielding around pairs of wires.

Example:

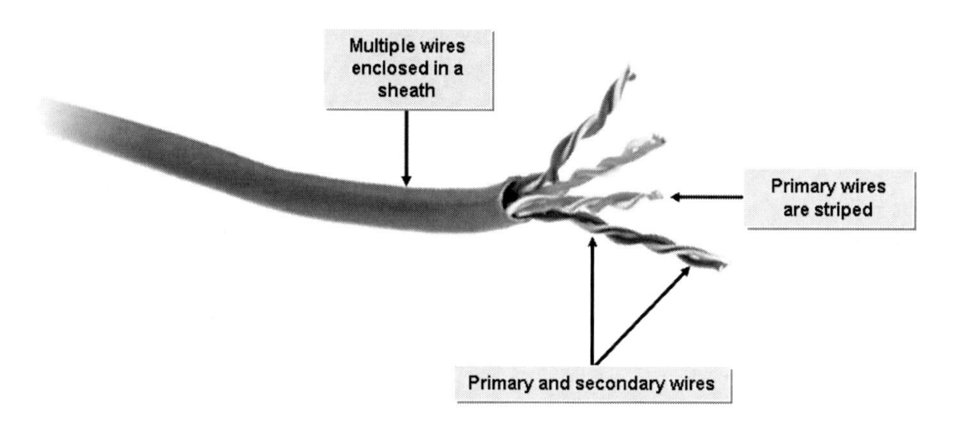

Figure 3-2: *Constituents of a twisted pair cable.*

RJ-45 Connectors

RJ-45 is an eight-pin connector used by twisted pair cables in networking. All four pairs of wires in the twisted pair cable use this connector.

The RJ in RJ-11 or RJ-45 is an abbreviation for "registered jack." An RJ-45 connector can also be called an 8P8C connector.

RJ-45 Wiring Schemes

There are two standard wiring schemes for RJ-45: T568A and T568B. It is important that you use the wiring scheme that matches the devices on your network even though all cables are the same.

Pin	T568A	T568B
1	White/green	White/orange
2	Green	Orange
3	White/orange	White/green
4	Blue	Blue
5	White/blue	White/blue
6	Orange	Green
7	White/brown	White/brown
8	Brown	Brown

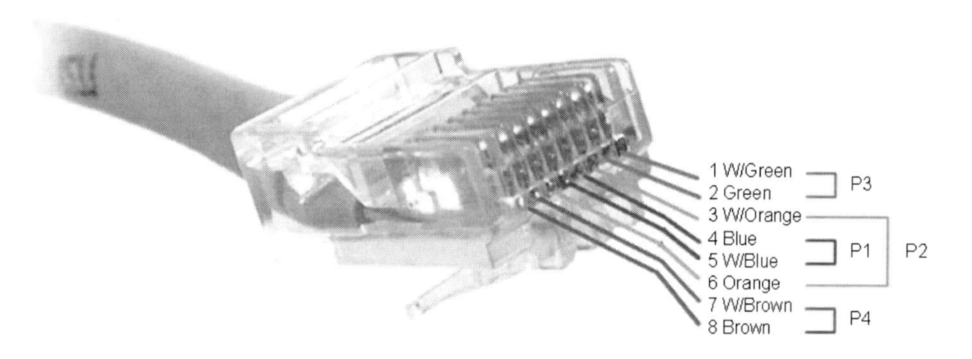

Figure 3-3: *Twisted pair connectors — RJ-45 wiring schemes.*

The RJ-11 Connector

The RJ-11 connector is used with Category 1 cables in telephone system connections and is not suitable for network connectivity. However, because the RJ-11 connector is similar in appearance to the RJ-45 connector, they are sometimes confused. RJ-11 connectors are smaller than RJ-45 connectors, and have either four or six pins.

Twisted Pair Cable Types

A twisted pair cable can be of two types: *Unshielded Twisted Pair (UTP)* or *Shielded Twisted Pair (STP)*.

Twisted pair cables are available in 2–pair, 4–pair, 6–pair, 25–pair, 100–pair, and larger bundles.

Cable Type	Description
UTP	There are different characteristics of UTP: • Does not include shielding around its conductors • Typically contains four pairs of stranded or solid conductors • Is inexpensive and reliable • Supports transmission distances of up to 100 meters • Supports data transfer rates of up to 1 Gbps
STP	There are different characteristics of STP. • Includes foil wrapper shielding around its conductors to improve the cable's resistance to interference and noise. • Typically contains four pairs of stranded or solid conductors • More expensive than UTP • Supports transmission distances of up to 100 meters • Supports data transfer rates of 10 to 100 Mbps.

Color Schemes

The conductors in older twisted pair cables used a solid color scheme. Old telephone cables used black, green, red, and yellow wires. The current color scheme uses striped colors.

Wire colors are standardized. The industry standard for twisted pair is one solid color and the same color with white. Consider the blue pair of wires: one wire will be mostly blue with white stripes. It will be identified on wiring diagrams as the blue/white wire. The corresponding wire in the pair will be mostly white with blue stripes, and be identified as the white/blue wire.

The first four standard color pairs are listed in the table.

Primary Wire	Secondary Wire
White/blue	Blue/white
White/orange	Orange/white
White/green	Green/white
White/brown	Brown/white

In the solid color scheme, red corresponds to blue/white, green to white/blue, yellow to orange/white, and black to white/orange.

Twisted Pair Cable Categories

A twisted pair cable comes in different grades, called categories, which support different network speeds and technologies.

Category	*Specifications*
1	**Network Type:** Voice transmission
	Maximum Speed: 1 Mbps
	CAT1 is not suitable for networking.
2	**Network Type:** Digital telephone and low-speed networks
	Maximum Speed: 4 Mbps
	CAT2 is not commonly used on networks.
3	**Network Type:** Ethernet
	Maximum Speed: 10 Mbps
	CAT3 is currently used for telephone wiring.
4	**Network Type:** IBM Token Ring
	Maximum speed: 16 Mbps
	CAT4 may also be used for 10 Mbps Ethernet.
5	**Network Type:** Fast Ethernet
	Maximum Speed: CAT5 supports a signaling rate of 100 Mbps.
5e	**Network Type:** Gigabit Ethernet
	Maximum Speed: CAT5e supports a signaling rate of 350 Mbps.
6	**Network Type:** Gigabit Ethernet
	Maximum Speed: 1 Gbps
	CAT6 supports a signaling rate of 250 MHz.
6a	**Network Type:** Gigabit Ethernet
	Maximum Speed: 1 Gbps
	CAT6a supports a signaling rate of 500 MHz.
7	**Network Type:** Gigabit Ethernet
	Maximum Speed: 1+ Gbps
	CAT7 supports a signaling rate of 1 GHz.

A twisted pair cable's category is typically printed on the cable itself, making identification easier.

Coaxial Cables

Definition:

A coaxial cable, or *coax*, is a type of copper cable that features a central conducting copper core surrounded by an insulator and braided or foil shielding. The *dialectric* insulator separates the conductor and shield and the entire package is wrapped in an insulating layer called a sheath or jacket. The data signal is transmitted over the central conductor. A coaxial cable is so named because the conductor and shield share the same axis, or center. They share a *co*mmon *ax*is or are "co-axial." This arrangement helps prevent electromagnetic interference from reaching the conductor.

Example:

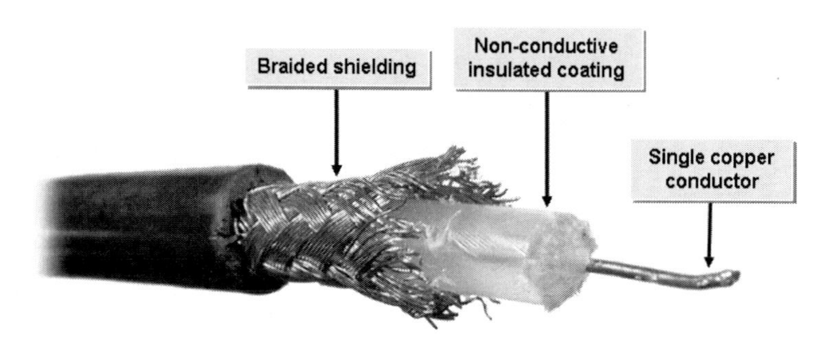

Figure 3-4: *Layers of a coaxial cable.*

Coaxial Cable Types

Many varieties of coax cables are available not all of which are used in computer networking.

Cable Type	*Characteristics*
RG58/U	A 5 mm (0.25 inch) coax cable with a solid core and 50 ohms impedance. RG58/U is used for Ethernet networking.
RG58A/U	A 5 mm (0.25 inch) coax cable with a stranded core and 50 ohms impedance. RG58A/U is used for Ethernet networking.
RG8	A 10 mm (0.5 inch) coax cable with a solid core and 50 ohms impedance. RG8 is used for Ethernet networking.
RG9	A 10 mm (0.5 inch) coax cable with a stranded core and 51 ohms impedance. RG9 is used for cable television transmission and cable modems.
RG62	A 5 mm (0.25 inch) coax cable with a solid core and 93 ohms impedance. RG62 is used for ARCNET networking.
RG59	A 6 mm (0.25 inch) coax cable with 75 ohms impedance. RG59 is used for low-power video connections such as digital receivers.
RG6	A coax cable with 75 ohms impedance. RG6 is preferred over RG59. This type of cable is often used in routing cable television signals.

Attached Resource Computer Network (ARCNET) is a LAN protocol widely used in microcomputers. It is similar to other major LAN technologies such as Ethernet, token ring, and FDDI.

Solid and Stranded Cores

The wires used in networking can be of two types: solid core and stranded core. A solid core wire is made of a single metal or a single strand. A stranded core wire consists of multiple strands or solid cores.

ThinNet

ThinNet is the name given to Ethernet networking over RG58/U or RG58A/U cabling. ThinNet is wired in a bus configuration in which segments can be up to 185 meters (607 feet) long. ThinNet connections are made with a BNC connector. Devices connect to the network with T-connectors and each end of the cable must be terminated with a 50-ohm resistor.

ThickNet

ThickNet is the name given to Ethernet networking over RG8 cabling. ThickNet is not commonly used today, but was popular as a network backbone because ThickNet segments can be up to 500 meters (or 1640 feet) long.

Networking devices are not directly connected to the ThickNet cable. Instead, transceivers are connected to the cable with *vampire taps*, which is a clamshell-like device that pierces an RG8 cable, to make contact with its conductors. This permits a networking device to connect to the ThickNet segment.

Transceivers can be installed as needed at intervals of 2.5 meters along the length of the cable. The networking device connects to the transceiver via a 15-pin *Attachment Unit Interface (AUI) connector* and a short section of cable called a drop cable. An AUI connector is also known as a DIX connector, which gets its name from the three companies that invented it: Digital Equipment Corporation (DEC), Intel, and Xerox.

Connections between ThickNet segments are made with a screw-type connector called an N-connector. ThickNet segments must be terminated with a 50-ohm resistor.

Coaxial Connector Types

Connectors are metal devices that are located at the end of a wire. Coaxial connectors are used to connect video equipment and network nodes in a LAN. Signals flow from the wire to network devices through connectors. All connectors are metal plated and some of the metals used are gold, silver, rhodium, nickel, or tin.

Two broad categories of connectors are typically used in coax cables: F and BNC connectors.

Connector Type	*Characteristics*
F	A coax connector type used with a 75-ohm cable to connect cable TV and FM antenna cables. It comes in a secure screw-on form or as a non-threaded slip-on connector.

Connector Type	Characteristics
BNC	A cable connector used to terminate a coaxial cable. It is usually used with the RG58/U cable. A Bayone-Neill-Concelman (BNC) connector has a center pin connected to the center cable conductor and a metal tube connected to the shield of the cable. A rotating ring outside the metal tube locks the cable to the connector. The types of BNC connectors include: • T-connectors • Barrel connectors

Coax cables are assigned a combination alphanumeric identity that indicates the size and electrical characteristics of that type of cable.

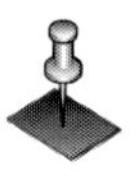

The RG specification codes come from their page numbers in the Radio Guide manual, the original military specification (Mil-Spec) for coax cables, which are no longer in use. For example, the RG8 specification appeared on page 8.

Termination

Coax network segments must be *terminated* to prevent signal reflections off the ends of the cable. Cables are terminated by installing a resistor of an appropriate rating, typically 50 ohms, at either end of the cable.

Network Media Performance Factors

Several factors can affect the performance of network media.

Factor	Description
Noise	Electromagnetic interference that disrupts the signal. The signal to noise ratio decreases as the transmitting distance increases.
Attenuation	The progressive degradation of a signal as it travels across a network medium. This is usually caused by an increase of noise or a decrease in the strength of the signal. The susceptibility to noise and attenuation depends on the types of media used; some media types are more susceptible to attenuation. Attenuation can also occur when the cable length exceeds the recommended length up to which signals can travel without distortion.
Impedance	The opposition to the flow of electricity in an *AC* circuit. Impedance is measured in *ohms* (Ω). An ohm is the value of electrical resistance through which one volt will maintain a current of one ampere.

Media Converters

A *media converter* enables networks running on different media to interconnect and exchange signals. Technically, a media converter is considered a transceiver because it transmits and receives signals. To install a media converter, simply connect terminated ends of the two media you want to bridge to the converter. You may need to provide electrical power to the converter, but may not need any additional configuration. Many converters are available that allow you to convert from one media type to another.

Different types of converters are available in market.

Converter Type	***Description***
Multimode fiber to Ethernet	Used to extend an Ethernet network connection over a multimode fiber backbone.
Fiber to Coaxial	Used to convert signals on fiber to a coaxial cable.
Singlemode to multimode fiber	Used to transmit multimode fiber signals over singlemode fiber devices and links. It supports conversion between multimode segments on a network that spans a wider coverage area.
Singlemode fiber to Ethernet	Used to extend an Ethernet network connection over a singlemode fiber backbone.

Structured Cabling

The *Telecommunications Industry Association (TIA)* and the *Electronic Industries Association (EIA)* developed the 568 Commercial Building Telecommunication Cabling standard. This standard defines the regulations on designing, building, and managing a cabling system that utilizes structured cabling according to specified performance characteristics to create a system of unified communications.

Structured cabling is based on a hierarchical design that divides cabling into six subsystems.

Subsystem	***Description***
Entrance facilities	Contains the telecommunication service entrance to the building, campus-wide backbone connections, and the interconnection to the local exchange carrier's telecommunication facilities. The network *demarcation point* is usually a foot away from where the carrier's facilities enter the building, but the carrier can designate a different measurement, depending on the needs of the facility.
Backbone wiring	Provides connections between equipment rooms and telecommunication closets. Backbone cabling runs through the floors of the building via risers or across a campus. The allowed distance measurements of this cabling depend on the type of cable and the facilities it connects.
Equipment room	Provides the main cross-connection point for an entire facility. Also provides a termination point for backbone wiring connected to telecommunication closets.

Subsystem	Description
Telecommunications closet	Houses the connection equipment for cross-connection to an equipment room along with workstations in the surrounding area. It contains horizontal wiring connections, and entrance facility connections. In an office building with multiple floors, depending on the floor plan, there can be as many telecommunications closets as needed.
Horizontal wiring	Runs from each workstation outlet to the telecommunication closet. The maximum allowed distance from the outlet to the closet is 295 feet. If patch cables are used, an additional 20 feet is allowed both at the workstation and the telecommunication closet, but the combined length cannot be more than 33 feet. Horizontal cabling specifications include: • Four-pair 100 ohms UTP cables • Two-fiber 62.5/125 mm fiber-optic cables • Multimode 50/125 mm multimode fiber-optic cables
Work area	Consists of wallboxes and faceplates, connectors, and wiring used to connect work area equipment to the telecommunications closet. It is required that a data and voice outlet be available at each wallbox and faceplate.

TIA/EIA-568

Telecommunications Industry Association/Electronic Industries Association (TIA/EIA) releases recommendations for how network media may best be installed to optimize network performance. They include:

- **568 C:** This current release is the third in the 568 series. 568C defines the standards for commercial building cabling. It covers the exceptions and allowances related to the commercial building cabling. It recognizes CAT6a as a media type. It also defines the minimum bend radius for twisted-pair cables, both shielded and unshielded. In addition, it specifies the maximum untwist value for the CAT6a cable termination.
- **568 B:** This earlier standard, in which some sections are now obsolete, defines the standards for preferred cable types that provide the minimum acceptable performance levels including:
    - 100 ohm twisted pair
    - STP
    - Optical fiber

568 A: This obsolete standard defined the standards for commercial buildings and cabling systems that support data networks, voice, and video. It further defined cable performance and technical requirements.

Premise Wiring

Premise wiring is defined as a hierarchical cable system architecture in which a *Main Cross-Connect (MCC)* is connected via a star topology across backbone cabling to *Intermediate Cross-Connects (ICC)* and *Horizontal Cross-Connects (HCC)*. Telecommunications design traditions have used a similar topology, and many people refer to the cross-connects of premise wiring by such nonstandard terms as distribution frames, *Main Distribution Frames (MDFs)*, *Intermediate Distribution Frames (IDFs)*, and wiring closets.

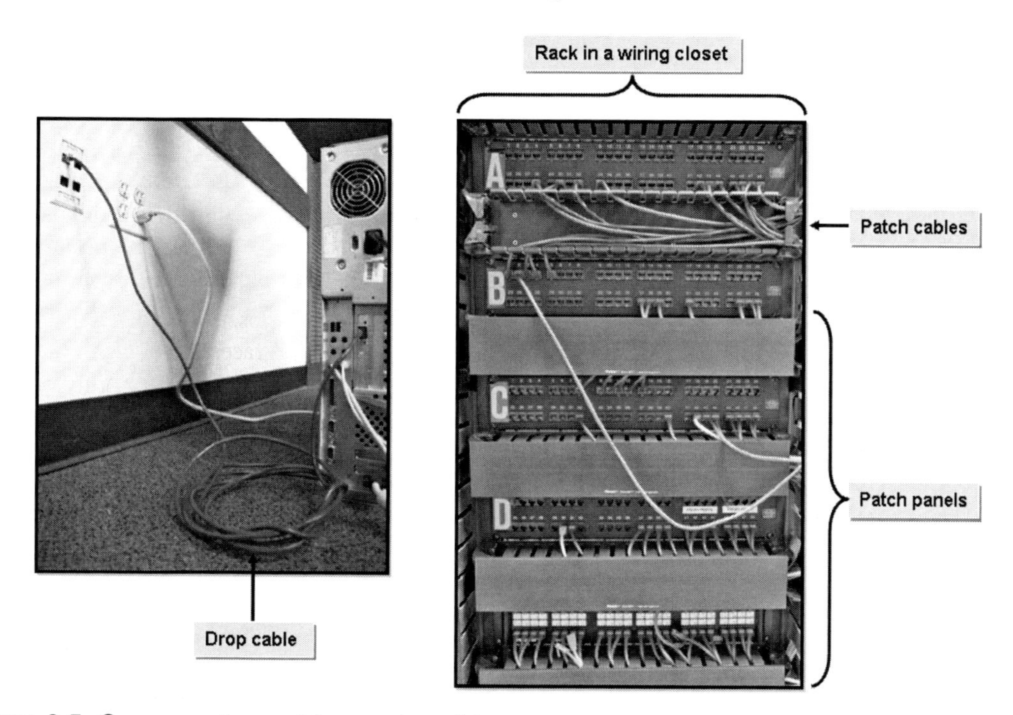

Figure 3-5: *Components used in premise wiring.*

Many components are used in premise wiring.

Premise Wiring Component	Description
Drop cable	The wire that runs to a PC, printer, or other device connected to a network.
Patch panel	A connection point for drop and patch cables. Typically, a patch panel has one or more rows of RJ-45 or other connectors. Drop cables are connected to the connectors. Cables run between the connectors to connect drop cables as needed.
Patch cable	A cable that is plugged into the patch panel to connect two drop cables. A patch cable might or might not be a crossover cable, where the transmit conductor at one end is connected to the receive conductor at the other.
Cross-connects	Individual wires that connect two drop cables to a patch panel. Cross-connects are rarely used in modern networks because they are built in the network components. However, they are still frequently used in telephone wiring.

Premise Wiring Component	Description
MDF	A cable rack that interconnects the telecommunications wiring between itself and any number of IDFs.
IDF	A cable rack that interconnects the telecommunications wiring between an MDF and any workstation devices.
Wiring closet	A small room in which patch panels are installed. Drop cables radiate out from the wiring closet to the components on the network.

Horizontal Cross-Connects

Horizontal cross-connects provide a point for the consolidation of all horizontal cabling, which extends in a star topology to individual work areas, such as cubicles and offices. Fiber optic horizontal cabling is limited to 90 meters. Optional consolidation points or transition points are allowable in horizontal cables, although many industry experts discourage their use.

Vertical Cross-Connects

Vertical cabling or *vertical cross-connects* are generally recognized as cables that run vertically between floors in a building, or vertically between equipment in an equipment rack. They are not defined as part of the Structured Cabling standards.

Plenum and PVC Cables

A *plenum cable* is a network cable that is jacketed tightly around conductors so that fire cannot travel within the cable. The jacket of the plenum cable does not emanate poisonous gases when it burns. Fire codes require that you install this special grade cabling in the *plenum*, an air handling space, including ducts and other parts of the *Heating, Ventilating, and Air Conditioning (HVAC)* system in a building, between the structural and suspended ceilings, and under raised floors, as well as in firebreak walls. Unlike non-plenum cables, plenum cables can run through the plenum and firebreak walls.

Polyvinyl chloride (PVC)-jacketed cabling is inexpensive and flexible. The PVC cable is also referred to as the non-plenum cable. However, when PVC burns, it gives off noxious or poisonous gases. Additionally, PVC jacketing is not formed tightly to the conductors it contains. Tests show that fire can travel within a PVC cable, passing through firebreaks.

Figure 3-6: *Plenum and PVC cables used in an office environment.*

Fiber Optic Cables

Definition:

A *fiber optic cable* is a network cable that has a core surrounded by one or more glass or plastic strands. In addition, it contains extra fiber strands or wraps, which are surrounded by a protective outer jacket. The core is the thin glass center through which light travels transmitting data. The core is between 5 and 100 microns thick with cladding made from optical materials such as silica.

The cladding reflects light back to the core in patterns determined by the transmission mode. A buffer, often made of plastic, surrounds the cladding and core. To add strength to the cable, strands of synthetic fiber surround the buffer. An outer jacket, sometimes called an armor, wraps and protects the whole assembly. Light pulses from a laser or high intensity LED are passed through the core to carry the signal. The cladding reflects the light back into the core, increasing the distance the signal can travel without a need for regeneration.

Example:

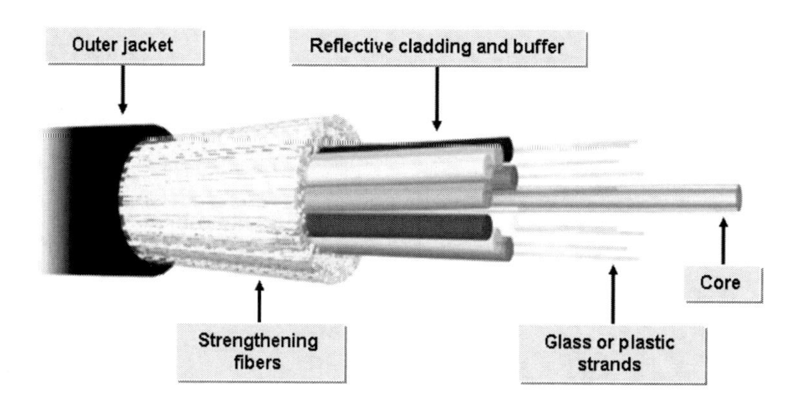

Figure 3-7: *Layers in a fiber optic cable.*

Fiber optic cables are the least sensitive of any cable type to electromagnetic interference.

You should not look into the end of an operating fiber optic cable. The intensity of light leaving the end of a singlemode fiber is strong enough to cause temporary or permanent damage to the eye.

Fiber Optic Cable Modes

Two modes of fiber optic cables are available in market: *multimode* and *singlemode*. Both modes of fiber optic cables have an outer diameter of 125 microns; that is, 125 millionths of a meter or 5 thousandths of an inch, which is just larger than a single human hair. The multimode fiber allows light to travel through its core in multiple rays or modes. Its core of 50 or 62.5 microns works with LED sources for slower networks and with laser for faster networks. At only 9 microns, the singlemode fiber is much less in diameter than the multimode fiber. Within the singlemode fiber, light travels unidirectionally. The singlemode fiber is used with laser to process telephony and cable TV transmissions.

Singlemode and multimode fibers have different characteristics.

Fiber Optic Cable Mode	*Description*
Singlemode fiber	Carries an optical signal through a small core, which allows only a single beam of light to pass. A laser, usually operating in the infrared portion of the spectrum, is modulated in intensity to transmit the signal through the fiber. It provides a bandwidth of up to 30 MHz.

Fiber Optic Cable Mode	*Description*
Step-index multimode fiber	Contains a core surrounded by cladding, each with its own uniform index of *refraction*. When light from the core enters the cladding, a "step down" occurs due to the difference in the refractive indices. Step-index fiber uses total internal reflection to trap light.
Graded-index multimode fiber	Possesses variations in the core glass to compensate for differences in the mode path length. Provides up to 2 GHz of bandwidth, which is significantly more than step-index fiber.

Refraction

Refraction occurs when a light ray passing from one transparent medium to another, bends due to a change in velocity. The change in velocity occurs due to the differences in the density of the two mediums. The angle of incidence is the same as in reflection. The angle between the normal and the light ray as light enters the second medium is called the angle of refraction.

Fiber Connectors

Various connectors are used with fiber optic cables.

It often takes a specially trained and certified technician, plus specialized equipment, to install fiber optic connectors. This is because the installation requires in-depth knowledge about fiber optic communication systems and fiber optic cables. Additionally, the installation involves various testing processes, which can be done only by a knowledgeable or certified technician.

Fiber Optic Connector	*Description*
Straight Tip (ST)	ST connectors are similar in appearance to BNC connectors and are used to connect multimode fibers. They have a straight, ceramic center pin and bayonet lug lockdown. They are often used in network patch panels. ST connectors are among the most popular types of fiber connectors. 

Fiber Optic Connector	Description
Subscriber Connector or *Standard Connector (SC)*	SC connectors are box-shaped connectors that snap into a receptacle. They are often used in a duplex configuration where two fibers are terminated into two SC connectors that are molded together. SC is used with a singlemode fiber. 
Face Contact (FC)	FC connectors use a heavy duty *ferrule* in the center for more mechanical stability than SMA or ST connectors. A ferrule is a tubular structure made of ceramic or metal that supports the fiber. These connectors are more popular in industrial settings where greater strength and durability is required. 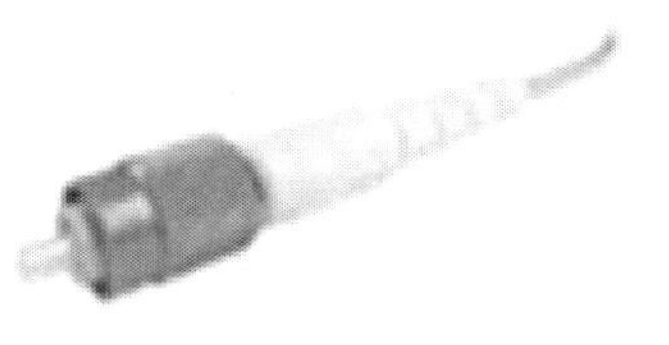
FDDI	FDDI connectors are used for multimode fiber optic cable and are a push/pull-type, two-channel snap-fit connectors. Also called a Media Interface Connector (MIC). 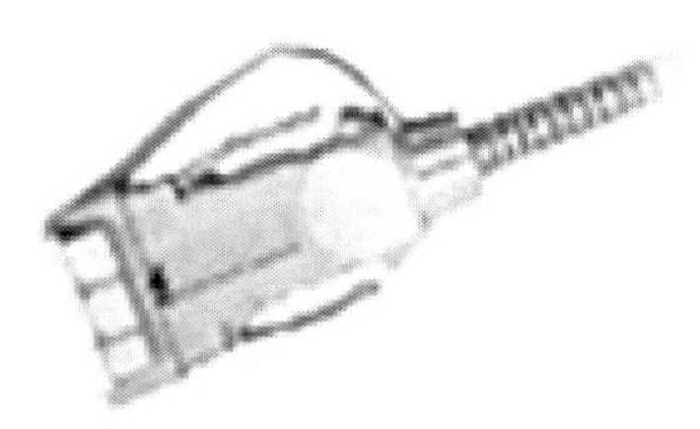
Biconic	The biconic connector is a screw-on type connector with a tapered sleeve that is fixed against guided rings and screws onto the threaded sleeve to secure the connection. When the connector is inserted into the receptacle, the tapered end of the connector locates the fiber optic cable into the proper position. The biconic connector is one of the earliest connector types. 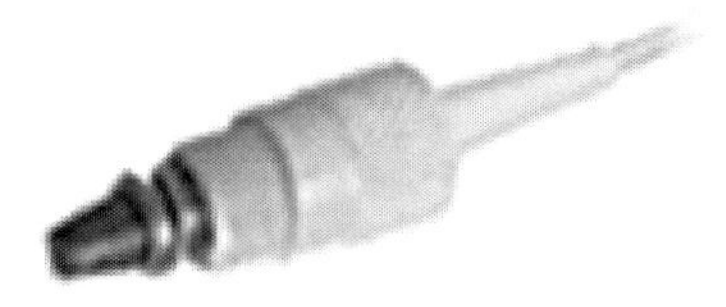

Fiber Optic Connector	Description
Local Connector (LC)	LC connectors are used for both singlemode and multimode fiber and a small form factor ceramic ferrule. It is about half the size of a SC or ST connector. LC connectors use an RJ-45-type latching and can be used to transition installations from twisted pair copper cabling to fiber. 
Sub Multi Assembly or Sub Miniature type A (SMA)	SMA connectors are similar to ST connectors, and use a threaded ferrule on the outside to lock the connector in place. It is typically used where water or other environmental factors necessitate a waterproof connection, unlike a bayonet-style connector. 
Mechanical Transfer Registered Jack (MT-RJ)	The MT-RJ connector, also called a Fiber Jack connector, is a compact snap-to-lock connector used with multimode fiber. Because the MT-RJ connector is compact, it is easy to use. It is similar in size to the RJ-45 connector. Two strands of fiber are attached with the MT-RJ connector. 

Cable Properties

Twisted pair, coaxial, and fiber optic cables have different properties with regard to transmission speed, distance, duplex, noise immunity, and frequency.

Cable Type	*Properties*
Twisted pair	**Transmission Speed:** • CAT 3 — UTP at 10 Mbps • CAT 5 — Up to 100 Mbps • CAT 6 — Up to 155 Mbps **Distance:** 1800 ft. **Duplex:** Supports full-duplex transmission **Noise Immunity (security, EMI):** 30 MHz **Frequency:** Up to 600 MHz
Coaxial	**Transmission Speed:** 10 Mbps **Distance:** Star topology – 2000 ft. Bus topology – 1000 ft. **Duplex:** Supports both half-duplex and full-duplex transmission **Noise Immunity (security, EMI):** High **Frequency:** 1 GHz to 10 GHz
Fiber optic	**Transmission Speed:** 40,000 Mbps **Distance:** Multimode fiber is typically used for shorter runs of up to 500 meters, and singlemode for longer runs. The ultra high-quality of some fiber cables allows runs of 62 miles or more between repeaters, which are rarely used now. **Duplex:** Supports full-duplex transmission as it consists of two fibers that can be used for simultaneous, bi-directional data transfer. **Noise Immunity (security, EMI):** High **Frequency:** Normally the frequency is very high and its range depends on the bandwidth and the device that you use.

Other Cable Media Types

Although twisted pair, coax, and fiber optic cables are the most prevalent types of cable media used in network installations, you might also encounter several other types of cables.

Cable Type	*Description*
Serial cable	A *serial cable* is a type of bounded network media that transfers information between two devices using serial transmission. Information is sent one bit at a time in a specific sequence. A serial cable most often uses an RS-232 connector. In networking, serial cables are often used to connect routers. Null modem serial cables are also used by networking professionals.

Cable Type	Description
IEEE 1394 (FireWire™)	While not as common as other bounded network media, IEEE 1394, commonly known as FireWire, can be used to connect up to 63 devices to form a small local network. FireWire cables use a shielded cable similar to STP with either four or six conductors. Connections to devices are made with either a six- or four-pin connector.
USB	A *USB connection* is a personal computer connection that enables you to connect multiple peripherals to a single port with high-performance and minimal device configuration. USB connections support two-way communications.

IEEE 1394 is commonly called FireWire, a name given to the standard by Apple, Inc. Sony names the same standard i.LINK™, which is often written as iLink.

Cables Used in Serial and Parallel Data Transmissions

The difference between serial and parallel cable is primarily the method that data is transmitted with. In parallel transmission, data (typically 8 bits) is transmitted simultaneously over several channels or wires.

USB Standards

USB 3.0 is the current standard that can transmit data at rates of up to 5 Gbps. USB 2.0 was the earlier standard that supported communication at up to 480 Mbps. It can communicate at up to 12 Mbps. A USB 2.0 device connected to a USB 1.1 hub or port will only communicate at USB 1.1 speeds, even though it might be capable of faster speeds. Windows will inform you of this when you connect the device.

FireWire vs. USB

FireWire predated USB and was faster than the original USB 1.1 standard. USB 3.0, with its increased speed, has largely superseded FireWire 3200. However, although USB 3.0 is faster than FireWire 3200 by the numbers, FireWire 3200 has better throughput, making it ideal for video or audio file transfers and external storage devices. A file transfer of 100 separate documents might be slightly faster on USB than FireWire, but a file transfer of a single 2 GB video file will be much faster in FireWire. Also, while USB provides a device with up to 5V power, FireWire maintains an edge in power management and provides up to 12V power on the wire.

ACTIVITY 3-1

Identifying Bounded Network Media

Scenario:

In this activity, you will identify the major types of bounded network media.

1. **Match the media type with its definition.**

___	IEEE 1394	a. Multiple insulated conductors clad in a protective and insulating outer jacket carry the signal.
___	Fiber optic	b. A shielded cable that is used to connect up to 63 devices to form a small local network.
___	Twisted pair	c. Light pulses from a laser or LED carry the signal through a core.
___	Coaxial	d. A central copper conductor carries the signal, surrounded by braided or foil shielding.

2. **Identify the type of network cabling shown in the graphic.**

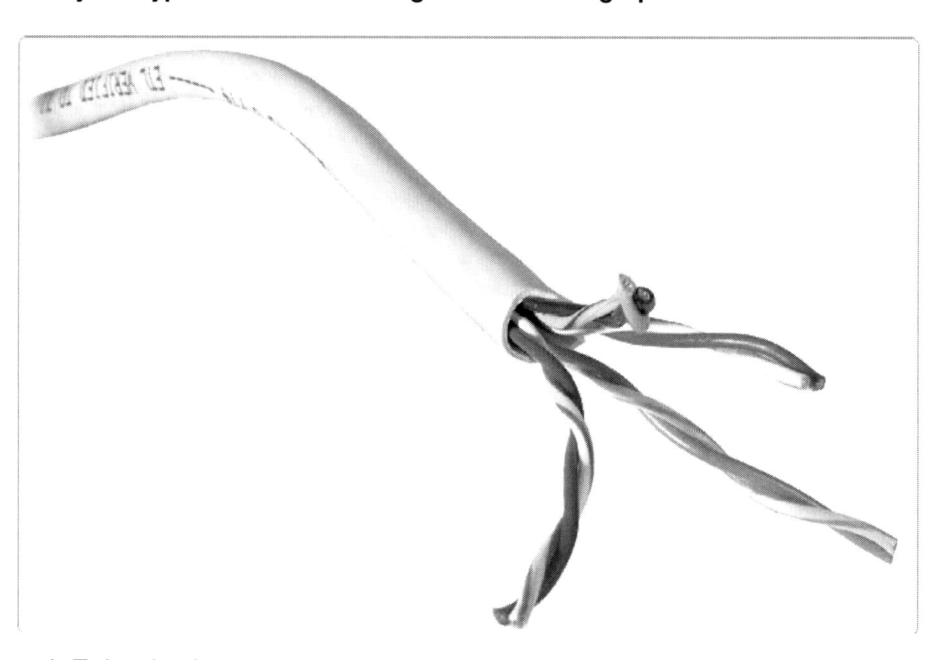

a) Twisted pair

b) Coax

c) Fiber optic

3. **Match the network media with the connector typically used with it.**

___	Coaxial cable	a.	RJ-45
___	Twisted pair cable	b.	MT-RJ
___	Fiber optic cable	c.	BNC

4. **Identify the type of network cabling shown in the graphic.**

a) Unshielded twisted pair

b) Shielded twisted pair

c) Coax

d) Fiber optic

5. **Why is a plenum cable commonly used in air handling spaces and run through fire-breaks?**

a) It does not give off poisonous gases when burning.

b) Fire cannot travel through the cable because of the insulated metal shield that surrounds the conductors.

c) Fire cannot travel through the cable because the jacket is closely bound to the conductors.

d) It is more durable than using a PVC cable.

ACTIVITY 3-2
Identifying Network Media

Scenario:

In this activity, you will identify the network media used on your local classroom network.

---

1. **Identify the cable types used to connect devices in the classroom.**

---

2. **Identify the types of connectors used in the classroom network.**

---

3. **Your instructor will provide samples of a variety of media and connector types. Identify each of the media and connectors.**

TOPIC B

Unbounded Network Media

In the previous topic, you identified bounded network media. With more and more wireless network implementations, you will need different types of media to meet the needs of your wireless network. In this topic, you will identify unbounded network media.

Unbounded media technologies have two distinct advantages for businesses over bounded media: first, they are generally easier to install and configure; and second, they afford clients a lot of mobility. They are usually not as secure as bounded media, as the signals are subject to interception. Wireless technologies implementations offer various advantages and you need to understand their limitations to compensate for their disadvantages in your network environments.

Wireless Communication

Definition:

Wireless communication is a type of communication in which signals are transmitted over a distance without the use of a physical medium. Information, data or voice, is transmitted as electromagnetic waves, such as radio and microwaves, or as light pulses. Wireless communication enables users to move around while remaining connected to the network. Wireless communication can be broadly classified as point-to-point communication such as cellular phones, multipoint communication such as wireless computer networks, and broadcast communication such as radio services.

Wireless media are also referred to as unbounded network media, where data signals are transmitted through the air instead of cables.

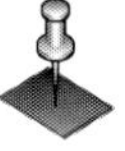

Wireless communication permits connections between areas where it would be difficult or impossible to connect using wires, such as in hazardous areas, across long distances, or inside historic buildings.

Example:

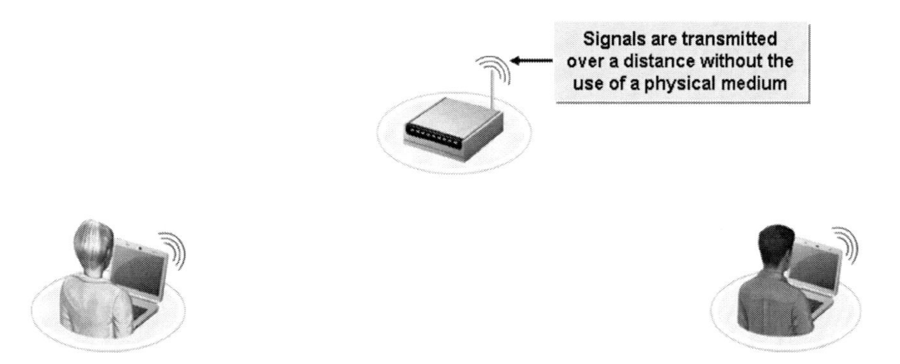

Figure 3-8: *Communication on a wireless network.*

Point-to-Point, Multipoint, and Broadcast Communications

Wireless connections can be point-to-point, multipoint, or broadcast.

Point-to-point communication is a direct connection between two nodes. Data transmitted by one node goes directly to the other. Cellular communications are point-to-point communications. Typically, point-to-point wireless connections are used to link distant buildings or networks as part of a CAN, a MAN, or a WAN.

Multipoint communication involves connections between many nodes. Each multipoint connection has more than two endpoints. A signal transmitted by any device through a medium is not private. All devices that share the medium can detect the signal but cannot receive it. Wireless computer networks are an example of multipoint communication.

Broadcast communication is a communication method in which data goes from a source node to all other nodes on a network. Each node receives and acts on the data. Radio communication is an example of a broadcast communication.

Radio Networking

Definition:

Radio networking is a form of wireless communications in which signals are sent via *Radio Frequency (RF)* waves in the 10 KHz to 1 GHz range. Radio networking is subject to electrical interference from power lines, a building's metal structural components, and atmospheric conditions.

U.S. regulatory agencies define the limits on which frequencies and how much power can be used to transmit radio signals. In the United States, the Federal Communications Commission (FCC) regulates radio transmission.

Example:

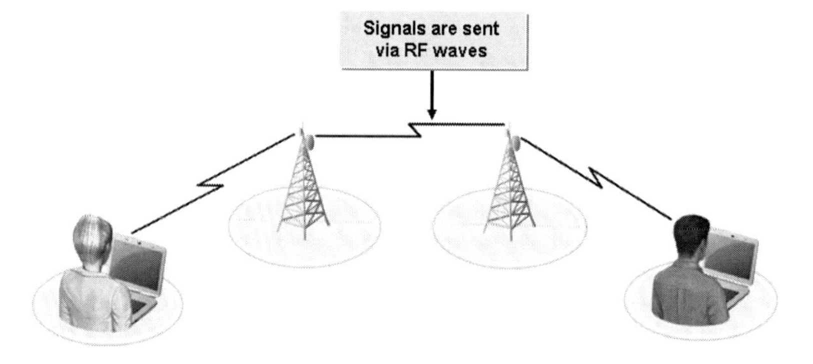

Figure 3-9: *Communications on a radio network.*

Broadcast Radio

Definition:

Broadcast radio is a form of RF networking that is non-directional, uses a single frequency for transmission, and comes in low- and high-power versions. Low-power RF transmission travel a short distance, often no more than 70 meters, but arc inexpensive and relatively easy to install. High-power RF transmission travel longer distances; however, specially-trained technicians are often required to install this more expensive type of system.

Example:

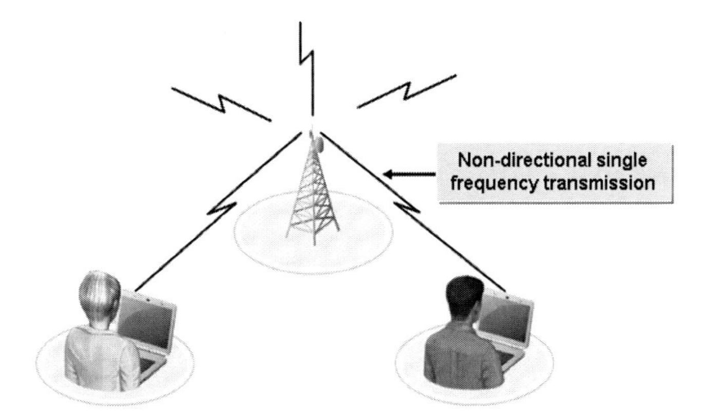

Figure 3-10: *Communications using broadcast radio.*

Spread Spectrum

Definition:

The spread spectrum is a form of radio transmission in which the signal is sent over more than one frequency. Because signals are transmitted over different frequencies, it is more difficult to eavesdrop and capture the signals. Additionally, distinguishing between the signal and background noise is often easier.

Example:

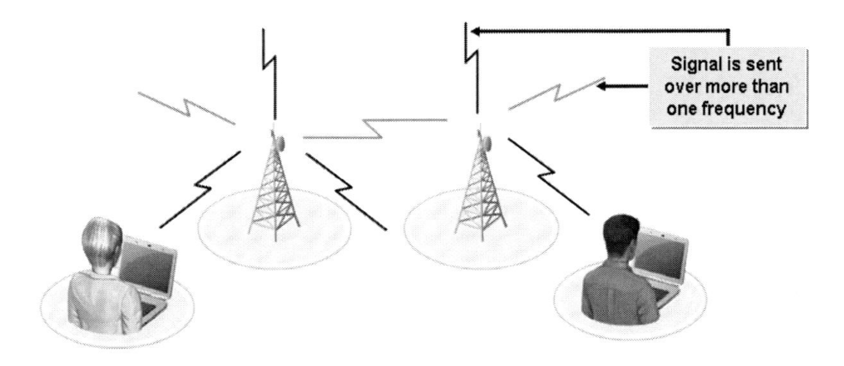

Figure 3-11: *Spread spectrum radio.*

Types of Spread Spectrum

The spread spectrum uses either frequency hopping or direct sequencing techniques to distribute the signal across the radio spectrum.

Spread Spectrum Type	Description
Frequency Hopping Spread Spectrum (FHSS)	*FHSS* sends signals on one channel at a time. The channel changes at fixed predetermined intervals. Both the sender and receiver use the same selection and order of frequencies so that communication is possible even as the frequency changes. FHSS does not significantly reduce noise or improve the signal-to-noise ratio.
Direct Sequence Spread Spectrum (DSSS)	*DSSS* uses multiple channels simultaneously to send data. Additionally, Error Detection And Correction (EDAC) techniques are used to reduce data transmission errors. In DSSS, a data signal is converted into multiple data signals called *chips*. The set of chips is sent across a wide band of adjacent channels. Upon receiving the data, the receiver combines and converts the signals back into the original. Because of the included EDAC information, the signal can often be reconstructed only if some of the channels are received clearly.

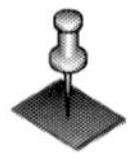

Eavesdroppers are less likely to be successful at listening in on an FHSS transmission than a normal radio transmission. It is unlikely that parties other than the sender and the receiver would know the selection and order of frequencies being used to communicate.

Infrared Transmission

Definition:

Infrared transmission is a form of wireless transmission over unbounded media in which signals are sent as pulses of infrared light. Infrared signals transmit at frequencies between 300 GHz and 300,000 GHz. Infrared frequencies transmit in the range just below visible light in the electromagnetic spectrum. Receivers need an unobstructed view of the sender to successfully receive the signal, though the signal can reflect off hard surfaces to reach the recipient. Many infrared-compatible devices follow the standards set forth by the Infrared Data Association (IrDA).

Example:

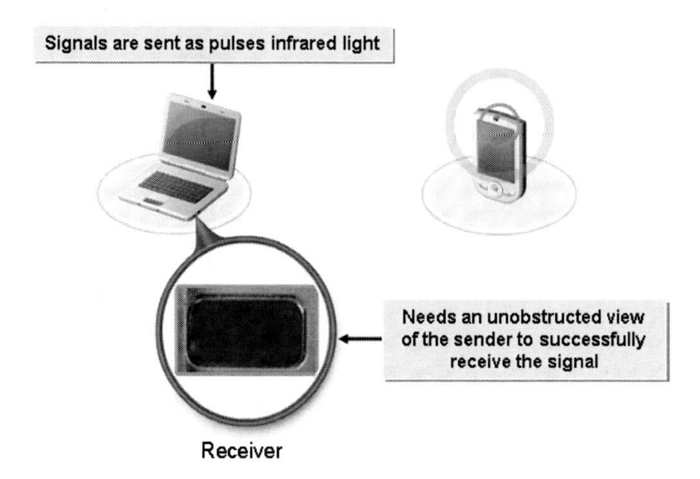

Figure 3-12: *Infrared transmission receiver.*

Infrared Transmission Rates

Infrared wireless networking offers transmission rates between 10 and 16 Mbps. Infrared compatible devices, such as a wireless mouse and keyboard, are limited to distances of approximately three feet and for that reason such devices are often used in Wireless Personal Area Networks (WPANs). Direct transmission and short distances between devices virtually eliminate eavesdropping and signal tampering, a key feature that makes IrDA the chosen standards for securing the transmission medium.

Infrared Specification	*Description*
Serial Infrared (SIR)	Discovery and negotiation of data connections is performed at 9.6 Kbps and speeds vary from 9.6 to 115.2 Kbps
Fast Infrared (FIR)	An obsolete term, but still used to describe 4 Mbps data transmission rates. FIR is also an informal reference to all speeds above SIR.
Very Fast Infrared (vFIR)	Supports data transmission speeds of up to 16 Mbps.
Medium Infrared (MIR)	An unofficial reference to data transmission speeds between 0.576 and 1.152 Mbps.

IrDA Data transfer

Support for IrDA functions is included with, or can be added to, many current operating systems including Windows, Mac OS X, and Linux. The IrDA specifications dictate a wide range of functions:

- **File transfer:** The IrDA Object Exchange (IrOBEX) protocol enables file transfer between IrDA devices.
- **Printing:** The IR Line Printer (IrLPT) protocol enables printing between IrDA devices such as laptops and IrDA printers.
- **Image transfer:** The IR Transfer Picture (IrTran-P) protocol enables easy image transfer between digital cameras and Windows devices.

- **Dial-up networking:** The IR Communications (IrCOMM) protocol enables dial-up Internet access through IR-enabled cell phones.
- **LAN access and peer-to-peer networking:** The IR Network (IrNET) protocol enables network access through IR-enabled access points.

Bluetooth

Bluetooth 1.1 is a wireless technology that facilitates short-range wireless communication between devices such as personal computers, laptops, cellular phones, and gaming consoles, thus creating a WPAN. A maximum of eight Bluetooth devices usually less than 30 feet apart can be connected to each other at a point in time. Bluetooth establishes a link using an RF-based media and does not need line-of-sight to make connections.

Bluetooth uses the 2.4 GHz spectrum to communicate a 1 Mbps connection between two devices for both a 232 Kbps voice channel and a 768 Kbps data channel. Bluetooth 2.0 will increase the overall speeds to a data rate of 2.1 to 3 Mbps. The latest version of Bluetooth—version 2.0 allows for communicating devices to be as far as 30 meters or 100 feet apart.

The "Bluetooth" technology is named in memory of a Danish king named Harald Bluetooth.

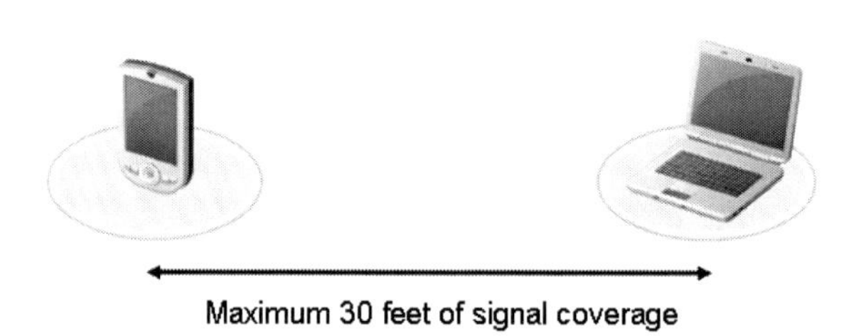

Figure 3-13: *Bluetooth communications.*

Although Bluetooth is used often in a WPAN, a small personal office or even a desktop allows you to connect other Bluetooth-enabled devices effectively.

Microwave Transmission

Definition:

Microwave transmission is a form of point-to-point wireless transmission over unbounded media in which signals are sent via pulses of electromagnetic energy in the microwave region of the electromagnetic spectrum. It transmits signals at a frequency range of 1 GHz to 300 GHz. Receivers need an unobstructed view of the sender to successfully receive the signal, and depending on the frequency in use, transmission can be affected by environmental conditions. Signals can be reflected off satellites to increase the transmission distance. Microwave transmission technologies are often used in WANs and MANs.

Example:

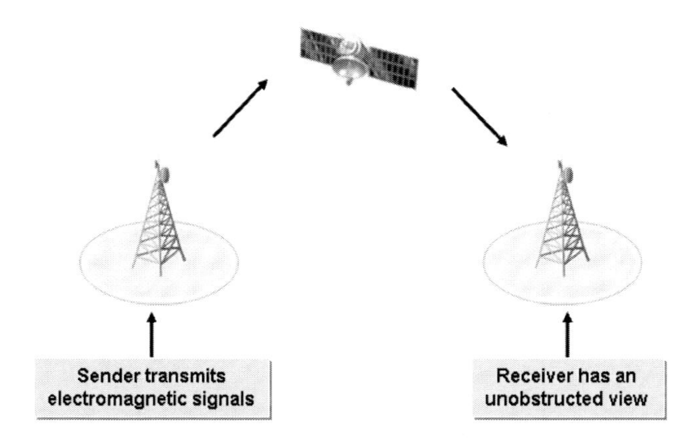

Figure 3-14: *Microwave transmission using satellites.*

Wireless Access Points

Definition:

A *Wireless Access Point (WAP)* is a device that provides a connection between wireless devices and can connect to wired networks. It has a network interface to connect to the wired network and an antenna or infrared receiver necessary to receive wireless signals. The *Service Set Identifier (SSID)* is a 32-bit alphanumeric string that identifies a WAP and all devices attached to it. Wireless connectivity devices such as the WAP or wireless routers come with a default SSID. Many access points include security features that enable you to specify which wireless devices can make connections to the wired network.

IEEE 802.11 does not specify how two WAPs should communicate. To ensure compatibility, it is best to use WAPs from the same manufacturer.

Example:

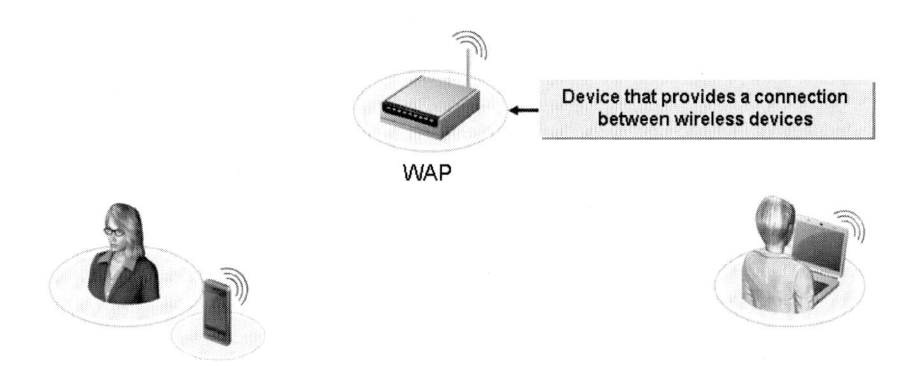

Figure 3-15: *A wireless access point connecting to a wired network.*

Enable and Disable SSIDs

Wireless connectivity devices such as a WAP or wireless routers come with a default SSID. An administrator can accept a device's default SSID or specify an SSID manually to more clearly identify the device.

Another method of securing a wireless connection is by disabling the broadcast of the SSID of the wireless device. Disabling the broadcast causes the wireless device to not appear on the network. Therefore, when a client device scans the network, it will not be able to locate the disabled SSID. Though disabling the broadcast of SSID is comparatively an easy task to do, this method is not very effective because hackers can still access the WLAN using sniffing software.

SSID Mismatches

A client device uses its SSID to identify itself to the wireless network. An SSID mismatch can occur when a device receives a packet that contains a different SSID than its own. Devices need to be configured with the same SSID as the WAP in order to communicate with it. A mismatch of SSIDs can block communication between the device and the WAP.

Steps to Install a WAP

How to Install a Wireless Access Point

Procedure Reference:

To install a WAP:

1. Select and purchase a WAP that meets your needs.
2. Determine placement for the WAP:
   - Where are the nodes you wish to connect to the router located?
   - How long will the cable connects the WAP to the wired network be?
   - Is there access to a power outlet?
   - Will the device be physically secure?
   - Do you need access to a wired network drop?
   - Consider wireless networking characteristics such as avoiding interference, signal range, and signal degradation.
3. Using a laptop, or a workstation at a desk or workbench, configure the WAP prior to deployment:
   a. Connect a network cable to the WAP's uplink port.
   b. Power on the WAP.
   c. Connect to the WAP via the built-in web interface, or by using manufacturer supplied configuration software.
   d. Configure the desired settings:
      - Consult your network documentation for configuration parameters such as the WAP's SSID, DHCP settings, and security settings.
      - Consult the device manufacturer's documentation for information on how to configure and use the device's capabilities and settings.
   e. Save the settings once configured.
   f. Test the WAP's functionality by connecting a wireless client to it:
      - Ping or use `traceroute` to test the connection to other computers and observe the results.
      - Use software tools to monitor the client's wireless signal strength and the WAP's behavior.
      - Connect to internal network shares.

- Connect to the Internet.

4. Place the WAP in the chosen location.
5. If necessary, run the appropriate type of cabling from the wired network to the WAP. Label the cable or drops on both ends so that there is no confusion as to where the cables go.
6. Power on the WAP.
7. Test the WAP's functionality in the live environment by repeating the tests from earlier installation.
8. Document your actions and their results, including any exceptions along the way.

ACTIVITY 3-3

Identifying Wireless Transmission Technologies

Scenario:

In this activity, you will identify and distinguish between the various types of unbounded media used to create wireless links between network nodes.

---

1. **Select the characteristic(s) of unbounded media.**
   a) Use a physical medium
   b) Transmit both voice and data signals
   c) Use electromagnetic energy
   d) Operate only within a 10 mile radius

---

2. **At what radio frequency does Bluetooth operate?**
   a) 5 GHz
   b) 2.4 GHz
   c) 300 GHz
   d) 100 GHz

---

3. **Which form of wireless transmission transmits signals in the 10 KHz to 1 GHz frequency range?**
   a) Radio
   b) Infrared
   c) Microwave

---

4. **What statements are true of data signaling in FHSS?**
   a) Consist of multiple chips transmitted across a different frequency.
   b) Sent over a single, high-frequency RF transmission band.
   c) Transmitted across a single frequency, and later sent over a randomly selected frequency.
   d) Less likely to be intercepted, but not significantly less susceptible to noise.

---

5. **Which forms of wireless media operate only when there are no obstacles in the transmission path?**
   a) Infrared
   b) Radio
   c) Microwave

---

6. Which unbounded media transmission method uses multiple frequencies to reduce interference and the likelihood of eavesdropping?

a) Infrared

b) Microwave

c) Spread spectrum

d) Broadcast radio

TOPIC C

Noise Control

You have identified both bounded and unbounded transmission media—the conduits over which network communications flow. This flow of communications can be impaired by interference such as noise. In this topic, you will describe noise and noise control techniques used on your network media.

Any number of things can cause interference with the transmission on your network—radio, TV, cell phones, and radar to name a few. The one constant is that noise always slows a network's performance and reduces its reliability. When the receiving node has to try to make sense of a mix of different signals, it ends up asking the sending node to resend data multiple times. In order to reduce noise on your network, you need to understand the sources of noise and how to protect your network against them.

Electrical Noise

Definition:

Electrical noise refers to unwanted signals that are present in the network media. Noise interferes with the proper reception of transmitted signals. Noise can come from natural sources, such as solar radiation or electrical storms, or from man-made sources, such as electromagnetic interference from nearby motors or transformers.

Example:

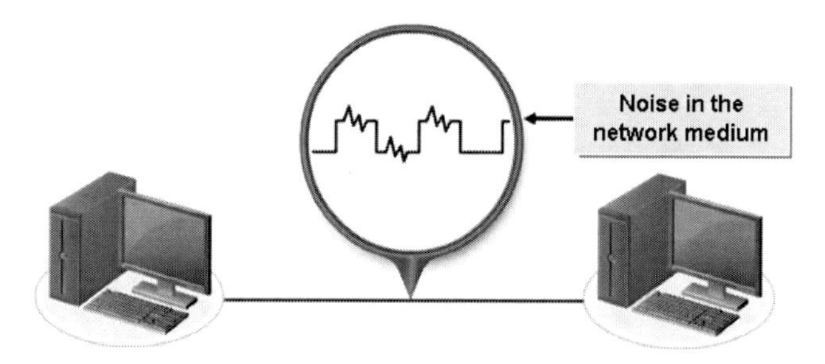

Figure 3-16: *Electrical noise on a signal transmission.*

Sources of Electrical Noise

A variety of sources contribute to electrical noise.

Noise Source	*Description*
Ambient noise	Ambient noise can come from many sources, including solar disturbances that affect the Earth's magnetosphere, or nearby radio broadcasting towers. These forms of noise affect both bounded and unbounded media, with longer network segments being affected more than shorter ones.
Power wires	High-tension power lines or a building's own electrical wiring can create electrical noise. Network cables that run parallel to electric wires are more susceptible to electrical noise than those that run perpendicular.

Noise Source	Description
Electric motors	Electric motors, such as those used in elevators, refrigerators, water fountains, and HVAC equipment, create noise while running, but this is more when they start up. Motors require a huge amount of electricity to start up, causing a burst of noise. These bursts can create temporary outages that resolve themselves when the motor reaches full speed or stops.
Electrical heat-generating devices	Like electric motors, electric heating elements use a lot of electricity and cause a significant amount of electrical noise while running.
Fluorescent, neon, and HID lights	Fluorescent, neon, and High-Intensity Discharge (HID) lighting devices produce a large amount of electrical noise, generally due to the transformers and ballasts required to make these lights work. Interior overhead lights, building security lights, and decorative lighting can create enough noise during operation to interfere with networking signals traveling over either bounded or unbounded media.

Other Effects of Noise

In addition to the noise that affects data networking media, noise can affect the electricity that powers computing devices. Surges or dips can result in the electric current, which can damage equipment, cause application or operating system software crashes, or even system restarts.

Electric motors, heating elements, solar disturbances, or natural disasters can cause transient power problems. Most devices include power conditioning components that handle at least some of these power fluctuations. However, sensitive equipment should be protected through the use of specialized power conditioning devices, such as an Uninterruptible Power Supply (UPS) or a surge protector.

Grounding

Grounding is the connection of a shield or conductor to an electrical ground point, such as a pipe or wire that is in contact with the ground. Grounding at one point in a segment helps prevent noise on the data conductor by shunting noise signals to ground. Connecting to ground at multiple points can introduce noise onto the line, degrading network performance.

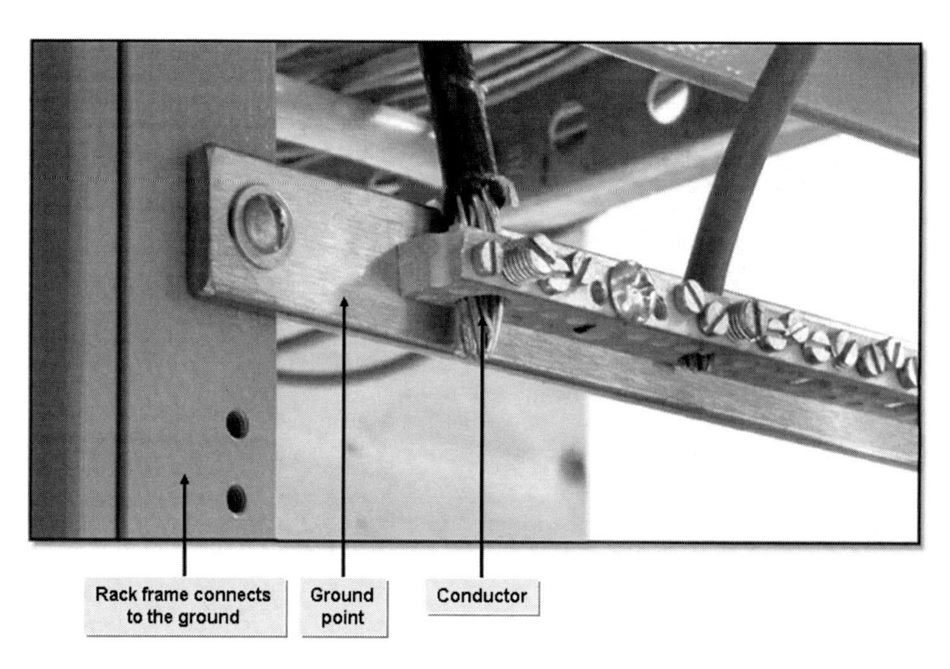

Figure 3-17: *Grounding using a rack frame.*

Grounding for Safety

Electrical devices often must be connected to a ground point for safety. In these situations, the ground connection serves as a way to direct high voltages safely away from humans and other devices, sending them instead into the ground.

Isolated Grounds

You should ground networking and other sensitive electronic equipment to dedicated ground points rather than to pipes and conduits. Electricians refer to this sort of ground connection as an isolated ground and will use an orange socket for such circuits.

Shielding

Definition:

Shielding is the method of placing the grounded conductive material around the media. This prevents the introduction of noise into the media by deflecting the noise to the ground. Because of this, the connection between the ground and the shield is called a *drain*. Shields are drained in only one location to prevent a ground loop, a phenomenon in which the shield introduces noise in the data signal.

Example:

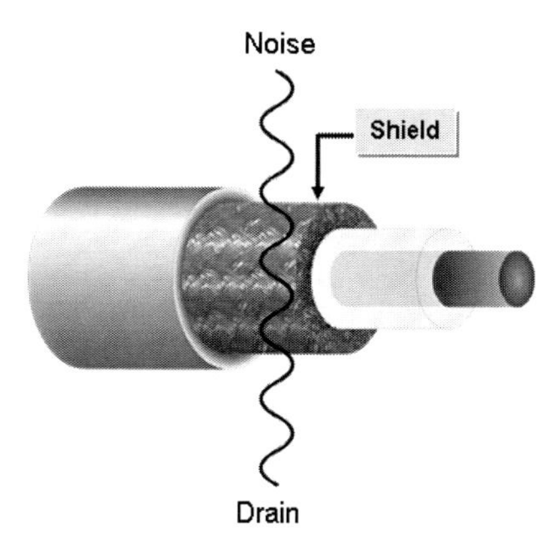

Figure 3-18: *Shielding used in Coax.*

Differential Signaling

Definition:

Differential signaling is a noise reduction technique in which signals from two inputs are compared; signals that are identical on both inputs are ignored, while those that are different on the inputs are accepted. Quite often, noise is constant on both inputs of a network cable. With differential signaling, such noise can be easily canceled out.

Example:

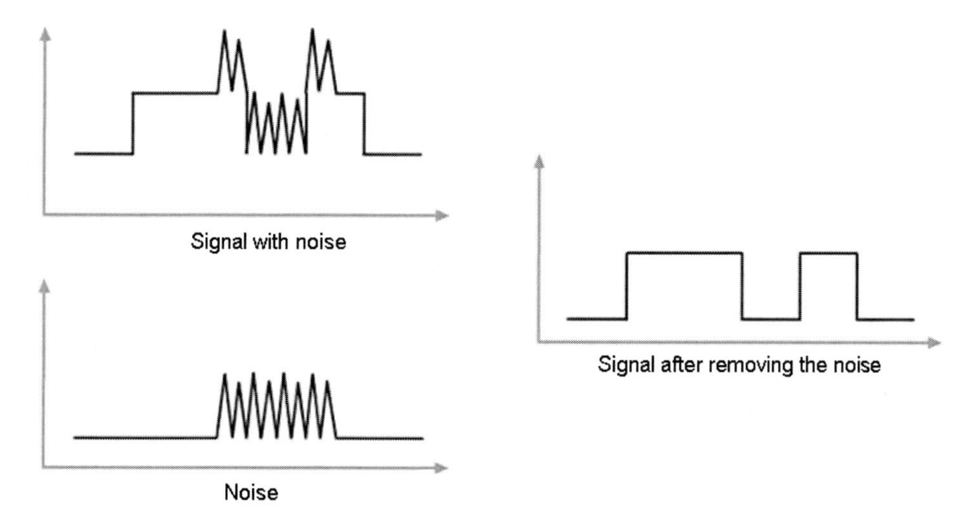

Figure 3-19: *Flow of signal in differential signaling.*

Noise Control with Twisted Pair

The twists in the twisted pair cable determine how resistant the cable will be to noise. When noise is introduced into a twisted pair cable in which pairs are closely wound, noise is deflected, minimizing the effect on the signal. When noise is introduced into a twisted pair cable in which pairs are loosely twisted, noise impinges on the conductor, adversely affecting the signal.

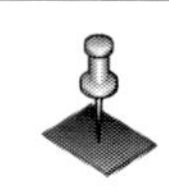

The tightness of the twists in twisted pair is called the "twist ratio."

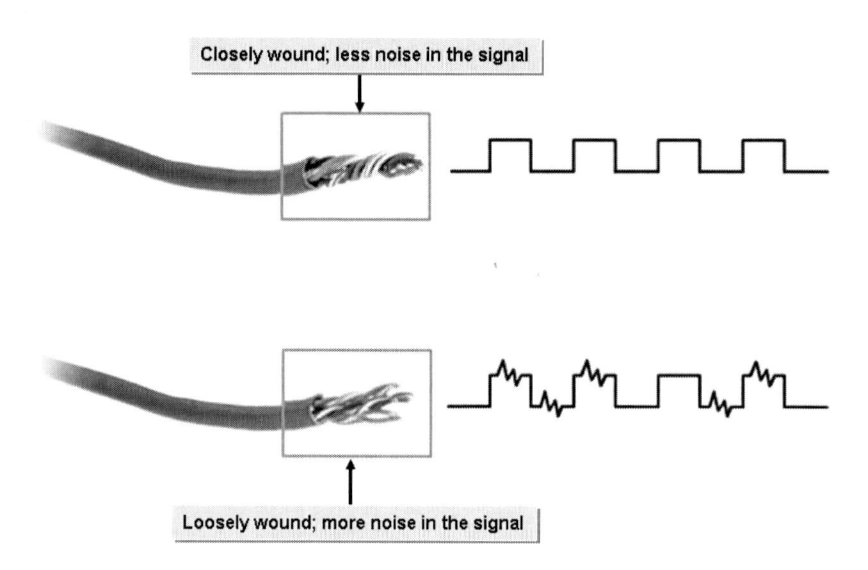

Figure 3-20: *Noise impact of different twists.*

Twists and Connectors

The primary difference between Category 3 and Category 5 twisted pair cables is the number of twists per inch, with Cat 5 being more tightly wound. However, to fully support the network speeds for which they are rated, you must take care when adding connectors to these cables. You should not unwind the pairs too much or you will eliminate the noise-canceling benefits of the twists. The more twists per foot and the more consistently the twists arranged are, the more resistant to noise a cable will be.

As a rule, you should not unwind to more than 3/8 of an inch (about 10 mm) for a Category 5 cable. A Category 3 cable is more tolerant to unwinding of twists. A Category 6 cable requires special connectors that maintain the twists inside the connector.

Termination

Termination is the application of a resistor or other device to the end of a cable. Adding such a *terminator* ensures that the ends of the cable do not represent an abrupt change in impedance, causing signal reflections and noise. The electrical characteristics of a terminator must match those of the cable and other components.

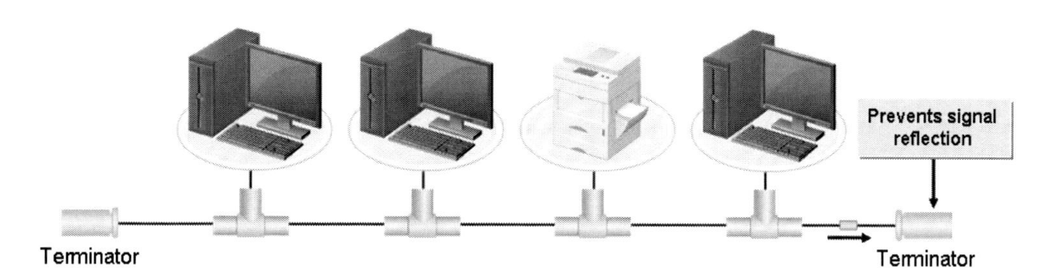

Figure 3-21: *Terminators used in a bus network.*

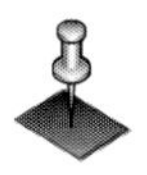

In legacy networking equipment, you had to install terminators yourself. They are now typically built into the networking devices you use.

Matching Impedance

Generally, you must match the impedance of all devices and cables to achieve proper signal flow. Signals can reflect off the points where impedance changes, such as at a connector between devices or cable segments of mismatched impedance. Signals flow smoothly across connections when impedances match.

A cable's impedance is typically marked on its outer jacket. If such a measure is a concern for a particular networking device, you will find markings on its case or in its manual stating the device's impedance.

Noise Reduction Considerations

The installation techniques you follow can affect the amount of noise introduced into a network cable. There are several considerations that you can use to limit the impact of noise on your network.

Consideration	*Description*
Separate data and electric cables	Do not run data and electricity cables in the same trays, raceways, and conduits. Avoid running network cables parallel to each other when you can, because crosstalk is worst when cables run parallelly.
Fluorescent lights	Keep network cables at least 20 inches from fluorescent lights as it can cause electromagnetic interference. If you must run data cables across or near these lights, do so in such a way that exposes the smallest length of cable to the light.

Consideration	Description
Power ground	Make sure to ground all equipment and electrical circuits according to the manufacturer's instructions and local building codes.
Connector installation	Follow standards, specifications, and manufacturer's directions when installing network cables. Do not unwind conductor pairs any more than required or allowed. Make sure connectors are firmly attached and connected to power outlets.

ACTIVITY 3-4

Identifying Electrical Noise Control Measures

Scenario:

In this activity, you will identify methods for controlling electrical noise.

---

1. **Choose the statement that defines electrical noise.**
    a) Solar radiation or man-made sources of data signals.
    b) Extraneous signals introduced onto network media.
    c) The reception of transmitted signals from a source.
    d) Extraneous signals that enhance the quality of received transmission.

---

2. **Select the items that are sources of electrical noise.**
    a) Fluorescent lights
    b) Solar storms
    c) Wind storms
    d) HVAC equipment

---

3. **True or False? Differential signaling reduces electrical noise by distinguishing between the signals on two different inputs.**

    __ True

    __ False

---

4. **What is the process of installing a resistor on the end of a cable to prevent signal reflections called?**
    a) Draining
    b) Grounding
    c) Terminating
    d) Shielding

---

5. Match the source of noise with the means by which you can lessen or eliminate its impact.

___	Fluorescent lights	a. Ensure that all equipment and electrical circuits follow the manufacturer's instructions and local building codes.
___	Power ground	b. Do not unwind conductor pairs any more than required or allowed.
___	Separate data and electric cables	c. Avoid running network cables parallel to each other when you can to avoid cross talk.
___	Connector installation	d. Keep cables at more than 20 inches distance from this source to avoid electromagnetic interference.

TOPIC D

Network Connectivity Devices

You are familiar with how network media, both bounded and unbounded, carry data across a network. Network connectivity devices transmit this data from one end to another. In this topic, you will identify the network connectivity devices and their purpose.

Network connectivity devices are the base connections upon which the structure of a network is established. Network connectivity devices connect clients to the network and assist in transfer of data on a network. Network devices can also boost the data signal to increase the distance your data transmission can travel and to ensure that they are usable at the destination.

NICs

Definition:

A *Network Interface Card (NIC),* also called a network adapter or network card, is a device that serves as an interface between a computer and the network. To connect to a network, a computer must have a NIC installed. NICs can be built into the motherboard of the computer, or can be connected using a USB, PC Card, CompactFlash or FireWire port; or it can also be an internal adapter card that is installed on one of the computer's expansion slots. NICs can connect to either wired or wireless networks.

Example:

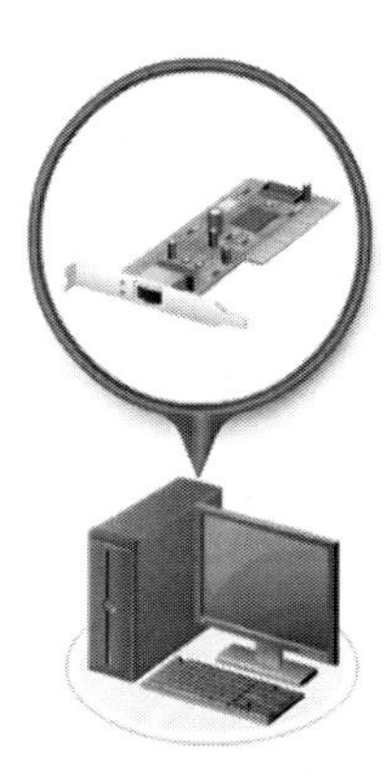

Figure 3-22: *A NIC on a computer.*

NIC Installation

Specific installation procedures for network cards might vary depending on the type of hardware used and its software features. You will need to customize the generic installation procedure to suit your specific situation. To install a NIC you need to:

1. Ensure that you take anti-static precautions by using an anti-static wrist strap or similar gear.
2. Power down the PC.
3. Disconnect the power and other cables.
4. Open the case for the CPU.
5. Locate the PCI or PCIx slot you want to install the card into.
6. Install the card into the slot and secure it with a screw.

7. Close the case and reconnect the cables.
8. Connect a network cable to the newly installed card.
9. Power on the PC.
10. Install the manufacturer provided drivers. The operating system may identify and install the driver automatically or you may have to install the driver manually.
11. Test the card's functionality.
    - Observe the card's LED lights to verify that it is operational.
    - Ping other computers on the network.
    - Connect to internal network share folders to check local network access.
    - Connect to the Internet.
12. Document the steps for the installation for future reference.

Full Duplex Support

Full Duplex is a feature of NIC that allows multiple devices to send and receive data simultaneously without data collision. Because a switch forms a miniature network between a node and itself, there is no chance of data collision. Thus, it does not need to use a conventional media access method, such as CSMA/CD. Instead, providing the node's NIC is properly configured, the switch can support a full duplex connection with each node over which data can be sent and received simultaneously. Full duplex operation may not be enabled by default on your NICs and switches. Taking the time to enable this feature using the NIC's properties can improve performance by doubling throughput on your network.

ACTIVITY 3-5

Identifying the Local Network Card

There is a simulated version of this activity available on the CD-ROM that shipped with this course. You can run this simulation on any Windows computer to review the activity after class, or as an alternative to performing the activity as a group in class. The activity simulation can be launched either directly from the CD-ROM by clicking the **Interactives** link and navigating to the appropriate one, or from the installed data file location by opening the C:\Data\Simulations\Lesson#\Activity# folder and double-clicking the executable (.exe) file.

Before You Begin:

Your user name is Child##\Administrator (where ## is your assigned student number). Your password is !Pass1234. The classroom main domain is named CLASSNET.

Scenario:

In this activity, you will identify the local network adapter card.

---

1. Log on to Windows Server 2008 R2.
   a. Press **Ctrl+Alt+Delete** to log on.
   b. In the log on screen, click **Switch User** and then click **Other User.**
   c. In the **User name** text box, type ***Administrator*** and press **Tab.** In the **Password** text box, enter ***!Pass1234***
   d. Close the Server Manager window.

---

2. Verify your log on identity.
   a. Click **Start.**
   b. Observe that your user name is displayed at the top of the **Start** menu.

   c. Choose **Control Panel** and, in the Control Panel window, click **User Accounts.**
   d. In the User Accounts window, in the right pane, click the **User Accounts** link.
   e. Click the **Manage User Accounts** link.
   f. Verify that your user name is selected and click **Properties.**

g. Observe your domain user name in the title of the dialog box. Close the **CHILD##\ Administrator Properties** and **User Accounts** dialog boxes.

3. Identify the network card type.

   a. In the User Accounts window, click the **Control Panel Home** link.

   b. In the Control Panel window, click the **Hardware** link.

   c. In the **Devices and Printers** section, click the **Device Manager** link.

   d. In the Device Manager window, in the objects list, double-click **Network adapters** to expand it.

Your card type might be different from the one displayed in the graphic of Step 2e.

   e. Identify the network card type and then close all open windows.

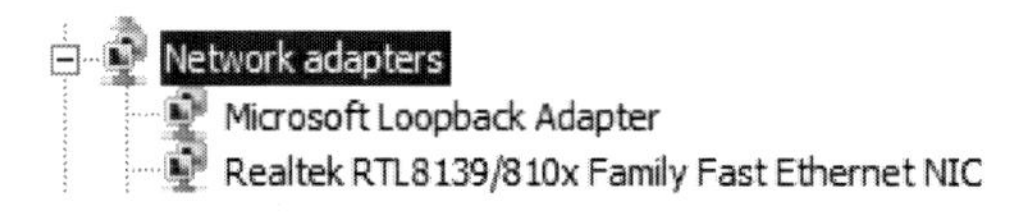

Transceivers

Definition:

A *transceiver* is a device that has both a transmitter and a receiver integrated into it and, as a result, can both send and receive data. Most modern transceivers are built into the network card. In networking, the transceiver supports the NIC in allowing data transmission through the medium.

Example:

Figure 3-23: *A transceiver on a network card.*

Example: GBIC

A *Gigabit Interface Converter (GBIC)* is a transceiver used to convert electrical signals into optical signals and vice versa. It is used as an interface for high-speed networking and to upgrade the network, without needing to replace all components in the motherboards. For instance, if different optical technologies are used, GBICs can be used to specifically configure that link on the network. Based on the wavelength of laser light generated within the GBIC generator, GBICs can be categorized into short-wave GBICs and long-wave GBICs. The short-wave GBIC is used for connecting devices that are between 0.5 meters and 500 meters apart. Meanwhile, the long-wave GBIC is used for connecting devices that are between 2 meters and 6 miles apart.

Example: SFP

A *Small Form Factor Pluggable (SFP)* transceiver is most commonly used in 2 Gbps and 4 Gbps fiber channel components to interconvert electrical signals and optical signals. SFPs are similar to GBICs in their architecture, but they allow higher port density than GBICs.

Switches

Definition:

A *switch* is a network device that acts as a common connecting point for various nodes or segments. Switches work with pairs of ports, connecting two segments into an isolated contention domain as needed. Switches check the MAC address of each packet before they forward the packet to one or more ports for transmission. Most switches can work with multiple pairs of ports simultaneously to improve performance. Switches are responsible for forwarding data from the source to the destination, but switches forward data packets only to nodes or segments to which they are addressed. Because switches forward each packet only to the required port, the chances of collision are greatly reduced, increasing performance.

Example:

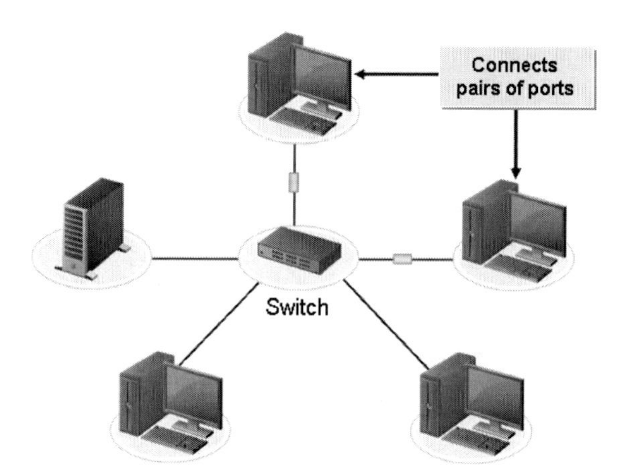

Figure 3-24: *Switches in a network.*

Managed Switches

A *managed switch,* also called an *intelligent switch,* is one that includes functions that enable you to monitor and configure its operation. Typically, you connect to the switch using special software or via a dedicated management port.

Port Mirroring

Port mirroring is the practice of duplicating all traffic on one port in a switch to a second port, effectively sending a copy of all the data to the node connected to the second port. Port mirroring is useful as a diagnostic tool when you need to monitor all traffic going to a particular port or node with minimal impact on the network performance.

Channel Bonding

Channel bonding is the process of increasing throughput as it uses channels to bind multiple NICs to a MAC address. Channel bonding is performed on the Data Link layer. Channel bonding is also referred to as NIC bonding.

Trunking

Trunking involves combining multiple network connections to increase bandwidth and reliability. Trunking is also known as link aggregation, port teaming, and NIC bonding, among other names. While there are a variety of manufacturer implemented techniques, IEEE 802.1AX-2008 defines a standard for link aggregation and resolves some issues with earlier definitions.

Linking two 1 Gbps ports on a server to two 1 Gbps ports on a switch can result in 2 Gbps aggregate throughput. Depending on the implementation, this can result in a redundant connection in case one of the cables or ports fails. However, this still leaves the possibility of the entire switch failing, so some hardware vendors provide proprietary methods for trunking ports across two physically separate switches. Trunking can be used to connect a variety of network hardware, including switch to switch, server to switch, server to server, or switch to router.

Steps to Install and Configure a Switch

Virtual Switches

A *virtual switch* is a software-based switch that provides functionality similar to physical switches. Used to connect systems on a virtual network, a virtual switch contains a core forwarding unit that forwards packets to the correct virtual systems. Virtual switches check the MAC address of each packet like a physical switch, and forwards the packet to one or more virtual ports for transmission. It also contains a VLAN tagging unit, a packet filtering unit, and a security unit. Traffic cannot directly flow from one virtual switch to another in the same host network. All network traffic from external virtual networks is routed through a physical switch to its destination. Two virtual switches or VLANs cannot communicate directly, and you need to configure a router to forward packets.

Switch Installation and Configuration

Procedure Reference:

To install and configure a switch:

1. Purchase a switch that will meet your network requirements.
2. Determine the placement for the switch. You will need to consider:
   - Where are the devices you wish to connect to the switch located?
   - How long will the cable run between the switch and each node be?
   - Is there access to a power outlet?
   - Will the switch need to be physically secured?
   - Do you need access to a wired network drop?
3. Run the appropriate cabling from each node to the switch.
   - Ensure that you properly terminate the cables at both ends.
   - Label the cables or drops on both ends so that there is no confusion as to how the cables need to be connected.
4. Plug the ends of the cables into the ports on the nodes and the switch.
5. Use an appropriate network cable to connect the switch to the rest of the network.

If you are connecting to another network device rather than an individual workstation and the switch has an uplink port, use it. You may need to use a crossover cable to make the connection.

6. Power on the switch.
7. Unmanaged switches do not need to be configured. If it is a managed switch, configure the desired settings:
   - Consult your network documentation for configuration parameters.
   - Consult the device manufacturer's documentation for information on how to configure and use the device's capabilities and settings.

8. Test the switch's functionality:
    - Check LED lights on the front of the switch to make sure it is operational and the necessary ports are active.
    - Ping other computers attached to both the switch and other portions of the network.
    - Use software tools to monitor the signal strength, packet loss, and connection speed.
    - Connect to internal network shared folders to check network access.
    - Connect to the Internet.
9. Document your actions and results, including any exceptions for future reference.

Routers

Definition:

A *router* is a networking device that connects multiple networks that use the same protocol. Routers send data between networks by examining the network addresses contained in the packets they process. Routers can work only with *routable protocols,* which are network protocols that provide separate network and node addresses. A router can be a dedicated device, incorporated into a multi-function device, or can be implemented as software running on a node, typically with two NICs, with one NIC being the node's primary network adapter and the other NIC acting as the router.

Example:

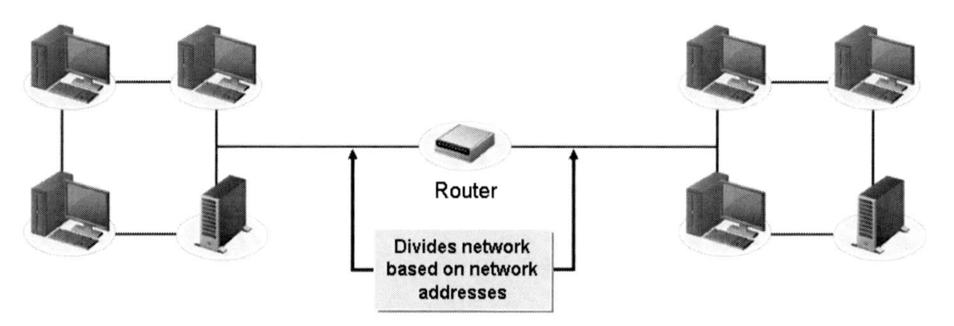

Figure 3-25: *Router on a network.*

Rollover Cables

A rollover cable is a cable used to connect a computer to a router. It is often necessary to use a rollover cable to perform initial setup and configuration, or troubleshooting of routers. The rollover cable connects to the router's console port on one end, and to a computer's serial port on the other.

The term "rollover" is used because the wires are reversed at one end; going from one to eight on end A and from eight to one on end B. Rollover cables are usually differentiated by being flat instead of round, and their outer jacket is often a unique color such as yellow or light blue. Some rollover cables have Ethernet connectors on both ends and will need a DB-9 (RS-232) or RJ-45 adapter to connect to a serial port.

Steps to Install and Configure a Router

Router Installation and Configuration

Procedure Reference:

To install and configure a router:

1. Ensure that you purchase a router that will meet the needs of your network.
2. Determine the correct placement for the router. You need to consider:
   - Where are the nodes you wish to connect to the router located?
   - How long will the cable run between the router and each node be?
   - Is there access to a power outlet?
   - Is the router physically secured?
   - Do you need access to a wired network drop?
   - Do you need to make considerations for wireless networking?
3. Run the appropriate type of cabling from each node to the router.
   - Ensure that all cables are properly terminated at both ends.
   - Label the cables or drops on both ends so that there is no confusion as to where the cables go.
4. Use an appropriate network cable to connect the router to the rest of the network.

If you are connecting to another network device rather than an individual workstation and the router has an uplink port, use it. You may need to use a crossover cable to make the connection.

5. Power on the router.
6. Configure the desired settings:
   - Consult the network documentation for configuration parameters such as subnetting parameters, routing protocol configuration, and router connection settings.
   - Consult the device manufacturer's documentation for information on how to configure and use the device's capabilities and settings.
7. Test the router's functionality:
   - Ping other computers attached to both the router and other portions of the network.
   - Run a `traceroute` command from your node to other nodes that you know the new router should be servicing.
   - Use software tools to monitor the signal strength, packet loss, and connection speed.
   - Connect to internal network shared folders to check network access.
   - Connect to the Internet.
8. Document your actions and their results, including any exceptions for future reference.

Gateways

Definition:

A *gateway* is a device, software, or a system that converts data between incompatible systems. This function differentiates it from the router, which can interconnect networks that use similar protocols only. Gateways can translate data between different operating systems, or email formats, or between totally different networks. A gateway can be implemented as hardware, software, or both. You can also install gateways as software within a router, allowing the router to act as a gateway when required, and eliminating the need for separate hardware.

It is important not to confuse a gateway with the default gateway in TCP/IP, which just forwards IP data packets.

Example:

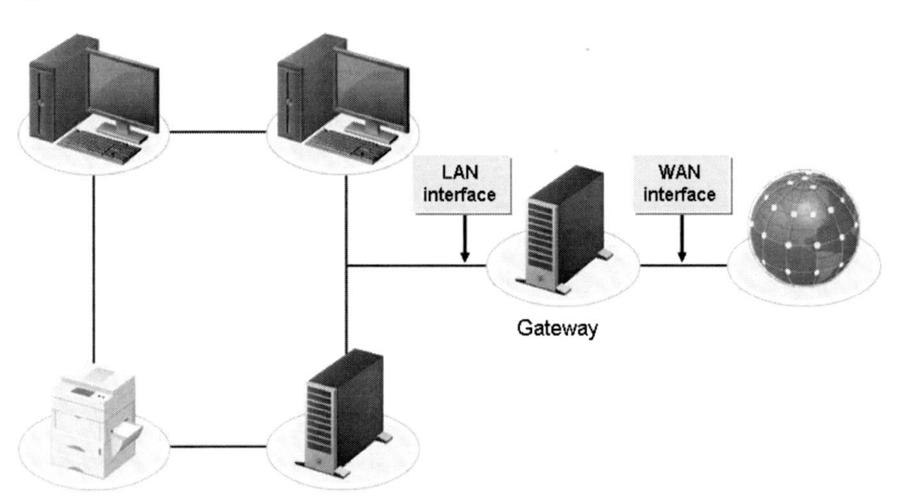

Figure 3-26: *A gateway connecting a LAN to a WAN.*

Virtual Servers

A *virtual server* is remote software that can run its own operating systems or applications, similar to a physical server. A virtual server is composed of only software components and behaves similar to a real computer. A virtual server has characteristics similar to a physical computer and contains its own virtual software-based CPU, RAM, hard drive, and NIC. An operating system will behave in the same manner on both virtual and physical servers because it cannot differentiate between the two. Similarly, there will not be any major functionality changes in the way applications or computer networks behave in a virtual server environment. Virtual servers offer distinct advantages over physical servers such as the ability to perform administrative tasks remotely and at lower costs.

Virtual Desktop

Virtual desktop is a feature of the operating system that allows multiple desktops to be open instead of the default single desktop. On the supported operating system, users can specify the default number of desktops. Virtual desktop is supported on most Linux distributions. Windows require additional software to be installed for enabling virtual desktop. Virtual desktop will be useful when a user needs to have multiple windows open without cluttering their desktop.

Virtual PBX

A *virtual PBX* is a private communications service provider that provides low cost PBX service. Traditionally, businesses use PBX technology to manage phone-based tasks such as voicemail, faxing, conference calling, and call routing. A physical PBX system involves a very high cost investment with expensive hardware that only large businesses could afford. Virtual PBXs allow smaller businesses to utilize PBX services without the need to purchase, install, or maintain a physical PBX. Virtual PBX utilizes the traditional Public Switched Telephone Network (PSTN) with *Voice over IP (VoIP)* technology.

PBX Parachute

Virtual PBX provides a service named the *PBX parachute* that acts as a disaster recovery capability and keeps the phone service running even in case of power failure.

NaaS

Organizations can purchase networking infrastructure. However, when they do not need it, they can lease the network 'as a service' to a client. In this method, service providers lease resources on the network such as communication services and infrastructure. *Network as a Service (NaaS)* includes offerings such as *Platform as a Service (PaaS)* and *Infrastructure as a Service (IaaS)*. PaaS includes infrastructure and tools from the service provider so that the client does not need to manage them. They can, however, modify the applications deployed and the configuration parameters. IaaS includes network resources such as storage systems. The client can deploy software and add network components such as firewalls. Wireless service providers provide their services to subscribers, which is also an implementation of NaaS.

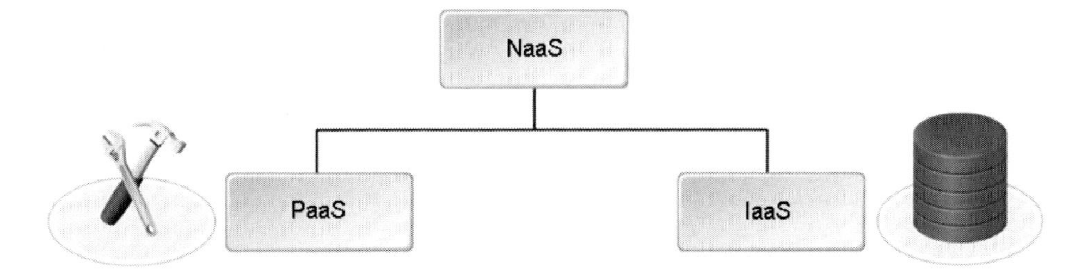

Figure 3-27: *NaaS Infrastructure.*

Legacy Network Connectivity Devices

Due to technological advancements in the field of networking, some of the network connectivity devices have become outdated. While some of them are no longer available as separate devices, their functionality is built into devices such as routers and switches.

Network Device	Description
Repeater	A *repeater* is a device that regenerates a signal to improve signal strength over transmission distances. By using repeaters, you can exceed the normal limitations on segment lengths imposed by various networking technologies. Repeaters are used frequently with coax media, such as cable TV, and were also deployed in networks that used coax cabling. Most networks today use twisted pair cabling, and repeaters are not commonly needed. Wireless network repeaters and bridges are frequently used to extend the range of a WAP.
Hub	A *hub* is a networking device used to connect the nodes in a physical star topology network into a logical bus topology. A hub contains multiple ports to which the devices can be connected. When a data packet from the transmitting device arrives at a port, it is copied and transmitted to all other ports so that all other nodes receive the packets. However, only the node to which it is addressed reads and processes the data while all other nodes ignore it. Two common types of hubs used were passive and active. A *passive hub* simply receives data transmitted from a device to one port and broadcasts it out to the devices connected on all other ports. An *active hub* performs the same "receive then broadcast" action as a passive hub, and also regenerates or boosts the signal much like a repeater.
Bridge	A *bridge* is a network device that divides a logical bus network into segments. Bridges examine the MAC address of each packet. If the packet is destined for a node connected to a different port, the bridge forwards the packet. If the packet is addressed to a node on its own segment, the bridge does not forward the packet. This arrangement reduces traffic between segments and improves overall network performance.

ACTIVITY 3-6

Identifying Network Connectivity Devices

Scenario:

In this activity, you will identify the primary types of network connectivity devices.

---

1. **You need to connect multiple networks that use the same protocol. Which networking device would best meet your needs?**
    a) Router
    b) Bridge
    c) Gateway
    d) Switch

---

2. **Which of these network devices is a common connecting point for various nodes or segments?**
    a) Hub
    b) Router
    c) Gateway
    d) Switch

---

3. **True or False? A gateway subdivides a LAN into segments.**
    __ True
    __ False

---

4. **Which statements are valid for a gateway?**
    a) It can connect networks with dissimilar protocols.
    b) It can be implemented in a router.
    c) It can be implemented only as a computer program.
    d) It can be implemented as hardware or software.

Lesson 3 Follow-up

In this lesson, you identified network media and networking devices. These components form the infrastructure of your network. Just as people do not commute without a road, train, or subway, your data cannot move from computer to computer without media and devices. Knowledge of the media and devices will help you better understand the flow of data, and detect and troubleshoot transmission issues as they arise on your network.

1. **Which will you use more frequently in your networks: bounded or unbounded media?**

2. **Of the various networking devices, which offers you the best mix of features and functionality?**

4 Network Implementations

Lesson Time: 1 hour(s), 50 minutes

Lesson Objectives:

In this lesson, you will identify the major types of network implementations.

You will:

- Identify the components of an Ethernet network implementation.
- Identify the components of a wireless network implementation.

Introduction

In the previous lesson, you identified the different types of transmission media, noise control, and the various network connectivity options. All of these network connectivity methods are used in different types of network implementations. In this lesson, you will identify the major types of network implementations.

Networking is a fundamental aspect of all computer infrastructure. The ability to link and communicate between clients, servers, and mainframes is vital for the dissemination of voice and data traffic. As a network engineer, you will need to handle different types of networks. You need to be aware of the characteristics of the different types of networks to implement the most suitable network such that its performance is fully optimized.

This lesson covers all or part of the following CompTIA® Network+® (Exam N10-005) certification objectives:

- Topic A:
  - 1.2 Classify how applications, devices, and protocols relate to the OSI model layers.
  - 1.3 Explain the purpose and properties of IP addressing.
  - 3.7 Compare and contrast different LAN technologies.
- Topic B:
  - 1.2 Classify how applications, devices, and protocols relate to the OSI model layers.
  - 2.2 Given a scenario, install and configure a wireless network.
  - 2.4 Given a scenario, troubleshoot common wireless problems.
  - 3.3 Compare and contrast different wireless standards.

TOPIC A
Ethernet Networks

In this lesson, you will identify major types of standard network implementations. The most pervasive standard in the majority of today's LAN implementations is Ethernet. In this topic, you will learn how devices and resources are connected using the Ethernet technology.

Ethernet continues to dominate the wired LAN scenario, and is known for its simplicity and wide applicability. Its popularity can be owed to its ease of installation and upgradability. Networks both large and small utilize the Ethernet technology to provide both backbone and end-user services. Due to the wide deployment of Ethernet today, you will be required to manage and troubleshoot Ethernet networks.

Ethernet

Ethernet is a set of networking technologies and media access methods specified for LANs. Ethernet allows computers to communicate over small distances using a wired medium. Ethernet has evolved as the most widespread technology for wired LANs. Most Ethernet networks use twisted pair cables in their subnetworks and optical fibers or coaxial cables in the network backbone. IEEE has defined the 802.3 specifications and standards for Ethernet implementations.

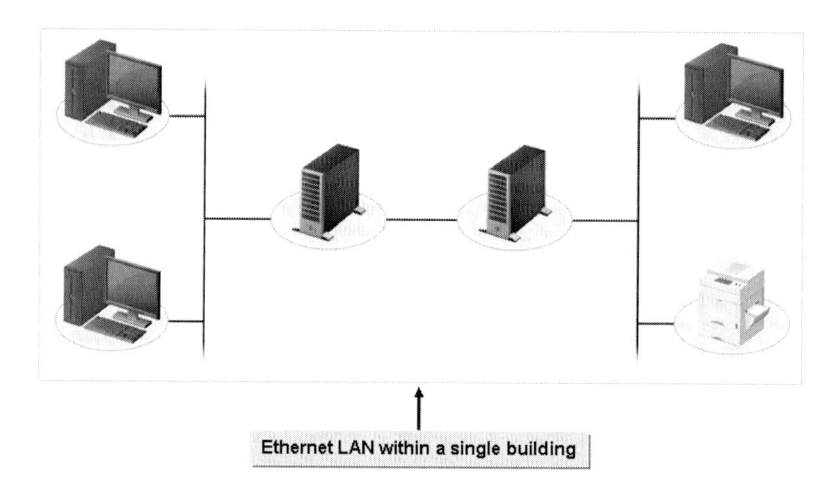

Figure 4-1: *An Ethernet network implementation.*

Switched Ethernet

Switched Ethernet is a LAN technology that connects computers using switches. The switch enables the device to utilize the full bandwidth of the medium. In switched Ethernet, switches recognize the destination address and route the packet only to the destination node. Thus, a switch can route multiple packets to different destinations simultaneously.

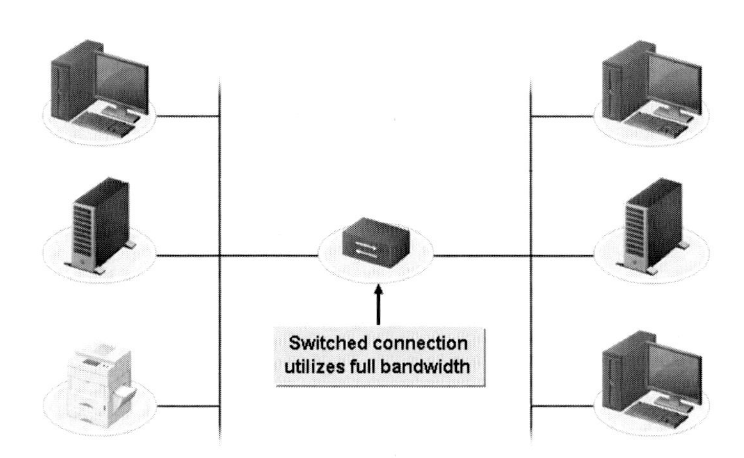

Figure 4-2: *Switches on an Ethernet network.*

Ethernet Frames

An *Ethernet frame* is a data packet that has been encoded on the Data Link layer for transmission from one node to another on an Ethernet network. The basic Ethernet frame is broken down into seven fields as shown in the graphic.

7 bytes	1 byte	6 bytes	6 bytes	2 bytes	n bytes	4 bytes
Preamble	Start-of-Frame Delimiter	Destination address	Source address	Frame type	Data	Frame Check Sequence

Figure 4-3: *Fields in an Ethernet frame.*

Ethernet Frame Field	***Description***
Preamble (PRE)	(7 bytes) A pattern of ones and zeros used to signal the start of the frame and provide synchronization and timing information. The preamble notifies all nodes that there is data to follow.
Start-of-Frame Delimiter (SFD)	(1 byte) The SFD identifies the beginning of the data field.
Destination Address (DA)	(6 bytes) This is the MAC address of the computer to which the frame is being transmitted; it can be a unicast, multicast, or broadcast address.
Source Address (SA)	(6 bytes) This is the MAC address of the computer transmitting data—the SA is always a unicast address.
Frame type	(2 bytes) This is the length of the entire Ethernet frame in bytes, or the frame type ID of the frame. This field can hold a value between 0 and 65,534, but the maximum value is usually less than 1500.
Data	(n bytes) The payload of the frame (or the information being sent). It must be a minimum of 46 bytes long and can be a maximum of 1500 bytes. If the length of data is less than 46 bytes, the data field must be extended by adding a filler to increase the length to a minimum of 46 bytes.

Ethernet Frame Field	Description
Frame Check Sequence (FCS)	(4 bytes) The FCS checks the frame using a 32–bit Cyclic Redundancy Check (CRC) value. The FCS allows the receiving device to detect errors in the Ethernet frame and reject it if it appears damaged.

MAC Addresses

Definition:

A *MAC address*, also called a physical address, is a unique, hardware-level address assigned to every networking device by its manufacturer. MAC addresses are six bytes long. The first three bytes uniquely identify the manufacturer and are referred to as the *Organizationally Unique Identifier (OUI).* The remaining three bytes identify the device itself and are known as the Universal LAN MAC address. MAC addresses make use of an IEEE standard called the Extended Unique Identifier (EUI). A host computer implemented with EUI-64 can assign to itself a 64-bit IPv6 interface identifier automatically.

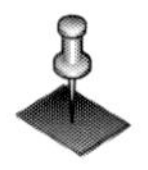

The OUI may also be called the Block ID and the Universal LAN MAC address may also be called the Device ID.

Example:

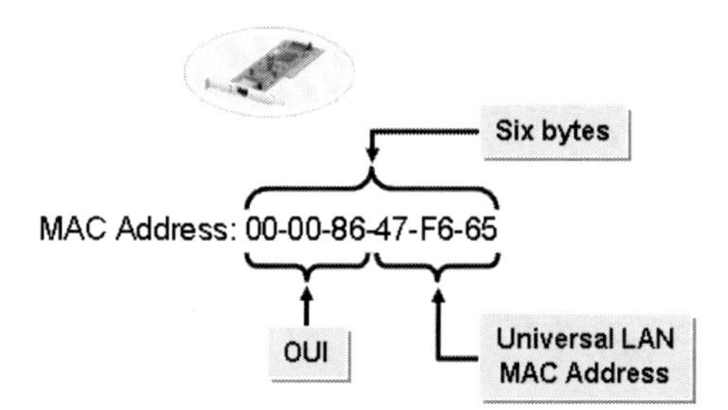

Figure 4-4: *A MAC address.*

ACTIVITY 4-1

Identifying the Local MAC Address

There is a simulated version of this activity available on the CD-ROM that shipped with this course. You can run this simulation on any Windows computer to review the activity after class, or as an alternative to performing the activity as a group in class. The activity simulation can be launched either directly from the CD-ROM by clicking the **Interactives** link and navigating to the appropriate one, or from the installed data file location by opening the C:\Data\Simulations\Lesson#\Activity# folder and double-clicking the executable (.exe) file.

Before You Begin:

You are logged in as the administrator for the domain Child##.Classnet. Your password is !Pass1234.

Scenario:

In this activity, you will identify your computer's MAC address.

1. Open the **Local Area Connection Status** dialog box.
   a. Choose **Start→Control Panel.**
   b. In the Control Panel window, click the **Network and Internet** link.
   c. In the Network and Internet window, click the **Network and Sharing Center** link.
   d. In the Network and Sharing Center window, on the left pane, click **Change adapter settings.**
   e. In the Network Connections window, right-click **Local Area Connection** and choose **Status.**

2. Identify your computer's MAC address.
   a. In the **Local Area Connection Status** dialog box, click **Details.**
   b. In the **Network Connection Details** dialog box, identify the **Physical Address** value to determine your computer's MAC address.
   c. Close all open dialog boxes and windows.

Networking Standards

Definition:

A *networking standard* is a set of specifications, guidelines, or characteristics applied to network components to ensure interoperability and consistency between them. Standards determine all aspects of networking such as the size, shape, and types of connectors on network cables as well as the number of computers that can connect to the network.

Example:

The IEEE 802.3 standard is used to standardize Ethernet network implementations by providing networking specifications and characteristics.

Formalization of Standards

Standards can be *de facto*, meaning that they have been widely adopted through use, or *de jure*, meaning that they are mandated by law or have been approved by a recognized body of experts.

To help recall which is which, you can think of words like jury and jurisdiction, which are words related to the legal system. These words, and the term *de jure*, come from the same Latin root.

Standards Organizations

Standards organizations issue standards that are important in the field of computer networking.

Standards Organization	***Description***
ISO	International Organization for Standardization, ISO, is the largest standards-development body in the world, comprising the national standards institutes of 162 countries. It is a non-governmental organization issuing voluntary standards in fields from agriculture to textiles. Of most significance for networking, in 1984, the ISO developed a reference model called the *Open Systems Interconnection (OSI)* model. The OSI model is a seven-layered framework of standards and specifications for communication in networks. The short name ISO is not an abbreviation for the name of the organization in any particular language, but was derived from the Greek word *isos*, meaning *equal.* Website: **www.iso.org**
IEEE	Institute of Electrical and Electronics Engineers, IEEE, is an organization dedicated to advancing theory and technology in electrical sciences. The standards wing of IEEE issues standards in areas such as electronic communications, circuitry, computer engineering, electromagnetics, and nuclear science. Website: **www.ieee.org**

Standards Organization	*Description*
ANSI	American National Standards Institute, ANSI, is the national standards institute of the United States that facilitates the formation of a variety of national standards, as well as promoting those standards internationally. Individually accredited standards bodies perform the standards development under ANSI's guidance. The best-known ANSI standard in the computer world is a method for representing keyboard characters by standard four-digit numeric codes. Website: **www.ansi.org**
TIA and EIA	Telecommunications Industry Association, TIA, and Electronic Industries Alliance, EIA, are two trade associations accredited by ANSI to develop and jointly issue standards for telecommunications and electronics. Website: **www.tiaonline.org** and **www.eia.org**
IETF	The Internet Engineering Task Force, IETF, an international open committee, consists of working groups, committees, and commercial organizations that work together to develop and maintain Internet standards and contribute to the evolution and operation of the Internet. All published Internet standards documents, known as Requests For Comments (RFCs), are available through the IETF. Website: **www.ietf.org**

IEEE 802.x Standards

The *802.x* standards are a family of networking standards developed by the IEEE in 1980 to address the rapid developments in the networking technology. The 802.x standards are divided into subcategories to address different networking requirements.

802.2 and 802.3 are two of the most commonly used IEEE standards in the 802.x series.

IEEE Standard	*Description*
802.2	The *802.2* standard was developed to address the need for MAC-sub-layer addressing in switches. The 802.2 standard specifies the frame size and transmission rate. Frames can be sent over Ethernet and *Token ring* networks using either copper or fiber media.
802.3	The original Ethernet network implementation was developed by Xerox® in the 1970s. The IEEE issued the *802.3* specification to standardize Ethernet and expand it to include a wide range of cable media. In addition to the media type, 802.3 also specifies transmission speeds and the signaling method. This type of network is most efficient in a physical star/logical bus topology.

The 10Base Standards

The *10Base standards* describe the media type and the speeds at which each type of media operates. The cable standard specification contains three components: a number indicating media speed, the signal type in baseband or broadband, and a code for either copper or fiber media.

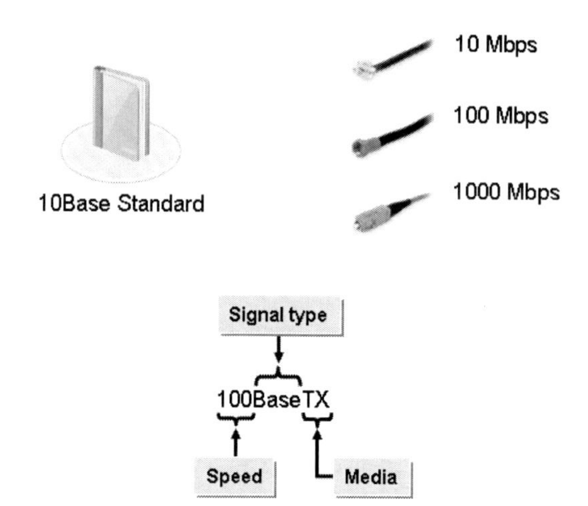

Figure 4-5: *Media types and the transmission speeds of the 10Base standard.*

10 Mbps Ethernet

There are several standards and specifications for 10 Mbps Ethernet.

Standard	*IEEE Specification*	*Medium*	*Distance (meters)*
10Base-2	802.3a	Thinnet coax	185
10Base-5	802.3	Thicknet coax	500
10Base-T	802.3i	CAT5 UTP	100
10Base-F	802.3j	Fiber	2000
10Base-FB	802.3j	Fiber	2000
10Base-FL	802.3j	Fiber	2000
10Base-FP	802.3j	Fiber	500

Fast Ethernet

Fast Ethernet is an Ethernet technology that can transmit data at speeds of 100 Mbps. The maximum length of the cable is limited to 250 meters and can use either coaxial cables or optical fibers. It is used as a backbone network to interconnect several LANs.

Fast Ethernet Standards

There are several standards and specifications for 100 Mbps or Fast Ethernet. In copper, 100Base-TX is the most widely used medium for Fast Ethernet. It uses two pairs of category 5 cables. 100Base-T2 uses two copper wire pairs. In fiber, 100Base-FX implements Fast Ethernet over optical fiber. It uses two strands of the fiber, one to transmit and the other to receive.

Standard	IEEE Specification	Medium	Distance (m)
100Base-T	802.3u	CAT5 UTP	100
100Base-T4	802.3u	CAT3, 4, or 5 UTP	100
100Base-TX	802.3u	CAT5 UTP	100
100Base-FX	802.3u	Multimode or single mode fiber	412 (half duplex), 2000 (full duplex), 15,000–20,000 (full duplex)

Gigabit Ethernet

Gigabit Ethernet is an Ethernet technology that can transmit data at speeds of 1000 Mbps and primarily uses optical fibers for transmission. It can be used for distances ranging from 500 to 5000 meters depending on the type of optical fiber used. The hardware required for Gigabit Ethernet is very expensive when compared with other types of Ethernet.

Gigabit Ethernet Standards

There are several standards and specifications for 1000 Mbps or Gigabit Ethernet.

Standard	IEEE Specification	Medium	Distance (m)
1000Base-T	802.3ab	CAT5 CAT6 UTP	100
1000Base-X	802.3z	Shielded Balanced coax	25 to 5000
1000Base-CX	802.3z	Shielded Balanced coax	25
1000Base-SX	802.3z	Multimode fiber Wavelength: 850 nm	550 in practice (220 per specification)

Standard	IEEE Specification	Medium	Distance (m)
1000Base-LX	802.3z	Single mode fiber Wavelength: 1300 nm	5000
1000Base-LX	802.3z	Multimode fiber Wavelength: 1300 nm	550
1000Base-LH	802.3z	Single mode fiber Wavelength: 1300 nm	10,000
1000Base-LH	802.3z	Multimode fiber Wavelength: 1300 nm	550

10 Gigabit Ethernet

10 Gigabit Ethernet is currently the highest speed at which Ethernet operates. It can achieve speeds of 10 Gbps, which is 10 times faster than Gigabit Ethernet. Still an emerging technology, it is also compatible with WAN. There are several standards and specifications for 10 Gbps or 10 Gigabit Ethernet.

Standard	IEEE Specification	Medium and Characteristics	Speed (in Gbps)	Distance (m)
10GBase-X	802.3ae	Multimode fiber Wavelength: 850 nm	9.9	65
10GBase-SR	802.3ae	Multimode fiber Wavelength: 850 nm	10.3	300
10GBase-SW	802.3ae	Multimode fiber Wavelength: 850 nm	9.9	300
10GBase-LR	802.3ae	Single mode fiber Wavelength: 1310 nm Dark fiber	10.3	10,000
10GBase-LW	802.3ae	Single mode fiber Wavelength: 1310 nm Synchronous Optical Network (SONET)	9.9	10,000
10GBase-ER	802.3ae	Single mode fiber Wavelength: 1550 nm Dark fiber	10.3	40,000
10GBase-EW	802.3a	Single mode fiber Wavelength: 1550 nm SONET	9.9	40,000

Standard	IEEE Specification	Medium and Characteristics	Speed (in Gbps)	Distance (m)
10GBase-T	802.3an	CAT5e, 6, or 7 UTP	10	100
10GBase-CX4	802.3ak	Four thin twin-axial cables	4 x 2.5	25

A nanometer (nm) is one trillionth of a meter (10^{-9}).

Ring-Based Networks

Token ring and Fiber Distributed Data Interface (FDDI) are commonly used ring-based LAN technologies deployed on Ethernet networks.

Ring-Based Network Types	Description
Token ring 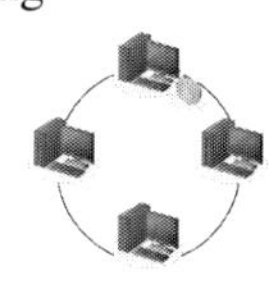	*Token ring* is a type of technology used on ring networks in which computers pass a special sequence of bits called a token between them. Only the node holding the token can transmit on the network. If it has no more data to transmit, the node passes the token to the next computer on the network. Standards dictate how long a node can hold a token and what happens if the token is damaged or lost. The damaged or lost tokens are renewed automatically every seven seconds.
FDDI 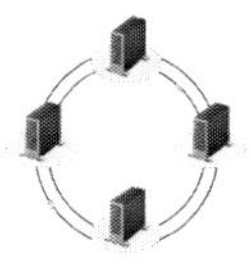	The *Fiber Distributed Data Interface (FDDI)* is a type of technology used on ring networks and uses single mode or multi mode fiber that transmits data at a rate of 100 Mbps. Although FDDI has dual fiber rings, only one ring carries data under normal conditions; the second ring is either idle or carries control signals. When the second ring is not needed for backup, it can carry data, extending the carrying capacity to 200 Mbps.

ACTIVITY 4-2

Describing Ethernet Networks

Scenario:

In this activity, you will describe the different types of Ethernet networks.

---

1. **On which networks is Ethernet implemented?**
   a) WANs
   b) MANs
   c) PANs
   d) LANs

---

2. **True or False? The 802.2 standard specifies the frame size and transmission rate of the Ethernet technology.**
   __ True
   __ False

---

3. **Which field of the Ethernet frame provides error detection information?**
   a) PRE
   b) FCS
   c) SFD
   d) SA

---

4. **Match the field of an Ethernet frame with its description.**

___	Preamble	a.	The MAC address of the computer receiving data.
___	Destination address	b.	Signals the start of a frame.
___	Source address	c.	The length of the Ethernet frame in bytes.
___	Frame type	d.	The MAC address of the computer transmitting data.

---

5. **You have a fiber-based ring network with dual fiber rings. Which technology have you implemented?**
   a) Token ring
   b) FDDI
   c) Switched Ethernet
   d) Fast Ethernet

TOPIC B

Wireless Networks

In the previous topic, you identified various types of wired LANs—that is, networks that use different types of cabling to connect the various nodes. There are also wireless networks that connect without using a physical media. In this topic, you will identify the components of a wireless LAN implementation.

Wireless networks are the network of choice in most environments today because they are relatively easy to install and are flexible. Even more importantly, with users increasingly needing to connect on the move using different devices, roaming users in both business and leisure environments want the freedom to use their computers for work or recreation wherever they are, without a physical connection to the network. With its increasing popularity and widespread appeal, you will undoubtedly be faced with installing, managing, or troubleshooting a wireless network.

WLANs

Definition:

A *Wireless LAN (WLAN)* is a self-contained network of two or more computers connected using a wireless connection. A WLAN spans a small area, such as a small building, floor, or room. A typical WLAN consists of client systems such as a desktop, laptop, or PDA and wireless connectivity devices such as access points. The access points interconnect these client systems in a wireless mode or can connect to a wired network. WLANs allow users to connect to the local network or the Internet, even on the move.

Example:

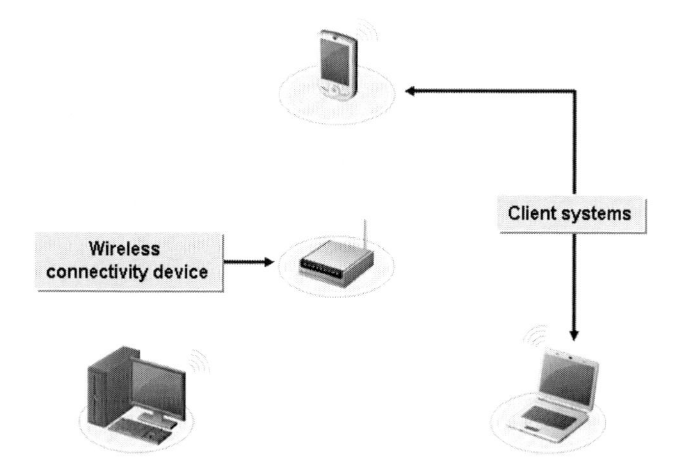

Figure 4-6: *Devices connected in a WLAN.*

WLAN Architecture

A WLAN architecture comprises several components.

WLAN Architecture Component	*Description*
Station (STA)	A device that connects an IEEE 802.11 conformant MAC interface to a wireless medium with an Ethernet-like driver interface. A wireless STA contains an adapter card, a PC card, or an embedded device to provide wireless connectivity.
Access Point (AP)	A device or software that facilitates communication and provides enhanced security to wireless devices. It also extends the physical range of a WLAN. The AP functions as a bridge between wireless STAs and the existing network backbone for network access.
Distribution System (DS)	A wired connection between a BSS and a premise-wide network that enables mobility to devices and provides access to available network resources.
Basic Service Set (BSS)	The service set defines the way a WLAN is configured. There are three ways to configure a WLAN—BSS, IBSS, and ESS. A set of devices with an AP connected to a wired network and one or more wireless stations or clients. A BSS can effectively extend the distance between wireless endpoints by forwarding signals through the WAP.
Extended Service Set (ESS)	A configuration of multiple BSSs used to handle mobility on a wireless network. BSSs are connected to a common distribution system such as a wired network. ESS enables users to move their mobile devices, such as laptop computers, outside of their home BSS while keeping their connection. It also enables data to be forwarded from one BSS to another through the network backbone.
Independent Basic Service Set (IBSS)	A peer-to-peer network where each wireless station acts as both a client and a wireless AP. Each wireless station can both transmit and receive data.

Wireless Antennas

Definition:

A *wireless antenna* is a device that converts high frequency signals on a cable into electromagnetic waves and vice versa. In wireless communication, an antenna is used to receive or transmit radio waves. The frequency at which an antenna can send or receive radio waves depends on the physical dimensions of the antenna. The larger the size of the antenna, the higher the frequency of the wave that antenna can transmit. You can choose different antenna types to use in different wireless networking situations. Different styles of antennas vary in their *gain* or signal strength, and the shape or the radiation pattern of the transmission beam.

Example:

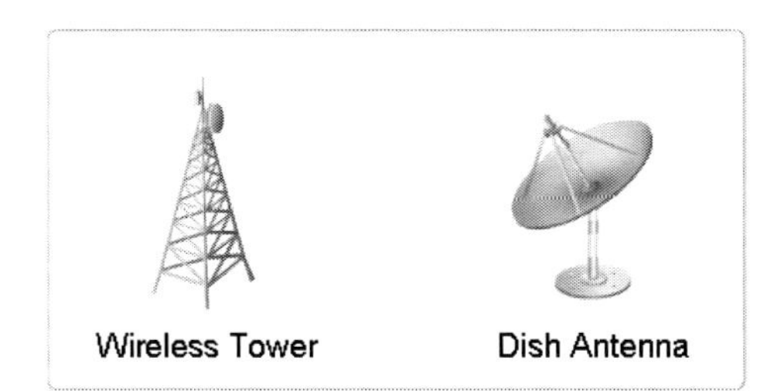

Figure 4-7: *A wireless antenna converts high frequency signals on a cable into electromagnetic waves.*

Gain

Gain is an increase in the amplitude of a radio wave. Gain can occur due to the use of external sources such as amplifiers that amplify a radio signal. It has both positive and negative effects. Typically, high gain is advantageous but there may be situations where the amplitude of a radio wave is already very close to the legal value and added power could be a serious problem.

Wireless Antenna Types

Antennas can be grouped into one of two broad categories.

Antenna Category	*Description*
Directional antenna	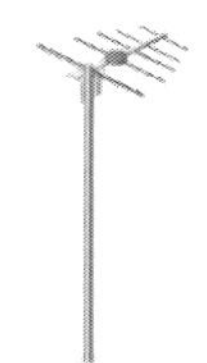 A type of antenna that concentrates the signal beam in a single direction. They have a relatively narrow, focused transmission beam and a relatively high gain. Since they transmit primarily in a single direction, the sending and receiving stations must be precisely aligned. The high gain provides for good signal quality and the narrow beam ensures that only a narrow transmission area needs to be clear of interference.Directional antennas are used in a point-to-point network to connect one station to another. Directional antennas include the parabolic dish antenna, backfire antenna, yagi antenna, and panel antenna.

Antenna Category	Description
Omni-directional antenna	 A type of antenna that radiates the signal beam out in all directions and has lower gain but a wider coverage area. The transmission radiates from the antenna in all directions, generally in a single horizontal or vertical plane, so that the sending and receiving stations do not need to be as precisely aligned. However, a wider coverage zone means there are more potential sources of interference, and there is lower gain because the signal power is not as focused.Omni-directional antennas are used in multipoint and distributed networks. Omni-directional antennas include the ceiling dome or "blister" antenna, blade antenna, and various rod-shaped antennas.

Wireless Antenna Performance Factors

It is important to consider various performance factors before installing antennas for infrared, radio, or microwave wireless technologies.

Wireless Technology Type	Performance Factors
Infrared	The maximum transmitting distance of an infrared wireless installation is affected by these factors: • Bright sunlight • Obstacles • Smoke, dust, or fog
Radio	The maximum transmitting distance of a radio wireless installation is affected by all of these factors: • Signal characteristics of the antenna • Environmental conditions • Ambient electrical noise • Conductive obstacles in the path • Presence of other electrical equipment • Data transmission rate

Wireless Technology Type	***Performance Factors***
Microwave	The maximum transmitting distance of a microwave wireless installation is affected by all of these factors: • Signal characteristics of the antenna • Line of sight • Distance between transmitting stations

The IEEE 802.11 Standard

The *802.11* standard is a family of specifications developed by the IEEE for the wireless LAN technology. 802.11 specifies an over-the-air interface between a wireless client and a base station or between two wireless clients. 802.11 defines the access method as CSMA/CA. It specifies spread spectrum radio devices in the 2.4 GHz band for reliability. The 802.11b standard also defines a multichannel roaming mode and automatic data rate selection.

802.11 Standards

The 802.11 standards provide specifications for different wireless technologies.

Standard	***Transmission Speed in Mbps***	***Frequency in GHz***	***Geographic Range in meters***	***MIMO Streams***
802.11	2	2.4	20	1
802.11a	54	5	20	1
802.11b	11	2.4	100	1
802.11g	54	2.4	100	1
802.11n	150	2.4 or 5	70	4

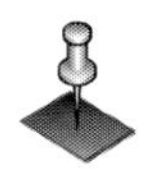

The 802.11a standard is not cross-compatible with 802.11b and g.

Latency

Latency is the time taken by a data packet sent through a wireless connection from a requesting device to the receiving device and back. Latency includes the time taken for checking the data packets, correcting errors, and resending data lost in transit. Some of the 802.11 specifications have higher latency when compared to Gigabit Ethernet.

Channels in 802.11b/g Implementations

The 802.11b and g specifications define a number of distinct channels within the 2.4 GHz band. Due to the way these channels are implemented, there is substantial overlap in the radio signals. This overlap can cause interference between adjacent APs and clients, resulting in reduced performance. The immediate result is that there are only three channels that are truly usable when you want to get the best possible performance out of your WLAN. These are channels 1, 6, and 11. In a single AP configuration, the choice of channel does not matter. When dealing with an implementation that requires multiple APs to ensure sufficient coverage, best practice is to set adjacent APs to use different channels, choosing from 1, 6, and 11.

802.11 Modes

The 802.11 standard supports two modes: the infrastructure mode and the ad-hoc mode.

Mode	Description
Infrastructure mode	The *infrastructure mode* utilizes one or more WAPs to connect workstations to the cable backbone. Infrastructure mode wireless networks use either BSS or ESS. 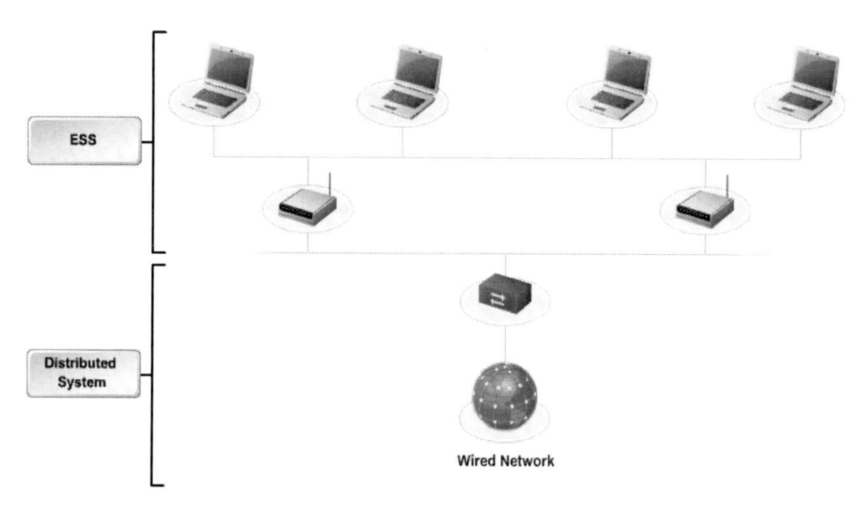
Ad-hoc mode	The *ad-hoc mode*, also referred to as IBSS, utilizes a peer-to-peer configuration in which each wireless workstation talks directly to other workstations. 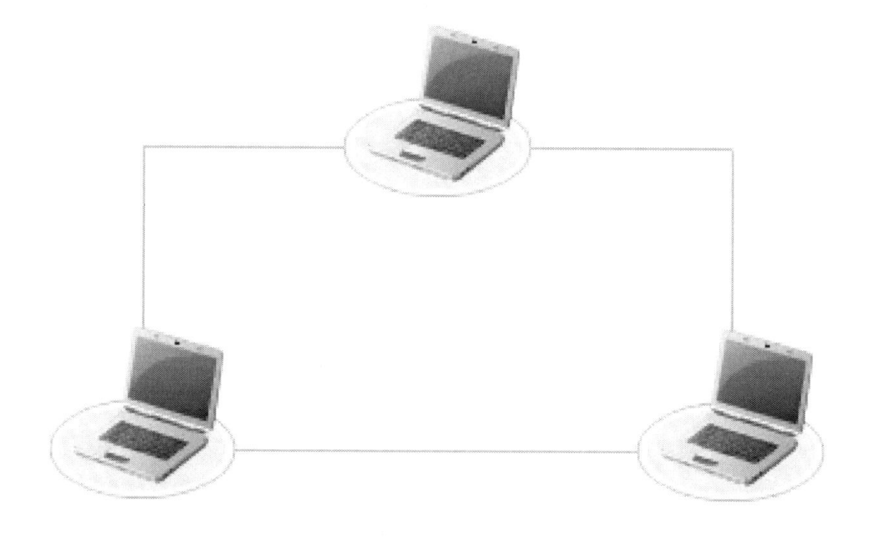

802.11 Beacon Frames

Beacon frames are management frames that are 50 bytes long and used to start and maintain wireless communications. They contain information about the communication process, such as the SSID, channel number, and security protocol information. Beacon frames are periodically sent by APs in 802.11 infrastructure networks, and can be configured to be sent at various intervals.

Basic Wireless Network Implementation

By considering several key factors of wireless network installation along with the cost of implementing and maintaining a secure wireless network, a network professional both demonstrates the proper installation methods and ensures maximum network functionality.

Guidelines

To implement a basic wireless network, follow these guidelines:

- Choose the appropriate 802.11 technology for your needs, such as 802.11a, b, g, or n.
- Choose the appropriate AP placement locations for your network.
  - Obtain a scale drawing of the building. This will assist you in all areas of AP placement.
  - Determine the range of the AP for the wireless technology you have chosen. This will help you to better determine how many APs you will need to ensure adequate coverage for the space.
  - Balance the number of users who will have access to the AP, and ensure that the AP can cover all employees in the range of the AP. More employees in a given area means more APs.
  - Tour the area in the range of the AP and check to see if there are any devices that will interfere with the wireless network. This can include devices such as microwave ovens, Bluetooth-enabled devices, or an existing wireless network—whether from a community network, a neighboring building, or another floor of your company's building. These devices or networks can possibly interfere with your new implementation.
  - Consider whether the AP will be exposed or concealed in the ceiling or placed in a secure room.
  - Ensure that there are no obstacles in the path of the AP, such as doors, closed windows, walls, and furniture, that the wireless signal will need to pass through on its way to a client. If there are too many obstacles in the path, adjust the placement of your AP accordingly.

- Install the APs. The specific steps for installing the AP will vary by vendor, but the common steps may include:
  - Connecting the AP to a router.
  - Configuring the DHCP service as appropriate.
  - Configuring the appropriate encryption schemes.
  - Configuring channels and frequencies.
  - Setting the ESSID and an 802.11 beacon.
  - If necessary, creating an Access Control List (ACL). The ACL contains a list of users who have access to the wireless network.
  - Configuring the network adapters of the devices that will connect to the AP.
- Test to ensure that the installation is appropriately-sized, secure, and operational.
- Document the steps and establish a baseline for future installations.

How to Install Wireless Clients

The specific installation procedure for installing wireless clients might vary depending on the hardware and software features of the device. The procedure for installing wireless clients will need to be customized to the requirement of the situation.

To install a wireless client on a computer:

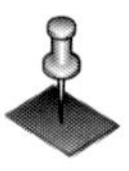

Some computers are pre-installed with a wireless client. In such computers, manual installation of a wireless client is not necessary.

1. Observe necessary anti-static precautions such as using an anti-static wrist strap to remove a buildup of static charges.
2. Power off the PC and disconnect the power and other cables.
3. Open the PC case and insert the wireless NIC into a PCI, PCIx, or USB slot.
4. Close the PC case and reconnect the cables.
5. Power on the PC.
6. Install the manufacturer-provided drivers and software.

   The operating system may identify and install the necessary drivers automatically; if not, you may need to install the drivers manually.
7. Connect to the wireless network with the operating system's built-in utilities (such as ZeroConf) or the manufacturer provided utility.

You may also need some access information in order for you to be able to use the wireless client to connect to the wireless network. The details include:

- The SSID of the wireless access point.
- A pre-shared password to access the wireless network.
- The MAC address of the wireless adapter you wish to add to connect to the access point.
- The login information for the administrative interface of the WAP.
- A pre-assigned static IP address.

8. Test the Wireless NIC's functionality. You can do this by performing one or more of these checks:
   - Check the adapter's LED lights to verify that it is connected and is operational.
   - Ping other computers on both the wireless and wired portions of the network.
   - Use software tools to monitor the signal strength, packet loss, and connection speed.
   - Connect to shared folders on the internal network, if available.
   - Connect to the Internet.
9. Document the steps for installing the wireless clients on a PC for future reference.

Wireless Access Point Placement

While deciding on placement of WAPs, you need to consider several important factors.

Factor	*Description*
Building layout	The building layout is a very important factor when deciding on the positions at which to place WAPs. A scaled building layout of the coverage area will help in deciding on the areas where you require wireless access. Also, the layout helps in locating strategic spots where you can place the WAPs.
Coverage area	The area covered by an access point is called a *cell*. If the cell area is large, then you need to consider increasing the number of WAPs. Overlapping cells with multiple access points provide continuous access for devices.
Clients	The number of clients accessing the WAP plays a major role in deciding on the placement of the WAP. Depending on the number of clients, you need to decide on the number of WAPs to install.
Obstacles	Obstacles in the path of transmission of RF waves sometimes absorb the signals when they pass through, resulting in signal loss. Avoiding obstacles such as doors, walls, and windows between access points and devices can considerably reduce signal loss.
Interference	Radio frequency interference from other devices can affect signals from WAPs. Removing other devices that can cause radio frequency interference will significantly reduce signal interference.

How to Install a Wireless Repeater

To install a wireless repeater, consider the following guidelines:

1. Determine the placement for a repeater.
   - Physically, where does performance drop off on the existing wireless network?
   - Is there access to a power outlet?
   - Will the device be physically secure?
   - If necessary, is there access to a wired network drop?
2. Set up the repeater to work with your wireless network.

   If your repeater has a wired network port:
   a. Connect one end of an Ethernet cable to an active network drop and connect the other end to a repeater.
   b. Plug-in and power-on the repeater.
   c. Enter the setup utility (usually on a ROM or through the device's built-in web interface).
   d. Configure the appropriate WLAN settings.
   e. Save the configuration.If your repeater does not have a wired network port:
   a. Make sure that the repeater is within range of the WLAN you wish to expand.
   b. Plug-in and power-on the repeater.
   c. Initiate the repeater's auto-setup functionality.
3. Test the repeater's functionality by connecting a wireless client to the WLAN:
   - Ping other computers and observe the round-trip latency.
   - Monitor the client's wireless signal strength using software tools.
   - Connect to shared internal network locations.
   - Connect to the Internet.
4. In case performance of the repeater does not improve, reassess its placement and configuration.

Example: Implementing a Wireless Network

As a network administrator, Matt is concerned with the proper implementation of his company's wireless network to ensure maximum company-wide efficiency. He has read through several reference materials related to wireless network installation, and has gathered the appropriate tools.

The company has many different available locations for access points, and Matt has decided where the best access points for the wireless network will be.

The installation of the access point covers several tasks including configuring the appropriate wireless encryption standards, as well as configuring all wireless channels and frequencies, along with setting the ESSID and beacon interval for the network.

Once the wireless network installation and implementation is complete, it needs to be verified. Matt accesses the network from both inside and outside the building, he attempts to log on using a non-corporate laptop, and he tries to capture data packets from the parking lot. He also wanders around the building with a laptop and notes where he loses the signal.

ACTIVITY 4-3

Identifying a Wireless Network Implementation

Scenario:

In this activity, you will identify the components of a wireless network implementation.

---

1. **True or False? Infrastructure mode wireless networks use either BSS or ESS.**

    __ True

    __ False

---

2. **Select the characteristics of directional antennas.**

    a) Used in point-to-point networks

    b) Have low gain

    c) Transmit narrow and focused beams

    d) Are prone to interference

---

3. **Your company has installed a wireless network. There are ceiling dome transmitters at various locations in your building, and you have upgraded the users' laptops with wireless NICs. There is one wireless antenna to serve the warehouse area. The coverage area is adequate; however, users in the warehouse report intermittent connectivity problems as they move in and out of the tall metal storage shelving. What problem do you suspect?**

Lesson 4 Follow-up

In this lesson, you identified the major types of network implementations. The knowledge of major network implementations and the advantages and disadvantages of these will allow you to choose the right implementation when you set up a network.

1. **What are some of the challenges that you might face when implementing a wireless network and how do you plan to overcome these challenges?**

2. **In your opinion, what is the significance of Ethernet standards on networks today?**

5 Networking Models

Lesson Time: 1 hour(s), 30 minutes

Lesson Objectives:

In this lesson, you will identify the components of a TCP/IP network implementation.

You will:

- Identify the constituent layers and purpose of the OSI model.
- Identify the constituent layers and purpose of the TCP/IP model.

Introduction

You are familiar with major types of network implementations. All networks follow a common network model to communicate and transmit data. In this lesson, you will identify the Open Systems Interconnection (OSI) and TCP/IP network models.

Data communication over a network is a structured process and is governed by certain models. The OSI model breaks the data communication process into simpler stages, which will help you learn it in a step-by-step manner for better understanding. The OSI model is the simplest model of its type, and understanding it will enable you to understand other models such as the TCP/IP network model. Being able to identify the various layers of network models and their purpose will enable you to design and troubleshoot different types of networks effectively and quickly.

This lesson covers all or part of the following CompTIA® Network+® (Exam N10-005) certification objectives:

- 1.1 Compare the layers of the OSI and TCP/IP models.
- 1.2 Classify how applications, devices, and protocols relate to the OSI model layers.
- 1.6 Explain the function of common networking protocols.

TOPIC A

The OSI Model

In the previous lesson, you identified the various network types of network implementations. These implementations are built on common network standards and models of networking to understand how these devices and protocols interconnect. In this topic, you will identify how these devices utilize an important common standard, the OSI model.

Data communication over a network is a structured process and is governed by certain models. The OSI model breaks the data communication process into definite stages with each stage corresponding to one of its layers. The OSI model has been implemented in many types of networks. Being able to identify the OSI layers and their purpose will enable you to plan the implementation of a network according to the devices, protocols, and transmission methods needed.

The OSI Reference Model

The *Open Systems Interconnection (OSI) reference model* is a network model developed by the ISO for communication in *open system networks*. The OSI reference model divides the data communication process into seven tasks, which are grouped into different layers. Each layer is a collection of related functions, protocols, and devices that work at that layer. Every layer is designed to link the layers above it. While a layer provides services to the layer above, it requests service from the layer below. The seven layers of OSI, from lowest to highest, are the Physical layer, the Data Link layer, the Network layer, the Transport layer, the Session layer, the Presentation layer, and the Application layer.

It can be difficult to remember the correct sequence of the OSI layers, it is easy to remember them from the top down, using the mnemonic “All People Seem To Need Data Processing.”

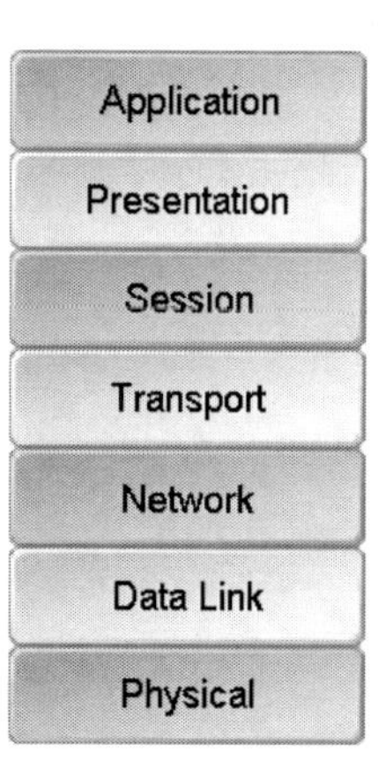

Figure 5-1: *Layers in the OSI reference model.*

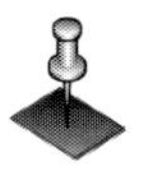

The OSI model was developed by the ISO in the early 1980s and the organization continues to maintain the standard.

Open System Networks

An open system network is a network that supports multiple communication protocol suites that different vendors develop. Prior to open system networks, communication protocols were largely vendor-specific and proprietary applications, such as Systems Network Architecture (SNA) by IBM®, Appletalk® by Apple®, and Internetwork Packet Exchange (IPX) by Novell®. Due to the lack of common communication protocols, the devices of one vendor were not compatible with those of another and so communication was not possible on a network that contained devices from different vendors. Open system networks were developed to create a common network standard and provide a common protocol suite to all the devices.

OSI Functional Blocks

The layers in the OSI reference model can be classified into two functional blocks: application support and network support.

Functional Block	*Description*
Application support	The application support block consists of the upper three layers: Application, Presentation, and Session. Connecting software programs to the network is the primary responsibility of this functional block.
Network support	The network support block is made up of the lower four layers: Transport, Network, Data Link, and Physical. Moving data on the network is the primary responsibility of this functional block.

Layer 1: The Physical Layer

The *Physical layer* provides the means for transmitting data packets over a physical medium. It specifies the electrical and mechanical characteristics, such as the voltage, frequency, and transmission medium of the network. The Physical layer receives fully formatted data packets from the Data Link layer and places them on the media. Network adapters and WAPs are some of the devices that operate at this layer. Therefore, the Physical layer determines the mode and medium of data transmission, which are factors that affect transmission speeds. Technologies that function at this layer include Ethernet, Fast Ethernet, *Asynchronous Transfer Mode (ATM)*, token ring, and FDDI.

Transmission of Data Packets

A *packet* is a unit of data transmitted on a network. All packets contain three parts: header, data, and footer or trailer. If a sender transmits a packet and the recipient is busy, the sender sits idle until it receives the acknowledgment, after which it sends the next packet.

Design Considerations at the Physical Layer

The Physical layer affects some of the network design considerations including:

- Bandwidth of the transmission medium
- Type of transmission medium
- Switching technologies
- Mode of transmission (wired or wireless)
- Analog or digital transmission
- Modulation

Multilayer Devices

Some network devices can perform tasks defined by more than one layer and function across layers. Such devices are known as multilayer devices. Some of the multilayer devices are WAPs and gateways. Hubs and repeaters were also multilayer devices.

Layer 2: The Data Link Layer

The *Data Link layer* is responsible for transferring data packets between adjacent network nodes without any errors. After sending the packets, the Data Link layer waits for an acknowledgment from the receiving devices. It performs many functions on the network and is responsible for:

- Grouping data bits into *frames* and attaching the address of the receiving node to each frame, thus forming a data packet.
- Error-free transfer of data packets between nodes on the network. After transmitting data packets, the Data Link layer awaits an acknowledgment from receiving devices to accomplish this.
- Adding error correction and detection codes to frames to perform error checks and corrections.

Switches operate at the Data Link layer. The *Point-to-Point Protocol (PPP)* and Serial Line Internet Protocol (SLIP) are protocols that operate at this layer.

The Data Link layer can be divided into two sub-layers: the *Logical Link Control (LLC)* sub-layer and the *Media Access Control (MAC)* sub-layer.

Sub-Layer	***Description***
LLC	The LLC sub-layer is responsible for identifying Network layer protocols and for encapsulating those protocols so that multiple upper-layer protocols can share the same media. It controls how frames are placed on the media by controlling the Physical layer device. The LLC sub-layer checks the CRC of the frame, and either ACKs or NACKs the data. It also controls data flow so that at any point, data transmission does not exceed the bandwidth of the network medium. An LLC header tells the Data Link layer how to handle the frame it receives.
MAC	The MAC sub-layer defines how packets are placed on the media. In a contention-based network, the MAC sub-layer is responsible for the carrier sense to detect collision; in a token passing network, it is responsible for the token. For example, in an Ethernet network, which uses contention-based media access, the MAC sub-layer controls elements of addressing such as error notification, the frame delivery sequence, and flow control.

Do not confuse the MAC sub-layer with the MAC address. While the MAC sub-layer defines how packets are transferred on the media, MAC address is a unique physical address that is assigned by the network manufacturer to each network device.

Network Acknowledgments

A *network acknowledgment* is a signal used by a communication protocol between nodes on a network to acknowledge the receipt of data. Typically, two types of acknowledgment notifications are sent on a network. Acknowledgment notifications can either be positive (ACK) to indicate successful receipt sent from the receiving node to the sending node once the token reaches its destination; or negative (NACK) that can indicate a bad transmission. Alternatively, a node can also send an REJ signal to indicate rejection of data or an Automatic Request for Retransmission (ARQ).

Layer 3: The Network Layer

The *Network layer* of the OSI model is responsible for addressing data packets, routing the packets from a source to the destination through the network, and ensuring data delivery. This characteristic differentiates the Network layer from the Data Link layer, which deals with the transmission of data only between adjacent nodes. The presence of too many packets on the network simultaneously may lead to collisions.

Routers and some switches operate at the Network layer. The responsibility of controlling congestion on the network by taking proper routing decisions belongs to this layer. It also defines protocols for interconnecting two or more similar networks such as: IP, *Address Resolution Protocol (ARP)*, *Dynamic Host Configuration Protocol (DHCP)*, *Internet Control Message Protocol (ICMP)*, *Routing Information Protocol (RIP)*, *Border Gateway Protocol (BGP)*, *Open Shortest Path First (OSPF)*, and *Internet Group Management Protocol (IGMP)*.

There are two main types of switches. Layer 2 switches operate at the Data Link layer of the OSI model. Layer 3 switches operate at the Network layer of the OSI model.

Layer 4: The Transport Layer

The *Transport layer* accepts data from upper layers, and breaks it into smaller units known as segments. It then passes these segments to the lower layers, and ensures that all segments arrive correctly at the receiving end. Because the segments may not be transmitted in sequence, they may arrive out of sequence. The Transport layer adds a sequence number to each segment, which helps reconstruct the original sequence of segments in case of out of order sequencing. The Transport layer is also responsible for error correction and sending acknowledgments at the network level.

The Transport layer also defines protocols for interconnecting networks that use different protocols. Gateways operate at this layer and at higher layers of the OSI model. Examples of protocols that function at this layer include TCP, *User Datagram Protocol (UDP)*, *IP Security (IPSec)*, *Point-to-Point Tunneling Protocol (PPTP)*, Remote Desktop Protocol (RDP), and *Layer Two Tunneling Protocol (L2TP)*.

Network- and Transport-Layer Protocols

The Network and Transport layers contain several protocol families that are categorized based on functions they perform.

Protocol Family	***Function***
Reliability protocols	Provide a method of ensuring reliable data transfer. For example, a header or trailer might contain a *Checksum* value or request that you need to acknowledge received data by sending an acknowledgment message back to the sender.
Connection protocols	Establish and maintain a connectionless or connection-oriented service for the upper layers. In a connection-oriented service, the sending and receiving nodes maintain constant communication to mediate the transfer of data. Sequencing, flow control, and reliability are monitored at both ends. In a connectionless service, the message is packaged, delivered, and sent. The message is transferred only if communication exists between the two nodes.
Routing protocols	Provide a method of ensuring data transfer to the correct destination. In an unswitched network, routing is virtually unnecessary because the nodes are directly connected. In a switched network, however, the routing protocol determines the path a packet will take to reach its destination. This function is particularly important and complex in a packet-switched network, because there can be many possible paths to a destination and many intermediary devices such as routers along the path. Routing protocols determine the strategies used to transmit data through the network.

TCP can fit into any of the three categories—reliability protocols, connection protocols, or routing protocols.

Checksum

The Checksum value lets the receiver test the integrity of received data. If the Checksum value is corrupted, the receiver fires back an error message to the sender, which then immediately retransmits the data.

Layer 5: The Session Layer

The *Session layer* establishes connections between devices and applications, maintains the connection, and then terminates or reestablishes it when required. This layer controls how, when, and for how long a device can transmit or receive data, and specifies procedures for the connection, termination, and reestablishment of sessions. It also specifies the procedures for synchronizing data transfer between two devices with different data transmission rates. Sockets and session establishment in TCP function at this layer.

Layer 6: The Presentation Layer

The *Presentation layer* is responsible for encoding data into a standard network-compatible format. Most programs contain data such as names, identification numbers, and passwords. These items may be represented as characters, integers, or floating numbers, and each device on a network may use a different code to represent the same data. Moreover, standard data formats are used to enable devices with different representation techniques to communicate with each other. This translation is only an intermediary format, and will change at the lower layers.

The Presentation layer also adds services such as data compression and encryption. Examples of technologies and protocols that function at this layer include *Mesh Made Easy (MME), Secure Sockets Layer (SSL), Transport Layer Security (TLS), Graphics Interchange Format (GIF), Joint Photographic Experts Group (JPEG),* and *Tagged Image File Format (TIFF).*

Technologies at the Presentation Layer

The protocols and file formats that work at the Presentation layer perform different functions. They include:

- MME is a protocol used for routing in wireless networks.
- GIF is a graphic interchange format primarily used on the Internet.
- JPEG is a compressed graphical file format that reduces the file size.
- TIFF is a digital format used to handle images used in publishing and photography.

Layer 7: The Application Layer

The *Application layer* provides utilities and services that allow applications to access the network and its resources. This layer defines protocols for tasks such as transferring files, sending emails, and saving data to a network server. It also advertises itself to the server resources available in each system for usage on the network. This is the only layer with which the user directly interacts. Examples of technologies, protocols, and services that function at this layer include HTTP, *Domain Name Service (DNS), File Transfer Protocol (FTP),* Gopher, *Network File System (NFS), Network Time Protocol (NTP), Simple Network Management Protocol (SNMP), Simple Mail Transfer Protocol (SMTP),* and *Telnet.*

Application-, Presentation-, and Session-Layer Protocols

The Application, Presentation, and Session layers contain several protocol families.

Protocol Family	***Functions***
Terminal-emulation protocols	Enable computers to act as standard terminals so that they can access hosts. This usually involves translation of keystrokes and video-display codes.
File access and file transfer protocols	Enable nodes to access files on the network. Different clients might use different file- and path-naming conventions. File access protocols provide a common means to access network files. File transfer protocols enable copying of files between network storage and other storage, such as a computer's local disk drive.
Email protocols	Provide for email delivery and handling of messages.

Protocol Family	Functions
Remote-action and multiple-session protocols	Determine whether processes should be performed remotely on a client node or directly by a server. RDP is an example of the remote-action protocol. These protocols are required for setting up a client-server relationship. Multiple-session protocols enable multiple network links to be established. TCP is an example of a multiple-session protocol.
Network management protocols	Provide tools for setting up and maintaining the network. As networks interconnect with other networks and become more complex, more sophisticated network management tools are necessary. SNMP is an example of a network management protocol.
Task-to-task protocols	Enable software processes to communicate over the network.
Codeset and data structure protocols	Define the representation of data. These protocols translate data for nodes that use different coding schemes.

The OSI Data Communication Process

Data transmission through the OSI reference model involves the following stages:

1. During transmission, data is added to the Application layer of the OSI reference model.
2. It is then forwarded to the lower layers in the OSI stack until the Physical layer transfers the data to the network media.
3. In the data reception process, data is first added to the Physical layer of the OSI reference model.
4. Data is then forwarded to the layers above it in the OSI stack until it reaches the Application layer. Each layer removes the information it needs before transmitting the remaining data to the next layer.

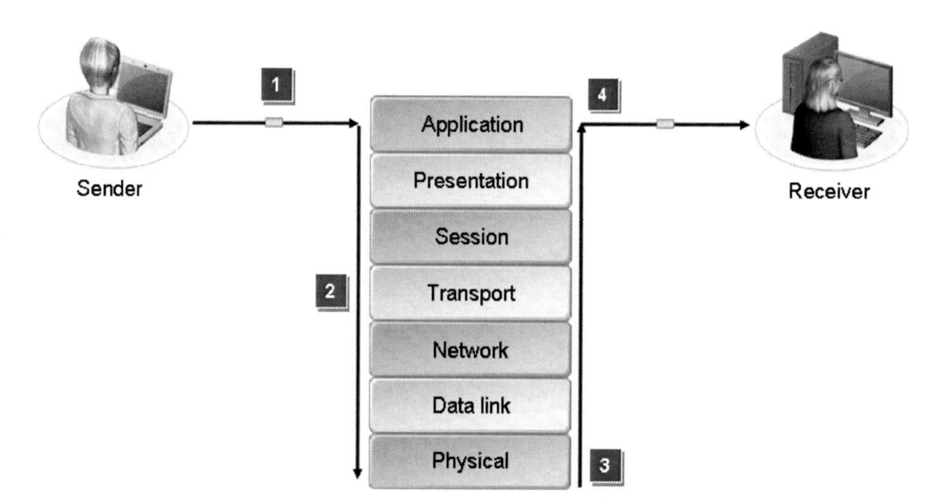

Figure 5-2: *Data communication through the OSI reference model.*

ACTIVITY 5-1

Identifying the Layers in the OSI Model

Scenario:

In this activity, you will identify the layers in the OSI model.

1. **Match each layer of the OSI model with a description of its function.**

	Layer		Description
___	Application	a.	Establishes, maintains, and terminates connections between network devices.
___	Presentation	b.	Ensures reliable data transmission by error detection.
___	Session	c.	Addresses and delivers packets across a network.
___	Transport	d.	Moves bits of data on and off the cabling media.
___	Network	e.	Translates data so that it can be moved on the network.
___	Data Link	f.	Enables applications to access a network and its resources.
___	Physical	g.	Ensures reliable data transmission by decreasing the packet size.

2. **At which OSI layer is the MAC address applied to a data packet?**
   a) Physical
   b) Network
   c) Transport
   d) Data Link

3. **In which layer of the OSI model does Telnet operate?**
   a) Data Link
   b) Physical
   c) Application
   d) Presentation
   e) Session

4. **Which OSI layer is responsible for establishing connections between two devices?**
   a) Session
   b) Presentation
   c) Application
   d) Physical
   e) Data Link

5. **Which layer divides the data received from the Network layer into frames that are capable of being transmitted by the Physical layer?**

    a) Presentation

    b) Session

    c) Transport

    d) Data Link

    e) Application

TOPIC B

The TCP/IP Model

You have identified the layers in the OSI model. Another common networking model is the TCP/IP model. In this topic, you will identify the layers in the TCP/IP model.

The protocols and services defined by the TCP/IP model are more suitable for practical use than those defined by OSI. To ensure that you are able to utilize the benefits of the TCP/IP model in your network, you first need to know the protocols and services defined by TCP/IP layers.

The TCP/IP Protocols

The *Transmission Control Protocol/Internet Protocol (TCP/IP)* is a network protocol suite that is routable and allows computers to communicate across all types of networks. The native protocol of the Internet, TCP/IP is nonproprietary and used for Internet connectivity.

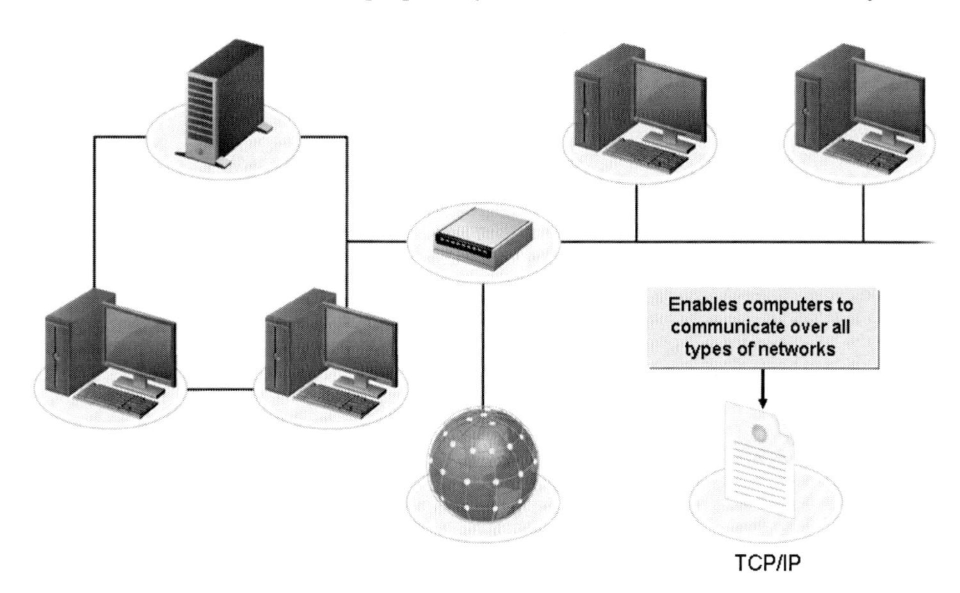

Figure 5-3: *The TCP/IP protocol used in networks.*

The TCP/IP protocol suite includes a network/node address structure, tools for static and dynamic address assignment, name resolution services, and utilities for testing and configuration.

The TCP/IP Network Model

The *TCP/IP model* is a four-layer model developed by the United States Department of Defense. To some extent, it is similar to the OSI model. The TCP/IP model was developed to allow the addition of new technologies and create a more flexible architecture which can easily allow the modification of existing protocols. This architecture later became known as the TCP/IP model after two of its most important protocols: TCP and IP.

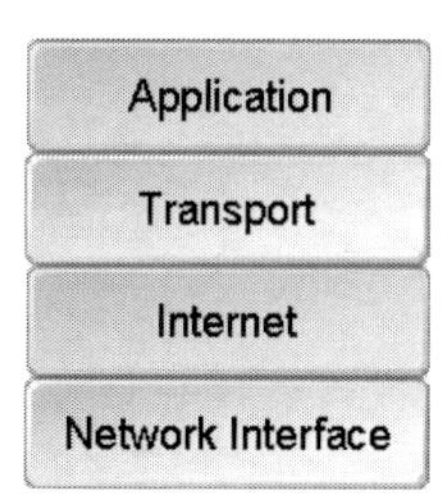

Figure 5-4: *The layers in the TCP/IP network model.*

Layers in the TCP/IP Network Model

The TCP/IP model defines four layers—the Application layer, the Transport layer, the Internet layer, and the Network Interface layer, which is also called the Link layer. Each layer in the TCP/IP model performs a specific function.

TCP/IP Layer	***Functions***
Application	Provides definition of protocols for file, email, and hypertext transfer. It also handles the encoding of data, controls the sessions, and defines socket services and other utilities over TCP/IP.
Transport	Provides connection establishment and communication services. It also defines protocols for end-to-end transfer of data, along with error and flow controls. In the TCP/IP model, there are two transport layer protocols: TCP and UDP.
Internet	Provides addressing and routing services. It also controls congestion on the network. This layer involves transferring data from a source to a destination network when multiple networks are connected together.
Network Interface	Provides services to send and receive data packets on the network. It defines protocols for moving data frames between adjacent nodes, and for accessing the medium by the devices. It defines the protocols for encoding and transmitting data over the network media.

Data Terminologies

Each layer uses different terminologies for a unit of information.

Layer	***Terminology Used***
Application	Data
Transport	Segment
Internet	Datagram or packets

Layer	Terminology Used
Network Interface	Frames

Comparison of the OSI and TCP/IP Models

In the TCP/IP model, the Application layer maps to the Application, Presentation, and Session layers of the OSI model. The Transport layer maps to the Transport layer in the OSI model. The Internet layer maps to the Network layer in the OSI model, and the Network Interface layer maps to the Data Link and Physical layers in the OSI model.

Similar to the OSI model, each layer of the TCP/IP model defines a set of functions and protocols and is designed to provide services to the layer above it. The data communication process through the TCP/IP layers is similar to the data communication process through the OSI layers. When data is transmitted on a network, it is added to the Application layer and then forwarded to the Network Interface layer. Data reception on the TCP/IP layers is the reverse process of transmission.

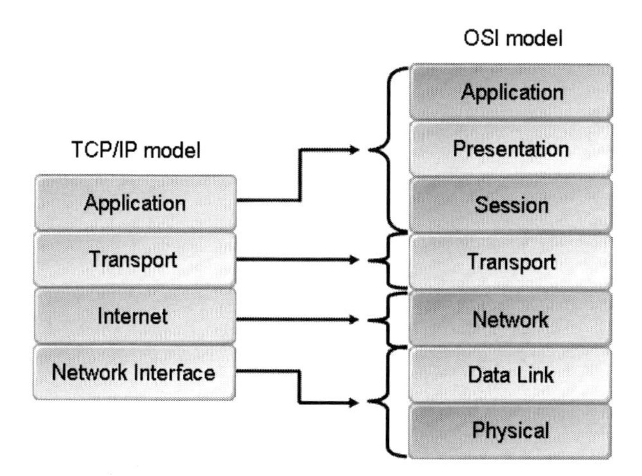

Figure 5-5: *The TCP/IP and OSI network models.*

There are several similarities and dissimilarities between the OSI and TCP/IP models.

Category	Description
Similarities	• Both models have a similar architecture. • Both models have an Application, Transport, and Network layer. • Both models have their lowest layer connected to the physical network.

Category	Description
Dissimilarities	• OSI was developed to standardize networking. However, TCP/IP was specifically developed to execute Internet-related tasks such as remote login, email, and resource sharing. • The OSI reference model consists of seven architectural layers whereas the TCP/IP only has four layers. The TCP/IP model does not have a Session or a Presentation layer. • The Application layer in TCP/IP handles the responsibilities of Application, Presentation, and Session layers in the OSI reference model. The TCP/IP model combines the OSI Data Link and Physical layers into the Network Interface layer. • The OSI reference model did not account for different protocols, and therefore the functionality of each layer is not clearly defined and optimized. In the TCP/IP model, the protocols define the functionality of each layer for optimal performance.

Flexibility of the TCP/IP Model

The functions and protocols defined in the TCP/IP model are more flexible than those in the OSI model. It has overshadowed the OSI model in its implementation on TCP/IP networks. The OSI model is now used to describe the concept of network models; most networks today, such as the Internet, follow the TCP/IP model.

Data Encapsulation

Encapsulation is the process of adding delivery information to the actual data transmitted on each layer. Encapsulation takes place in the transmission end as data is passed down the layers. At the receiving end, the reverse process of removing the added information is done as data passes to the next higher layer. This process is called *de-encapsulation*. The added information is called a header if it is before the data, or a trailer if it is added after the data.

If an application is initiated on the TCP/IP network, data is sent from the Application layer to the Transport layer. The Transport layer adds a header to the datagram and moves the datagram to the Internet layer. In the Internet layer, another header is added to the datagram and passed to the Network Interface layer, which adds a header and a trailer. The entire packet with the header and trailer information is sent to ensure its proper delivery. Upon receiving the data, the computer removes the corresponding header and trailer from the data and moves it to the Application layer.

Protocol Binding

Assigning a protocol to a NIC is referred to as *protocol binding*. As protocols govern data transmission, it is critical to bind the protocol to the network interface as it creates a path for the flow of data. Multiple protocols can be bound to a NIC, and the NIC can use any of the protocols that are bound to it to communicate with other nodes on the network.

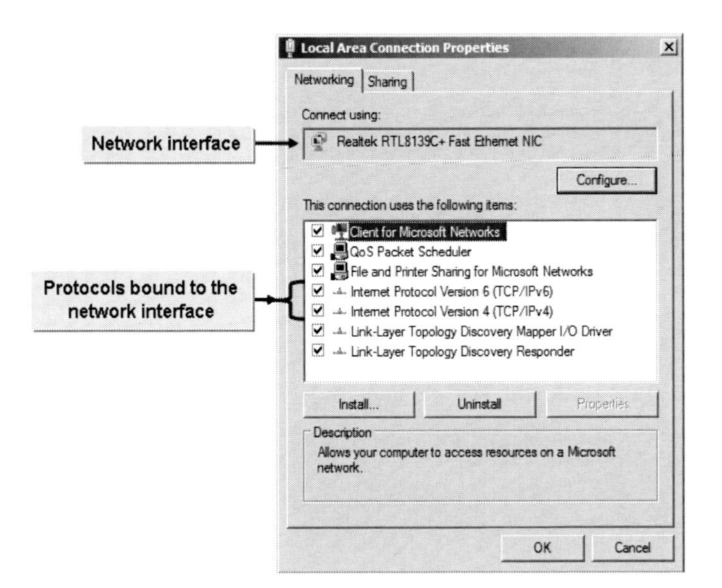

Figure 5-6: *Protocols bound to a NIC.*

Binding Order

In a scenario where a network interface is bound with multiple protocols, it attempts to connect to a receiving node by sequentially testing the available protocols until it gets a response from the receiving node using a protocol. This carries an inherent risk that the protocol that the node responds to might not be the most efficient one—it is simply the first compatible protocol in the sender's protocol list that the two nodes have in common.

In Windows, you can specify the binding order in which to bind protocols to a network interface. When you set the binding order to prefer the protocol you most frequently use on your network, your system does not attempt to use other protocols to access the network, thus increasing the efficiency of the connection.

ACTIVITY 5-2

Identifying the Layers of the TCP/IP Network Model

Scenario:

In this activity, you will identify the layers of the TCP/IP network model.

1. **Match the OSI layers with the TCP/IP layers.**

___	Application, Presentation, Session	a.	Network Interface
___	Transport	b.	Transport
___	Network	c.	Application
___	Data Link, Physical	d.	Internet

2. **Which TCP/IP layer provides addressing and routing services?**
   a) Application
   b) Internet
   c) Transport
   d) Network Interface

3. **Which layers of the OSI model are included in the Network Interface layer of the TCP/IP model?**
   a) Physical
   b) Network
   c) Data Link
   d) Transport

4. **At which TCP/IP layer is information called a datagram or packet?**
   a) Application
   b) Network Interface
   c) Internet
   d) Transport

5. **Match each layer with its corresponding data terminology.**

___	Application	a.	Data
___	Transport	b.	Frame
___	Internet	c.	Segment
___	Network Interface	d.	Datagram

ACTIVITY 5-3

Identifying Protocol Binding on a NIC

There is a simulated version of this activity available on the CD-ROM that shipped with this course. You can run this simulation on any Windows computer to review the activity after class, or as an alternative to performing the activity as a group in class. The activity simulation can be launched either directly from the CD-ROM by clicking the **Interactives** link and navigating to the appropriate one, or from the installed data file location by opening the C:\Data\Simulations\Lesson#\Activity# folder and double-clicking the executable (.exe) file.

Scenario:

In this activity, you will verify that the TCP/IP protocol is currently bound to your NIC.

---

1. Verify that the TCP/IP protocol is bound to your NIC.
    a. Choose **Start→Control Panel.**
    b. In the Control Panel window, click the **Network and Internet** link.
    c. In the Network and Internet window, click the **Network and Sharing Center** link.
    d. In the Network and Sharing Center window, in the left pane, click the **Change adapter settings** link.
    e. In the Network Connections window, right-click the **Local Area Connection** object and choose **Properties.**

f. In the **Local Area Connection Properties** dialog box, verify that the **Internet Protocol Version 4 (TCP/IPv4)** check box is checked and then select the **Internet Protocol Version 4 (TCP/IPv4)** option.

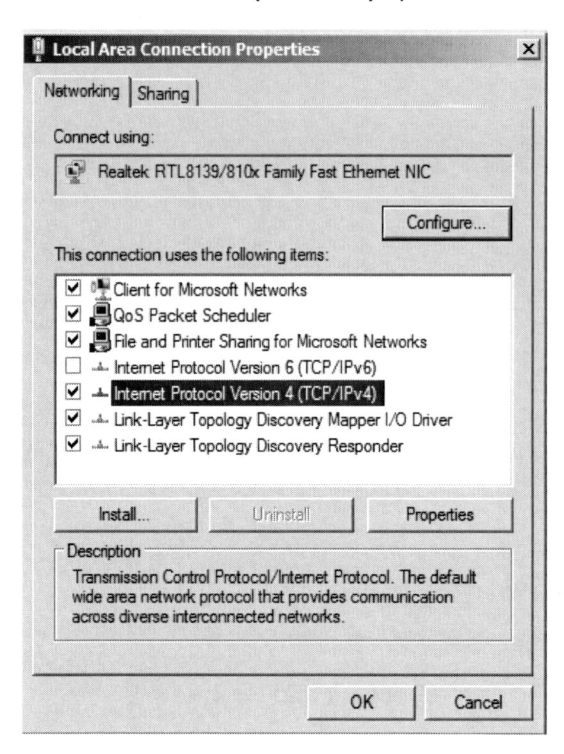

g. Read the protocol description and then click **OK** to close the **Local Area Connection Properties** dialog box.

h. Close the Network Connections window.

Lesson 5 Follow-up

In this lesson, you identified the two main network models that are used in computer networks—the OSI model and the TCP/IP model. Your ability to identify the various layers of the TCP/IP and OSI models will enable you to plan the implementation of a network according to the devices, protocols, and transmission methods needed for your network.

1. **What are the Physical layer devices that you have come across in your network?**

2. **What are the similarities and differences between OSI and TCP/IP models?**

6 TCP/IP Addressing and Data Delivery

Lesson Time: 2 hour(s), 40 minutes

Lesson Objectives:

In this lesson, you will identify TCP/IP addressing and data delivery methods.

You will:

- Identify the key protocols in the TCP/IP protocol suite.
- Identify data addressing on TCP/IP networks.
- Identify a default IP addressing scheme.
- Create custom IP addressing schemes.
- Implement IP version 6.
- Identify techniques to ensure reliable network data delivery.

Introduction

You are familiar with the TCP/IP model of networking. As a Network+ technician, apart from the network model, you need to be aware of TCP/IP addressing and data delivery methods to implement TCP/IP on your network. In this lesson, you will identify the addressing and data delivery methods of TCP/IP.

As a Network+ technician, you must be able to identify each individual system that is connected, and the addressing scheme and data flow on the network. This knowledge will become necessary to perform fault management and zero in on the faulty node. It will also allow you to isolate the system from the network, and recognize and troubleshoot the problem while ensuring that the network is fully functional.

This lesson covers all or part of the following CompTIA® Network+® (Exam N10-005) certification objectives:

- Topic A:
  - 1.2 Classify how applications, devices, and protocols relate to the OSI model layers.
  - 1.4 Explain the purpose and properties of routing and switching.
  - 1.6 Explain the function of common networking protocols.
- Topic B:

  - 1.2 Classify how applications, devices, and protocols relate to the OSI model layers.
  - 1.3 Explain the purpose and properties of IP addressing.
  - 1.6 Explain the function of common networking protocols.
- Topics C, D, and E:
  - 1.2 Classify how applications, devices, and protocols relate to the OSI model layers.
  - 1.3 Explain the purpose and properties of IP addressing.

TOPIC A
The TCP/IP Protocol Suite

In this lesson, you will learn about TCP/IP addressing and data delivery, which is performed by the TCP/IP protocol suite. TCP/IP consists of a suite of complementary protocols and standards that work together to provide the functionality on TCP/IP networks. In this topic, you will identify the protocols that are in use on a TCP/IP network.

The TCP/IP protocol suite includes many services that made TCP/IP the universal *de facto* standard networking protocol. The TCP/IP protocol suite defines how applications on separate nodes establish a connection and track communications. To ensure that your network is receiving the benefits that the TCP/IP suite of protocols and standards provide, you need to learn what those protocols are, and how they can benefit your network.

TCP

The TCP/IP protocol suite includes two Transport-layer protocols: *Transmission Control Protocol (TCP)* and *User Datagram Protocol (UDP)*. TCP is a connection-oriented, guaranteed-delivery protocol used to send data packets between computers over a network such as the Internet. It is part of the Internet protocol suite along with the *Internet Protocol (IP)*. TCP is responsible for breaking up data into datagrams, reassembling them at the other end, resending data lost in transit, and resequencing data. It sends data, waits for an acknowledgement, and fixes erroneous data.

TCP Analogy

Mr. TCP's boss gives him a letter to send to a client. TCP sends it via certified mail with delivery confirmation and waits by the mailbox. In a few days, he gets a notice in the mail that the letter is delivered. However, if the notice does not come in a timely manner, Mr. TCP knows he has to resend the letter.

Connection-Oriented and Connectionless Protocols

Protocols can be divided into two categories depending upon the types of connections they establish. They are connection-oriented and connectionless protocols. Connection-oriented protocols require a logical connection before transfer of data. Connectionless protocols, however, do not establish a connection between devices.

Connection-oriented protocols operate in three phases. In the first phase, a connection is established and the devices negotiate the parameters for the connection. During the second phase, the devices transfer data. And in the third phase, the connection held by the devices is released and is torn down as it is no longer required.

Connectionless protocols do not have any explicit setup or release phases, and are always in the data transfer phase. If a device has data to be sent to the other, it just sends it. Connection-oriented systems can function only in bidirectional communication environments.

Connectionless communication is achieved when information is transmitted from a source to a destination without checking to see if the destination is prepared to receive the information. In environments where it is difficult to transmit data to a destination, the sender may have to retransmit the information multiple times before the destination receives the complete message.

IP

Internet Protocol (IP) is a Network-layer protocol that is responsible for routing individual datagrams and addressing. Responsible for packet formats and the addressing scheme, IP is a connectionless protocol and acts as an intermediary between higher protocol layers and the network. It makes no guarantees about packet delivery, corruption of data, or lost packets. IP usually works in concert with TCP, which establishes a connection between a source and the destination. TCP/IP not only enables computers to communicate over all types of networks but also provides network addressing and naming, and data delivery. TCP/IP is the native protocol of the Internet and is required for Internet connectivity.

The IP Data Packet Delivery Process

IP assigns the correct destination IP address to a data packet. The process of delivering a data packet by IP consists of three steps:

1. When a service establishes a connection to the receiving node at the Transport layer, it resolves the name of the receiving node to that node's IP address.
2. The IP address is then passed from the Transport layer to the Internet layer.
3. IP uses a *subnet mask* to determine if the receiving node is on the same subnet or a remote network, and delivers the packet.

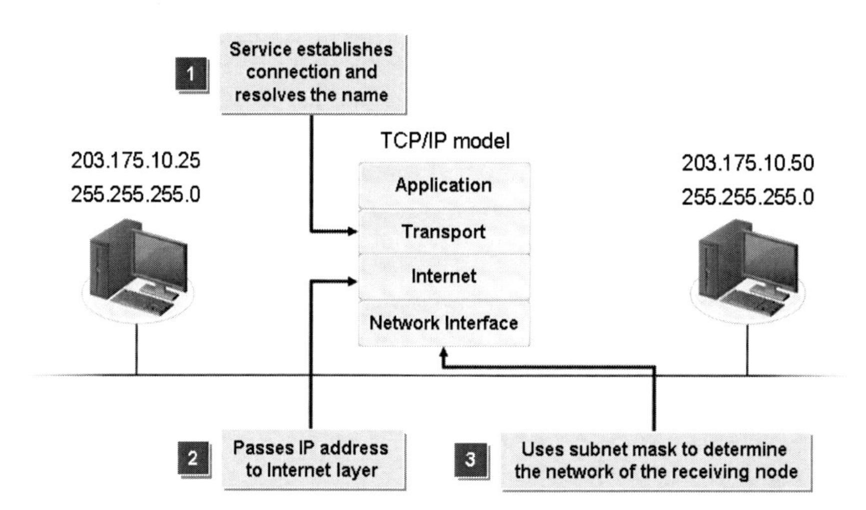

Figure 6-1: *The process of IP data packet delivery.*

UDP

The User Datagram Protocol (UDP), also known as the Universal Datagram Protocol, is a connectionless Transport-layer protocol in the Internet protocol suite. A connectionless, best-effort delivery protocol, UDP is used with IP like TCP. It transmits data and ensures data integrity as TCP does. UDP, however, lacks reliability, flow-control, and error-recovery functions. It is less complex than TCP, and since it is a connectionless protocol, it provides faster service.

UDP Analogy

Ms. UDP's boss gives her a letter to send, which she sends via regular mail. She does not wait by the mailbox or give the letter a second thought. She assumes that it reached its destination. If Ms. UDP's letter does not reach its destination, the receiving party has to call UDP's boss and ask for the letter to be resent. Ms. UDP has done her best job and is out of the picture.

Store and Forward

Because UDP is connectionless, it can send data using the *store and forward* method. For example, if a network is congested and data is sent via UDP to a router, the router may store the data until the next router or *hop* becomes available. When data reaches a router, that is considered a hop. So, if data passes through three routers on its way to its destination, it has made three hops.

ARP

The *Address Resolution Protocol (ARP)* maps an IP address to a physical or MAC address recognized within a local network. ARP resides on the Data Link layer of the Network Interface layer, encapsulated by an Ethernet header. Because the MAC address of a network device is 48 bits long and an IP address is only 32 bits, ARP's protocol rules help make suitable correlations.

Address resolution in ARP is performed in the following three steps:

1. ARP receives an IP address from IP.
2. If ARP has the MAC address in its cache, it returns it to IP. If not, it issues a broadcast to resolve the IP address.
3. A target node with the corresponding IP address responds with a unicast that includes its MAC address. ARP adds the MAC address into its cache and then sends it to IP as requested.

ARP supports IP by resolving IP addresses to MAC addresses.

MAC Address Resolution

ARP plays a critical role in address resolution. If IP needs to deliver a packet to an IP address on the local subnet, it needs to obtain the MAC address of the destination node directly from ARP. However, if IP needs to deliver a packet to an IP address on a remote subnet, it needs only the MAC address of the default gateway, and not of the destination node.

Once IP sends the packet to the default gateway, the default gateway will undertake its own MAC address resolution process to locate the MAC address of the next hop, and then forward the packet to other routers and networks as needed. Because the first step in the route to the destination is always on the local network, ARP resolution broadcasts can be confined to the local subnet.

Reverse Address Resolution Protocol

The *Reverse Address Resolution Protocol (RARP)* allows a node on a LAN to discover its IP address from a router's ARP table or cache. With RARP, a network administrator creates a table on the LAN's router that maps each node's MAC address to its corresponding IP address. When a node is added to the network, its IP address is requested by the RARP client program from the RARP server on the router. The IP address is returned to the node by the RARP server if the router table has set up that entry, so that it is stored for future use. RARP is available for Ethernet, FDDI, and Token Ring LANs.

ICMP

The *Internet Control Message Protocol (ICMP)* is used with IP that attempts to report on the condition of a connection between two nodes. ICMP messages notify a sender of network conditions by reporting on errors. If a node is sending data so fast that the receiving node's buffers flood, the receiving node sends an ICMP source quench message to slow down data transmission from the sending node.

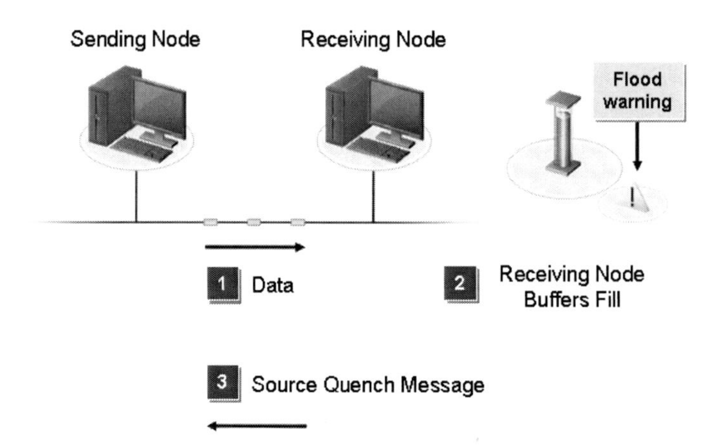

Figure 6-2: *ICMP reports on the condition of a connection between two nodes.*

IGMP

The *Internet Group Management Protocol (IGMP)* is a protocol in the TCP/IP suite that supports multicasting in a routed environment. It is used to inform all systems on a network as to what host currently belongs to which multicast group. The routers need to support IGMP and multicast packet routing. Routers use IGMP to periodically send out queries to hosts enquiring about group membership. IGMP on the node responsible for multicast traffic sends a message to the router informing it of the multicast session in progress. The router uses IGMP to poll its interfaces for members of the multicast group, and then forwards the multicast transmission to group members. Hosts send out notifications, called host membership reports, as response to the query. Upon receiving the response from hosts, routers forward the multicast transmission to group members.

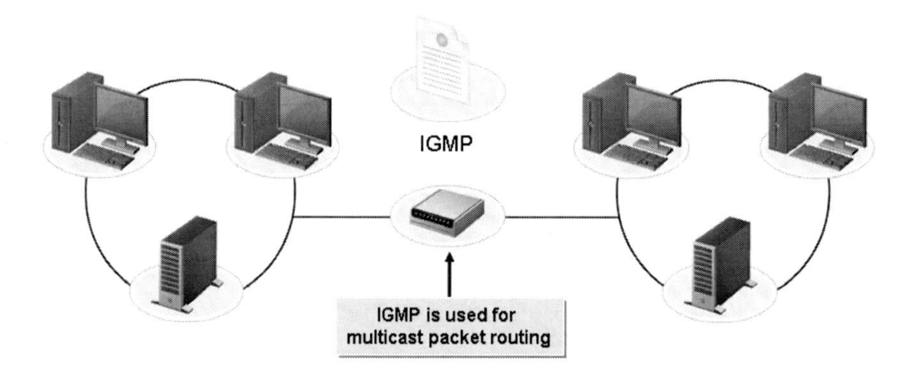

Figure 6-3: *IGMP directs multicast traffic to members of the multicast group.*

ACTIVITY 6-1

Identifying Protocols on a TCP/IP Network

Scenario:

In this activity, you will identify the protocols that are in use on TCP/IP networks.

---

1. **Which protocol lets systems on the network know which host belongs to which multicast group?**
   a) IP
   b) TCP
   c) ICMP
   d) IGMP

---

2. **Which is a function of ICMP?**
   a) Controls multicast sessions
   b) Controls data transfer speeds
   c) Resolves IP addresses to MAC addresses
   d) Provides best-effort data delivery

---

3. **Arrange the following phases of the working of ICMP on an IP network.**

   Data transmission

   ICMP source quench message

   Buffer flood

---

4. **True or False? ARP uses a multicast session to resolve an IP address to a MAC address it does not have in its cache.**
   __ True
   __ False

---

5. **What are the functions of TCP?**
   a) Breaking up data
   b) Routing data
   c) Reassembling data
   d) Addressing
   e) Resending lost data

TOPIC B

IP Addressing

You are familiar with different protocols and their functions on a TCP/IP network. To ensure that a network request arrives at its intended destination, you need to ensure that it follows the correct data addressing scheme. There is an addressing scheme followed on TCP/IP networks. In this topic, you will identify the methods used for packaging and addressing of data so that it can be accurately delivered to its intended destination.

Data, while being sent or received on a TCP/IP network, is packaged with the addresses of the sending and receiving nodes. Packaging data for delivery so that it can be routed to the correct destination is the cornerstone of networking. Incorrectly packaging or addressing data will result in users' experiencing symptoms of network communication problems. If you understand how a client packages data and then addresses it to travel to its destination on your network, you can use this information to detect causes of network communication problems.

Data Packets

Definition:

A *data packet* is a unit of data transfer between computers that communicate over a network. In general, all packets contain three parts: a header, data, and a trailer or footer. The header part contains the destination and source addresses. The footer part contains an error checking code. The data part contains the actual information or data that is to be transmitted.

Typically, a sender transmits a data packet and waits for an acknowledgement of its receipt from a recipient—an "ACK" signal. If the recipient is busy, the sender waits until it receives an ACK, after which it transmits the next packet. Throughput can increase if data is sent as larger packets, with the recipient needing to send fewer acknowledgements. The contents of a packet depend on the network protocol in use.

Frames, Packets, and Datagrams

The terms frame, packet, and datagram are sometimes used interchangeably when referring to data being transmitted over a network. With reference to the OSI model, frames occur at Layer 2 and packets are a feature of Layer 3. A datagram is a self-contained, independent piece of data with enough information to move from a source to a destination. The terms "packet" and "datagram" are used interchangeably in IP networks, but a packet refers to any message formatted as a packet; datagrams usually work with an unreliable service, such as UDP, that does not require an acknowledgement of delivery.

Example:

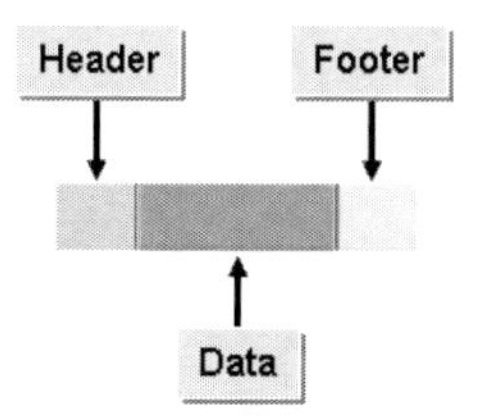

Figure 6-4: *Parts of a data packet.*

Network Addresses

Definition:

A *network address* is a protocol-specific identifier assigned to a node. A network address typically includes two parts: the first part identifies the network, and the second identifies a node on the network. A network address can be a number that maps to the MAC address by software running on nodes. The combination of the network address and host address is called an IP address.

Example:

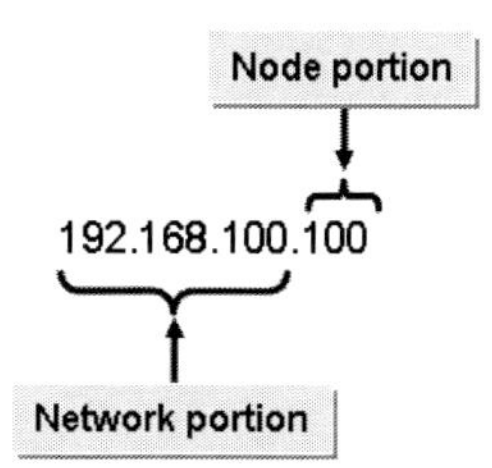

Figure 6-5: *A network address contains the network and node portions.*

Network Names

Definition:

A *network name* is a name assigned to a node to help users and technicians recognize the device more easily. A naming service, enabled by software running on one or more nodes, maps a network name to a network address or MAC address.

Example:

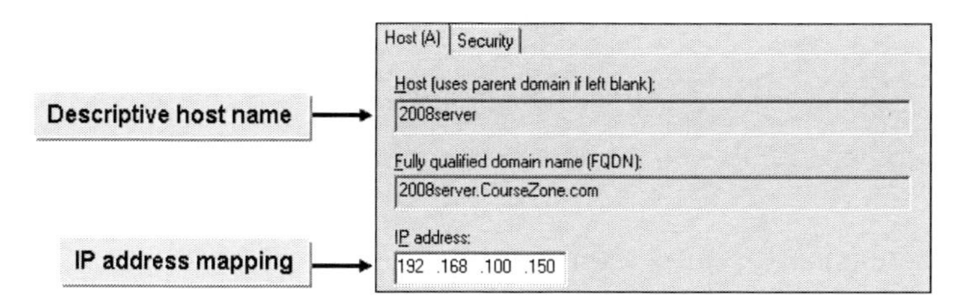

Figure 6-6: *Network names allow users to recognize the device.*

Naming Services

Naming services map network names to network addresses.

Naming Service	*Description*
Domain Name System (DNS)	The naming service used on the Internet and many TCP/IP-based networks. For example, the IP address 209.85.165.99 might map to **www.google.com**. In an organization's network, the IP address 128.4.20.100 might map to Server1.
NetBIOS	A simple, broadcast-based naming service. A NetBIOS name can be any combination of alphanumeric characters excluding spaces and the following characters: / : * ? " ; \ I The length of the name cannot exceed 15 characters. The 16th character is reserved.

Naming Service	Description
Windows Internet Naming Service (WINS)	An older type of naming service used on Windows-based networks.

IP Addresses

An *IP address* is a unique 32-bit binary address assigned to a computer so that it can communicate with other computers and devices on a TCP/IP network. An IP address consists of two portions: the network address portion common to all hosts and devices on a physical network, and the host address portion unique to the network host. All devices on a TCP/IP network, such as computers, routers, and printers, each have a unique IP address. Two types of IP addresses are available: classful or default IP addresses, and classless or custom IP addresses. IP addresses belonging to the first type are grouped into five different classes ranging from Class A to Class E.

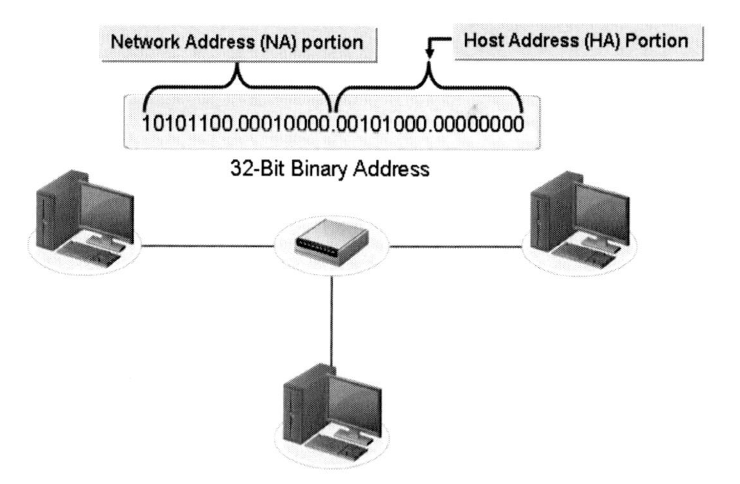

Figure 6-7: *An IP address enables a computer to connect with other devices.*

Depending upon the number of hosts a transmitting terminal addresses, an IP address can be further classified as unicast, multicast, or broadcast. You can easily recognize an IP address by its dotted decimal notation.

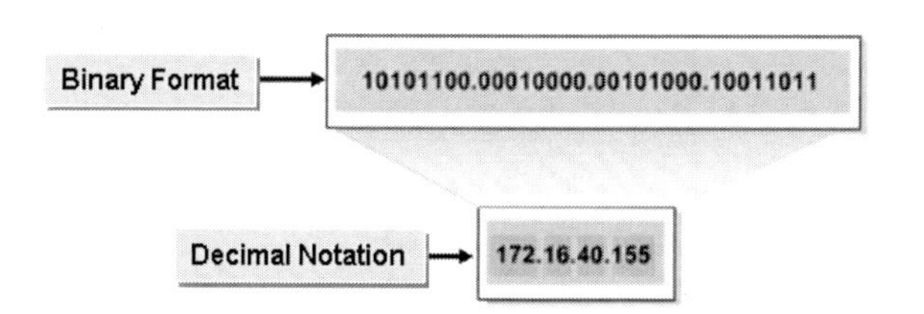

Figure 6-8: *Decimal notation of an IP address.*

The technique of assigning IP addresses is called IP addressing.

IPv4 Addresses

A 32-bit binary IPv4 address is usually separated by dots into four 8-bit octets for readability, and each octet is converted to a single decimal value. Each decimal number can range from 0 to 255, but the first number cannot be 0. In addition, all four numbers cannot be 0 (0.0.0.0) or 255 (255.255.255.255).

For more information on IP address assignments, see **www.iana.org/assignments/ipv4-address-space/**.

The Dotted Decimal Notation

TCP/IP addresses are usually displayed in the dotted decimal notation rather than in binary. The dotted decimal notation consists of four decimal numbers separated by three dots. Each decimal number is called an octet and represents eight binary bits. When pronouncing a dotted decimal number, include the separator dots. For example, the IP address 208.123.45.18 is pronounced "two oh eight dot one twenty-three dot forty-five dot eighteen."

ARIN

The Regional Internet Registry (RIR) is an organization that supervises how Internet numbers are allocated and registered in a particular geographical region. There are five RIRs in operation now and the American Registry for Internet Numbers (ARIN) is responsible for the United States, Canada, and parts of the Caribbean.

The services provided by ARIN include:

- IP address allocation.
- Registration transaction information with the help of WHOIS, a query/response protocol that is used to query an official database to determine the owner of a domain name, or an IP address on the Internet.
- Routing information with the help of RIRs that manage, distribute, and register public Internet number resources within their respective regions.

Mailing Address Analogy

Some of the numbers in an IP address identify the network segment on which a computer resides, just as a person's mailing address uses a street name to identify the street on which he or she lives. The rest of the numbers in the IP address uniquely identify the computer on a network, just as the house number portion of the mailing address uniquely identifies a specific house on a street.

Subnets

Definition:

Subnetting is the process of logically dividing a network into smaller subnetworks or *subnets*, with each subnet having a unique address. The conventional addressing technique has IP addresses with two hierarchical levels, namely the network ID and host ID. However, in subnet addressing, the host portion is further subdivided into the subnet ID and host ID. Therefore, subnet addressing is designed with three hierarchical levels: a network ID, subnet ID, and host ID.

To create subnets, a network administrator configures each node with an IP address and a subnet mask, which is used to identify the subnet to which the node belongs in order to divide the network into subnetworks. Routers and switches act as border devices for each subnet and manage traffic within and between subnets on a network. The subnet can be on a separate physical segment, or it can share segments with other logical subnets.

Analogy:

The three address parts of a subnet address can be compared to a telephone number, which consists of an area code, an exchange number, and the customer code.

Example:

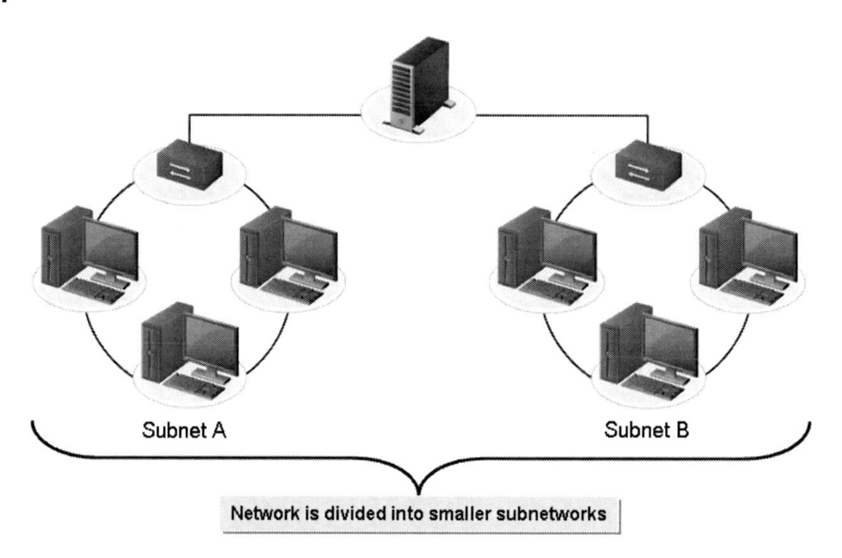

Figure 6-9: *A network divided into two subnets.*

Benefits of Subnets

Two main benefits of creating subnets are to improve network performance and to provide a more secure network environment. For performance enhancement, an administrator would most likely divide the network into groups of devices that frequently interact with each other, and for security enhancement, the administrator might divide the network based on servers that have restricted applications or sensitive data.

Subnet Masks

A *subnet mask* is a 32-bit number assigned to each host for dividing the 32-bit binary IP address into network and node portions. This segregation makes TCP/IP routable. A subnet mask uses the binary AND operation to remove the node ID from the IP address, leaving just the network portion. Default subnet masks use the value of eight 1s in binary, or 255 in decimal, to mask an entire octet of the IP address.

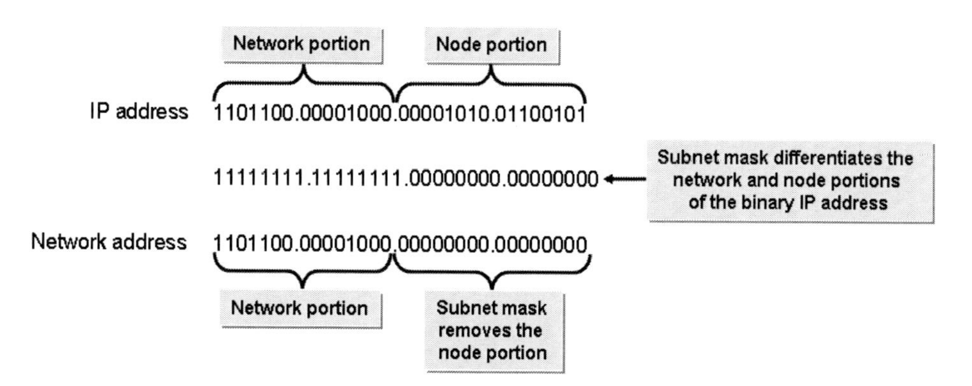

Figure 6-10: *The subnet mask of an IP address.*

Subnet Mask Values

The first number of a subnet mask must be 255; the remaining three numbers can be any of the following values: 255, 254, 252, 248, 240, 224, 192, 128, and 0.

Default Subnet Masks

Groups of IP addresses have specific default subnet masks, based on the range of values of the first octet of the IP address.

Default Subnet Mask	*Value of the First Octet of IP Address*
255.0.0.0	1–126
255.255.0.0	128–191
255.255.255.0	192–223

ACTIVITY 6-2
Identifying TCP/IP Information

There is a simulated version of this activity available on the CD-ROM that shipped with this course. You can run this simulation on any Windows computer to review the activity after class, or as an alternative to performing the activity as a group in class. The activity simulation can be launched either directly from the CD-ROM by clicking the **Interactives** link and navigating to the appropriate one, or from the installed data file location by opening the C:\Data\Simulations\Lesson#\Activity# folder and double-clicking the executable (.exe) file.

Scenario:

As the network administrator, you need to identify the IPv4 and MAC addresses of few computers to create a subnet. You also need to identify the names of a few computers so that you can join them to the domain on your network. You need to reassign the computers to a different subnet on your organization's network and you have been asked to gather information such as the subnet mask and default gateway. You need to check this TCP/IP information on each computer.

---

1. Display system properties.
   a. Choose **Start→Control Panel.**
   b. In the Control Panel window, click the **System and Security** link.
   c. In the System and Security window, click the **System** link to display the system properties.

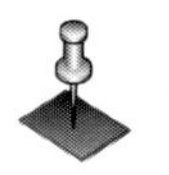

Your computer's full name might differ from the name displayed in the graphic.

   d. In the System window, in the **Computer name, domain, and workgroup settings** section, in the **Full computer name** field, identify your computer's full name.

Computer name, domain, and workgroup settings

Computer name:	Computer01
Full computer name:	Computer01.Child01.Classnet.com
Computer description:	
Domain:	Child01.Classnet.com

   e. Close the System window.

---

2. View the TCP/IP information assigned to your NIC.
   a. Choose **Start→Control Panel.**

b. In the Control Panel window, click the **Network and Internet** link.

c. In the Network and Internet window, click the **Network and Sharing Center** link.

d. In the Network and Sharing Center window, click the **Change adapter settings** link.

e. Right-click **Local Area Connection** and choose **Status.**

f. In the **Local Area Connection Status** dialog box, click **Details.**

g. In the **Network Connection Details** dialog box, in the properties list, identify the physical address, IPv4 address, subnet mask, DHCP server, and DNS server information.

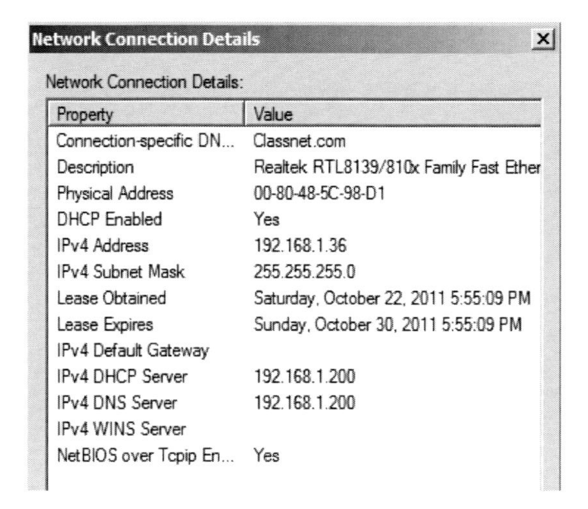

h. Close all open dialog boxes and windows.

Subnet Mask Structure

To conform to TCP/IP standards, subnet masks must follow a set of rules:

- The ones in the mask always start at bit 32, to the left of the mask.
- The zeros in the mask always start at bit 1, to the right of the mask.
- The ones in the mask must be contiguous, with no zeros interspersed between the ones.

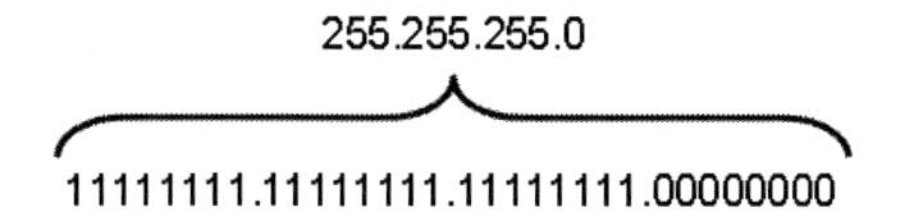

Figure 6-11: *Structure of a subnet mask.*

IP Address Assignment Rules

While assigning IP addresses to nodes in a network, certain rules are to be followed:

- Each node that connects to the network must have a unique IP address.
- If the network has subnets, each node connected must be assigned to a subnet on the network.
- Each subnet must have a unique network ID.
- All devices on a subnet must share the same network ID.
- Nodes on a local subnet must have unique node IDs.
- Nodes on different subnets can have the same node IDs if the network IDs are different.
- The node address cannot be all ones or all zeros.
- The IP address 127.0.0.1 is reserved for testing and cannot be used as a node ID.

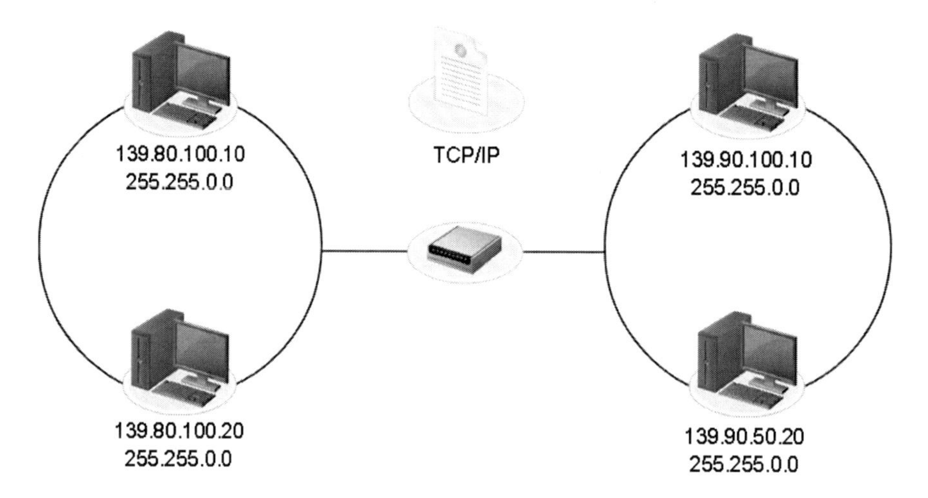

Figure 6-12: *IP addressing on subnets.*

Binary and Decimal Conversion

Binary is a base 2 numbering system in which any bit in the number is either a zero or a one. Each bit has a weight, or place value, which is a power of two. The place value is determined by the bit's location in the binary number. The value of a binary number is the sum of the place values of all one bits in a number.

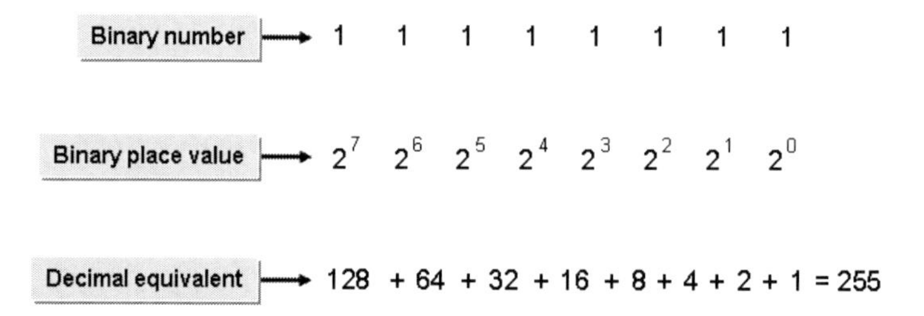

Figure 6-13: *Binary and decimal equivalents.*

Binary Exponents

For a given value of n ranging from zero to two, the decimal values of 2^n vary accordingly.

Exponent Value	*Decimal Value*
2^0	1
2^1	2
2^2	4
2^3	8
2^4	16
2^5	32
2^6	64
2^7	128

Binary to Decimal Equivalents

8-bit binary numbers can be converted to their decimal equivalents using powers of two.

Binary Number	*Conversion*	*Decimal Value*
00000001	$0+0+0+0+0+0+0+2^0$	1
00000011	$0+0+0+0+0+0+2^1+2^0$	3
00000111	$0+0+0+0+0+2^2+2^1+2^0$	7
00001111	$0+0+0+0+2^3+2^2+2^1+2^0$	15
00011111	$0+0+0+2^4+2^3+2^2+2^1+2^0$	31
00111111	$0+0+2^5+2^4+2^3+2^2+2^1+2^0$	63
01111111	$0+2^6+2^5+2^4+2^3+2^2+2^1+2^0$	127
11111111	$2^7+2^6+2^5+2^4+2^3+2^2+2^1+2^0$	255

Windows Calculator

The Calculator accessory that is built in to Windows operating systems can be very useful when converting decimal and binary numbers. Switch the calculator to the Scientific view, type a number, and use the **Dec** and **Bin** radio buttons to convert the number from one format to another.

Binary ANDing

To apply a subnet mask, both the IP address and subnet mask are converted to binary. The two binary numbers are ANDed together. The zeros in the subnet mask convert all bits in the node portion of the IP address to zeros, leaving the network portion of the address intact. The binary AND operation involves two rules:

- Zero AND any value equals zero.
- One AND one equals one.

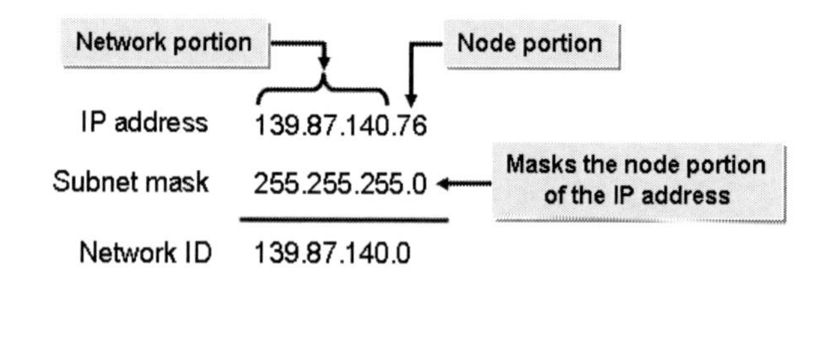

IP address in binary 10001011.01010111.10001100.01001100
Subnet mask in binary 11111111.11111111.11111111.00000000
ANDing 10001011.01010111.10001100.00000000

Figure 6-14: *Applying a subnet mask.*

Custom Subnetting

Because the binary value of 255 is all ones (11111111), you can easily identify the network portion of an IP address with any of the three default subnet masks applied without converting to binary. However, you can subdivide your IP network address by borrowing a part of your network's host addresses to identify subnet addresses. In these cases, the network portion of the IP address is not so easily identified, and it may be necessary to convert to binary to determine the network and node portions of the IP address.

ACTIVITY 6-3

Identifying IP Addressing

Scenario:

In this activity, you will identify IP addressing concepts.

1. **Match a component of a data packet with its contents.**

___	Header	a.	An error checking code.
___	Data	b.	Destination and source addresses.
___	Footer	c.	Data to be transmitted.

2. **Select the example of an IP address.**

   a) webserver1

   b) 201.183.100.2

   c) 00-08-02-D4-F6-4C

   d) M123-X7-FG-128

3. **Match the binary value with its decimal equivalent.**

___	01100100	a.	100.100.2.1
___	11100000	b.	100
___	11111111.11111111. 11110000.00000000	c.	127.0.0.1
___	01100100.01100100. 00000010.00000001	d.	224
___	01111111.00000000. 00000000.00000001	e.	255.255.240.0

4. **Which is the default subnet mask value for the addresses whose first octet ranges from 192 to 223?**

   a) 255.255.0.0

   b) 255.255.255.0

   c) 255.0.0.0

   d) 254.255.0.0

5. **True or False? Default subnet masks use the value of eight 0s in binary.**

   __ True

   __ False

TOPIC C
Default IP Addressing Schemes

In the previous topic, you identified the addressing schemes for the protocols and standards that can be used on a TCP/IP network. Now that you are aware of the protocols, you can identify the ways by which IP addresses are assigned. In this topic, you will identify the default addressing schemes used in TCP/IP networks.

On the Internet, TCP/IP addresses must be regulated with a common scheme to ensure that there are no duplicate addresses worldwide. Companies and Internet Service Providers (ISPs) often lease addresses for their networks and customers to gain Internet access as it is expensive for a company to lease IP addresses for every client that needs Internet access. To lease the required IP addresses easily, you need to first understand the default IP address classes, their reserved purposes, and where to lease the IP addresses you need.

ICANN

The IP address of every node on the Internet must be unique. An international organization called the *Internet Corporation for Assigned Names and Numbers (ICANN)* controls the leasing and distribution of IP addresses on the Internet. Companies lease their IP addresses from ICANN to ensure that there are no duplicate IP addresses.

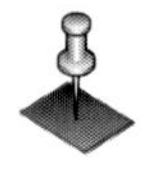

In 1993, an international organization called the *Internet Assigned Number Authority (IANA)* was established to govern the use of Internet IP addresses. Today, that function is performed by ICANN.

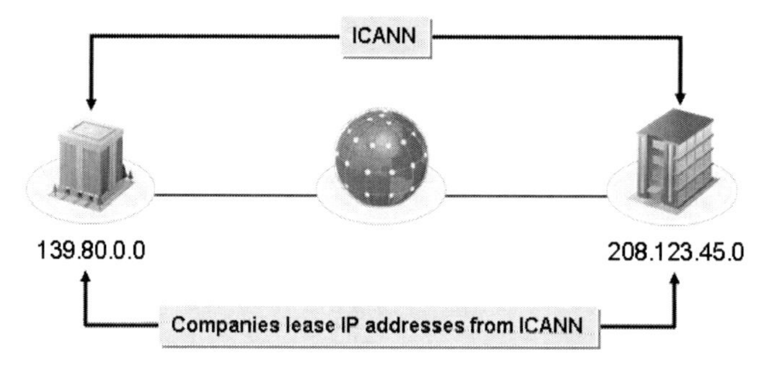

Figure 6-15: *ICANN leases IP addresses on the Internet.*

IP Address Classes

The TCP/IP suite consists of five blocks of addresses, called address classes, for use on specific networks based on their size.

Address Class	Description
Class A	*Class A* addresses provide a small number of network addresses for networks with a large number of nodes per network. Used only by extremely large networks, Class A addresses are too extensive for use by most organizations. • **Address range:**1.0.0.0 to 127.255.255.255 • **Number of networks:**126 (The IP address 127.0.0.1 is reserved.) • **Number of nodes per network:**16,777,214 • **Network ID portion:**First octet • **Node ID portion:**Last three octets • **Default subnet mask:**255.0.0.0 Example of a Class A address: 10.28.220.19
Class B	*Class B* addresses provide a balance between the number of network addresses and the number of nodes per network. Most organizations lease Class B addresses for use on networks that connect to the Internet. • **Address range:**128.0.0.0 to 191.255.255.255 • **Number of networks:**16,382 • **Number of nodes per network:**65,534 • **Network ID portion:**First two octets, excluding Class A addresses • **Node ID portion:**Last two octets • **Default subnet mask:**255.255.0.0 Example of a Class B address: 155.128.20.106
Class C	*Class C* addresses provide a large number of network addresses for networks with a small number of nodes per network. • **Address range:**192.0.0.0 to 223.255.255.255 • **Number of networks:**2,097,150 • **Number of nodes per network:**254 • **Network ID portion:**First three octets, excluding Class A and Class B addresses • **Node ID portion:**Last octet • **Default subnet mask:**255.255.255.0 Example of a Class C address: 201.208.120.86
Class D	*Class D* addresses are set aside to support multicast transmissions. Any network can use them, regardless of the base network ID. A multicast server assigns a single Class D address to all members of a multicast session. There is no subnet mask. Class D addresses are routable only with special support from routers. **Address range:**224.0.0.0 to 239.255.255.255 Example of a Class D address: 230.43.160.48

Address Class	Description
Class E	*Class E* addresses are set aside for research and experimentation. **Address range:**240.0.0.0 to 255.255.255.255 Example of a Class E address: 250.217.39.190

Special Addresses in Default Address Classes

Because neither the node portion nor the network portion of an IP address can be all 1s or all 0s, certain host addresses in each address class are invalid for individual hosts. For example, in Class A only, the host address 10.0.0.0 is not valid because the host portion is all 0s—the address is identical to the network address. Similarly, the Class A address 120.255.255.255 is not valid because the host portion is all 1s. A host address with all 1s has a special purpose; it is used as a broadcast address. The address 127.255.255.255 would be used for broadcasts to the local subnet.

Available Host and Network Addresses

The number of host addresses or network addresses available on networks in each class depends upon how many bits are in the network portion or host portion of the address. The formula to calculate available host addresses is 2^x-2, where x is the number of host bits. Two addresses in each block are unavailable because host addresses cannot be all ones or all zeros.

Similarly, the formula to calculate available network addresses is 2^y-2, where y is the number of network bits.

Restricted IP Addresses

Some IP addresses have special uses and cannot be assigned to networks and hosts. For example, IP address 127.0.0.1 is reserved for testing. It identifies your network and host on the Internet.

Restriction	Reason	Example
A network address of 0 is not permitted.	When the network address is set to 0, TCP/IP interprets the IP address as a "local" address, meaning that the data packet does not need to be transmitted through a router.	The 0.0.0.22 address identifies host 22 on the local network.
A node address of 0 is not permitted.	When the node address is set to 0, TCP/IP interprets the address as a network address and not a node address.	The address 122.0.0.0 identifies the network whose address is 122.
The network address of 127 is reserved.	Messages addressed to a network address of 127 are not transmitted out onto the network; instead, these messages are sent back to the transmitting node. The address of 127 is used to test the configuration of TCP/IP.	127.0.0.1 is referred to as the loopback address. It is a shorthand way for any host to refer to itself.

Restriction	***Reason***	***Example***
Neither the network address nor the host address can be just 255.	The 255 address is reserved for broadcasts.	255.255.255.255 is a broadcast address. Data packets will be sent to all hosts on all networks. 187.205.255.255 is also a broadcast address and data packets will be sent to all hosts on network 187.205.
Network address 1.1.1.1 is not permitted.	TCP/IP identifies all hosts with that address.	1.1.1.1 refers to every host.

To test your node, enter `ping 127.0.0.1`, `ping loopback`, or `ping localhost` to check if TCP/IP is functioning on your node.

Private IP Addresses

Private IP addresses are addresses that organizations use for nodes within enterprise networks requiring IP connectivity and not external connections to the Internet. IP addresses in each of the Classes A, B, and C are reserved as private IP addresses. When an Internet router receives a data packet bound for one of these reserved IP addresses, it recognizes the address as nonroutable and does not forward it outside the network. Private IP addresses can be used freely on internal networks. Because they are not routable, private IP addresses do not cause duplicate IP address conflicts on the Internet.

An organization can use private IP addresses without contacting an Internet registry or the ICANN. These addresses are not injected into the global Internet routing system. Therefore, different organizations can use the address space simultaneously. Problems arising due to the shortage of IP addresses are partly resolved by private IP addresses.

In order for a computer with an assigned nonroutable IP address to access Internet resources or other external networks, the private IP address needs to be converted to a routable address. This is usually accomplished through a gateway or by a router.

Private IP Address Ranges

The private, nonroutable IP address ranges are:

- 10.0.0.0 to 10.255.255.255
- 172.16.0.0 to 172.31.255.255
- 192.168.0.0 to 192.168.255.255

The Local and Remote Addressing Process

In the local and remote addressing process:

1. A network node uses a subnet mask to determine whether a data packet is bound for the local subnet or must be routed to a remote subnet.
2. The node applies the subnet mask to its own IP address to determine its own network ID.
3. It then applies the subnet mask to the packet's destination address to determine the destination network ID.
4. Once the node has applied the subnet mask, it compares the two network IDs.
5. If they are the same, then the two nodes are on the same subnet and the node can deliver the packet.
6. If the two networks are different, then the two nodes are remote to each other and the data is routed to the remote network.

The process of determining local and remote addresses based on IP addresses falls under the Network layer's routing protocol function.

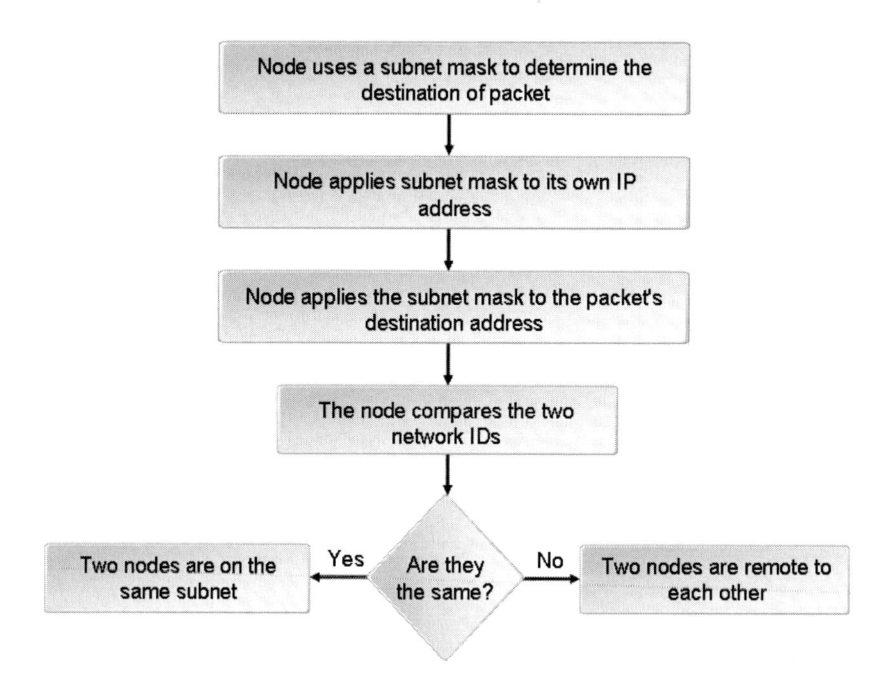

Figure 6-16: *Steps involved in local and remote addressing process.*

Default Gateways

Definition:

A *default gateway* is the IP address of a router that routes remote traffic from the computer's local subnet to remote subnets. Typically, it is the address of the router connected to the Internet. A TCP/IP host does not need a default gateway address if the computer does not need to communicate with computers outside its local subnet. You need to configure a node with an IP address, a subnet mask, and a default gateway to communicate on the Internet. You will need only an IP address and a subnet mask to communicate with other nodes on your network.

You can enter `ipconfig` on your command prompt to view the TCP/IP parameters on your computer.

Example:

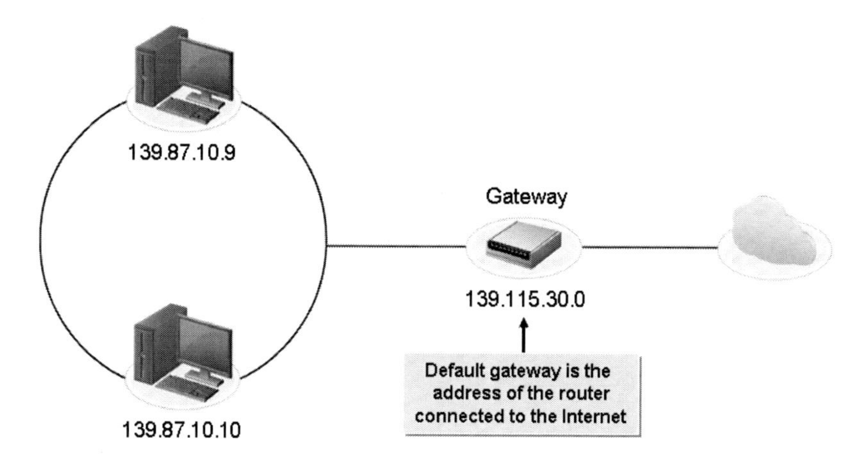

Figure 6-17: *The default gateway routes traffic to remote subnets.*

ACTIVITY 6-4
Identifying Default IP Addressing Schemes

Scenario:
In this activity, you will identify the characteristics of default IP addressing schemes.

---

1. Match the IP address range with its class.

___	Class A	a.	1.0.0.0 to 127.255.255.255
___	Class B	b.	128.0.0.0 to 191.255.255.255
___	Class C	c.	224.0.0.0 to 239.255.255.255
___	Class D	d.	192.0.0.0 to 223.255.255.255
___	Class E	e.	240.0.0.0 to 255.255.255.255

---

2. Select the IP address classes that can be assigned to hosts.

a) Class A

b) Class B

c) Class C

d) Class D

e) Class E

---

3. What is the term used to denote the IP address of a router that routes remote traffic from the computer's local subnet to remote subnets?

a) Subnet mask

b) Default gateway

c) Private IP address

d) Loopback address

---

4. True or False? A TCP/IP host needs a default gateway address to communicate with computers within its local subnet.

__ True

__ False

TOPIC D

Create Custom IP Addressing Schemes

In the previous topic, you identified the various IP addressing schemes. Administrators can also create customized IP address schemes. In this topic, you will learn how to construct custom IP addressing schemes.

Because of the fixed number of default networks and hosts on Class B and Class C networks, many companies were forced to either lease Class B networks and then divide them up into multiple subnetworks within their company, or combine multiple smaller subnets into one highly subnetted network using Class C networks to facilitate the total number of nodes. As a network administrator, you will need to know how to create subnets that meet the requirements of the current IP addressing scheme and are fully functional on any IP network.

Custom TCP/IP Subnets

Definition:

A *custom TCP/IP subnet* is a class of leased addresses that are divided into smaller groups to serve a network's needs. A custom TCP/IP subnet has a custom subnet mask ANDed to the IP address, so that what the node sees as its local network is a subset of the whole default network address block. A default gateway is configured for each subnet to route traffic between subnets.

Example:

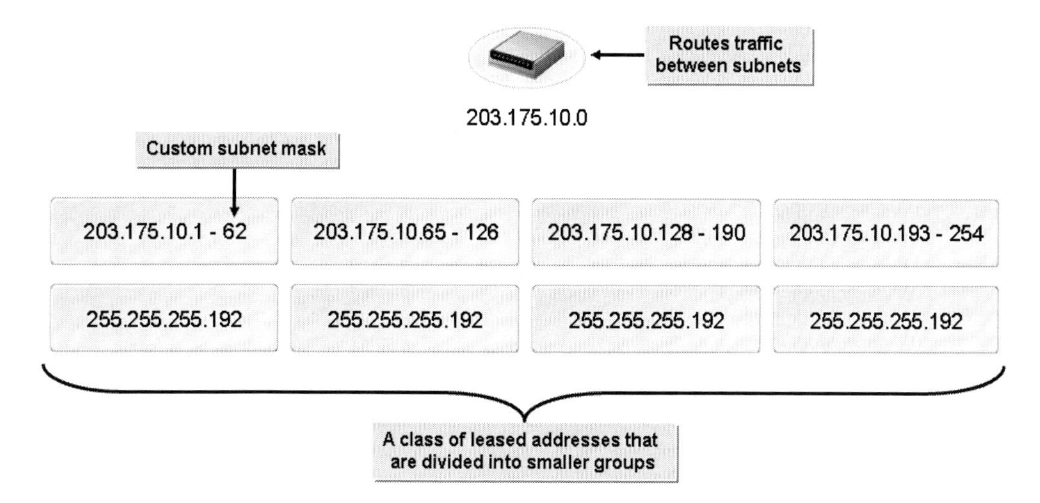

Figure 6-18: *A custom subnet mask ANDed to the IP address.*

Custom Subnet Masks

You can use a custom subnet mask to divide a single IP address block into multiple subnets. A custom subnet mask borrows node bits in a contiguous block from the left side of the node portion of the address, and uses them as network bits. This divides a single network address into multiple networks, each containing fewer nodes.

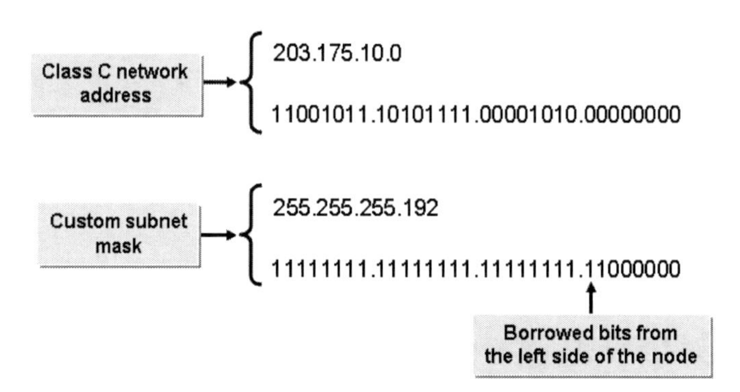

Figure 6-19: *A custom subnet mask borrows node bits in a contiguous block.*

Custom Subnet Masks on Class C Networks

There are different possible combinations of custom subnet masks on a Class C network.

Last Octet of New Mask (Binary)	*New Mask (Decimal)*	*Number of Added Networks*	*Nodes per Network*
10000000	255.255.255.128	2	126
11000000	255.255.255.192	4	62
11100000	255.255.255.224	8	30
11110000	255.255.255.240	16	14
11111000	255.255.255.248	32	6
11111100	255.255.255.252	64	2
11111110	255.255.255.254	Not allowed in Class C	
11111111	255.255.255.255	Not allowed in Class C	

Determining Available Host Addresses

The number of host addresses on a custom subnet is a function of the total number of address bits available for host addressing. The formula is 2^x-2, where x is the number of host bits. Two addresses in each block are unavailable because host addresses cannot be all ones or all zeros.

So, with a subnet mask of 255.255.255.248 (11111111.11111111.11111111.11111000 in binary), three bits available for host addresses (2^3=8), less two unavailable addresses leaves a total of six available host addresses per network.

Variable Length Subnet Masks

Definition:

A *Variable Length Subnet Mask (VLSM)* can be used for creating subnets that have different numbers of nodes. In a standard subnet, the number of addresses is identical within each subnet. The custom subnet mask must accommodate the subnet with the greatest number of nodes. However, such a scheme can waste addresses on smaller subnets. A VLSM applies the custom subnet mask, which provides the number of nodes required for each subnet.

The downside of carefully tailoring a subnet mask to each subnet is that you limit your capacity for future node growth on each subnet. Ideally, you want some room for future growth, but predicting how much growth you need is more of an art than an exact science.

Example: Variable Subnet Masks on a Network

A Class C network might contain 3 subnets, with 5 hosts on subnet 1, 12 hosts on subnet 2, and 28 hosts on subnet 3. You could use a custom subnet mask of 255.255.255.224 to allow each subnet to have 30 addresses. However, applying this subnet mask would waste 25 IP addresses on subnet 1, 18 IP addresses on subnet 2, and 2 IP addresses on subnet 3. By applying a variable subnet mask of 255.255.255.248 to subnet 1, 255.255.255.240 to subnet 2, and 255.255.255.224 to subnet 3, you only waste one IP address on subnet 1, and two IP addresses each on subnets 2 and 3.

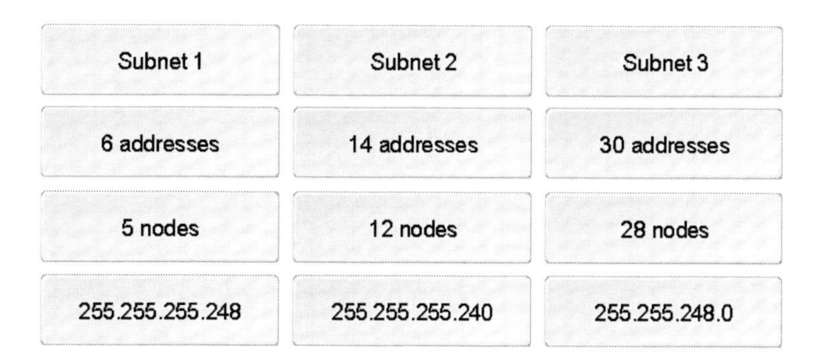

Figure 6-20: *VLSM creates subnets containing different numbers of nodes.*

Classless Inter Domain Routing

Classless Inter Domain Routing (CIDR) is a classless addressing method that considers a VLSM as a 32-bit binary word. Mask bits can move in one-bit increments to provide the exact number of nodes and networks required. The CIDR notation combines a network address with a number to represent the number of one bits in the mask. With CIDR, multiple class-based networks can be represented as a single block.

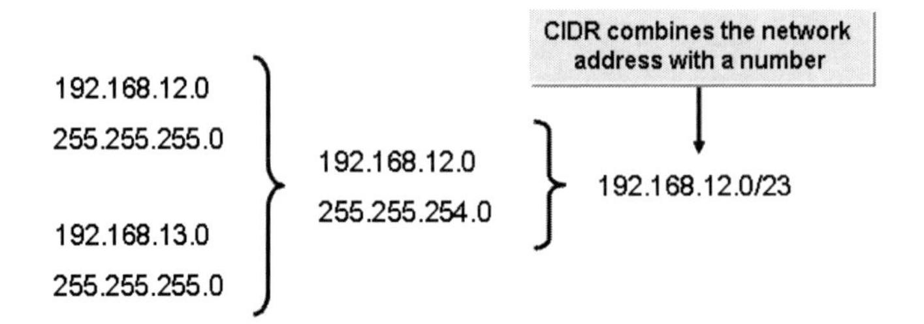

Figure 6-21: *A classless addressing method that considers a VLSM as a 32-bit binary word.*

CIDR can also be referred to as classless routing or supernetting. Because of its efficiencies, CIDR has been rapidly adopted, and the Internet today is largely a classless address space.

CIDR Subnet Masks

There are different values possible for each CIDR subnet mask. The /24, /16, and /8 CIDR masks correspond with the classful ranges of Class C, Class B, and Class A, respectively.

CIDR Mask (Number of Network Bits)	*Number of Possible Nodes*	*Standard Subnet Mask in Dotted Decimal*
/32	N/A	255.255.255.255
/31	N/A	255.255.255.254
/30	2	255.255.255.252
/29	6	255.255.255.248
/28	14	255.255.255.240
/27	30	255.255.255.224
/26	62	255.255.255.192
/25	126	255.255.255.128
/24	254	255.255.255.0
/23	510	255.255.254.0
/22	1,022	255.255.252.0
/21	2,046	255.255.248.0
/20	4,094	255.255.240.0
/19	8,190	255.255.224.0
/18	16,382	255.255.192.0
/17	32,766	255.255.128.0
/16	65,534	255.255.0.0

CIDR Mask (Number of Network Bits)	Number of Possible Nodes	Standard Subnet Mask in Dotted Decimal
/15	131,070	255.254.0.0
/14	262,142	255.252.0.0
/13	524,286	255.248.0.0
/12	1,048,574	255.240.0.0
/11	2,097,150	255.224.0.0
/10	4,194,304	255.192.0.0
/9	8,386,606	255.128.0.0
/8	16,777,214	255.0.0.0
/7	33,554,430	254.0.0.0
/6	67,108,862	252.0.0.0
/5	134,217,726	248.0.0.0
/4	268,435,544	240.0.0.0
/3	536,870,910	224.0.0.0
/2	1,073,741,824	192.0.0.0
/1	N/A	N/A

A CIDR Application

The CIDR address 192.168.12.0/23 applies the network mask 255.255.254.0 to the 192.168.0.0 network, starting at 192.168.12.0. On a VLSM-enabled router, this single routing entry can define a supernet that includes the address range from 192.168.12.0 to 192.168.13.255. Compare this to traditional class-based networking, where this range of addresses would require separate routing entries for each of two Class C networks—192.168.12.0 and 192.168.13.0—each using the default Class C subnet mask of 255.255.255.0.

How to Create Custom IP Addressing Schemes

Procedure Reference: Calculate the Base Network ID of a Custom Subnet

To calculate the base network ID of a custom subnet:

1. Isolate the octet that has shared network and node bits. This is the only octet you need to focus on. The other octets will be either all network bits or all node bits.
2. Convert the shared octet for the IP address to binary.
3. Apply the mask from the shared octet of the subnet mask to the shared octet of the IP address to remove the node bits.
4. Convert the shared portion of the IP address back to decimal.

Example: Calculate a Network ID

To determine the network ID of the IP address 206.234.120.87/20:

1. Isolate the octet that has shared network and node bits.

   The subnet mask for /20 is 11111111 11111111 11110000 00000000

   The third octet is shared between nodes and networks.

2. Convert the shared octet for the IP address to binary; add leading zeros as needed to create an 8-bit number.

   The third octet is 120; the binary equivalent is 1111000. Add a leading zero to create an 8-bit number.

   206.234.01111000.87

3. Apply the mask from the shared octet of the subnet mask to the shared octet of the IP address to remove the node bits.

   Because the fourth octet involves node bits, all of it will change to zeros. The first and second octets are totally network bits and will drop through the mask.

   206.234.01111000.87

   255.255.11110000.0

   206.234.01110000.0

4. Convert the shared portion of the IP address back to decimal.

   01110000 = 112

   The base network ID is 206.234.112.0.

DISCOVERY ACTIVITY 6-5

Creating Custom IP Addressing Schemes

Scenario:

You have been asked to implement TCP/IP on a divided network. There are three subnets separated by two Layer 3 network devices and no Internet connection. Subnet 1 has 120 nodes, Subnet 2 has 1,350 nodes, and Subnet 3 has 240 nodes. You need to create a custom addressing scheme by selecting the appropriate network IDs.

---

1. **How many individual network IDs do you need?**
   a) One
   b) Two
   c) Three
   d) Four

---

2. **If you were going to use default subnet masks for the networks, which default subnet would be applied to each network?**

---

3. **Which is a valid example of an appropriate IP address and subnet mask for subnet 1?**
   a) IP address: 192.168.10.0; subnet mask: 255.255.255.0
   b) IP address: 172.16.0.0; subnet mask: 255.255.0.0
   c) IP address: 192.168.10.0; subnet mask: 255.255.0.0
   d) IP address: 172.16.0.0; subnet mask: 255.255.255.0

TOPIC E

Implement IPv6 Addresses

In the previous topics, you learned about IPv4, which is the original version of the TCP/IP protocol and is in use on thousands of networks. In contrast, IP version 6 (IPv6) is a new standard that is currently being implemented on networks and is expected to replace IPv4 very shortly. In this topic, you will implement IPv6 addresses.

As a network professional who supports TCP/IP networking, you will be aware of the limitations of the IPv4 addressing scheme. IPv6 is an addressing scheme available to network administrators who need to overcome these limitations. If you support or configure networks that include this new IP addressing scheme, you will need to understand its characteristics as well as how it can interoperate with existing IPv4 implementations.

IPv4 Address Space Limitations

Limitations of the IPv4 address space include:

- The 32-bit IP address space itself, which provides only a theoretical maximum of 2^{32}, or approximately 4,295 billion, separate addresses.
- The division of the address space into fixed classes, with the result that node addresses falling either between classes or between subnets are unavailable for assignment.
- The fact that IP address classes provide a small number of node addresses, leading to difficulty matching IP address leases to a company's needs and IP addresses being wasted.
- The depletion of Class A and Class B IP address assignments.
- Unassigned and unused address ranges within existing Class A and Class B blocks.

IPv6

IP version 6, or *IPv6,* the successor to IPv4, is an addressing scheme that increases the available pool of IP addresses by implementing a 128-bit binary address space. IPv6 also includes new features, such as simplified address headers, hierarchical addressing, support for time-sensitive network traffic, and a new structure for unicast addressing.

IPv6 is not compatible with IPv4, so at present it is narrowly deployed on a limited number of test and production networks. Full adoption of the IPv6 standard will require a general conversion of IP routers to support interoperability.

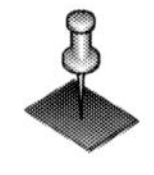

For more information on IPv6, see the IETF's IP Version 6 Working Group charter at **www.ietf.org/html.charters/ipv6-charter.html**.

Simplified Headers

One of the goals of IPv6 is to keep the IP headers as small as possible, to make access to the address more efficient and quicker. Non-essential information in IPv6 headers is moved to optional extension headers.

Hierarchical Addressing

In IPv6, address blocks are automatically assigned hierarchically by routers. Top-level routers have top-level address blocks, which are automatically divided and assigned as routers, and segments are added to them. This divides the address space logically instead of randomly, making it casicr to manage.

Time-Sensitive Data Support

A new field in the IP header of IPv6 packets enables IP to guarantee the allocation of network resources when requested by time-dependent services such as voice and video transmission.

Unicast Address Structure

IPv6 replaces classful addresses with a more flexible and logical unicast addressing structure. There are different categories of unicast addresses that serve different functions. Each network interface on a typical IPv6 host will be logically multihomed, which means that it will have more than one type of unicast address assigned.

Unicast Address Type	***Description***
Global addresses	Globally routable public addresses. Also known as aggregatable global unicast addresses, they are designed in such that they can be summarized for efficient routing. Global addresses are the equivalent of the entire IPv4 public address space.
Site-local addresses	Addresses used for internal networks that are not routable on the Internet. The equivalent of the IPv4 private, nonroutable address blocks.
Link-local addresses	Addresses that are used to communicate and automatically assigned on private network segments with no router. The equivalent of APIPA addressing in IPv4.
IPv6 transitional addresses	Addresses are used on mixed networks to support routing of IPv6 data across IPv4 networks. This class will be phased out when all routers convert to IPv6.

IPv6 Addresses

An *IPv6 address* is a 128-bit binary number assigned to a computer on a TCP/IP network. Some of the bits in the address represent the network segment; the other bits represent the host itself. For readability, the 128-bit binary IPv6 address is usually separated by colons into eight groups of four hexadecimal digits: 2001:0db8:85a3:0000:0000:8a2e:0370:7334. While all eight groups must have four digits, leading zeros can be omitted: 2001:db8:85a3:0:0:8a2e:370:7334 and groups of consecutive zeros replaced with two colons: 2001:db8:85a3::8a2e:370:7334. To avoid ambiguity, the double-colon substitution can only be performed once per address.

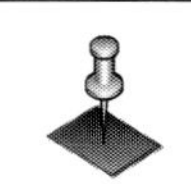

A 128-bit address provides 2^{128} potential address combinations.

The IPv6 Address Space

A 128-bit address provides $2^{\wedge 128}$ potential address combinations.

IPv4 vs. IPv6

IPv4 addresses differ from IPv6 addresses in several ways.

- IPv4 addresses use 32 bits as opposed to the 128 bits used in IPv6 addressing.
- While implementing IPv4 addresses, IPSec is optional. However, IPSec is not optional in IPv6 addresses.
- The header information structure is different between IPv4 and IPv6 addresses.

Implement IPv6 Addresses

IPv6 has many advanced features that are not available in IPv4. Although IPv6 is being implemented in test and production networks, IPv4 is implemented on a larger scale. As there are many IPv4 networks, when implementing IPv6 on a network, you need to follow these guidelines to ensure backward compatibility with IPv4.

Guidelines

To implement IPv6 on an IPv4 network, follow these guidelines:

- Implement IPv6 in phases throughout the organization.
- Ensure interoperability between IPv4 and IPv6 during the initial phase of the transition from IPv4 to IPv6, rather than trying to replace IPv4 completely with IPv6.
- Avoid using subnet masks while migrating your network to IPv6 as it is not necessary to use subnet masks in networks that implement IPv6. In case the existing IPv4 network uses subnet masks, they can be avoided.
- Remember that the network classes used in IPv4 will not apply to IPv6.
- Configure AAAA DNS records for IPv6 although IPv4 DNS services make use of A records.
- Upgrade the necessary hardware to support IPv6. This includes all nodes, hosts, and routers on the network.
- Ensure that the IPv6 environment, once implemented, is scalable to support the future requirements of your network.
- Ensure that IPv6 packets that are sent on an IPv4 network are encapsulated. This can be done by *tunneling*.

Example:

Jason Smith is the network administrator in OGC Technologies. His team was recently involved in migrating the IPv4 address space to IPv6. In the deployment planning meeting, the team agreed to implement IPv6 progressively to ensure that any issues that came up during transition could be resolved. As most of the hardware, such as routers, needed to be replaced before the actual implementation, Jason placed procurement orders for all IPv6–compatible hardware that would be needed.

The team also updated current A records in the DNS to AAAA which IPv6 supported. As the network classes used in the IPv4 environment no longer applied to IPv6, he created new network classes to suit IPv6. Since OGC had planned to progressively migrate to IPv6, a considerable part of the network was still working on IPv4. The IPv6 data packets were also encapsulated so that they could be transmitted on the IPv4 network.

ACTIVITY 6-6
Implementing IPv6 Addressing

Scenario:

In this activity, you will identify components of the IPv6 protocol.

---

1. **Which is not a limitation of IPv4?**
    a) 128–bit address space.
    b) Depletion of Class A and B network addresses.
    c) Unassigned and unused address ranges.
    d) Division of the address space into fixed classes.

---

2. **True or False? IPv6 data packets cannot be sent on IPv4 networks.**
    __ True
    __ False

---

3. **What are the factors that an organization may need to consider before upgrading to IPv6?**

---

4. **True or False? DNS A records are compatible with IPv6.**
    __ True
    __ False

---

5. **What will be the reasons for the widespread future deployment of IPv6?**

TOPIC F
Delivery Techniques

In terms of network data delivery, you have identified two pieces of the puzzle—data addressing and network connection mechanisms. Once you have the data properly packaged and addressed, and a functional network connection established between the source and destination computers, you are ready to transmit data across the network. In this topic, you will identify the techniques that ensure that data is transmitted completely and accurately across a network.

Data that is sent through a network can encounter several variables that can delay or even alter the data before it is received. The challenge for network administrators is to implement delivery techniques within the network to ensure the integrity of data transmission across the network. When implemented, these delivery techniques can detect errors in data transmissions and recover from the errors using recovery mechanisms.

Connections

A *connection* is a virtual link between two nodes established for the duration of a communication session. Connections provide flow control, packet sequencing, and error recovery functions to ensure reliable communications between nodes.

Connection Services

Connection services ensure reliable delivery by detecting and attempting to correct transmission problems.

Connection Service	*Description*
Unacknowledged connectionless	This service provides no acknowledgement of successfully transmitted data. The application must provide its own reliability checks. Simplex communications use this type of service.
Acknowledged connectionless	Nodes do not establish a virtual connection. However, they do acknowledge the successful receipt of packets. Web (HTTP) communications use this type of connection service.
Connection-oriented	Nodes establish a virtual connection for the duration of the session. Nodes negotiate communication parameters and typically share security information to establish a connection. This connection service provides the means for flow control, packet sequencing, and error recovery functions. Traditional, non-web-based networking applications often use connection-oriented services.

Connection Modes

There are three commonly used connections modes.

Connection Mode	Description
Simplex	The *simplex* mode of communication is the one-way transmission of information. There is no return path. Because the transmission operates in only one direction, simplex mode can use the full bandwidth of the medium for transmission. Radio and television broadcasts are simplex mode transmissions.
Half duplex	The *half duplex* mode of communication permits two-way communications, but in only one direction at a time. When one device sends, the other must receive; then they can switch roles to transfer information in the other direction. Half duplex mode can use the full bandwidth of the medium because the transmission takes place in only one direction at a time.
Full duplex	The *full duplex* mode of communication permits simultaneous two-way communications. A device can both send and receive data simultaneously. Sending and receiving can occur over different channels or on the same channel. Generally, neither the sender nor the receiver can use the full bandwidth for their individual transmission because transmissions are allowed in both directions simultaneously. Full duplex mode also may be called a bi-directional transmission. If someone speaks about "duplex" transmissions, they likely are referring to the full-duplex mode. Telephone systems are full duplex devices—all persons involved can talk simultaneously. Many modern networking cards support the full duplex mode.

There are full bandwidth transmissions in some network environments, namely full-duplexed switched Ethernet.

Flow Control

Flow control is a technique for optimizing data exchange between systems. If too much data is sent at once, the receiving node can become overwhelmed, dropping packets that arrive too quickly to process. If too little data is sent, the receiver sits idle waiting for more data to arrive. Buffering and data windows are two flow control techniques commonly used in computer networking.

Buffering

Definition:

Buffering is a flow control technique in which data received is stored on a temporary high-speed memory location, called a buffer, until the main system components are ready to work with the data. In a networking situation, the network card itself handles buffering so that the processor does not have to become involved. Buffering is also used when reading information from the disk or RAM, in which case the buffer is more often called a *cache.*

Example: Cache Controller

A cache controller, a specialized processor chip, manages caching so that the processor does not have to.

Flooding

Even with a high-speed buffer, data can sometimes arrive too quickly to be handled. This situation is called *flooding*. To avoid flooding, receiving devices typically send a squelch signal to the sender when the buffer is approximately 75 percent full. Upon receiving a squelch signal, the sender will slow or halt further data transmissions until the receiver catches up.

Data Windows

Data windows constitute a flow control technique in which multiple packets are sent as a unit called a block or a window. The recipient acknowledges each window rather than each packet, resulting in higher throughput. Two types of data windows are available: fixed length and sliding. Data windows define how much data can be sent without waiting for an acknowledgment. The flow control window, whose size is set by the receiver, ensures that packets are sent in the same speed as the receiver's processing. The size of a data window is set by a sender.

In the simplest case, a sender transmits one packet and then waits for an acknowledgement from the recipient, an ACK signal. If the recipient is busy, the sender sits idle until it receives the ACK, after which it sends the next packet. Throughput can be increased if data is sent in larger packages, with the recipient sending fewer acknowledgements.

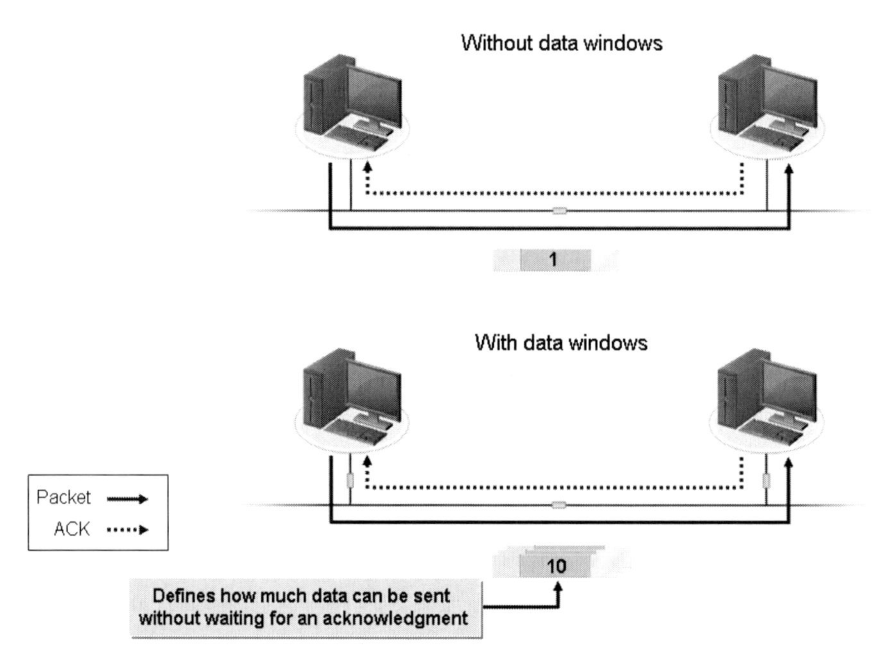

Figure 6-22: *Multiple packets sent as a block.*

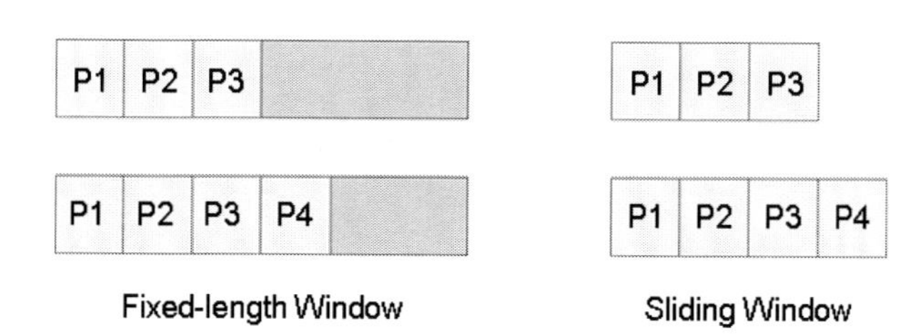

Figure 6-23: *Data window sizes can be fixed or variable.*

Fixed Length and Sliding Windows

The data window size can be fixed or variable. With *fixed length windows*, every block contains the same number of packets. To avoid flooding the buffers of some devices, fixed length windows are typically small. So, while fixed length windows are more efficient than sending individual packets, they are less efficient than sliding windows.

Sliding windows use variable block sizes. The first block sent contains a small number of packets. Each subsequent block is a bit larger, until the sender floods the buffers of the recipient. Upon receiving the squelch signal, the sender reduces the window size and resumes transmission. The window size is continually reevaluated during transmission, with the sender always attempting to send the largest window it can to speed throughput.

Error Detection

Error detection is the process of determining if transmitted data has been received correctly and completely. Typically, the sender attaches extra bits in the form of an *Error Detection Code (EDC)* to the footer of the transmitted data to indicate its original contents. The receiver generates an EDC and compares it with the transmitted EDC to determine if the data has been altered en route.

- If the EDCs match, the receiver processes the data.
- If the receiver finds an error, it requests retransmission of data.

Error detection can also include a correction component, *Error Detection and Correction (EDAC)*, wherein if data has an error, the receiver can rebuild the data.

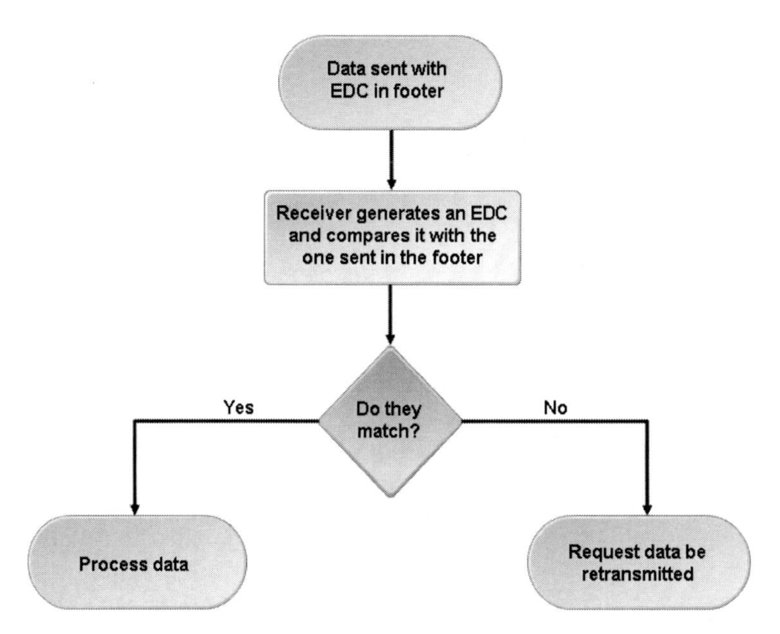

Figure 6-24: *The error detection process.*

Parity Check

Parity check is a process used to detect errors in memory or data communication. In this process:

1. A computer checks the data sent and received on a word-by-word basis.
2. The sender adds one bit to each word of the data and then transmits to the receiver.
3. The receiver compares the number of ones within a transmitted byte to those received.
4. If the count matches, the data is assumed to be valid. If a word is determined to be corrupt, the receiver requests retransmission of the data.

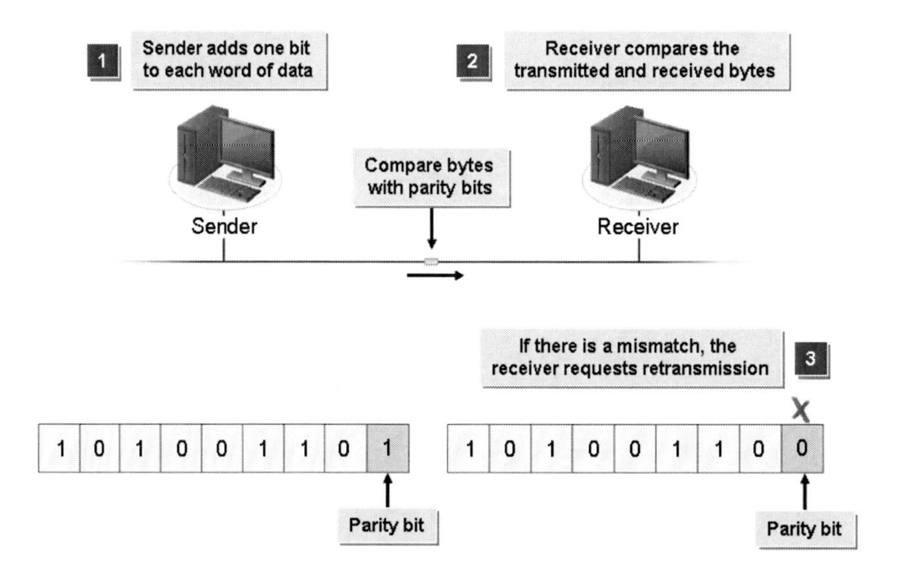

Figure 6-25: *Parity check detects errors during data communication.*

Cyclic Redundancy Check

Cyclic Redundancy Check (CRC) is an error detection method in which a predefined mathematical operation is used to calculate a CRC code. In this error detection process:

1. The sender attaches the CRC to a block of data and transmits it to a receiver.
2. The receiver calculates its own CRC value for the data block and compares it to the transmitted CRC.
3. If the values match, the receiver assumes the data was unaltered during transmission.

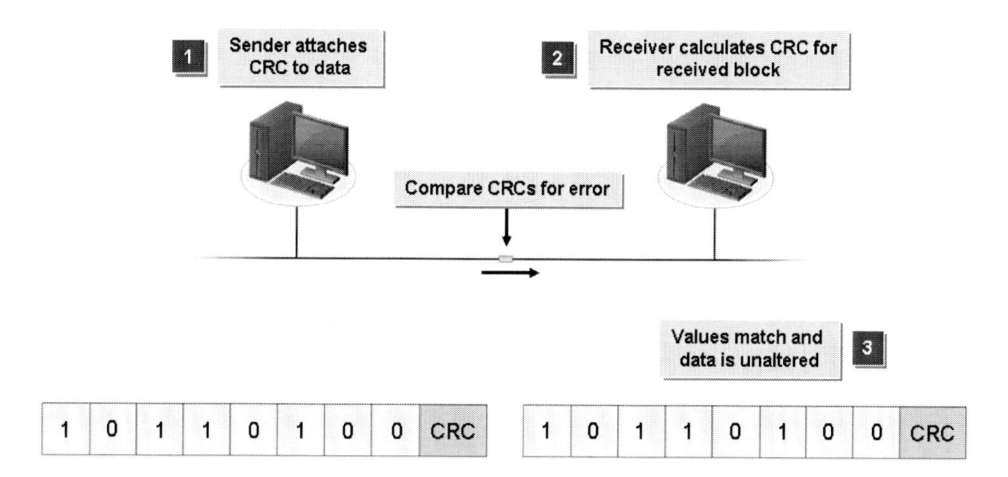

Figure 6-26: *CRC used to detect errors in transmitted data.*

CRC Considerations

Typically, CRC checks are applied to large blocks of data, such as all the data sent in a packet. Thus, fewer error detection bits must be transmitted with the data in a packet. However, if a CRC check fails, the entire block must be retransmitted. In general, though, CRC checking uses less network bandwidth than parity checking.

ACTIVITY 6-7
Identifying Data Delivery Techniques

Scenario:
In this activity, you will identify the characteristics of reliable data delivery techniques.

---

1. **Which are techniques for error detection?**
   a) Sliding windows
   b) Parity checking
   c) CRC
   d) EDAC

---

2. **True or False? Parity checking adds overhead to network transmissions.**
   __ True
   __ False

---

3. **Which statement is true of sliding and fixed length windows?**
   a) Sliding windows are groups of packets selected at random from transmitted data, whereas fixed length windows always include the same sequence of packets.
   b) Fixed length windows always contain the same number of packets, while sliding windows contain 8, 16, or 32 packets.
   c) Sliding windows contain a variable number of packets in a block, while fixed length windows always contain the same number.
   d) Fixed length windows contain a variable number of packets in a block, while sliding windows always contain the same number.

---

4. **Buffer flooding is the process of:**
   a) Sending data at a speed the receiver can handle.
   b) Corrupting the buffers in the receiver.
   c) Filling the buffer of the receiver with padding (empty) packets.
   d) Overfilling the buffers in the receiver.

---

5. **Match the error detection technique with the amount of data that it checks.**

___	Parity check	a. Packet
___	CRC	b. Block
___	EDAC	c. Byte

Lesson 6 Follow-up

In this lesson, you learned how data is delivered to its intended destination reliably and unaltered by using data addressing, connection mechanisms, and techniques that ensure the reliable delivery of data. Using this knowledge, you can ensure that when users make a request for a network service or send data across your network, their request or data arrives at the intended destination.

1. **In your opinion, which class of IP address will suit your organization?**

2. **Which delivery techniques will you implement most often on your network?**

7 TCP/IP Services

Lesson Time: 3 hour(s), 20 minutes

Lesson Objectives:

In this lesson, you will identify the major services deployed on TCP/IP networks.

You will:

- Assign IP addresses statically and dynamically.
- Identify host name resolution methods on a TCP/IP network.
- Identify common TCP/IP commands and their functions.
- Identify the common protocols and services in use on a TCP/IP network.
- Identify various TCP/IP interoperability services.

Introduction

In the previous lesson, you learned how the TCP/IP protocol suite uses IP addressing on networks to enable communication. The TCP/IP protocol suite also includes services that aid in managing your TCP/IP network. In this lesson, you will learn how the services that are part of the TCP/IP protocol suite can be used on your network.

To manage a TCP/IP network, you need to understand IP addressing methods. But you also have to be able to implement an addressing scheme, and support it on an ongoing basis. To do that, you will need to understand and use TCP/IP services and tools that enable you to configure, monitor, and troubleshoot your TCP/IP network.

This lesson covers all or part of the following CompTIA® Network+® (Exam N10-005) certification objectives:

- Topic A:
  - 1.2 Classify how applications, devices, and protocols relate to the OSI model layers.
  - 1.3 Explain the purpose and properties of IP addressing.
  - 1.5 Identify common TCP and UDP default ports.
  - 1.6 Explain the function of common networking protocols.
  - 2.3 Explain the purpose and properties of DHCP.
  - 4.3 Given a scenario, use appropriate software tools to troubleshoot connectivity issues.
- Topic B:

    - 1.2 Classify how applications, devices, and protocols relate to the OSI model layers.
    - 1.6 Explain the function of common networking protocols.
    - 1.7 Summarize DNS concepts and its components.
- Topic C:
    - 1.2 Classify how applications, devices, and protocols relate to the OSI model layers.
    - 4.3 Given a scenario, use appropriate software tools to troubleshoot connectivity issues.
- Topic D:
    - 1.6 Explain the function of common networking protocols.
- Topic E:
    - 1.6 Explain the function of common networking protocols.
    - 5.2 Explain the methods of network access security.

TOPIC A

Assign IP Addresses

You have learned that each node needs an IP address to communicate on a TCP/IP network. An administrator can manually assign these IP addresses or the assignment can be done automatically without manual intervention. In this topic, you will learn the different methods for assigning IP addresses to your nodes, and how to use the tools that support IP address assignment.

Depending on the scope and size of your network, it may be just as easy to manually assign IP addresses to all your nodes as it is to install and maintain a service to do it for you dynamically. By understanding the different methods available to you for assigning IP addresses, you can choose the method that best suits your network.

Static and Dynamic IP Addressing

On a TCP/IP network, you can assign IP address information statically to nodes by manually entering IP addressing information on each individual network node. Or, you can assign IP addresses dynamically, by using the *Dynamic Host Configuration Protocol (DHCP)* service.

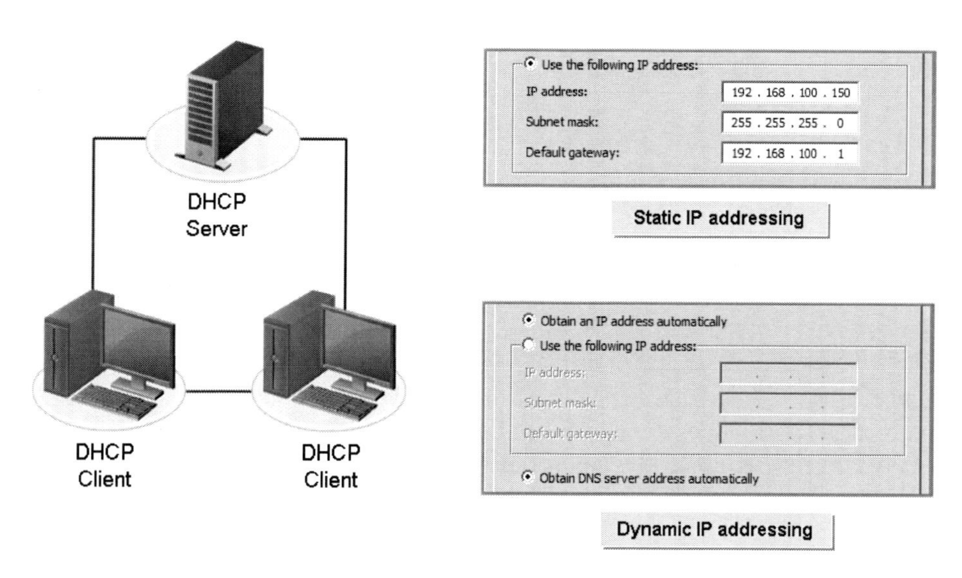

Figure 7-1: *Static and dynamic IP addresses assignment.*

Static IP Address Assignment

Configuring TCP/IP statically on a network requires that an administrator visit each node to manually enter IP address information for that node. If the node moves to a different subnet, the administrator must manually reconfigure the node's TCP/IP information for its new network location. In a large network, configuring TCP/IP statically on each node can be very time consuming, and prone to errors that can potentially disrupt communication on the network. Static addresses are typically only assigned to systems with a dedicated functionality, such as router interfaces, network-attached printers, or servers that host applications on a network.

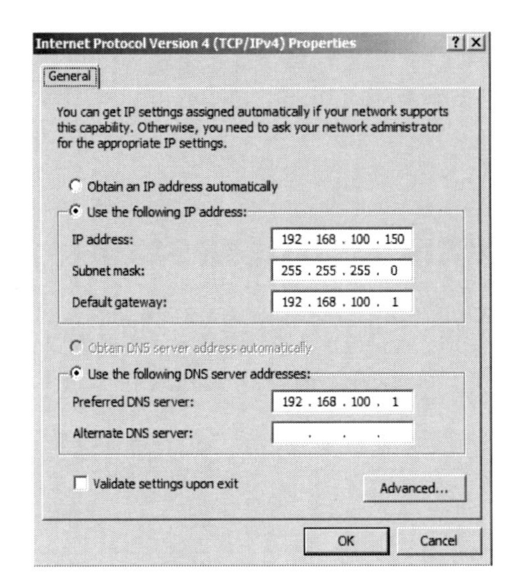

Figure 7-2: *Static IP address assignment using the Internet Protocol (TCP/IP) Properties dialog box.*

DHCP

DHCP is a network service that automatically assigns IP addresses and other TCP/IP configuration information on network nodes configured as DHCP clients. A DHCP server allocates IP addresses to DHCP clients dynamically, and should be configured with at least one DHCP *scope*. The DHCP server is configured with IP addresses that it can use, called a scope.

When a DHCP server enables the scope, it automatically leases TCP/IP information to DHCP clients for a defined lease period. The scope contains a range of IP addresses and a subnet mask, and can contain other options, such as a default gateway and DNS addresses. A scope also needs to specify the duration of the lease, and usage of an IP address after which the node needs to renew the lease with the DHCP server. The DHCP server determines this duration, which can be set for a defined time period or for an unlimited length of time.

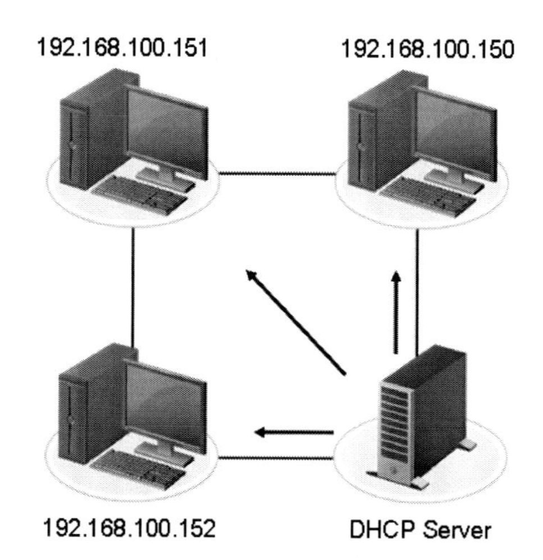

Figure 7-3: *A DHCP server dynamically assigns IP addresses to clients.*

DHCP Options

DHCP options allow you to enable and configure specific values and their assignment and distribution to DHCP clients based on the different parameters such as the scope, server, class or client-specific levels. DHCP options allow you to specify the names of DNS servers and domain suffixes. This will be useful when there are a number of DNS servers on the same network and you want to specify a particular DNS server or a specific domain for your DHCP client. The DHCP options can be modified from the **DHCP Options Properties** dialog box.

There are different categories of options for DHCP. These options will always apply to all clients unless overridden by other settings at the client's end.

Category	*Description*
Global options	Includes options that are applicable globally for all DHCP servers and their clients.
Scope options	Includes options that are applicable to clients that obtain leases within a particular scope.
Class options	Includes options that are applicable to clients that specify a class when obtaining a scope lease.
Reserved client options	Includes options that are applicable to any client with a scope reservation for its IP address.

DHCP Reservations

Reservations are lease assignments in DHCP that allow you to configure a permanent IP address for a particular client on the subnet. Reserved IP addresses differ from statically configured IP addresses; in case of any changes in network parameters on the DHCP server, IP addresses receive the changes when they renew their lease.

The DHCP Lease Process

The DHCP lease process comprises several steps.

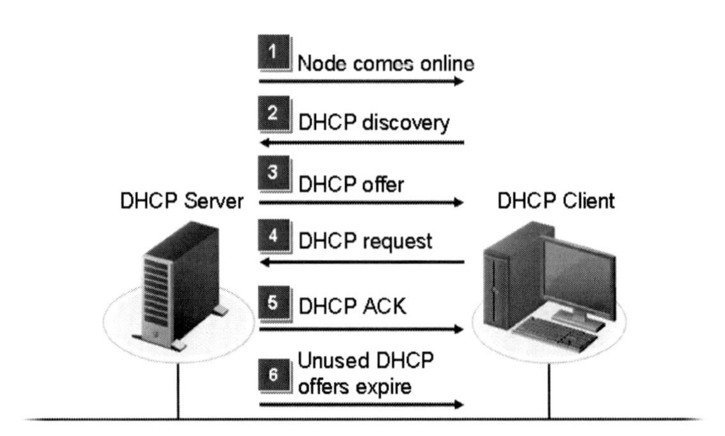

Figure 7-4: *Steps in the DHCP lease process.*

Step	***Description***
Step 1: Node comes online	A node configured to use DHCP comes online and loads a simple version of TCP/IP.
Step 2: DHCP discovery	After a node comes online and is ready to communicate with a DHCP server, it transmits a Bootstrap Protocol (*BOOTP*) broadcast, called a DHCP discover, to the network's broadcast address of 255.255.255.255 to check if any DHCP servers are online, and request an IP address.
Step 3: DHCP offer	DHCP servers that are online respond with a directed lease offer packet that contains an IP address that the node can lease.
Step 4: DHCP request	The node accepts the first offer it receives, and returns a request to lease the IP address from the DHCP server, called a DHCP request.
Step 5: DHCP ACK	The DHCP server acknowledges the request from the node with a DHCP ACK, that has the IP address and settings required for the leasing time and starts the lease. The DHCP server also updates the IP address in its database as being in use to avoid reassigning the address.
Step 6: Unused DHCP offers expire	When the unused offers expire, all the other DHCP servers return the offered IP addresses to the common pool in their DHCP scopes.

Use the acronym DORA to remember the steps in DHCP lease process: **D**iscover, **O**ffer, **R**equest, **A**cknowledge.

All DHCP servers respond to clients the same way despite which vendor they are manufactured by because the process follows a standard methodology.

BOOTP

Any device on the network will need to know its IP address before it can communicate. Although usually a host can read this information from its internal disk, some devices do not have storage, so they need other devices on the network to provide them with an IP address and other information so that they can become IP hosts. This process is called bootstrapping, and to provide this capability, BOOTP was created.

BOOTP is a UDP network protocol. BOOTP servers assign IP addresses from a pool of available addresses. BOOTP enables "diskless workstation" computers to obtain an IP address prior to loading an advanced operating system.

DHCP Relay Agent

A DHCP relay agent is a service that captures a BOOTP broadcast and forwards it through the router as a unicast transmission to the DHCP server on another subnet. BOOTP uses a local broadcast that cannot be sent through routers on the network. As an administrator of a TCP/IP network using DHCP, you must either have a DHCP server on each subnet and configure the router to forward the broadcasts, or configure a *DHCP relay agent.* Having multiple DHCP servers also ensures a higher degree of fault tolerance as the unavailability of a DHCP server on a subnet does not prevent nodes from requesting or renewing their leases.

The DHCP server returns an offer to the relay agent, which in turn presents the offer to the client. Once the client has its lease, it also has the DHCP server's IP address, so it does not need to use the relay agent to renew the lease. An important factor you need to consider on a network with multiple subnets is that the routers on the network must be RFC 1542–compliant to allow a DHCP server to receive the broadcast message from a node.

IP Addresses Recovery

The DHCP lease process is important to the overall performance of a DHCP system. By leasing addresses to clients instead of permanently assigning them, a DHCP server can recover addresses leased to offline clients that no longer need the addresses.

APIPA

Automatic Private IP Addressing (APIPA) is a service that enables a DHCP client computer to configure itself automatically with an IP address in the range of 169.254.0.1 to 169.254.255.254, in case no DHCP servers respond to the client's DHCP discover broadcast. In case of a DHCP server failure, when the clients on the network cannot obtain IP addresses, the clients can use APIPA to assign themselves an IP address in the 169.254.x.x address range to enable communication with other clients. Thus, APIPA enables DHCP clients to initialize TCP/IP and communicate on the local subnet even in the absence of an active DHCP scope. APIPA addresses are not routable, so computers with APIPA addresses cannot communicate outside of the local subnet.

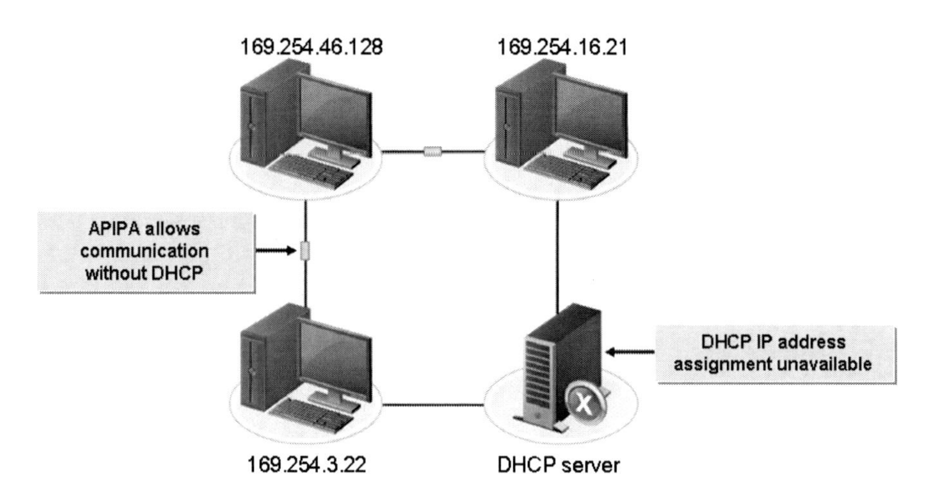

Figure 7-5: *Automatic assigned private IP addresses.*

If a client cannot reach destinations outside of the local subnet, check the machine's IP address. If the client shows an APIPA address, it signals that the DHCP server is unavailable.

APIPA Support

APIPA is available on client systems including: Windows XP, and Windows 7 and server operating systems including: Windows 2008 and Windows 2008 R2. Because APIPA requires no administrative configuration, APIPA addressing can be used for small offices where local subnet communication is all that is required.

IP Configuration Utilities

You can use the IP configuration utility for your operating system to see TCP/IP configuration information.

Utility	*Description*
ipconfig	Displays connection-specific DNS suffix, IP address, subnet mask, and default gateway information. Must be run from a command line. To display additional information about the IP configuration, use the `ipconfig /all` parameter with the command. Supported on server systems including Windows Server 2008 and Windows Server 2008 R2, and client systems including Windows 7, Windows XP, Windows NT, and Novell® NetWare®.
ifconfig	Displays the status of currently active network interface devices. Using options, you can dynamically change the status of the interfaces and their IP address. Supported on Linux and UNIX.
dhclient	Allows you to configure and manage DHCP settings on the network interfaces of a computer. Supported on Linux and UNIX.

ipconfig Options for DHCP

The Windows `ipconfig` utility provides options for managing dynamic address leases:

- `ipconfig /release` forces the release of an IP address used by a client.
- `ipconfig /renew` requests the renewal of an IP address for a client.

The system first attempts to obtain a DHCP address, and if a DHCP server fails to respond, it will switch to APIPA addressing.

The ping Command

The `ping` command is used to verify the network connectivity of a computer, and also to check to see if the target system is active. It verifies the IP address, host name, and reachability of the remote system by using and listening for echo replies. `ping` uses ICMP to check the connections with remote hosts by sending out echo requests as `ICMP ECHO_REQUEST` packets to the host whose name or IP address you specify on the command line. `ping` listens for reply packets.

`ping` is an acronym for packet Internet groper.

```
C:\>ping 192.168.1.200
Pinging 192.168.1.200 with 32 bytes of data:
Reply from 192.168.1.200: bytes=32 time<1ms TTL=128
Reply from 192.168.1.200: bytes=32 time<1ms TTL=128
Reply from 192.168.1.200: bytes=32 time<1ms TTL=128
Reply from 192.168.1.200: bytes=32 time<1ms TTL=128

Ping statistics for 192.168.1.200:
    Packets: Sent = 4, Received = 4, Lost = 0 (0% loss),
Approximate round trip times in milli-seconds:
    Minimum = 0ms, Maximum = 0ms, Average = 0ms
```

Figure 7-6: *Using ping tests the connectivity between two hosts.*

Syntax of ping command

The syntax of the `ping` command is:

`ping` *`target`*

The *`target`* variable specifies the IP address or DNS name of a computer on the network. Ping uses the DNS setting to resolve the DNS name into an IP address.

ping Options

You can ping a computer or an IP address. You can also ping the loopback address (127.0.0.1) to test whether TCP/IP has initialized on an individual system. If the computer has a default gateway, you can ping remote systems.

To list other options for the `ping` command, enter `ping/?` at the command prompt. Some of the options include setting the packet size, changing the *Time To Live (TTL)* value, and specifying how many times to ping the host.

- **Packet size:** By default, data packets are sent as 32 bytes. You can specify a larger size to test response time, the maximum size being 65,500 bytes. To change the packet size, use the `-l` option followed by the packet length.

  `ping` *`target`* `[-l` *`size`*`]`

- **TTL:** A value that determines how many hops an IP packet can travel before being discarded.

  `ping` *`target`* `[-i` *`TTL`*`]`

- **Packet Count:** Specifies the number of packets with which a remote host is pinged. The default is four packets. You can specify a higher number of packets with the `-n` option.

  ping *target* [-n *packet count*]

ping Blocking

As a security measure, some public Internet hosts and routers might be configured to block incoming packets that are generated by the `ping` command. (They might also block packets from other TCP/IP diagnostic utilities such as the `tracert` command.) Pinging these hosts will fail even if the host is online. Keep this in mind when you try to ping large public Internet sites; if you are trying to determine if one of these sites is up and running, a better method is simply to use a web browser to connect to the site directly.

Ports

Definition:

In TCP and UDP networks, a *port* is the endpoint of a logical connection. Client computers connect to specific server programs through a designated port. All ports are assigned a number in a range from 0 to 65,535. The IANA separates port numbers into three blocks: well-known ports, which are preassigned to system processes by IANA; registered ports, which are available to user processes and are listed as a convenience by IANA; and dynamic ports, which are assigned by a client operating system as needed when there is a request for service.

Three well recognized blocks of port numbers are available for use in DHCP.

Block	*Description*
Well-known ports	**Port range:** 0 to 1,023 These ports are preassigned for use by common, or well-known services. Often the services that run on these ports must be started by a privileged user. Services in this range include HTTP on TCP port 80, IMAP on TCP port 143, and DNS on UDP port 53.
Registered ports	**Port range:** 1,024 to 49,151 These ports are registered by software makers for use by specific applications and services that are not as well-known as the services in the well-known range. Services in the registered port range include SOCKS proxy on TCP port 1080, Kazaa peer-to-peer file sharing on TCP port 1214, and Xbox Live on TCP and UDP port 3074.
Dynamic or private ports	**Port range:** 49,152 to 65,535 These ports are set aside for use by unregistered services, and by services needing a temporary connection.

Example:

Well-Known TCP Port Numbers

The commonly used TCP port numbers are listed in the table along with the services run using the ports.

Port Number	Service Name	Service
7	echo	Ping
20	ftp-data	File Transfer [Default Data]
21	ftp	File Transfer [Control]
22	ssh	SSH
23	telnet	Telnet
25	smtp	SMTP
53	dns	DNS
67	bootps	DHCP (BOOTP) server
68	bootpc	DHCP (BOOTP) client
80	http	HTTP
110	pop3	POP3
137	netbios	NetBIOS naming service
143	imap	IMAP
194	irc	Internet Relay Chat (IRC)
389	ldap	LDAP
443	https	HTTP-secure
546	dhcpv6-client	DHCPv6 client
547	dhcpv6-server	DHCPv6 server
3389	rdp	RDP

The complete list of well-known TCP ports and other port number assignments is available online at **www.iana.org/assignments/port-numbers**

Well-Known UDP Port Numbers

The commonly used UDP port numbers are listed in the table along with the services run using the ports.

Port Number	Service Name	Service
7	echo	Ping
22	ssh	SSH
23	telnet	Telnet
53	dns	DNS
67	bootps	DHCP (BOOTP) server
68	bootpc	DHCP (BOOTP) client
69	tftp	TFTP
123	ntp	NTP
137	netbios	NetBIOS naming service

Port Number	Service Name	Service
143	imap	IMAP
161	snmp	SNMP
389	ldap	LDAP
546	dhcpv6-client	DHCPv6 client
547	dhcpv6-server	DHCPv6 server
3389	rdp	RDP

The complete list of well-known UDP ports and other port number assignments is available online at **www.iana.org/assignments/port-numbers**

Sockets

Definition:

A *socket* is a communication endpoint in an IP-based network. In TCP/IP, a socket links an IP address with the port number of a service. Sockets help in delivering data packets to the appropriate application process running in the target node. A socket address is the combination of the protocol, IP address, and port number.

Socket Format

Used to identify the target node, a socket employs the format:

```
{protocol, ip address, port number}
```

Example:

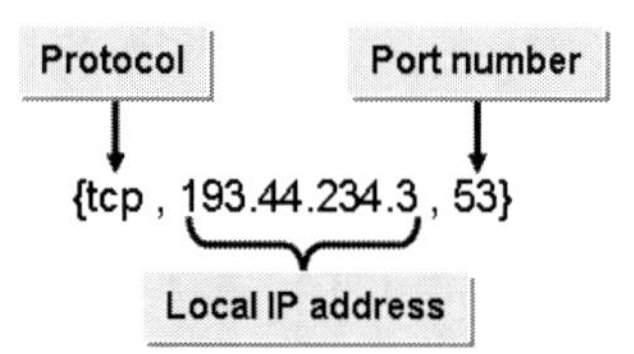

Figure 7-7: *Format of an IP address socket.*

How to Assign IP Addresses

Procedure Reference: Assign IP Addresses

To assign IP addresses:

1. Choose **Start→Network.**
2. In the Network window, on the toolbar, click **Network and Sharing Center.**
3. In the Network and Sharing Center window, in the left pane, click the **Change adapter settings** link.
4. Right-click your Local Area Connection object and choose **Properties.**
5. In the Local Area Connection Properties dialog box, in the **This connection uses the following items** section, select **Internet Protocol Version 4 (TCP/IPv4).**
6. Click **Properties,** and in the **Internet Protocol Version 4 (TCP/IPv4) Properties** dialog box, on the **General** tab, assign an IP address to your system.
   - To use automatic IP addressing for the IP address, subnet mask, and default gateway, select the **Obtain an IP address automatically** option.
   - To manually configure a static IP address, subnet mask, and default gateway.
     a. Select the **Use the following IP address** option.
     b. In the **IP address, Subnet mask,** and **Default gateway** text boxes, enter the TCP/IP information for your network.
7. In the **Internet Protocol Version 4 (TCP/IPv4) Properties** dialog box, configure the IP address of your DNS server.
   - To automatically configure the IP address for a DNS server, select the **Obtain DNS server address automatically** option.
   - To manually configure a static DNS server address.
     a. Select the **Use the following DNS server addresses** option.
     b. In the **Preferred DNS server** and **Alternate DNS server** text boxes, enter the DNS server addresses for your network.
8. Click **OK** to close the **Internet Protocol Version 4 (TCP/IPv4) Properties** dialog box.
9. Click **Close** to close the Local Area Connection Properties dialog box for your selected network connection.

ACTIVITY 7-1

Assigning IP Addresses Manually

There is a simulated version of this activity available on the CD-ROM that shipped with this course. You can run this simulation on any Windows computer to review the activity after class, or as an alternative to performing the activity as a group in class. The activity simulation can be launched either directly from the CD-ROM by clicking the **Interactives** link and navigating to the appropriate one, or from the installed data file location by opening the C:\Data\Simulations\Lesson#\Activity# folder and double-clicking the executable (.exe) file.

Before You Begin:

Your computer is currently configured to lease an IP address from the classroom DHCP server.

Scenario:

You are a network administrator for a start-up company with leased addresses from their ISP in the range of 192.168.1.25 to 192.168.1.95. The subnet mask is 255.255.255.0, and the IP address of the DNS server is 192.168.1.200. The DNS server is also the default gateway on the network. You have been assigned the task of configuring their computers to use the IP addresses provided to them by their ISP.

This activity uses internal IP addresses in the 192.168.1.x range for demonstration purposes. An ISP would not allocate addresses in this range.

---

1. Configure your computer with a static IP address.

- IP address = 192.168.1.##, where .##, is your student number.
- Subnet mask = 255.255.255.0
- Default gateway = 192.168.1.200
- DNS server = 192.168.1.200

a. Choose **Start→Control Panel.**

b. In the Control Panel window, in the **Adjust your computer's settings** section, click the **Network and Internet** link.

c. In the Network and Internet window, click the **Network and Sharing Center** link.

d. In the Network and Sharing Center window, in the left pane, click the **Change adapter settings** link.

e. Right-click **Local Area Connection** and choose **Properties.**

f. In the **Local Area Connection Properties** dialog box, in the **This connection uses the following items** section, select **Internet Protocol Version 4 (TCP/IPv4).** and click **Properties.**

g. In the **Internet Protocol Version 4 (TCP/IPv4) Properties** dialog box, on the **General** tab, select the **Use the following IP address** option.

h. In the **IP address** text box, click and type ***192.168.1.##***, where ***##*** is your student number.

i. Click the **Subnet mask** text box.

j. Observe that the default subnet mask for the IP address is auto populated.

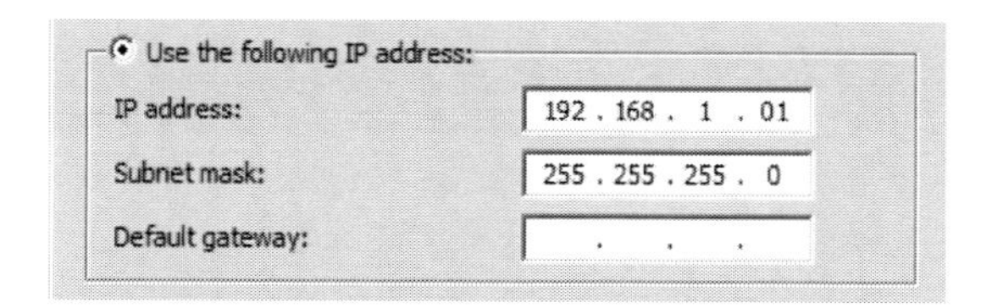

k. In the **Default gateway** text box, click and type ***192.168.1.200***

l. Verify that the **Use the following DNS server addresses** option is selected and in the **Alternate DNS server** text box, ***192.168.1.200*** is entered.

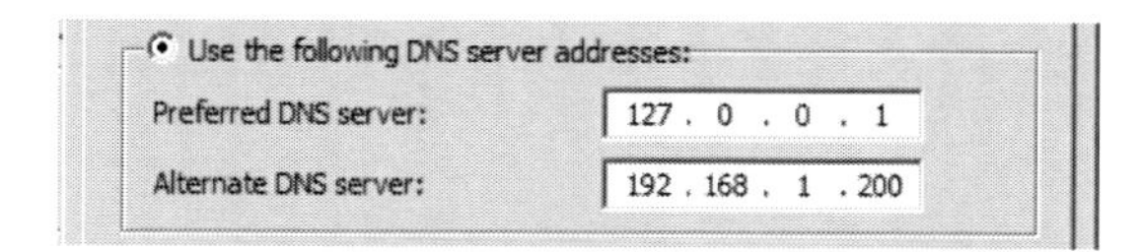

m. Click **OK** to close the **Internet Protocol Version 4 (TCP/IPv4) Properties** dialog box.

n. Click **Close** to close the **Local Area Connection Properties** dialog box. Close the Network Connections window.

---

2. Verify your IP information.

a. Choose **Start→Command Prompt** to open the Command Prompt window.

b. At the command prompt, enter **`ipconfig /all`** to view the network details.

c. Verify that, in the Command Prompt window, the **Ethernet adapter Local Area Connection** section displays the IP address, subnet mask, default gateway, and DNS server information you entered.

```
Ethernet adapter Local Area Connection:

   Connection-specific DNS Suffix  . :
   Description . . . . . . . . . . . : Realtek RTL8139/810x Family Fast Ethernet
 NIC
   Physical Address. . . . . . . . . : 00-80-48-5C-98-D1
   DHCP Enabled. . . . . . . . . . . : No
   Autoconfiguration Enabled . . . . : Yes
   IPv4 Address. . . . . . . . . . . : 192.168.1.1(Preferred)
   Subnet Mask . . . . . . . . . . . : 255.255.255.0
   Default Gateway . . . . . . . . . : 192.168.1.200
   DNS Servers . . . . . . . . . . . : 192.168.1.200
   NetBIOS over Tcpip. . . . . . . . : Enabled
```

---

3. Test your ability to communicate over TCP/IP with the DNS server.

a. At the command prompt, enter **`ping 192.168.1.200`**

```
C:\Users\Administrator.CLASSNET>ping 192.168.1.200

Pinging 192.168.1.200 with 32 bytes of data:
Reply from 192.168.1.200: bytes=32 time<1ms TTL=128
Reply from 192.168.1.200: bytes=32 time<1ms TTL=128
Reply from 192.168.1.200: bytes=32 time<1ms TTL=128
Reply from 192.168.1.200: bytes=32 time<1ms TTL=128

Ping statistics for 192.168.1.200:
    Packets: Sent = 4, Received = 4, Lost = 0 (0% loss),
Approximate round trip times in milli-seconds:
    Minimum = 0ms, Maximum = 0ms, Average = 0ms
```

b. Observe that the `ping` command returns four replies indicating that the connection to the server was successfully established.

c. Close the Command Prompt window.

ACTIVITY 7-2

Assigning IP Addresses Using APIPA

There is a simulated version of this activity available on the CD-ROM that shipped with this course. You can run this simulation on any Windows computer to review the activity after class, or as an alternative to performing the activity as a group in class. The activity simulation can be launched either directly from the CD-ROM by clicking the **Interactives** link and navigating to the appropriate one, or from the installed data file location by opening the C:\Data\Simulations\Lesson#\Activity# folder and double-clicking the executable (.exe) file.

Before You Begin:

Instructor Only Steps (to be performed only on the DC)

To deactivate the DHCP scope:

1. Log in as **Administrator** with ***!Pass1234*** as the password.
2. Choose **Start→Administrative Tools→DHCP.**
3. Expand your DHCP server object for IPv4.
4. Select and then right-click the scope object.
5. Choose **Deactivate.**
6. In the **DHCP** dialog box, click **Yes.**
7. Minimize the DHCP window.

Scenario:

You have been notified that there is a problem with the DHCP server and it will be unavailable for several hours. You need to use a TCP/IP addressing scheme so your client workstations can still communicate with one another using APIPA while the DHCP server is down.

---

1. Configure your computer to use APIPA.

a. Choose **Start→Control Panel.**

b. In the Control Panel window, in the **Adjust your computer's settings** section, click the **Network and Internet** link.

c. In the Network and Internet window, click the **Network and Sharing Center** link.

d. In the Network and Sharing Center window, in the left pane, click the **Change adapter settings** link.

e. Right-click **Local Area Connection** and choose **Properties.**

f. In the **Local Area Connection Properties** dialog box, in the **This connection uses the following items** section, select **Internet Protocol Version 4 (TCP/IPv4)** and click **Properties.**

g. In the **Internet Protocol Version 4 (TCP/IPv4) Properties** dialog box, select the **Obtain an IP address automatically** option and click **OK.**

h. In the **Local Area Connection Properties** dialog box, click **Close.**

i. Close Network Connections and the Network and Sharing Center windows.

---

2. Verify your IP information.

a. Choose **Start→Command Prompt** to open the Command Prompt window.

b. At the command prompt, enter **`ipconfig /all`**

> APIPA configuration can take a moment because the system first attempts to contact a DHCP server before self-assigning the APIPA address. If `ipconfig /all` shows your IP address and subnet mask as null (all zeros), wait a minute and run `ipconfig /all` again or type `ipconfig /renew`.

c. Verify that the **Ethernet adapter Local Area Connection** section displays the IP address and subnet mask from the 169.254.0.0 APIPA network.

```
Ethernet adapter Local Area Connection:

   Connection-specific DNS Suffix  . :
   Description . . . . . . . . . . . : Realtek RTL8139/810x Family Fast Ethernet
 NIC
   Physical Address. . . . . . . . . : 00-80-48-5C-98-D1
   DHCP Enabled. . . . . . . . . . . : Yes
   Autoconfiguration Enabled . . . . : Yes
   Autoconfiguration IPv4 Address. . : 169.254.206.67(Preferred)
   Subnet Mask . . . . . . . . . . . : 255.255.0.0
   Default Gateway . . . . . . . . . :
   NetBIOS over Tcpip. . . . . . . . : Enabled
```

---

3. Test your ability to communicate over TCP/IP with the DNS server.

a. At the command prompt, enter **`ping 192.168.1.200`**

b. Verify that the destination is unreachable and the error message "PING: transmit failed. General failure" is displayed. Because you are using a nonroutable APIPA address, you cannot communicate with the DNS server.

```
C:\Users\Administrator>ping 192.168.1.200

Pinging 192.168.1.200 with 32 bytes of data:
PING: transmit failed. General failure.
PING: transmit failed. General failure.
PING: transmit failed. General failure.
PING: transmit failed. General failure.

Ping statistics for 192.168.1.200:
    Packets: Sent = 4, Received = 0, Lost = 4 (100% loss),
```

---

4. Test your ability to communicate with another computer on the APIPA network.

a. At the command prompt, enter **`ping 169.254.`**`#.#` , where `#.#` is a part of the address of another computer in the classroom.

```
C:\Users\Administrator>ping 169.254.105.38

Pinging 169.254.105.38 with 32 bytes of data:
Reply from 169.254.105.38: bytes=32 time<1ms TTL=128
Reply from 169.254.105.38: bytes=32 time<1ms TTL=128
Reply from 169.254.105.38: bytes=32 time<1ms TTL=128
Reply from 169.254.105.38: bytes=32 time<1ms TTL=128

Ping statistics for 169.254.105.38:
    Packets: Sent = 4, Received = 4, Lost = 0 (0% loss),
Approximate round trip times in milli-seconds:
    Minimum = 0ms, Maximum = 0ms, Average = 0ms
```

b. Observe from the results that you are able to communicate with the other system on the APIPA network.

c. Close the Command Prompt window.

ACTIVITY 7-3
Assigning IP Addresses with DHCP

There is a simulated version of this activity available on the CD-ROM that shipped with this course. You can run this simulation on any Windows computer to review the activity after class, or as an alternative to performing the activity as a group in class. The activity simulation can be launched either directly from the CD-ROM by clicking the **Interactives** link and navigating to the appropriate one, or from the installed data file location by opening the C:\Data\Simulations\Lesson#\Activity# folder and double-clicking the executable (.exe) file.

Before You Begin:

Instructor Only Steps (to be performed only on the DC)

To activate the DHCP scope:

1. Maximize the DHCP window.
2. Right-click the scope object.
3. Choose **Activate.**
4. Close the DHCP window.

Scenario:

Your company has been experiencing problems with the DHCP server and it has been offline for several hours. You have just been notified that the server is back up and you can change the APIPA addressing back to DHCP addressing.

---

1. Force your computer to lease an IP address from the DHCP server.

   a. Choose **Start→Command Prompt** to open the Command Prompt window.

   b. In the Command Prompt window, enter **`ipconfig /renew`**

   c. Observe that the IPv4 address 192.168.1.## is obtained from the DHCP server.

---

2. Test your ability to communicate over TCP/IP with the DNS server.

   a. At the command prompt, enter **`ping 192.168.1.200`** to ping the DNS server.

   b. Observe that you are able to communicate with the DNS server. Enter **`exit`** to close the Command Prompt window.

TOPIC B

Domain Naming Services

Each node that has an IP address assigned to it also has a descriptive name that is more commonly used to identify it on the network. These descriptive names are easier for users to remember and use than their 32-bit IP addresses. In this topic, you will identify methods for host name resolution for TCP/IP networks.

Without host name resolution services, you have to connect to other computers and websites using their numeric IP addresses. However, for a user, it is easier to remember a descriptive name like **www.ourglobalcompany.com**, than its assigned 32-bit IP address: 74.43.216.152. When you configure host name resolution services on your network, you can connect to other computers and websites using their names rather than a string of numbers.

Host Names

Definition:

A *host name* is a unique name given to a node on a TCP/IP network. A host name combined with the host's *domain name* forms the node's *Fully Qualified Domain Name (FQDN)*. A name resolution service maps the FQDN of the node to its IP address so that users can use names instead of IP addresses to communicate with other network nodes and the Internet.

Example:

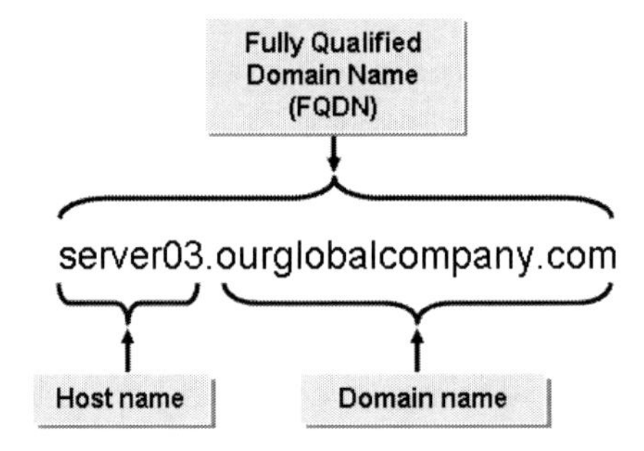

Figure 7-8: *A host name is a part of the FQDN of a server.*

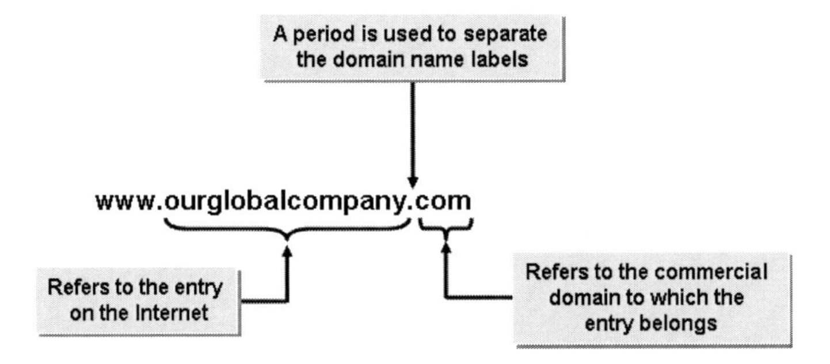

Figure 7-9: *Components of a domain name.*

FQDN

FQDNs are written using standard dot-delimited notation, and a dot separates each section of the name. The maximum length of an FQDN is 255 characters; each dot-delimited section can be up to 63 characters long. A network node can have more than one host name assigned to it. Its primary name is its host name; the other names are called canonical names (CNAMEs), also known as aliases.

Domains

A *domain* is a grouping of computers on the Internet based on the nature of their operations. A domain enables communication between its systems as a unit and other networks on the Internet, instead of maintaining individual connections for each of its systems. Although there are several types of domains, some of the common ones are commercial, governmental, and educational domains. Domains are identified by their unique names; for example, com, gov, and edu.

Domain Names

A domain name is a unique name that identifies an entity on the Internet. Also known as site names, domain names appear as part of the complete address of a web resource. They are usually registered by organizations as their website address. A period is used to separate domain name labels, which can have no more than 63 characters. Domain names are not case sensitive and they can be up to 255 characters in length.

Domain Names vs. Host Names

A domain name identifies a collection of computers and devices on the network of a particular domain. A host name is a unique name that identifies a specified computer or device in a network. Therefore, host names are subsets of domain names.

ACTIVITY 7-4

Identifying the Local Host Name

There is a simulated version of this activity available on the CD-ROM that shipped with this course. You can run this simulation on any Windows computer to review the activity after class, or as an alternative to performing the activity as a group in class. The activity simulation can be launched either directly from the CD-ROM by clicking the **Interactives** link and navigating to the appropriate one, or from the installed data file location by opening the C:\Data\Simulations\Lesson#\Activity# folder and double-clicking the executable (.exe) file.

Scenario:

In this activity, you will use different tools to identify your computer's host name.

---

1. Identify the host name and FQDN by using System Properties.

a. Choose **Start→Control Panel.**

b. In the Control Panel window, in the **Adjust your computer's settings** section, click the **System and Security** link.

c. In the System and Security window, in the right pane, in the **System** section, click the **See the name of this computer** link.

d. In the System window, in the **Computer name, domain, and workgroup settings** section, identify the computer's name.

e. In the **Full computer name** section, identify the computer's FQDN.

Computer name, domain, and workgroup settings

Computer name:	Computer01
Full computer name:	Computer01.Child01.Classnet.com
Computer description:	
Domain:	Child01.Classnet.com

f. Identify the host name from the first portion of the FQDN.

---

2. Identify the host name by using the `hostname` command.

a. Choose **Start→Command Prompt** to open the Command Prompt window.

b. In the Command Prompt window, enter **`hostname`** to display the host name of the system.

c. Observe the host name that is displayed.

---

3. Identify the FQDN by using the `ipconfig` command.

a. Enter **`ipconfig /all | more`** to view the first page of the network details.

b. Identify the host name and press the **Spacebar** to view the next page of the network details.

c. In the **Ethernet adapter Local Area Connection** section, in the **Connection-specific DNS Suffix** section, identify the DNS suffix.

d. Close the Command Prompt and System windows.

DNS

The *Domain Name System (DNS)* is a TCP/IP name resolution service that translates FQDNs into IP addresses. It consists of a system of hierarchical databases that are stored on separate DNS servers on all networks that connect to the Internet. These servers list IP addresses and related computer names. Because DNS servers store, maintain, and update databases, they respond to DNS client name resolution requests to translate host names into IP addresses. All these servers work together to resolve FQDNs. On internal networks, a local DNS service can resolve host names without using external DNS servers.

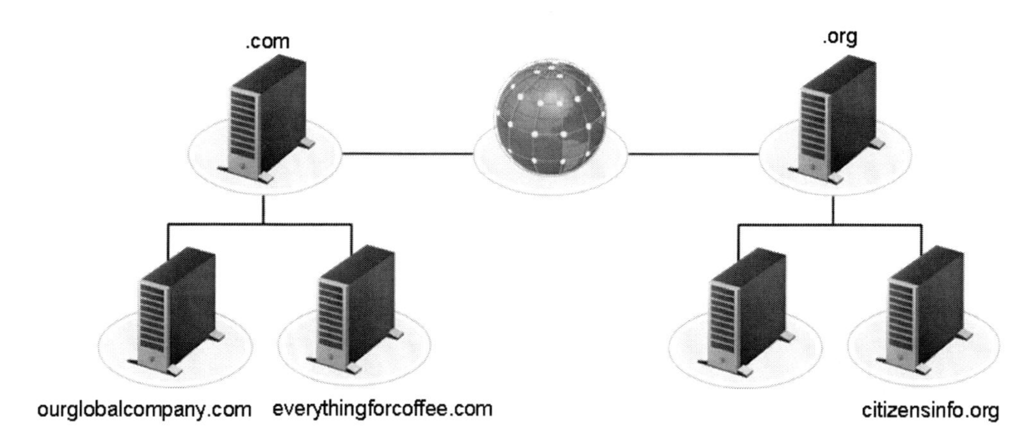

Figure 7-10: *DNS server domains.*

DNS Components

The DNS database is divided logically into a hierarchical grouping of domains. It is divided physically into files called *zones*. The zone files contain the actual IP-to-host name mappings for one or more domains. The zone file is stored on the DNS server that is responsible for resolving host names for the domains contained in the zone. For example, a zone might be responsible for mapping host names to IP addresses within the ourglobalcompany domain within the .com namespace. Each network node in that domain will have a host record within the domain's zone file. The record includes the node's host name, FQDN, and assigned IP address.

For example, a host named 2008srv in the ourglobalcompany.com domain might have an IP address of 74.43.216.152. That host would have a host record that maps the 2008srv.ourglobalcompany.com name to the IP address of 74.43.216.152. That host record will appear in the ourglobalcompany.com zone file on the DNS server that is responsible for the ourglobalcompany.com domain.

Static vs. Dynamic Records

Records can be entered into a DNS database either statically or dynamically. A static record is entered manually by an administrator and does not change unless the administrator manually updates it. A network node can request to add a dynamic DNS record that can change dynamically. For example, if a client is using DHCP to get its IP address, each time it leases a new address, it can request an update of its DNS host record.

Types of DNS Records

Different types of DNS records are available that serve specific purposes.

Record Type	***Purpose***
Address (A)	Maps a host name to its IP address using a 32-bit IPv4 address.
IPv6 address (AAAA)	Maps a host name to its IP address using a 128-bit IPv6 address.
Canonical name (CNAME)	Maps multiple canonical names (aliases) to an A record.
Mail Exchange (MX)	Maps a domain name to a mail exchange server list.
Name Server (NS)	Assigns a DNS zone to access the given authoritative name servers.
Pointer (PTR)	Maps an IP address to the host name for the purpose of reverse lookup.
Start of Authority (SOA)	Specifies authoritative information about a DNS zone.
Service Locator (SRV)	Specifies a generic service location record for newer protocols.

Authoritative Name Servers

An *Authoritative Name Server (ANS)* is a name server that responds to name-related queries in one or more zones. The most important function of the ANS is delegation, which means that part of a domain is delegated to other DNS servers. SOA is the first resource recording the zone.

The DNS Hierarchy

DNS names are built in a hierarchical structure. This allows DNS servers on the Internet to use a minimum number of queries to locate the source of a domain name. The top of the structure—represented by a period—contains root name servers. Below that is the top-level domain name, then the first-level domain name, and so on, until the FQDN for an individual host is complete.

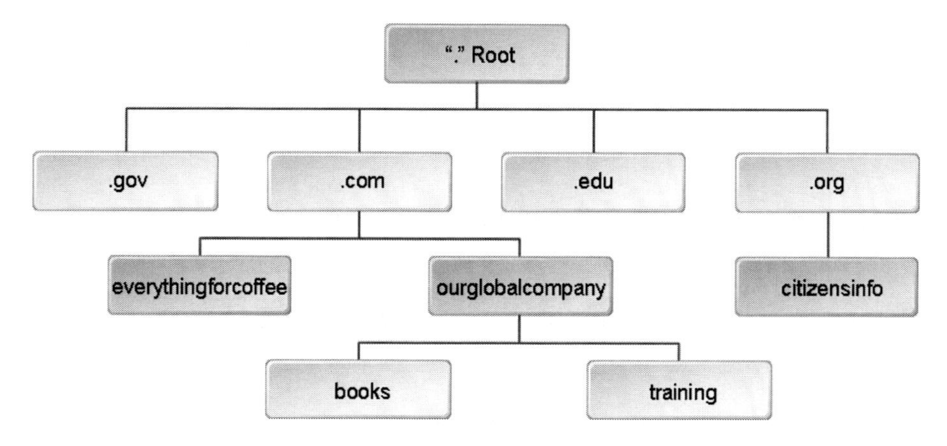

Figure 7-11: *Hierarchical structure of a DNS.*

The DNS Name Resolution Process

In the DNS process, DNS servers work together as needed to resolve names on behalf of DNS clients.

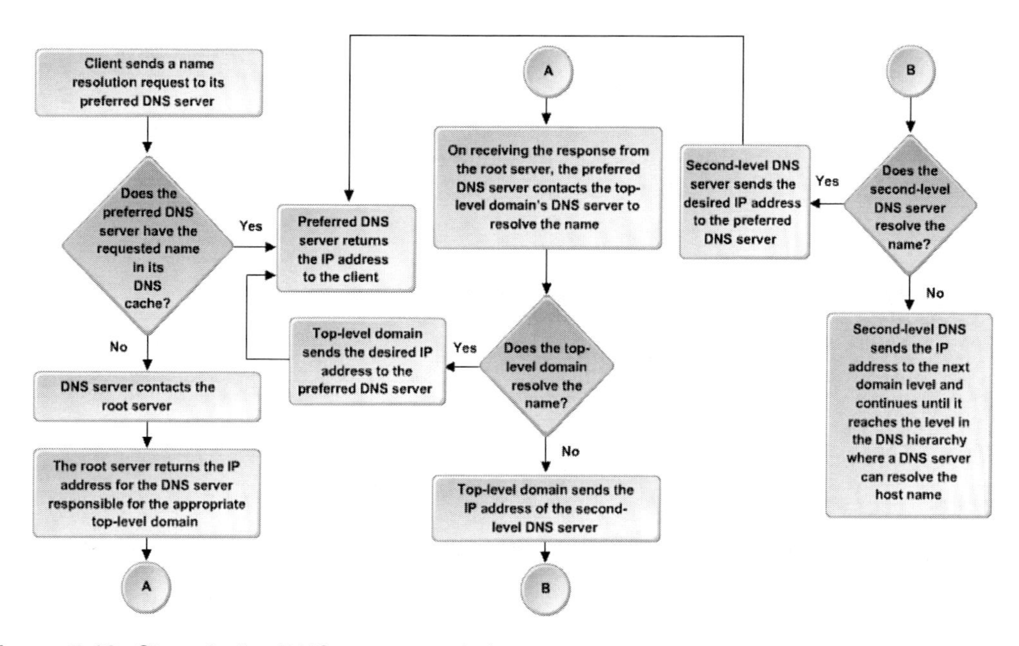

Figure 7-12: *Steps in the DNS name resolution process.*

Step	***Description***
Step 1: Client request	When a client needs to resolve a DNS name, it sends a name resolution request to the DNS resolver. A DNS name resolution request message is generated by the resolver, which is transmitted to the DNS server address specified during configuration.

Step	Description
Step 2: Preferred DNS server	The DNS server, upon receiving the request, checks if the requested name is in its DNS cache entries or its local DNS database, and returns the IP address to the client. If there is no match for the requested name, the DNS server forwards the request to a root name server asking which DNS server has the entries for the appropriate top-level domain.
Step 3: Root name server	Upon receiving the request, the root name server, reads the top-level domain of that name and sends a message that contains the IP address of the server for that top-level domain. The root name server then sends a reply to the client's DNS server.
Step 4: Top-level domain server	The client's DNS server contains the IP address of the top-level domain of the requested name. The DNS server then contacts the top-level domain's DNS server to resolve the name. The top-level domain server reads the second-level domain of the requested name, and if it can resolve the name, it sends the desired IP address back to the client's DNS server.
Step 5: Other domain servers	If the top-level domain cannot resolve the name because of additional levels in the FQDN, it sends the IP address to the second-level DNS server.
Step 6: Host name resolution	This communication between DNS servers continues until it reaches the level in the DNS hierarchy where a DNS server can resolve the host name.
Step 7: Host address	The preferred DNS server provides the client with the IP address of the target host.

Recursive and Iterative Name Queries

There are two kinds of DNS queries: recursive and iterative. A *recursive query* is when the client requests that its preferred DNS server find data on other DNS servers. A recursive request starts with the client requesting a name to be resolved to an IP address of its preferred DNS server. If the preferred server cannot resolve the name, it sends a request, on behalf of the client, to another DNS server.

An *iterative query* occurs when the client requests only the information a server already has in its cache for a particular domain name. If the receiving server cannot resolve the request, it notifies the client, but does not forward the request on to any other server.

Recursive queries usually take place between end-user client systems and their preferred DNS servers. Once the recursive query is in process, queries between DNS servers are usually iterative.

Primary and Secondary DNS Servers

When configuring a client's DNS settings, it is common to specify both a primary and a secondary DNS server to provide a more reliable name resolution process. When two DNS servers are listed, the client queries the primary server first. If the primary server does not answer, the client queries the secondary server. If the primary server returns a "Name Not Found" message, the query is over and the client does not query the secondary server. This is because both DNS servers can do recursive and iterative queries, and both primary and secondary servers should be able to contact the same resources. If one cannot access the resource, the other will not be able to either.

The HOSTS File

A *HOSTS file* is a plaintext file configured on a client machine containing a list of IP addresses and their associated host names, separated by at least one space. Comments may be included after the host name if preceded by the # symbol and separated from the host name by at least one space.

The HOSTS file provides an alternative method of host name resolution. An external client can use a HOSTS file to resolve names on your internal network without accessing your internal DNS server. You have to manually configure each host name entry in a HOSTS file.

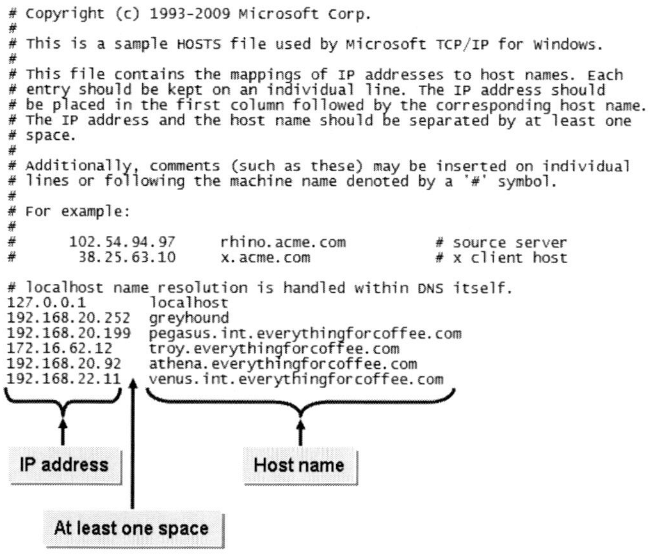

```
# Copyright (c) 1993-2009 Microsoft Corp.
#
# This is a sample HOSTS file used by Microsoft TCP/IP for Windows.
#
# This file contains the mappings of IP addresses to host names. Each
# entry should be kept on an individual line. The IP address should
# be placed in the first column followed by the corresponding host name.
# The IP address and the host name should be separated by at least one
# space.
#
# Additionally, comments (such as these) may be inserted on individual
# lines or following the machine name denoted by a '#' symbol.
#
# For example:
#
#      102.54.94.97     rhino.acme.com          # source server
#       38.25.63.10     x.acme.com              # x client host

# localhost name resolution is handled within DNS itself.
127.0.0.1       localhost
192.168.20.252  greyhound
192.168.20.199  pegasus.int.everythingforcoffee.com
172.16.62.12    troy.everythingforcoffee.com
192.168.20.92   athena.everythingforcoffee.com
192.168.22.11   venus.int.everythingforcoffee.com
```

IP address

Host name

At least one space

Figure 7-13: *Entries in a HOSTS file.*

HOSTS File Usage

The HOSTS file, however, requires a lot of maintenance, so it is recommended that you use it only when other methods of host name resolution are not supported, or temporarily unavailable for troubleshooting purposes.

ACTIVITY 7-5
Creating a DNS Record

There is a simulated version of this activity available on the CD-ROM that shipped with this course. You can run this simulation on any Windows computer to review the activity after class, or as an alternative to performing the activity as a group in class. The activity simulation can be launched either directly from the CD-ROM by clicking the **Interactives** link and navigating to the appropriate one, or from the installed data file location by opening the C:\Data\Simulations\Lesson#\Activity# folder and double-clicking the executable (.exe) file.

Scenario:

As a networking professional, you need to protect your server from external attacks. As the first step in protecting your DNS server, you decide to hide the actual server name from being displayed anywhere on the network by creating aliases to confuse the attacker.

---

1. Display the **New Host** dialog box.

a. Choose **Start→Administrative Tools→DNS.**

b. If necessary, in the DNS Manager window, in the left pane, expand the server object.

c. Expand the **Forward Lookup Zones** object and select **Child##.Classnet.com**, where ## is the student number.

d. Choose **Action→New Host (A or AAAA)** to display the **New Host** dialog box.

---

2. Add a new host entry for your server with an associated pointer record.

a. In the **New Host** dialog box, in the **Name** text box, type ***Server##*** and press **Tab** two times.

b. In the **IP address** text box, type ***192.168.1.##*** to specify the IP address of your server.

c. Check the **Create associated pointer (PTR) record** check box.

d. Check the **Allow any authenticated user to update DNS records with the same owner name** check box.

e. Click **Add Host** to add the new host entry for your server.

f. In the **DNS** message box, observe that "The host record Server##.Child##.Classnet.com was successfully created." message is displayed, and click **OK.**

g. In the **New Host** dialog box, click **Done.**

---

3. Check the connectivity with your server.

a. Choose **Start→Command Prompt** to open the Command Prompt window.

b. At the command prompt, enter `ping Server##`

c. Observe that you are able to communicate with the server and get four successful responses. Enter **`exit`** to close the Command Prompt window.

```
C:\Users\Administrator.CLASSNET>ping Server01

Pinging server01.Child01.Classnet.com [192.168.1.36] with 32 bytes of data:
Reply from 192.168.1.36: bytes=32 time<1ms TTL=128
Reply from 192.168.1.36: bytes=32 time<1ms TTL=128
Reply from 192.168.1.36: bytes=32 time<1ms TTL=128
Reply from 192.168.1.36: bytes=32 time<1ms TTL=128

Ping statistics for 192.168.1.36:
    Packets: Sent = 4, Received = 4, Lost = 0 (0% loss),
Approximate round trip times in milli-seconds:
    Minimum = 0ms, Maximum = 0ms, Average = 0ms
```

d. Close the DNS Manager window.

ACTIVITY 7-6

Discussing DNS Name Resolution

Scenario:

In this activity, you will identify components of DNS and the name resolution process.

---

1. **Which are fully qualified domain names?**

   a) www.everythingforcoffee.com

   b) \\fs001\data\new\accounts.mdb

   c) data1.ourglobalcompany.dom.\users\home

   d) citizensinfo.org

---

2. **What is the name of the top of the DNS hierarchy?**

   a) Host record

   b) Zone

   c) Root

   d) First-level domain

---

3. **True or False? If a preferred DNS server cannot resolve a client's name request, it contacts the DNS server immediately above it in the hierarchy.**

   __ True

   __ False

---

4. **True or False? An advantage of using a HOSTS file for DNS name resolution services is that updates to the file are automatic.**

   __ True

   __ False

---

5. **Which DNS record type is used to map a host name to its IP address for name resolution?**

   a) Name Server

   b) Pointer

   c) Canonical name

   d) Address

   e) Start of Authority

TOPIC C

TCP/IP Commands

You have learned about host name resolution for TCP/IP networks. The TCP/IP protocol suite provides commands you can use to troubleshoot and configure connectivity and name resolution. In this topic, you will identify the commands in the TCP/IP protocol suite that can help you ensure smooth connectivity in your TCP/IP network.

TCP/IP commands allow you to gather information about how your systems are communicating over a TCP/IP network. When used for troubleshooting, these commands can provide critical information about communication lapses and their causes.

The tracert Command

The *tracert* command determines the route data takes to get to a particular destination. The ICMP protocol sends out "Time Exceeded" messages to each router to trace the route. Each time a packet is sent, the TTL value is reduced before the packet is forwarded, thus allowing TTL to count how many hops it is away from the destination.

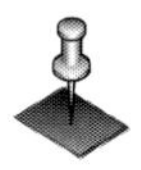

`traceroute` is the Linux equivalent of the `tracert` command, which is Windows-based.

If you run the `tracert` command repeatedly for the same destination, you will normally see different results. This is because TCP/IP is auto-correcting and takes the fastest route possible across the global network of Internet routers.

```
C:\>tracert www.everythingforcoffee.com

Tracing route to www.everythingforcoffee.com [74.43.216.150]
over a maximum of 30 hops:

  1    69 ms    69 ms    66 ms  220.224.141.145
  2    52 ms    38 ms    51 ms  220.224.157.141
  3    62 ms    55 ms    69 ms  124.124.239.185
  4   104 ms   112 ms   171 ms  so-5-1-0.0.cjr01.mmb003.flagtel.com [62.216.145.229]
  5   134 ms   153 ms   131 ms  so-7-0-0.0.ejr03.sin001.flagtel.com [62.216.128.73]
  6   315 ms   322 ms   303 ms  so-0-2-0.0.pjr02.hkg005.flagtel.com [85.95.26.125]
  7   223 ms   235 ms   209 ms  so-0-2-0.0.pjr02.wad001.flagtel.com [85.95.25.189]
  8   317 ms   328 ms   318 ms  so-4-2-0.0.ejr02.pao001.flagtel.com [62.216.128.62]
  9   329 ms   317 ms   319 ms  pao.paix.frontiernet.net [198.32.176.27]
 10   331 ms   322 ms   324 ms  ae2---0.cor02.plal.ca.frontiernet.net [74.40.3.169]
 11   341 ms   322 ms   348 ms  ae1---0.cor01.slkc.ut.frontiernet.net [74.40.5.62]
 12   370 ms   362 ms   376 ms  ae3---0.cor02.chcg.il.frontiernet.net [74.40.5.57]
 13   365 ms   450 ms   395 ms  ae0---0.cor01.chcg.il.frontiernet.net [74.40.3.241]
 14   375 ms   371 ms   377 ms  ae1---0.cor02.roch.ny.ny.frontiernet.net [74.40.5.21]
 15   384 ms   385 ms   379 ms  ge--0-0-0---0.car02.roch.ny.frontiernet.net [74.40.5.78]
 16   372 ms   380 ms   382 ms  74.45.102.10
 17     *        *        *     Request timed out.
 18     *        *        *     Request timed out.
 19     *        *        *     Request timed out.
 20     *        *        *     Request timed out.
 21     *        *        *     Request timed out.
 22     *        *        *     Request timed out.
 23     *        *        *     Request timed out.
 24     *        *        *     Request timed out.
 25     *        *        *     Request timed out.
 26     *        *        *     Request timed out.
 27     *        *        *     Request timed out.
 28     *        *        *     Request timed out.
 29     *        *        *     Request timed out.
 30     *        *        *     Request timed out.

Trace complete.
```

Total number of hops to remote host

Response time at each router

Routers in trace path to destination

Figure 7-14: *tracert output of everythingforcoffee.com.*

Network Firewalls

If a network firewall is configured to not allow a `tracert` or `ping` through, you might not be able to trace the route all the way to the end; it might appear to end at the firewall. If you get the message "Destination Unreachable", a router is not able to figure out how to get to the next destination. Even though it does not tell you what is wrong, it alerts you to the router where the problem is occurring.

tracert Options

You can use various options with the `tracert` command.

Option	*Description*
`-d`	If you are having trouble resolving host names when using `tracert`, use the `-d` option to prevent `tracert` from trying to resolve host names. It also speeds up response time since it is not spending time resolving host names.
`-h max_hops`	The default number of hops `tracert` will attempt to reach is 30. Using the `-h` option, you can specify more hops or fewer for it to check.
`-j [router] [local_computer]`	With loose source routing, you specify the destination router and your local computer using the `-j` option. It lets you trace the round trip rather than the default, which is to get to the destination.
`-w timeout`	If many of your responses on the `tracert` are timing out, using the `-w` option, you can increase the number of milliseconds to wait before continuing. If, after increasing the value, destinations are then reachable, you probably have a bandwidth issue to resolve.

The pathping Command

The *pathping* command provides information about latency and packet loss on a network. `pathping` combines the functionality of the `ping` and `tracert` commands. Similar to `ping`, `pathping` sends multiple ICMP echo request messages to each router between two hosts over a period of time, and then displays results based on the number of packets returned by each router.

It is similar to `tracert` as it identifies the routers that are on the path. In the output, it also displays the path to the remote host over a maximum of 30 hops. In addition, it displays details of packet transfer between the hosts in a time span of over 25 seconds, and the system names and their IP addresses. `pathping` can be used to isolate a router or subnet with issues as it can display the degree of packet loss at any given router or link.

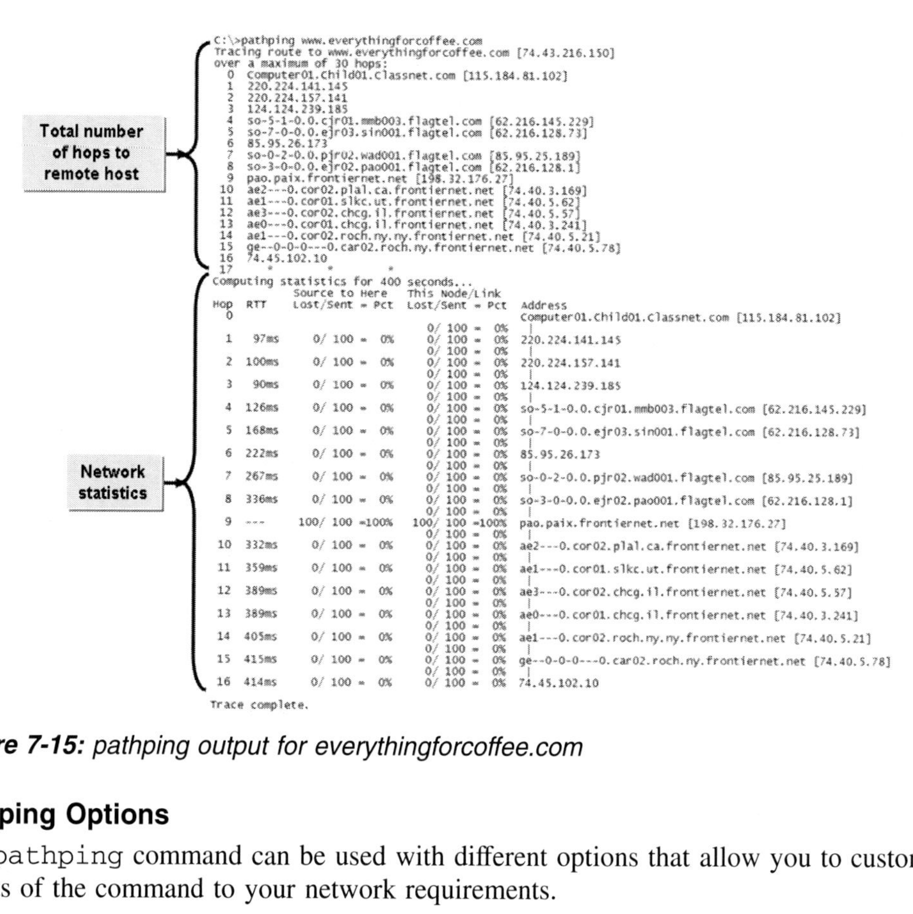

Figure 7-15: *pathping output for everythingforcoffee.com*

pathping Options

The `pathping` command can be used with different options that allow you to customize the results of the command to your network requirements.

Option	***Description***
`-h` *`maximum hops`*	Specify the maximum number of hops to locate a destination.
`-i` *`address`*	Specify a source IP address.
`-n`	Specify that host name resolution can be skipped.
`-4` *`address`*	Specify the IPv4 addresses that are to be used.
`-6` *`address`*	Specify the IPv6 addresses that are to be used.

The MTR Utility

The My traceroute (*MTR*) utility combines `ping` and `traceroute` into a single function. MTR displays the routers traversed, the average time taken for round trip, and packet loss of each router. This utility helps network administrators identify latency or packet loss between two routers. MTR is used on Unix-based systems.

The General Public License (GNU) is responsible for licensing and distributing MTR.

ACTIVITY 7-7
Using TCP/IP Commands

There is a simulated version of this activity available on the CD-ROM that shipped with this course. You can run this simulation on any Windows computer to review the activity after class, or as an alternative to performing the activity as a group in class. The activity simulation can be launched either directly from the CD-ROM by clicking the **Interactives** link and navigating to the appropriate one, or from the installed data file location by opening the C:\Data\Simulations\Lesson#\Activity# folder and double-clicking the executable (.exe) file.

Scenario:

A node on the network has problems communicating with the DNS server. As the network administrator, you have reconfigured the network setting on the node. You want to ensure that the connectivity is successful before you reassign the system to a user.

---

1. Use the `ping` command to verify that the DNS server is available.
   a. Choose **Start→Command Prompt** to open the Command Prompt window.
   b. In the Command Prompt window, enter **`ping DC`**
   c. Observe that the results display the DNS server's IP address as 192.168.1.200.

```
C:\Users\Administrator.CLASSNET>ping DC

Pinging DC.Classnet.com [192.168.1.200] with 32 bytes of data:
Reply from 192.168.1.200: bytes=32 time<1ms TTL=128
Reply from 192.168.1.200: bytes=32 time<1ms TTL=128
Reply from 192.168.1.200: bytes=32 time<1ms TTL=128
Reply from 192.168.1.200: bytes=32 time<1ms TTL=128

Ping statistics for 192.168.1.200:
    Packets: Sent = 4, Received = 4, Lost = 0 (0% loss),
Approximate round trip times in milli-seconds:
    Minimum = 0ms, Maximum = 0ms, Average = 0ms
```

---

2. Use the `tracert` command to trace the route from your system to the DNS server.
   a. In the Command Prompt window, enter **`tracert /?`** to view the syntax of the `tracert` command.
   b. Observe the syntax of the command displayed in the **Usage** section and the various options of the command along with their description.

```
C:\Users\Administrator.CLASSNET>tracert /?

Usage: tracert [-d] [-h maximum_hops] [-j host-list] [-w timeout]
               [-R] [-S srcaddr] [-4] [-6] target_name

Options:
    -d                 Do not resolve addresses to hostnames.
    -h maximum_hops    Maximum number of hops to search for target.
    -j host-list       Loose source route along host-list (IPv4-only).
    -w timeout         Wait timeout milliseconds for each reply.
    -R                 Trace round-trip path (IPv6-only).
    -S srcaddr         Source address to use (IPv6-only).
    -4                 Force using IPv4.
    -6                 Force using IPv6.
```

   c. In the Command Prompt window, enter **`tracert -d 192.168.1.200`**

d. Verify that there was only one hop because it is on the same local network as your system.

```
C:\Users\Administrator.CLASSNET>tracert -d 192.168.1.200

Tracing route to 192.168.1.200 over a maximum of 30 hops

  1    <1 ms    <1 ms    <1 ms  192.168.1.200

Trace complete.
```

e. Enter **`cls`** to clear the screen.

---

3. Use the `pathping` command to display statistics related to network traffic.

a. At the command prompt, enter **`pathping DC`**

b. Observe that the results display the IP address and the system name. Verify that there are no packet errors.

```
C:\Users\Administrator.CLASSNET>pathping DC

Tracing route to DC.Classnet.com [192.168.1.200]
over a maximum of 30 hops:
  0  Computer01.Child01.Classnet.com [192.168.1.36]
  1  DC [192.168.1.200]

Computing statistics for 25 seconds...
            Source to Here   This Node/Link
Hop  RTT    Lost/Sent = Pct  Lost/Sent = Pct  Address
  0                                           Computer01.Child01.Classnet.com [1
92.168.1.36]
                                0/ 100 =  0%   |
  1    0ms     0/ 100 =  0%     0/ 100 =  0%  DC [192.168.1.200]

Trace complete.
```

c. Close the Command Prompt window.

TOPIC D
Common TCP/IP Protocols

You have identified the common TCP/IP commands and their functions. The TCP/IP protocol suite also includes protocols that work at different layers of the protocol stack. In this topic, you will identify the common TCP/IP protocols and services and the functions they provide on your network.

Once network communication has been established at the lower layers of the protocol stack, users will deploy applications to complete tasks using that communication link. These tasks can include transferring and sharing files, reading and sending email, reading and posting messages on a newsgroup, and browsing the web. The TCP/IP upper-layer protocols and services make accomplishing these tasks possible. By understanding the function of each of the TCP/IP protocols, you can choose the appropriate protocol for the desired user task.

FTP

The *File Transfer Protocol (FTP)* is a TCP/IP protocol that enables the transfer of files between a user's workstation and a remote host. With FTP, a user can access the directory structure on a remote host, change directories, search for and rename files and directories, and download and upload files. The FTP *daemon* or service must be running on the remote host and an FTP utility may need to be installed on the client. FTP commands must be entered in lowercase and are available both as DOS and UNIX commands. It works on the Application layer of the OSI and TCP/IP models.

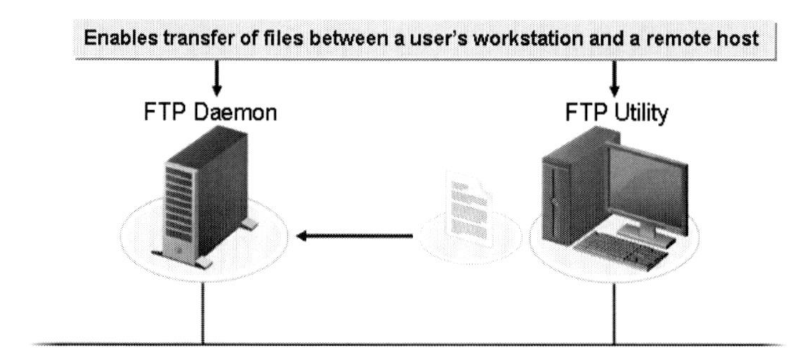

Figure 7-16: *The FTP utility enabling a client to access the FTP server.*

FTP works on two TCP channels: TCP port 20 for data transfer and TCP port 21 for control commands. These channels work together to allow users to execute commands and transfer data simultaneously. A server-based program answers requests from FTP clients for download. A command line utility allows users to connect to an FTP server and download files. You can initiate an FTP session by entering:

`ftp FQDN/IP address of remote host.`

Daemons

A daemon is a background process that performs a specific operation. Daemon is a UNIX term, though daemons are supported on other operating systems. Daemons on Windows are referred to as system agents or services.

FTP Options

You can use several options with the FTP command line utility.

Option	Used To
-v	Prevent remote server command responses being shown.
-n	Suppress auto-logon at initial connection.
-i	Disable interactive prompting when transferring multiple files.
-d	Enable debugging, displaying all commands passed between the FTP client and server.
-g	Disable wildcard character support.
-s: [*filename*]	Run all the FTP commands contained in the [*filename*] file.
-a	Allow use of any local interface during data connection binding.
-w: [*windowsize*]	Override the default transfer buffer size.

TFTP

Trivial File Transfer Protocol (TFTP) is a simple version of FTP that uses UDP as the transport protocol, and does not require log on to the remote host. As it uses UDP, it does not support error correction but provides for higher data integrity. It is commonly used for bootstrapping and loading applications and not for file transfer.

Internet Browsers and FTP

Most Internet browsers can support FTP in a GUI mode. A connection to an FTP site can be made by browsing the Internet, logging on, and connecting. Once connected, you can drag files on and off the FTP site the same way you would from Windows Explorer. There are also a number of third-party FTP utilities that can be used for connecting and loading files to your FTP site.

Troubleshooting FTP Access

To access most FTP servers, the client needs to connect using a valid user name and password. Some FTP servers allow limited access through an anonymous connection. If anonymous access is disabled on the remote host, users will need login credentials. To use this option, log on using the user name *anonymous*, and enter your email address for the password.

When connecting to an FTP server, logging on poses the biggest problems. You need to provide the correct credentials to log on to the FTP server. Most users are only granted read permissions, and to upload files you need to ensure that you have the necessary permissions.

NTP

The *Network Time Protocol (NTP)* is an Internet protocol that synchronizes the clock times of computers in a network by exchanging time signals. It works on the Application layer of the TCP/IP and OSI models. Synchronization is done to the millisecond against the U.S. Naval Observatory master clocks. Running continuously in the background on a computer, NTP sends periodic time requests to servers to obtain the server time stamp and then adjusts the client's clock based on the server time stamp received.

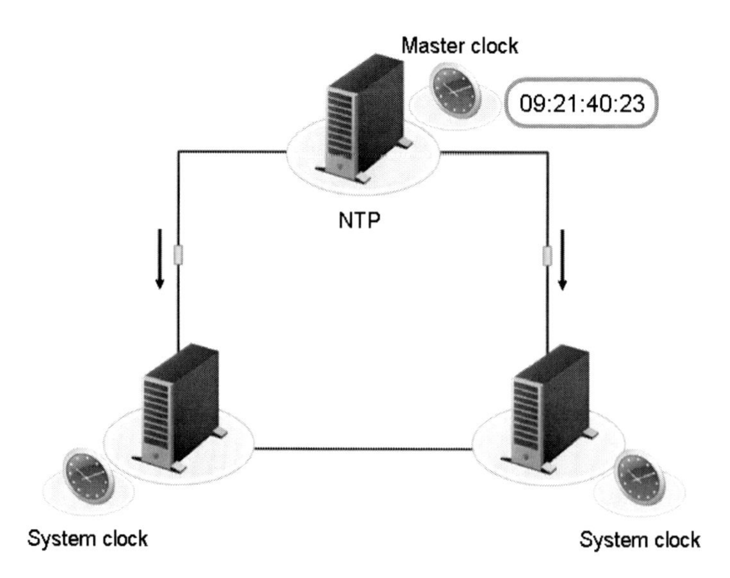

Figure 7-17: *Clocks synchronized using NTP.*

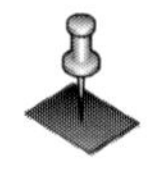

The master time clocks are located in Washington, D.C., and Colorado Springs, Colorado.

SMTP

TCP/IP has two services that operate in the Application layer of the OSI model and support the sending and receiving of email—*Simple Mail Transfer Protocol (SMTP)* and *Post Office Protocol version 3 (POP3).*

SMTP is a communications protocol used to format and send email messages from a client to a server or between servers. It uses a store-and-forward process. In SMTP, the sender starts the transfer. SMTP can store a message until the receiving device comes online. At that point, it contacts the device and hands off the message. If all devices are online, the message is sent quickly. An SMTP message consists of a header and a content section. The header, or envelope, contains the delivery information of the message and uses a colon (:) as a separator character. The content portion contains the message text, which is a sequence of ASCII characters.

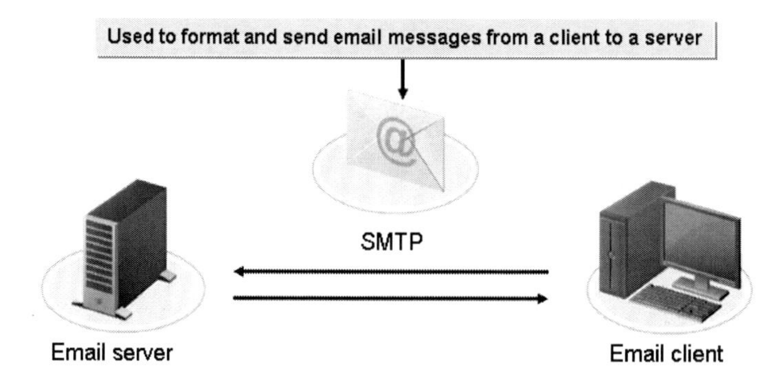

Figure 7-18: *Sending email messages using SMTP.*

Using SMTP on Unreliable WAN Links

Because of SMTP's store and forward capability, it is used to send data through unreliable WAN links if delivery time is not critical. Data is sent to the endpoint and continues to hop from server to server until it eventually reaches its destination.

Limitations of SMTP

SMTP has a few limitations. The first one is related to the size of messages. Messages that are more than 64 Kb cannot be handled by some older implementations. Another limitation involves timeouts. If the client and server timeouts are different, one of the systems may give up when the other is still busy, resulting in termination of the connection unexpectedly. Sometimes SMTP may also trigger infinite mail storms.

For example, consider host 1 with Mailing List A containing a few entries and host 2 with Mailing List B containing both its own entries and that of Mailing List A. In such a case, email sent to Mailing List A and copied to Mailing List B could trigger sending multiple copies of the same email to the same set of recipients. Furthermore, if host 1 fails when mail is being forwarded, host 2 will try resending it to host 1. This generates a heavy amount of traffic on the network.

Extended SMTP (ESMTP) extends the capabilities of SMTP and helps to overcome some of these limitations.

POP3

POP3 is a protocol used to retrieve email messages from a mailbox on a mail server. With POP3, email messages wait in the mailbox on the server until the client retrieves them. The client can start the transfer on a set schedule, or transfer messages manually. Once the client retrieves and downloads the messages, the server deletes them unless the client configures options to leave the messages on the server. The client then works with the locally cached email messages.

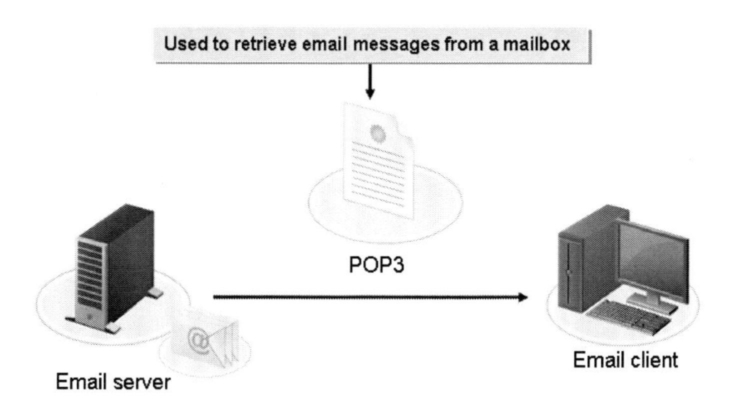

Figure 7-19: *Retrieving email message using POP3.*

POP3 and Multiple Computers

Because POP3 is designed by default to download messages to the local computer and delete them from the email server, it is not the best email protocol to use when users need to access their email from multiple computers. This is because when they use POP3, they end up with their email messages downloaded and split among the computers they use instead of having all their messages in one central location. Or, if they leave their messages on the server, they will have to delete old messages manually to avoid exceeding mailbox size limits, which may also lead to messages being split across multiple computers.

IMAP4

Internet Message Access Protocol version 4 (IMAP4) is a protocol used for retrieving messages from a mail server. Though it is similar to POP3, IMAP4 is more powerful and offers several functions. They include:

- A user can check an email header and also look for a specific string of characters in the contents of an email before downloading it.
- Messages can also remain on the server while the client works with them as if they were local.
- Users can search through messages by keywords, and to choose which messages to download locally.
- Messages in the user's mailbox can be marked with different status flags, such as deleted or replied to. The messages and their status flags stay in the mailbox until explicitly removed by the user.
- An email message containing multimedia files can be partially downloaded, saving bandwidth.
- A user can create, rename, or delete mailboxes on a mail server, and also arrange mailboxes in a hierarchical manner in a folder for email storage.
- Unlike POP3, IMAP4 enables users to access folders other than their mailbox.

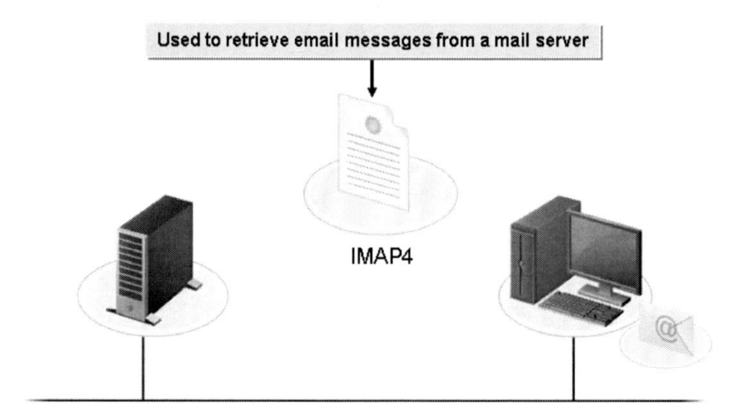

Figure 7-20: *Retrieving email messages using IMAP4.*

Because IMAP4 is designed to store messages on the server, it is much easier for users to access their email messages—both new and saved—from multiple computers.

IMAP was developed at Stanford University in 1986.

NNTP

The *Network News Transfer Protocol (NNTP)* is a protocol used to post and retrieve messages from the worldwide bulletin board system called USENET, which is a global bulletin board. It contains more than 14,000 forums, called newsgroups. Users use newsgroups to post queries relating to a particular topic. NNTP only submits and retrieves new or updated news articles from the server. With NNTP, postings to newsgroups are stored in a database, from which individual users, called subscribers, can select only those items they wish to read. *RSS feeds*, which allow users to subscribe to and receive updates made to web pages, are based on NNTP.

USENET is an acronym for User's Network.

HTTP

The *HyperText Transfer Protocol (HTTP)* is a network protocol that works on the Application layer of the OSI and TCP/IP models. HTTP enables clients to interact with websites by allowing them to connect to and retrieve web pages from a server. It defines the format and transmission of messages, as well as what actions web servers and client's browser should take in response to different commands. A stateless protocol where each command executes independently of any prior commands, HTTP not only supports persistent connections to web resources to reduce reconnection times, but also pipelining and buffering to help in the transfer process.

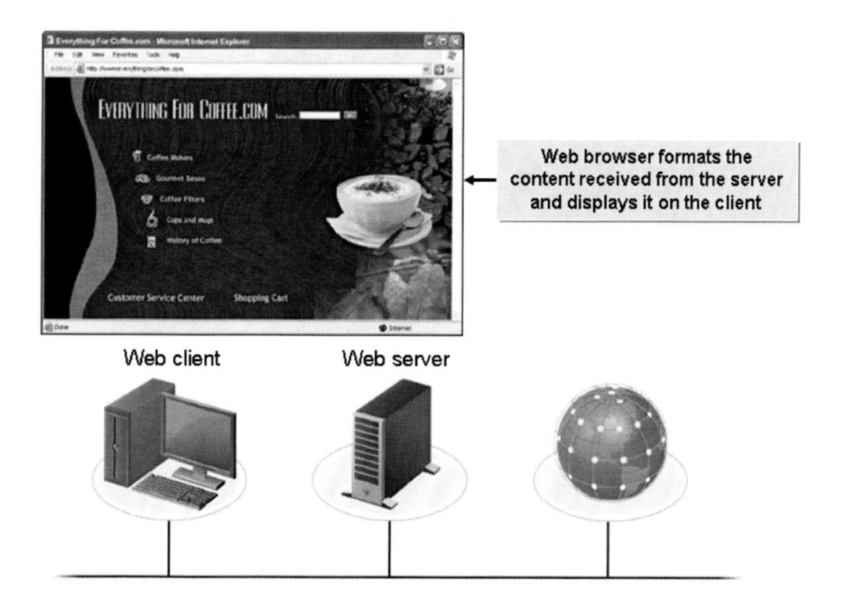

Figure 7-21: *Web clients using HTTP to access a website.*

Because HTTP is stateless, it is difficult to implement websites that react intelligently to user input. This limitation can be overcome with a number of add-on technologies, such as ActiveX, Java, JavaScript, and cookies.

HTTPS

HTTP Secure (HTTPS) is a secure version of HTTP that provides a secure connection between a web browser and a server. HTTPS uses the *Secure Sockets Layer (SSL)* security protocol to encrypt data. Not all web browsers and servers support HTTPS, though.

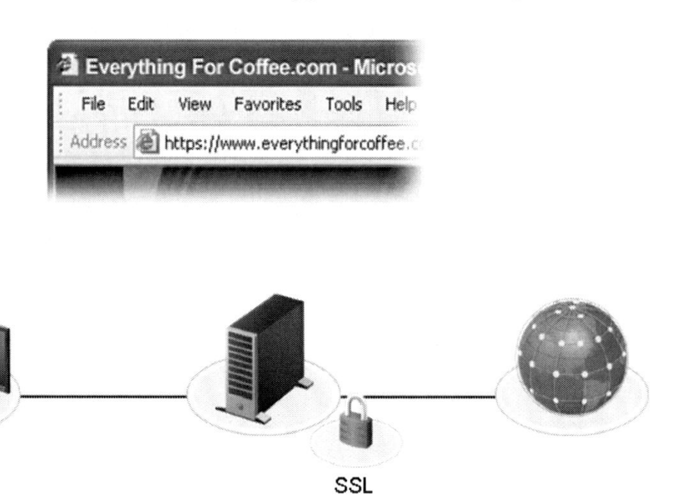

Figure 7-22: *Websites that use HTTPS for secure transactions.*

HTTPS is also referred to as HTTP over SSL.

ACTIVITY 7-8

Identifying Common TCP/IP Protocols

Scenario:

In this activity, you will identify common TCP/IP protocols.

---

1. **What are the differences between accessing email from multiple systems using IMAP4 and POP3?**

    a) POP3 does not maintain a copy of the email once it is downloaded from a mail server.

    b) POP3 does not maintain a copy of the outgoing email.

    c) Accessing email using POP3 is faster than IMAP4.

    d) IMAP4 is the messaging protocol used to access email.

---

2. **Your sales department wants to sell supplies over the Internet and wants to make sure that the transactions are secure. Which protocol should be configured on the web server?**

    a) FTP

    b) HTTPS

    c) NNTP

    d) SMTP

---

3. **Your company has a production floor with several shared computers. The production staff needs to be able to check their email from whichever computer is free. Which email protocol should you use?**

    a) POP3

    b) NTP

    c) IMAP4

    d) NNTP

---

4. **True or False? NTP is a protocol that allows users to connect to a USENET system and read newsgroup messages.**

    __ True

    __ False

---

5. **Your sales force needs to retrieve sales prospective documents and upload completed sales order forms to corporate headquarters while they are on the move. What service should you use?**

    a) HTTP

    b) NNTP

    c) NTP

    d) FTP

TOPIC E
TCP/IP Interoperability Services

In the previous topic, you identified various TCP/IP protocols. The TCP/IP protocol suite includes services for the purpose of providing interoperability between dissimilar systems. In this topic, you will identify the different TCP/IP interoperability services and the functions they can provide on your network.

Networks are established so that individual devices can communicate with each other and share resources. Most networks are made up of devices that are not natively compatible. When these devices are running TCP/IP, you can use the interoperability services that run on TCP/IP to create a network where dissimilar systems can securely communicate and share resources.

NFS

The *Network File System (NFS)* is a client/server application that enables users to access shared files stored on different types of computers, and work with the files as if they were stored locally. It also allows a user to share local files and act as a file server for other client computers. The functioning of NFS is independent of the type of computer, operating system, network architecture, and transport protocol on which it is deployed. Part of the TCP/IP protocol suite, NFS works on the Application layer of the OSI model and enables you to share printers on the network.

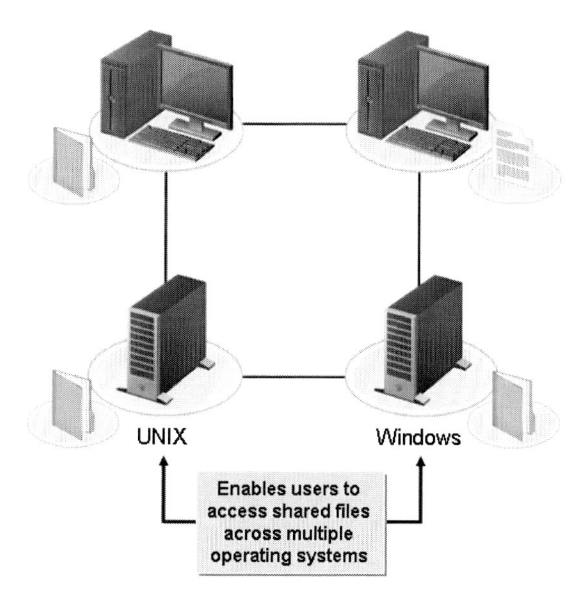

Figure 7-23: *NFS on UNIX and Windows systems.*

On TCP/IP networks, NFS uses an interface known as Virtual File System (VFS) that runs on TCP/IP.

SSH

Secure Shell (SSH) is a program that enables a user or an application to log on to another computer over a network, execute commands, and manage files. It creates a shell or session with a remote system, and offers strong authentication methods and ensures that communications are secure over insecure channels. It replaces UNIX-based remote connection programs that transmit unencrypted passwords. With the SSH `slogin` command, the login session, including the password, is encrypted and protected against attacks. Secure Shell works with many different operating systems, including Windows, UNIX, and Macintosh.

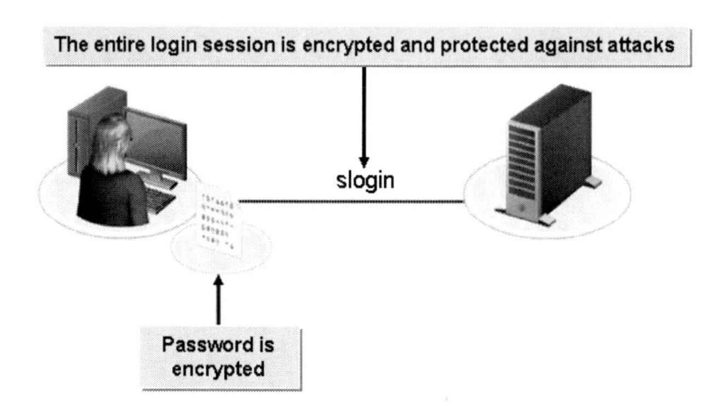

Figure 7-24: *An SSH session that uses slogin.*

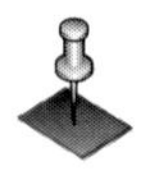

SSH is a replacement for the UNIX-based `rlogin` command, which can also establish a connection with a remote host, but transmits passwords in cleartext.

SSH1 and SSH2

There are two versions of Secure Shell available: SSH1 and SSH2. They are two different protocols and encrypt different parts of a data packet. To authenticate systems, SSH1 employs user keys, to identify users; host keys, to identify systems; session keys, to encrypt communication in a single session; and server keys, which are temporary keys that protect the session key. SSH2 is more secure; it does not use server keys. SSH2 includes a secure replacement for FTP called *Secure File Transfer Protocol (SFTP)*. Because they are different protocol implementations, SSH1 and SSH2 are not compatible with each other.

Note that the acronym SFTP is used both for Secure File Transfer Protocol as well as for the now obsolete Simple File Transfer Protocol.

Network Protection with SSH

All traffic (including passwords) are encrypted by SSH to eliminate connection hijacking, eavesdropping, and other network-level attacks, such as IP source routing, IP spoofing, and DNS spoofing. When you implement SSH with encryption, any attacker manages to gain access to your network can neither play back the traffic nor hijack the connection. They can only force SSH to disconnect.

SCP

The *Secure Copy Protocol (SCP)* is a protocol that uses SSH to copy files securely between a local and a remote host, or between two remote hosts. SCP can also be implemented as a command-line utility that uses either SCP or SFTP to perform secure copying.

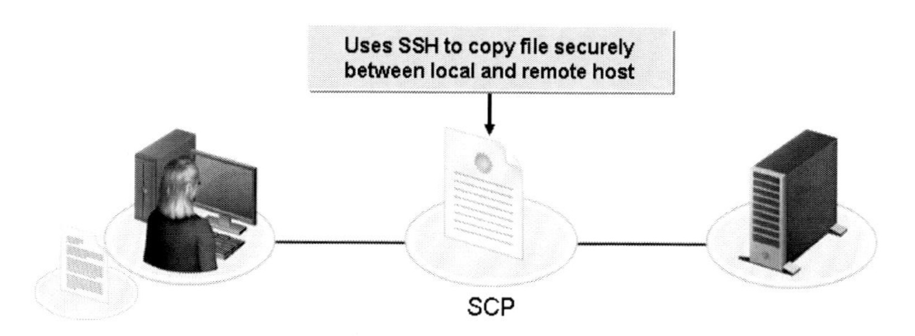

Figure 7-25: *SCP transfers using SSH.*

Telnet

Telecommunications Network (*Telnet*) is a terminal emulation protocol that allows users at one site to simulate a session on a remote host as if the terminal were directly attached. It performs this simulation by translating keystrokes from the user's terminal into instructions that the remote host recognizes, and then carrying the output back and displaying it in a format native to the user's terminal. You can connect to any host that is running a Telnet daemon or service. Connection-oriented, Telnet handles its own session negotiations and assists network administrators in remote administration such as connecting to a remote server or to a service such as FTP.

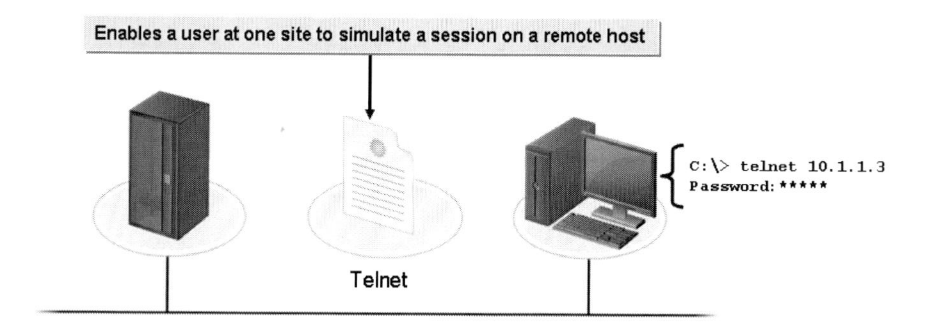

Figure 7-26: *A Telnet session.*

Telnet on Server Systems

Many systems, such as a UNIX host or an IBM mainframe running TCP/IP, include Telnet daemons. There is also a Telnet server service in Windows XP and Windows Server 2003. Telnet is not installed by default in Windows Server 2008 R2. Microsoft provides directions for installing Telnet; you can view them by visiting the URL: **http://technet.microsoft.com/en-us/library/cc770501(WS.10).aspx**

Windows Telnet Client

Windows includes a basic Telnet client utility. It is installed when you install TCP/IP on your Windows system. It includes VT100, VT52, and TTY terminal emulation. It does not include the Telnet daemon or service, but the Telnet service can be enabled on Windows Server computers.

Telnet Defaults

Telnet is defined in RFC 854, and uses the following defaults:

- Uses TCP Port 23; however, you can specify a different port if the host to which you are connecting is configured to use a different port.
- Uses 25 lines in the buffer, but you can configure it for up to 399 lines.
- Uses Video Terminal 100 (VT100) as the default terminal emulation, but some versions allow you to configure your system with VT220, VT52, and TeleTYpe (TTY) terminal emulation support.

SMB

The *Server Message Block (SMB)* is a protocol that works on the Application layer and helps share resources such as files, printers, and serial ports among computers. In a TCP/IP network, NetBIOS clients, such as Windows systems, use NetBIOS over TCP/IP to connect to servers, and then issue SMB commands to complete tasks such as accessing shared files and printers.

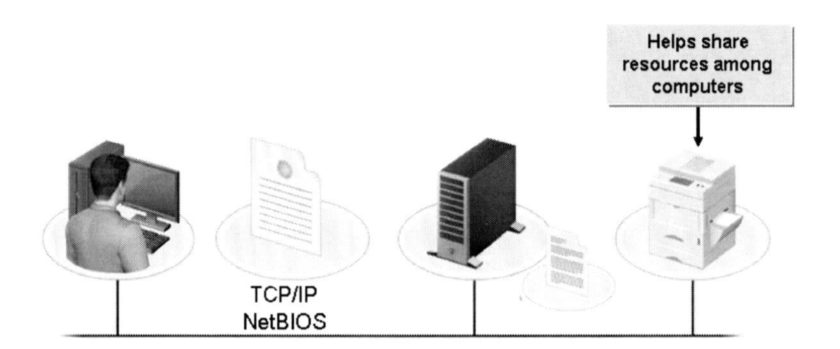

Figure 7-27: *Resource sharing using SMB.*

Samba

Samba is a well-known open-source product that uses SMB to enable UNIX and Windows machines for sharing directories and files. Although the SMB protocol is primarily used in Microsoft networks, there are products using SMB to facilitate file sharing across different operating system platforms.

LDAP

The *Lightweight Directory Access Protocol (LDAP)* is a protocol that defines how a client can access information, perform operations, and share directory data on a server. It was designed for use over TCP/IP networks in general, and on the Internet in particular. In most implementations, LDAP relies on DNS that enables clients to locate servers that host the LDAP directory, and then the LDAP servers enable clients to find the directory objects.

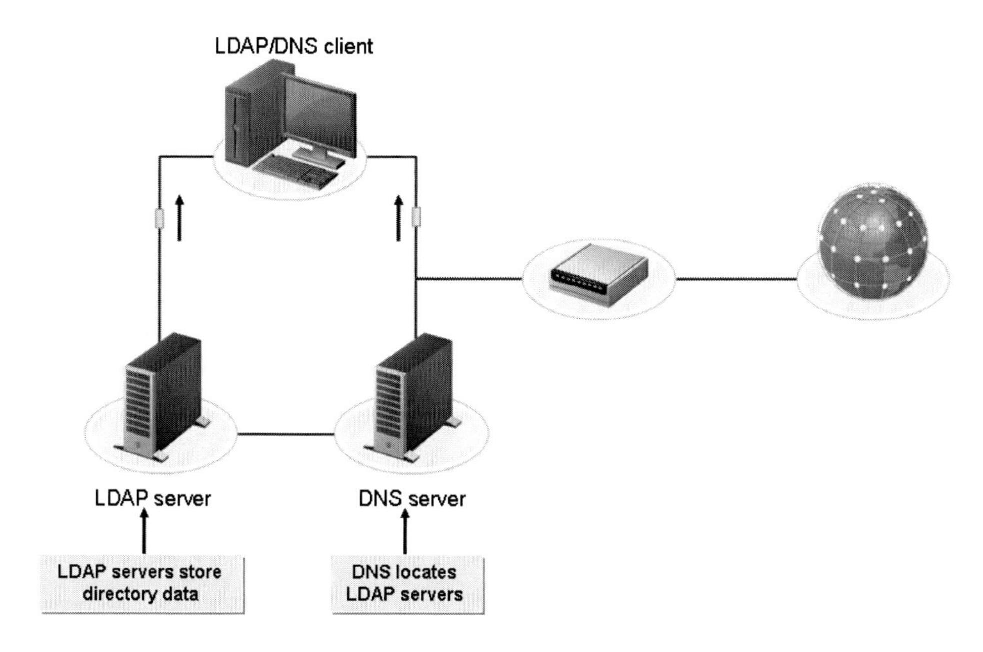

Figure 7-28: *LDAP on a network.*

Microsoft's Active Directory directory service implements LDAP and supports LDAP versions 2 and 3. The Novell directory services NDS® and eDirectory™ and Apple's Open Directory are also LDAP-compliant.

Zeroconf

Zero Configuration Networking (Zeroconf) is a set of standards that provides for automatic configuration and IP address allocation on both Ethernet and wireless networks. Used as alternatives, Zeroconf networks can exist without central control or configuration services such as DHCP or DNS. Protocols supporting Zeroconf can use configuration information if available, but do not require it. Zeroconf typically uses MAC addresses as parameters because they are unique and available on most network devices.

Networks implementing Zeroconf must include methods for four functions:

- Network-layer address assignment.
- Automatic address assignment using multicast.
- Translation between network names and network addresses.
- Location or discovery of network services by name and protocol.

Universal Plug and Play (UPnP) is another technology that facilitates automatic configuration and IP address allocation on networks.

Zeroconf Implementations

Microsoft's APIPA addressing and the Rendezvous product from Apple Inc., use addresses in the 169.254.0.0 /16 address range for automatic configuration. For more information, visit **www.zeroconf.org**

ACTIVITY 7-9

Identifying TCP/IP Interoperability Services

Scenario:

In this activity, you will identify the TCP/IP interoperability services.

---

1. **Which service states what a client should do to access information, perform operations, and share directory data on a directory server?**
   a) Zeroconf
   b) LDAP
   c) SMB
   d) NFS

---

2. **Which services work together to securely transfer computer files between a local and a remote host, or between two remote hosts?**
   a) SMB and NFS
   b) SCP and SSH
   c) NFS and LDAP
   d) NFS and SSH

---

3. **Which service enables users to access shared files stored on different types of computers?**
   a) NFS
   b) SCP
   c) LDAP
   d) SSH

---

4. **Match the TCP/IP interoperability service with its description.**

	Service		Description
___	NFS	a.	Enables sharing resources, such as files, printers, and serial ports, between computers.
___	SSH	b.	Enables users to access shared files stored on other computers and work with them as if they are stored locally.
___	SMB	c.	States client actions to access information, perform operations, and share directory data on a server.
___	LDAP	d.	Enables a user or an application to run commands on a remote machine, and transfer files from one machine to the other.

Lesson 7 Follow-up

In this lesson, you identified how you can use the services that are part of the TCP/IP protocol suite on your network. By implementing the TCP/IP services and utilities that match your network, you will be able to manage the network and optimize its functionality.

1. **What TCP/IP services and utilities do you currently implement in your organization?**

2. **Which TCP/IP command will you use commonly on your network?**

8 LAN Infrastructure

Lesson Time: 1 hour(s), 55 minutes

Lesson Objectives:

In this lesson, you will identify the components of a LAN implementation.

You will:

- Describe the functions of switches and switching technologies.
- Enable static routing.
- Implement dynamic IP routing.
- Identify the components and functionalities of a VLAN implementation.
- Plan a SOHO network.

Introduction

In the previous lessons, you have learned about components and technologies that can be used on different networks. These technologies can be deployed both in LANs and WANs. In this lesson, you will identify the components of a LAN implementation.

Any organization, however small it may be, will need to have its computers and resources interconnected. LANs are the simplest and most common network type used to provide communication over a small area. Understanding LANs and the technologies that make them functional will enable you to choose and implement the right type of LAN for your organization.

This lesson covers all or part of the following CompTIA® Network+® (Exam N10-005) certification objectives:

- Topic A:
  - 1.2 Classify how applications, devices, and protocols relate to the OSI model layers.
  - 3.4 Categorize WAN technology types and properties.
- Topic B:
  - 1.2 Classify how applications, devices, and protocols relate to the OSI model layers.
  - 2.1 Given a scenario, install and configure routers and switches.
  - 3.4 Categorize WAN technology types and properties.
- Topic C:

    - 1.2 Classify how applications, devices, and protocols relate to the OSI model layers.
    - 1.4 Explain the purpose and properties of routing and switching.
    - 2.1 Given a scenario, install and configure routers and switches.
- Topic D:
    - 1.2 Classify how applications, devices, and protocols relate to the OSI model layers.
    - 2.1 Given a scenario, install and configure routers and switches.
- Topic E:
    - 1.2 Classify how applications, devices, and protocols relate to the OSI model layers.
    - 2.6 Given a set of requirements, plan and implement a basic SOHO network.

TOPIC A

Switching

In the previous lesson, you learned about the services of the TCP/IP protocol suite that can be used on your network. Before you start setting up a network, you need to be aware of the devices that you need on a network. In this topic, you will identify switching technologies and the functions of switches.

Switches are fundamental network connectivity devices, so you are likely to encounter them in the network environments that you support. In addition, switches provide features and functions that make them slightly more complex to implement and manage. Understanding the capabilities of these devices will prepare you to support switching in your network environments.

Switches and Network Performance

Switches are designed to add functionality and increase performance on networks. The main purpose of a switch is to optimize performance by providing users with higher bandwidth for transmission. Switches inspect data packets as they receive them from a source device and forward packets only to the port of a destination device. The traffic between two devices can be streamlined to allow the switch port and destination device to operate in the full duplex mode. Because a switch forwards data directly to the intended destination, it significantly increases network performance. Broadcast transmissions, however, do not gain from the performance advantages because they must be repeated on all other ports.

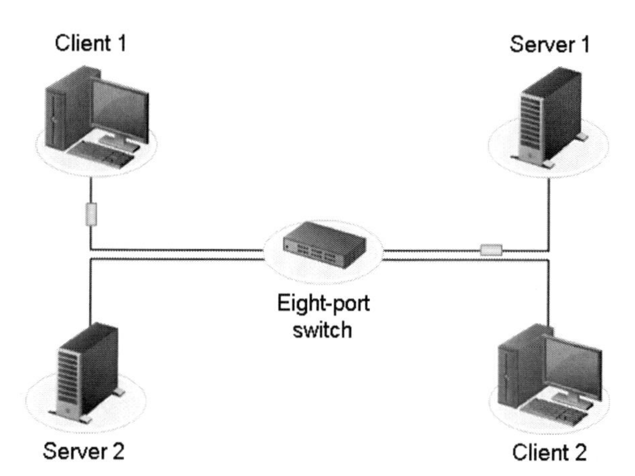

Figure 8-1: *An eight-port switch connecting several devices.*

Types of Switches

There are several types of switches available for your network.

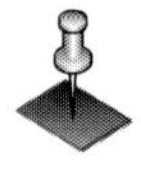

Basic or traditional switches operate at the Data Link layer of the OSI model (Layer 2). However, modern switches include more complex capabilities and can operate at the Network (Layer 3), and Transport layers (Layer 4). Higher layer switches are often called application or routing switches.

Switch Type	***Description***
Cut-through	A cut-through switch forwards a data packet as soon as it receives it; no error checking or processing of the packet is performed. This switch performs the address table lookup immediately upon receiving the destination address field in the packet header. The first bits in a packet are sent out of the outbound port on a switch immediately after it receives the bits. The switch does not discard packets that are corrupt and fail error checking.
Fragment-free	A fragment-free switch scans the first 64 bytes of each packet for evidence of damage by a collision. If no damage is found, it forwards the packet; otherwise, it discards it. Thus a fragment-free switch reduces network congestion by discarding fragments. It is similar to the cut-through switching method, but the switch waits to receive 64 bytes before it forwards the first bytes of the outgoing packet.
Store-and-forward	A store-and-forward switch calculates the CRC value for the packet's data and compares it to the value included in the packet. If they match, the packet is forwarded. Otherwise, it is discarded. This is the slowest type of switch. The switch receives the entire frame before the first bit of the frame is forwarded. This allows the switch to inspect the *Frame Check Sequence (FCS)* before forwarding the frame. FCS performs error checking on the trailer of an Ethernet frame.
Multilayer	A multilayer switch performs both routing and switching. This type of switch is relatively new, and there is no industry standard to define what qualifies as a multilayer switch. A multilayer switch is also called a Layer 2 router, Layer 3 switch, IP switch, routing switch, switching router, and wirespeed router. But, the term multilayer switch is the most prevalent.
Content	A content switch is used for load balancing among server groups and firewalls, and web cache and application redirection. Content switches are often referred to as 4-7 switches as they primarily work on Layers 4 and 7 of the OSI model. They make intelligent decisions about data by analyzing data packets in real time, and understanding the criticality and type of the request. Content switching supports load balancing for servers by directing traffic to assigned server groups that perform the function. This increases the response time for requests on the network. Although complex to implement, a content switch can perform many critical functions on a network and increase throughput.

Circuit Switching Networks

Definition:

Switching is a technique used for transmitting information over a network to the destination network device. The two types of switching are circuit switching and packet switching. In *circuit switching,* one end point creates a single path connection to another, depending on the requirement. In circuit switching, the word "circuit" refers to the connection path between endpoints. Once the circuit is established, data is transmitted through that path until the circuit is active. Bandwidth is dedicated to the connection until it is not needed any more. There is no guarantee that data will be transmitted through the same path through the network in different sessions.

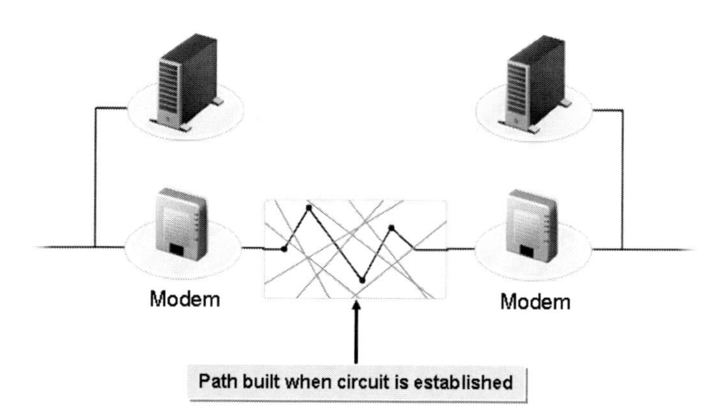

Figure 8-2: *Transfer of data in a circuit switching network.*

Example: PSTN

PSTN is an example of a circuit switching network.

Packet Switching Networks

In *packet switching networks,* data to be transmitted is broken into small units known as packets that move in sequence through the network. Each packet takes the best route available at any given time rather than following an established circuit path. Each data packet contains all of the routing and sequencing information required to transmit it from one endpoint to another, after which the data is reassembled. Packet switching assumes that a network is constantly changing and adjustments need to be made to compensate for network congestion or broken links.

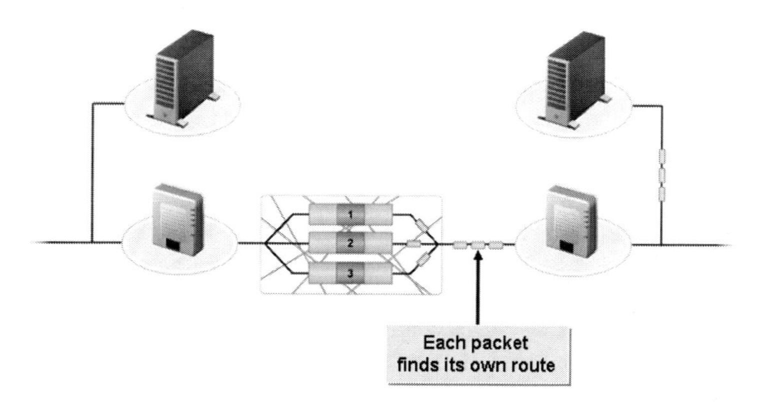

Figure 8-3: *Transfer of data in a packet switching network.*

Streaming Media and Live Video

Packet switching is not the best choice for streaming media such as live video and audio feeds. Because all packets do not necessarily arrive at the destination in order, or soon after each other, time-sensitive applications can end up stuttering or delayed, or a streaming connection may drop entirely.

Virtual Circuit Switching

Virtual circuit switching is a switching technique to transfer packets on logical circuits that do not have physical resources, such as frequencies or time slots allocated. This technique merges both packet and circuit switching techniques to its advantage. These logical paths are assigned to identities rather than physical locations and can be either permanent or switched. Each of the packets carries a Virtual Circuit Identifier (VCI) that is local to a link and updated by each switch on the path, from the source to the destination of the packet.

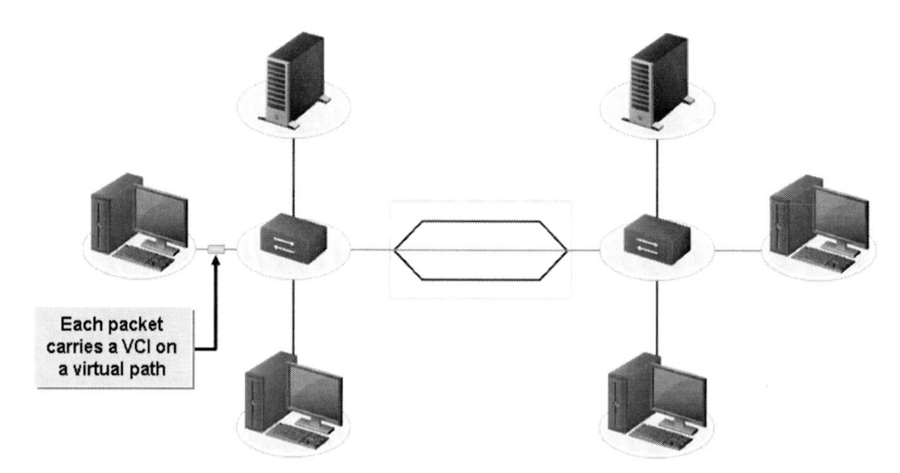

Figure 8-4: *Packets flow in a virtual circuit using VCI.*

There are two types of virtual circuits: Permanent Virtual Circuits (PVCs) and Switched Virtual Circuits (SVCs).

Virtual Circuit Type	***Description***
Permanent	*PVCs* are usually associated with leased lines. They connect two endpoints and are always on, which is why they are referred to as permanent. When a PVC is established, it is manually built and maintained by a telephone company (telco). The telco identifies the endpoints with a Data Link Connection Identifier (DLCI). PVCs provide a fast, reliable connection between endpoints because the connection is always on. Customers pay a fixed monthly fee per connection.
Switched	*SVCs* are associated with dial-up connections. SVCs provide more flexibility than PVCs and allow a single connection to an endpoint to be connected to multiple endpoints as needed. When a network device attempts to connect to a WAN, an SVC is requested and the carrier establishes the connection. Customers typically pay by connection time (like a long-distance phone call) and the monthly charge is less than that of a PVC. SVCs are useful when you need a part-time connection. But keep in mind that connection time can be slow, and if usage increases, so can an SVC's cost.

Cell Switching Networks

Cell switching networks are very similar to packet switching networks except that data is transmitted as fixed-length cells instead of variable-length packets. If data does not fill up an entire cell, the remainder of the space is filled with blank or filler data until the cell reaches its fixed size. The advantage of cell switching over packet switching is its predictability. Cell switching technologies make it easy to track how much data is moving on a network.

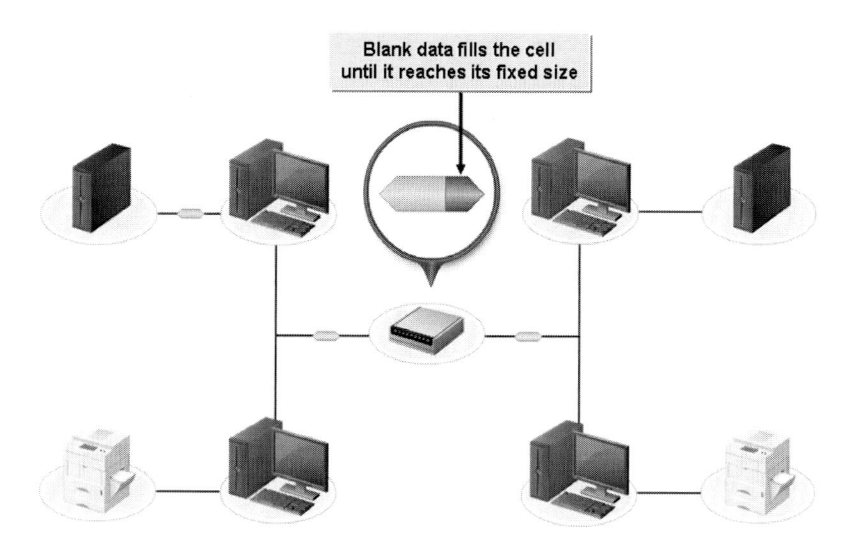

Figure 8-5: *Cell switching uses fixed-length cells instead of variable-length packets.*

ACTIVITY 8-1
Describing Switching

Scenario:
In this activity, you will identify switches and switching technologies.

1. Match the switch type with its description.

___	Store-and-forward	a.	Performs both routing and switching functions.
___	Multilayer	b.	Performs load balancing among server groups.
___	Content	c.	Calculates CRC for data and compares it to the value in the packet.

2. True or False? The difference between cell switching and packet switching networks is that in cell switching data is divided into fixed-length packets.

__ True

__ False

3. In which type of switching is a single path from one endpoint to another built when a connection is needed?

a) Cell

b) Circuit

c) Packet

4. Which switching techniques use the same path for all data traffic between two endpoints in a single session?

a) Packet

b) Circuit

c) Virtual circuit

d) Cell

TOPIC B

Enable Static Routing

In the previous topic, you identified switches and their role in networks. Switches function well in many networking situations, but in most large TCP/IP networks, you will need the advanced traffic-control capabilities of a router. In this topic, you will identify the components of a static IP routing implementation.

It is not enough to just know how millions of networks across the globe connect to form a single network. You should also know how these interconnected networks talk to each other, share data, and how information is transferred from a source to a destination almost instantaneously. Because routers are the workhorses of all internetworks, including the Internet, you will need to understand routing basics no matter what kind of network you support.

Routing

Definition:

Routing is the process of selecting the best route for transferring a packet from a source to its destination on a network. A router applies appropriate algorithms to generate and maintain an information base about network paths. It considers various routing metrics such as the bandwidth and reliability of the path, and communication costs while evaluating available network paths to determine the optimal route for forwarding a packet. Once the optimal route for a packet is assigned, packet switching is done to transport the packet from the source host to a destination host.

Example:

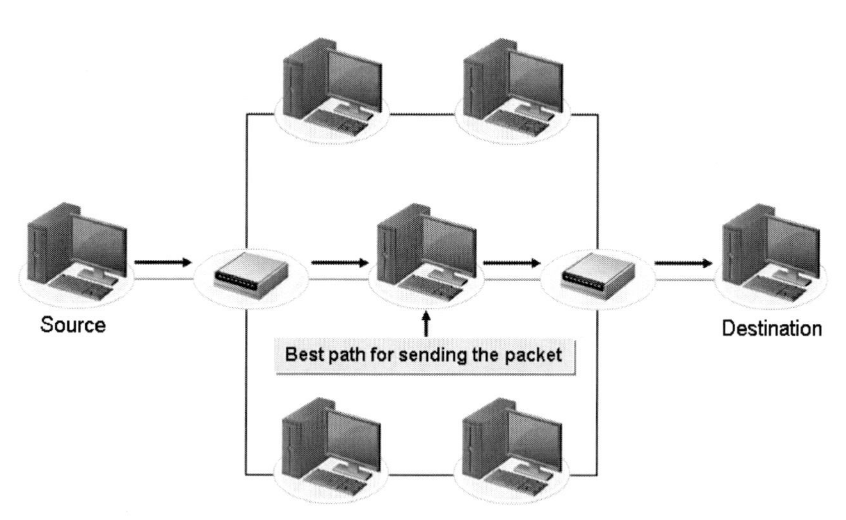

Figure 8-6: *A router selects the best path for transferring packets.*

Route

Route is the path used by data packets to reach the specified destination using the gateway as the next hop. Routes are added in the routing table that store information about connected and remote networks. Connected networks are directly attached to one of the router's interfaces, which are the gateways for the hosts on different local networks. Because remote networks are not directly connected to the router, routes to these networks must be manually configured on the router by the network administrator or set automatically using dynamic routing protocols.

Software-Based Routing in Windows Server

Although not as common as hardware-based routers, Windows Server® computers with two or more NICs installed can use the Routing and Remote Access software to function as routers. For testing purposes, instead of installing two NICs, you can install a software-based interface called the Microsoft® Loopback Adapter on your Windows system, which can simulate the presence of an additional NIC.

Static Routing

Static routing uses table mappings that the network administrator established manually in the router prior to routing. Static route mappings do not change unless the network administrator alters them. Static routes remain in a routing table, and traffic is forwarded regardless of whether the destination is active or inactive.

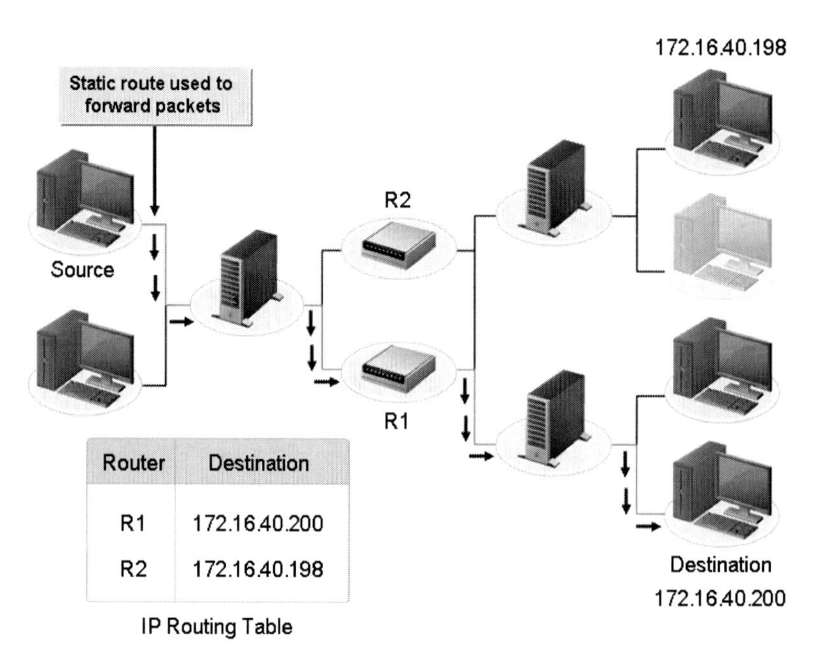

Figure 8-7: *Static routes can be altered only by a network administrator.*

Types of Routers

Routers can be classified into three main categories: access, distribution, and core.

Router Type	*Description*
Access routers	Routers used in *SOHO* networks. They are located at customer sites and are inexpensive.
Distribution routers	Routers that collect data from multiple access routers and redistribute them to an enterprise location such as a company's headquarters. The routing capabilities of a distribution router are greater than those of access routers.
Core routers	Core routers are located at the center of network backbones. They are used to connect multiple distribution routers located in different buildings to the backbone.

Routers vs. Switches

When computers communicate with different networks through switches, they are limited to adjacent networks because switches use the MAC address of a device to locate it. Routers, on the other hand, are designed to interconnect multiple networks and support connectivity to distant networks. They use a map of the network to make decisions on where to forward data packets. Routers primarily determine the next hop for data. Another advantage that a router has over a switch is that it can read the port number and determine not only the data's destination using the IP address but also what kind of data it is transmitting. Broadcasts can either be forwarded or dumped based on the settings of the router.

Unmanaged vs. Managed Switches

Unmanaged switches are devices that perform switching without user intervention. In other words, the functions of an unmanaged switch cannot be controlled. On the other hand, a managed switch provides complete control over how the device functions. It has its own IP address and a web interface through which the configurations can be managed. Managed switches allow users to create VLANs within the network.

Routing Tables

Definition:

A *routing table* is a database created manually or by a route-discovery protocol that contains network addresses as perceived by a specific router. Routers refer to this table to determine where to forward packets. If a router attached to four networks receives a packet from one of them, it would have to determine which of the three other networks is the best route to transfer the packet to its destination. Each router uses its routing table to forward a packet to another network or router until the packet reaches its destination. The action of forwarding a packet from one router to the next is called a *hop*. You can specify the number of hops packets can take from a sender to a receiver.

Example:

Figure 8-8: *A routing table.*

Route Cost

The number of hops along a route between two networks constitutes that route's *cost*. However, a cost can also consist of other specifications such as the transmission speed. Typically, a router maintains the most cost-effective route in its table.

Static Routing Tables

Static routing tables are manually configured on a router. They are easy to set up and are sometimes used on a small network. Also, as long as a network is relatively unchanging, static routing tables are ideal for an extranet where the border router of an *Autonomous System (AS)* is pointed toward the border router of an external network.

The advantage of static routing is that it does not cause additional network traffic by sending routing table updates to other routers. It provides extra security from other systems' rogue routers sending information to the AS routers. Also, the routing table can be configured to cover only the necessary portion of the network. That way, the router does not expend resources for maintaining its routing table.

The biggest disadvantage of static routing tables is that it requires manual maintenance. Network changes need to be updated manually on all routers affected by the change. Because of this, static routing is prone to configuration errors, and is less efficient than dynamic routing. However, if using static routing tables, it is crucial to maintain detailed documentation.

Routing Table Entries

Routing table entries fall into four general categories:

- Direct network routes, for subnets to which the router is directly attached.
- Remote network routes, for subnets that are not directly attached.
- Host routes, for routes to a specific IP address.
- Default routes, which are used when a better network or host route is not found.

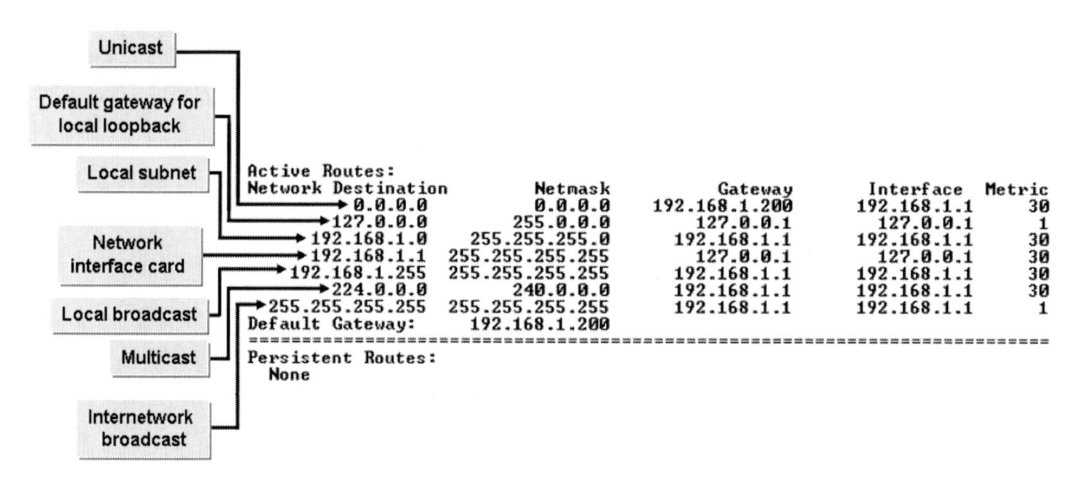

Figure 8-9: *A routing table with entries.*

All IP host computers have a routing table with default entries so that the host can deliver packets to common destinations.

Entry	***Description***
Default gateway (destination: 0.0.0.0)	The default gateway entry appears if the local host has been configured with a default gateway address.
Local loopback (destination: 127.0.0.1)	The local loopback entry provides a delivery route for packets addressed to the local loopback address (127.0.0.1).

Entry	***Description***
Local subnet (destination: network portion of local IP address plus host address of all 0)	The local subnet entry identifies the route to the local network. An example of a destination address can be 140.125.0.0.
Network interface (destination: local IP address)	The network interface entry identifies the route to the host's local network card. An example of a destination address can be 140.125.10.25.
Subnet broadcast address (destination: network portion of local IP address plus host address of all .255)	The subnet broadcast entry identifies the route for broadcasts on the local subnet. An example of a destination address can be 140.125.255.255.
Multicast broadcast address (destination: 224.0.0.0)	The multicast broadcast entry identifies the address for sending multicast transmissions.
Internetwork broadcast address (destination: 255.255.255.255)	The internetwork broadcast entry identifies the route for broadcasts to the entire network. However, most routers will not pass these broadcasts.

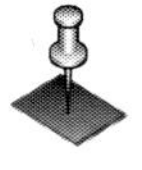

When reading routing tables, it can be helpful to think of each row as a single routing table entry, and each column as a characteristic of that route.

Routing Entry Components

Routing entries are entries in routing tables that provide routing information to a router. There are several components to each entry in a routing table.

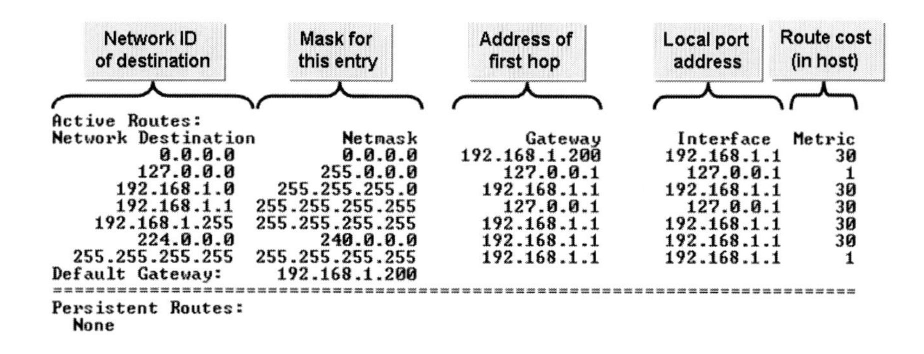

Figure 8-10: *Components of a routing table entry.*

Routing Entry Component	Description
Network destination or network address	The destination field contains the network ID of a destination address and is the search point when processing the routing table. It can be listed as a complete address, but the router will be more efficient if destination entries are listed as network IDs. This way, only one entry is added to the routing table for an entire subnet, no matter how many nodes are on it.
Network mask	A network mask is specific to a routing entry. It determines to what extent does a packet's destination address need to match the network destination field of a routing entry before that route is used to deliver the packet.
Gateway	The gateway field indicates the address to which the packet is delivered on its first hop. It can be the local loopback address, a local IP address, the host's own default gateway address, or the address of an adjacent router.
Interface	The interface is the IP address of the local port that a host uses to send data. Once a destination entry is found, data is sent to the interface entry listed in the same line as the destination.
Metric	A metric is the cost of the route, and it is determined by the number of hops. The metric is used to determine which route to use when there are multiple routes to a destination.

The route Command

Routes to destinations that are not in the default routing table must be added manually. On Windows Server 2008 R2, you can use the `route` command to manage the static routing table.

Command	Used To
route print	Display the routing table entries.
route add	Add static entries.
route delete	Remove static entries.
route change	Modify an existing route.
route -p	Make the specified route persistent across reboots, when used in conjunction with the `add` command.
route -f	Clear a routing table off all entries.

The Routing Process

There are three steps in the routing process:

1. A router receives data, reads its destination IP address and tries to find the shortest path to the destination.
2. The router reads its routing table, which lists the locations of other routers on the network.
3. Once it decides on a route, it removes the old destination MAC address and attaches the MAC address of the next hop in the data's path. The packet's ultimate destination IP address never changes. By enabling the router to change the MAC address, the data moves through multiple local networks.

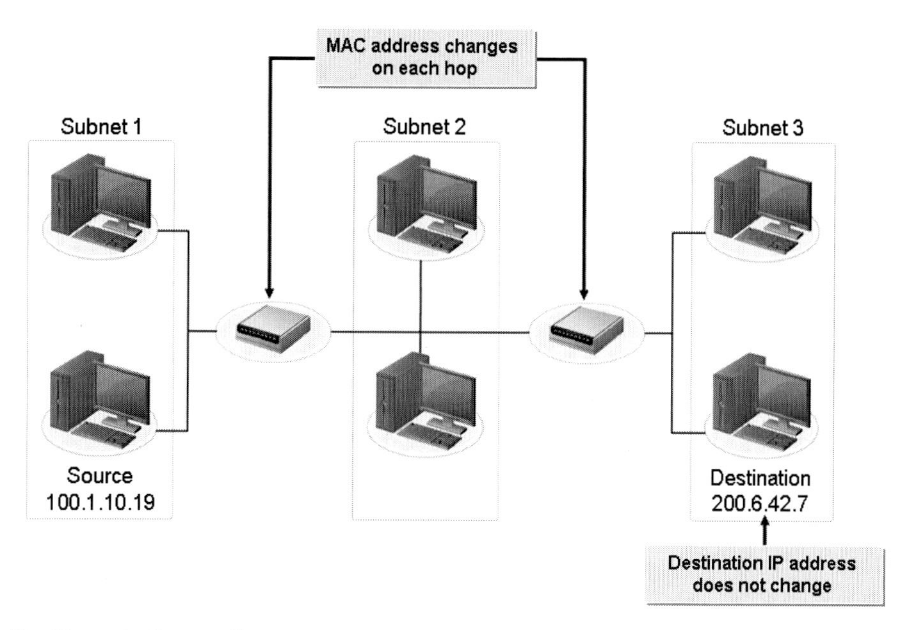

Figure 8-11: *Steps in the routing process.*

Autonomous Systems

Definition:

An *Autonomous System (AS)* or a *routing domain* is a self-contained network or group of networks governed by a single administration. All the routers in an AS share and conform to a single routing policy. An AS can connect to other networks or other autonomous systems, but does not share routing information outside of the AS. Each AS has a unique identification number assigned by the IANA. Depending on whether routing takes place within an autonomous system or among different autonomous systems, it is referred to as *intra-domain routing* or *inter-domain routing*. Each autonomous system may choose different routing algorithms for intra-domain routing, but only one algorithm can be used for inter-domain routing.

Example:

Company A's routers are owned, configured, and managed by the company itself. Each router in Company A is address-aware within the network that it serves as well as of the best output interface (port).

Example:

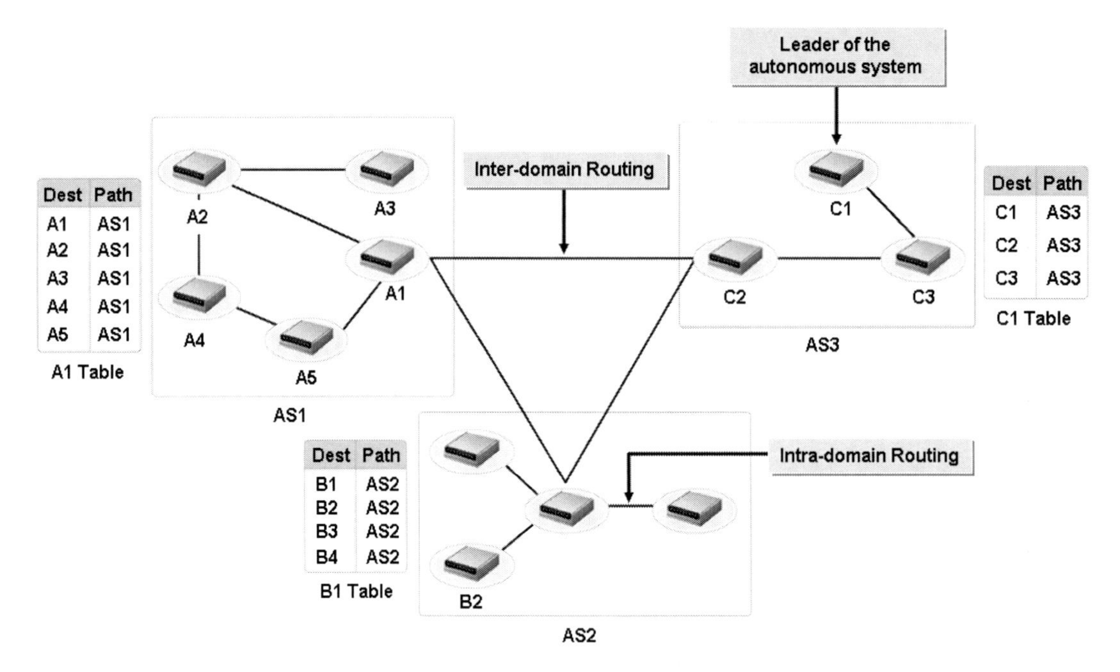

Figure 8-12: *Routing in an autonomous system.*

Classification of Autonomous Systems

Autonomous systems can be classified as *transit* and *stub autonomous systems*.

Autonomous System	*Description*
Transit	The source or destination node does not reside within an autonomous system. The autonomous system allows the traffic to reach another network. ISPs are examples of transit autonomous systems.
Stub	Either the source node or destination node must exist within an autonomous system. The stub autonomous system does not allow transit traffic.

Router Roles in Autonomous Systems

Routers can play three different roles in autonomous systems.

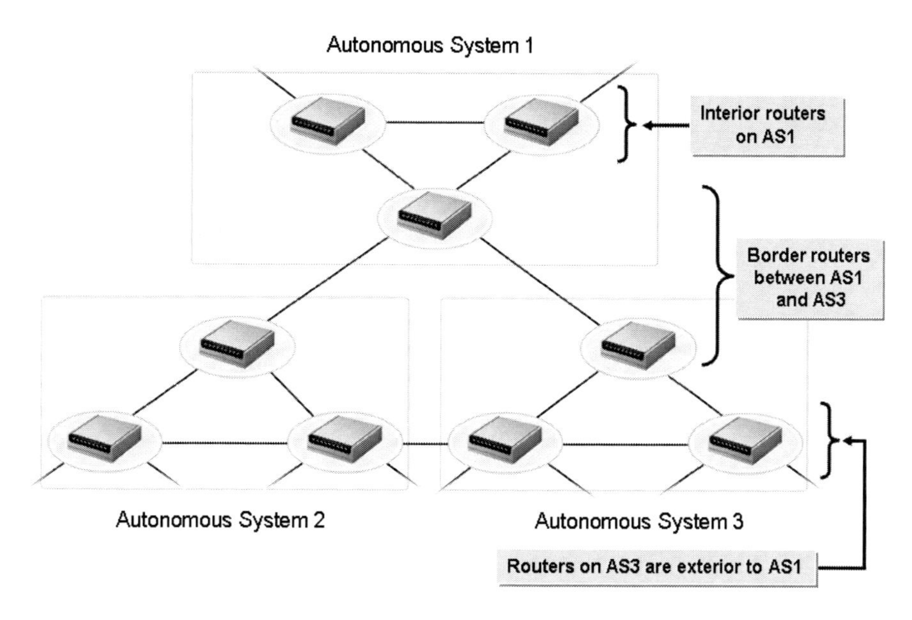

Figure 8-13: *Router roles in an autonomous system.*

Router Role	Description
Interior router	*Interior routers* are arranged inside an AS and the AS administrator controls them. All interfaces on an interior router connect to subnets inside the AS. Interior routers do not provide connections to external networks.
Exterior router	*Exterior routers* are entirely outside of an AS. These routers only matter to the AS if they handle data from the AS. Routers that operate on the Internet backbone are exterior routers.
Border router	*Border routers* are situated on the edge of an AS. They have one or more interfaces inside the AS and one or more interfaces that provide a connection to remote networks. Border routers are usually managed by the administrator of an AS and can be placed between two private networks or between a private network and its ISP to direct requests to the Internet.

IGP vs. EGP

Interior Gateway Protocol (IGP), as the name suggests, is the protocol responsible for exchanging routing information between gateways within an AS. In contrast, *Exterior Gateway Protocol (EGP)* exchanges routing information between two neighboring gateways. EGP can also utilize IGP to resolve a route within the AS.

Routing Methods in Autonomous Systems

There are different methods for routing inside an autonomous system, between adjacent networks, and between distant networks.

Routing Method	*Description*
Inside an autonomous system	When routing inside an autonomous network, data transmission begins at a workstation and does not leave the AS. That means that when any node sends data, it can send it only to a node on the same local network. Nodes use ARP to obtain the local destination's MAC address. When a node needs to send data to a remote network, it sends it to the IP address configured as the node's default gateway. When a node sends data to an address on its own subnet, it sends it directly to the address. When a node needs to send data to a node anywhere inside the AS, all routers in the AS should be aware of the path to the destination node.
Between adjacent networks	Adjacent networks share border routers, and because any router inside an AS knows a direct path to the adjacent network, it knows how to deliver data to the correct border router. That border router then passes the data on to the appropriate network. This configuration gives an AS a single point of contact between adjacent networks.
Between distant networks	Distant networks are not directly aware of the location of a destination network. You have accessed a distant network if you have sent a request to the Internet for a web page. An AS router cannot know all of the details in the path to a website. In this situation, the routers send the data to a default gateway. If the router serving as the default gateway does not know the destination, it transmits the packet to its own default gateway. Data moves from default gateway to default gateway until it either reaches a router that knows a route to the destination, or the TTL expires and the packet expires on the network.

How to Configure Routing and Remote Access

Procedure Reference: Configure Routing and Remote Access

To configure routing and remote access:

1. Choose **Start→All Programs→Administrative Tools→Server Manager.**
2. In the Server Manager window, under **Roles,** add the role **Network Policy and Access Services.**
3. From the **Roles Service** list, check the **Routing and Remote Access Services** check box and install the role.
4. In the Server Manager window, expand **Roles→Network Policy and Access Services.**
5. In the **Routing and Remote Access Server Setup Wizard,** set the required routing and remote access settings.
6. Close the Server Manager window.

ACTIVITY 8-2

Enabling Static Routing

There is a simulated version of this activity available on the CD-ROM that shipped with this course. You can run this simulation on any Windows computer to review the activity after class, or as an alternative to performing the activity as a group in class. The activity simulation can be launched either directly from the CD-ROM by clicking the **Interactives** link and navigating to the appropriate one, or from the installed data file location by opening the C:\Data\Simulations\Lesson#\Activity# folder and double-clicking the executable (.exe) file.

Scenario:

You work for a startup that plans to implement software-based routing by using Windows Server 2008 R2 routing features. You are going to test a router in a lab environment to simulate the production router. You need to enable routing on the server that you will be testing.

---

1. Enable routing and remote access.

a. Choose **Start→All Programs→Administrative Tools→Server Manager.**

b. In the Server Manager window, right-click **Roles** and choose **Add Roles.**

c. In the Add Roles Wizard, click **Next.**

d. In the **Roles** list, check the **Network Policy and Access Services** check box and click **Next.**

e. On the **Network Policy and Access Services** page, click **Next.**

f. On the **Select Role Services** page, in the **Role services** list, check the **Routing and Remote Access Services** check box and click **Next.**

g. Click **Install** and then click **Close.**

---

2. Verify that routing and remote access is enabled.

a. In the Server Manager window, in the left pane, expand **Roles→Network Policy and Access Services** and select **Routing and Remote Access.**

b. Choose **Action→Configure and Enable Routing and Remote Access.**

c. In the **Routing and Remote Access Server Setup Wizard,** click **Next.**

d. Verify that the **Remote access (dial-up or VPN)** option is selected and click **Next.**

e. Check the **VPN** check box and click **Next.**

f. From the **Network interfaces** list, select the **Loopback Adapter** option and click **Next.**

g. Verify that the **Automatically** option is selected, and click **Next** to assign IP addresses automatically to remote clients.

h. Verify that the **No, use Routing and Remote Access to authenticate connection requests** option is selected and click **Next.**

i. Click **Finish** and if necessary, click **OK.**

j. Observe that the Routing and Remote Access service has been enabled, indicated by the green upward pointing arrow next to the Routing and Remote Access object on the left pane. Close the Server Manager window.

DISCOVERY ACTIVITY 8-3

Identifying Routing Entries

Scenario:

You want to identify the default routing entries on the Windows Server 2008 R2 computer that you have enabled as a router. Refer to the IPv4 route table shown below to complete this activity.

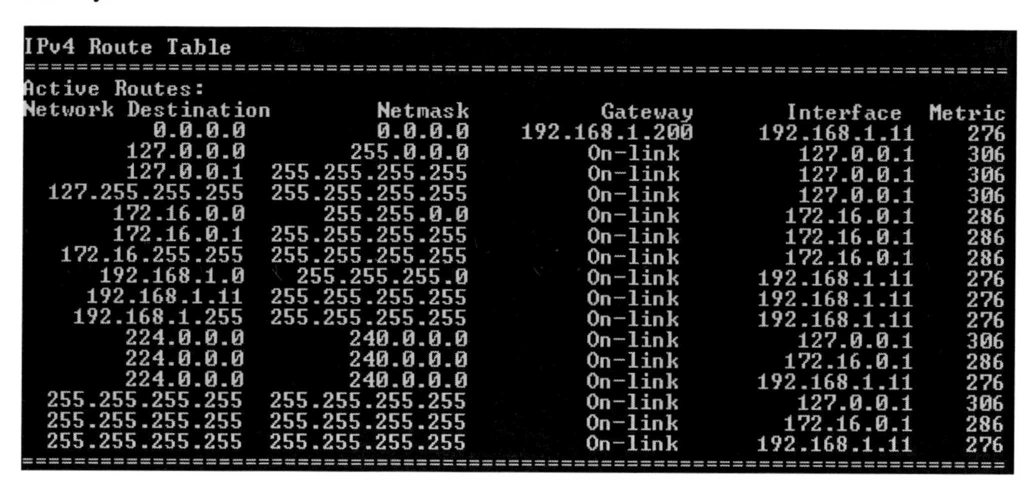

IPv4 Route Table

Active Routes:

Network Destination	Netmask	Gateway	Interface	Metric
0.0.0.0	0.0.0.0	192.168.1.200	192.168.1.11	276
127.0.0.0	255.0.0.0	On-link	127.0.0.1	306
127.0.0.1	255.255.255.255	On-link	127.0.0.1	306
127.255.255.255	255.255.255.255	On-link	127.0.0.1	306
172.16.0.0	255.255.0.0	On-link	172.16.0.1	286
172.16.0.1	255.255.255.255	On-link	172.16.0.1	286
172.16.255.255	255.255.255.255	On-link	172.16.0.1	286
192.168.1.0	255.255.255.0	On-link	192.168.1.11	276
192.168.1.11	255.255.255.255	On-link	192.168.1.11	276
192.168.1.255	255.255.255.255	On-link	192.168.1.11	276
224.0.0.0	240.0.0.0	On-link	127.0.0.1	306
224.0.0.0	240.0.0.0	On-link	172.16.0.1	286
224.0.0.0	240.0.0.0	On-link	192.168.1.11	276
255.255.255.255	255.255.255.255	On-link	127.0.0.1	306
255.255.255.255	255.255.255.255	On-link	172.16.0.1	286
255.255.255.255	255.255.255.255	On-link	192.168.1.11	276

1. **Which route determines the destination for packets to the 172.16.0.0 network? What adapter will they be delivered to?**

2. **Which interfaces will receive internetwork broadcasts?**

3. **Why is there no route to the 0.0.0.0 network destination on the 172.16.0.1 interface?**

4. **If you wanted packets to a specific network to be routed to the 172.16.0.1 network interface instead of to the default gateway, what would you do?**

TOPIC C
Implement Dynamic IP Routing

In the previous topic, you identified the components of a static routing implementation. Routing can also be implemented dynamically. In this topic, you will implement dynamic routing.

Dynamic routing, like dynamic IP addressing, is the technology of choice in larger network environments. As a network professional, you should understand dynamic routing technologies and how you can implement them so that you can support routed environments of all sizes and types. This will ensure that each device is properly identified on the network.

Dynamic Routing

Routers that support dynamic routing perform route discovery operations to build and update routing tables themselves using specially designed software. Routers transmit data to adjacent routers providing information about the networks they are currently connected to and networks they can reach. In the dynamic routing process, routing entries are dynamically created. Dynamically built routing tables can show a more accurate picture of a network as it is updated more often than static tables because the routers, and not the administrator, update the tables. If the network suffers traffic congestion or device failures, a router running dynamic routing protocols can automatically detect the problem and calculate a different routing path. This feature is a huge advantage on large networks with many routers or multiple paths to each endpoint.

Static Routing vs. Dynamic Routing

In static routing, routing entries are created manually in configuration files. This file is loaded when the router starts. Static routing is used when there are fewer devices on the network. Dynamic routing uses special software designed for routing devices. This software automatically creates routing entries for the router to connect all devices on the network.

Distance-Vector Routing

In *distance-vector routing,* each router passes a copy of its routing table to its neighbors. It also maintains a table of minimum distances to every node. The neighbor adds the route to its own table, incrementing the metric to reflect the extra distance to the end network. The distance is given as a hop count; the vector component specifies the address of the next hop. When a router has two routes to the same network, it selects the one with the lowest metric, assuming that it is faster to route through fewer hops. *Routing Information Protocol (RIP)* implements distance-vector routing.

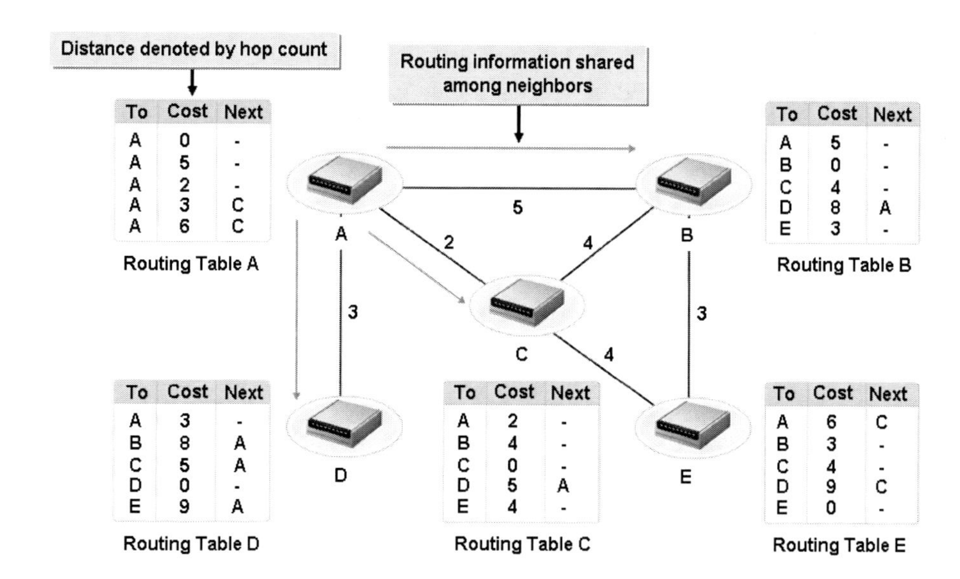

Figure 8-14: *Routers maintain a table of minimum costs.*

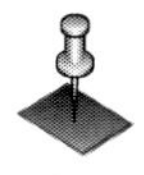

Distance-vector protocols use the Bellman-Ford algorithm to calculate route paths.

Link State Routing

Link state routing floods routing information to all routers within a network. It attempts to build and maintain a more complex route database with more information about the network. Routers can exchange information about a route, such as its quality, bandwidth, and availability. This way, the routers can make a decision about sending data through the network based on more information than just the hop count.

Link state algorithms broadcast small updates and converge quickly, a feature that makes them less prone to routing loops. However, link state algorithms are more expensive to implement because they require more power and memory. The *Open Shortest Path First (OSPF)* protocol implements link -state routing.

Link State vs. Distance-Vector Routing

To understand the difference between link state and distance-vector routing, consider a situation in which a single dial-up connection or two separate T1 links can deliver a packet. Distance-vector prefers dial-up based on the hop count alone; link-state prefers the two-hop route through the higher bandwidth connection. Also, link state is more complicated to set up and maintain than distance-vector. An administrator has to configure more information about the routers' local routes. However, link state routers are a must in situations with multiple routes through different types of connections, such as border routers.

Distance-Vector vs. Hybrid Routing

Distance-vector routing uses hop counts and routing table updates to prevent routing loops. They also alert neighboring routers about broken routing paths. Hybrid routing uses both distance-vector and link state routing methods. In hybrid routing, various factors such as the link cost and network bandwidth are considered before deciding upon the best route.

Path-Vector Routing

Path-vector routing is used in inter-domain routing, and a router keeps track of the route from itself to the destination. However, rather than recording every individual node, path-vector routing can treat entire autonomous systems as nodes. As the AS border or exterior routers pass routing information from one to the next, each adds its presence to the path and forwards the route to the next autonomous system in the chain. If the destination address is within an AS, the border router passes the packet on to interior routers.

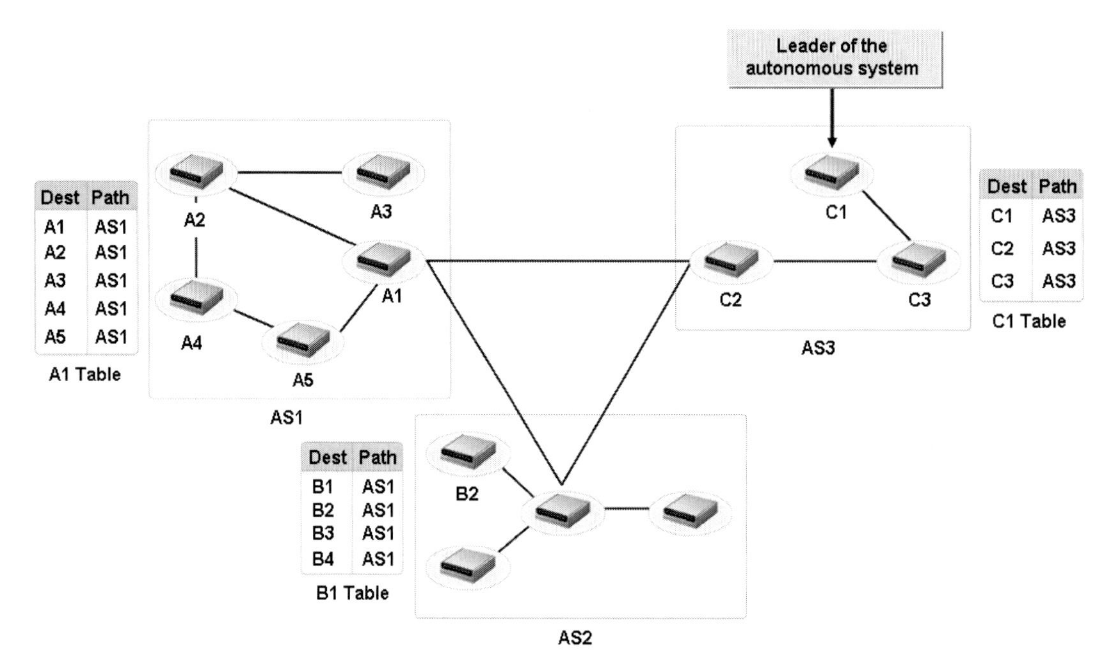

Figure 8-15: *The path vector routing table of different autonomous systems.*

Path-vector routing is enhanced by its inclusion of routing policies, which are implemented by administrators to enable routers to react to situations such as network congestion, offline nodes, and potentially duplicate routes. Path-vector routing has roots in distance-vector routing, but was designed to scale up to much larger networks. The *Border Gateway Protocol (BGP)* implements path vector routing.

Route Convergence

In dynamic routing, when the network topology or conditions change, each router must first learn of the change and then calculate the effect and update its routing tables. *Route convergence* is the period of time between a network change and the router updates to reach a steady state once again. During route convergence, data delivery can be unreliable as the routing table may not be updated with the route information.

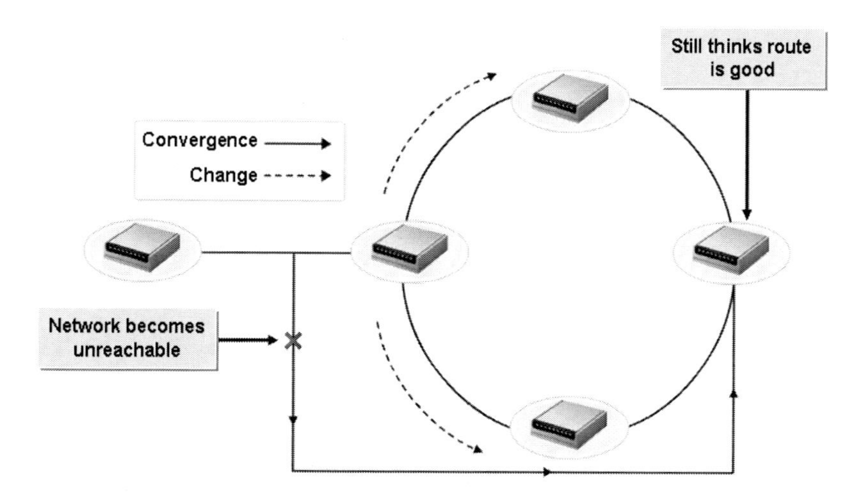

Figure 8-16: *A router changes the route when a part of the network becomes unreachable.*

Routing Loops

Definition:

A *routing loop* is a routing process in which two routers discover different routes to the same location that include each other, but have incorrect information and thereby never reach the endpoint. Data caught in a routing loop circles around until its TTL expires. Routing loops can be difficult to detect and to troubleshoot; the best prevention is proper router configuration.

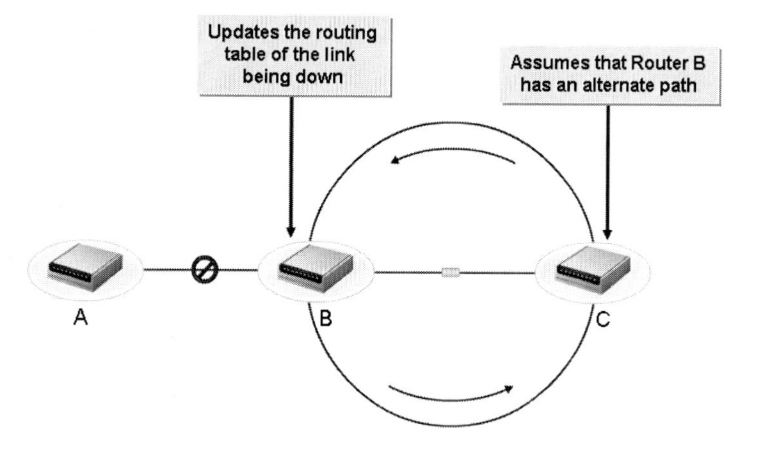

Figure 8-17: *A routing loop created between routers B and C.*

Example: Routers in a Loop

For example, Routers A, B, and C are connected in a line. When the link between A and B goes down, it prompts B to update its routing table. But, this update does not reach C on time, and it sends its regular update to B. This leads B to assume that C has found an alternate path to reach A. An endless loop is created because B tries to send packets addressed to A via C, which redirects the packets to B. This routing loop continues until the TTL of the data expires.

Count-to-Infinity Loops

Definition:

A count-to-infinity loop can occur when a router or network goes down and one of the other routers does not realize that it can no longer reach the route. This loop results in the remaining routers broadcasting incorrect information and updating each other's routing tables to create an endless cycle of hop count recalculation. This cycle continues to infinity, which is configured as 16 hops in most routing implementations.

Example: Routers in a Count-to Infinity Loop

A network contains four routers that connect five networks. In calculating the cost to network E, router 3 figures its cost to be one hop, router 2 figures two hops, and router 1 figures three hops. If router 4 fails, router 3 must recalculate its routing table using information from other routers. However, router 3 still thinks that it can reach network E, and uses information advertised from router 2 to calculate its table.

According to router 2, network E is still two hops away, so router 3 broadcasts that its cost to network E is three hops. Router 1 receives the new information from router 3, updates its table, and then broadcasts this information. Router B also recalculates accordingly and the infinite loop continues.

Split Horizon and Poison Reverse

One workaround to the count-to-infinity problem is the *split horizon* method, where a router does not include any routes to the router from which it discovered its own location in its broadcasts.

Another workaround to the count-to-infinity problem is called a *poison reverse*. Unlike in split horizon, routers using poison reverse broadcast routes back to the router from which they calculated their location, but instead of giving a true hop count, to discourage use of the route, the router broadcasts a hop count of 16, as a warning not to use the value specified and as an intimation that the route was learned from router 1.

Split horizon and poison reverse are not used together. Split horizon is enabled when poison reverse is disabled, and vice versa.

Router Discovery Protocols

Router discovery protocols are used to identify routers on the network.

Protocol	***Description***
RIP	*RIP* is a distance-vector routing protocol that is easy to configure, works well inside simple autonomous systems, and is best deployed in small networks with a fewer numbers of routers and in a non-dynamic environment. Most equipment that supports RIP is lower in cost than that that supports more complicated router discovery protocols. RIP broadcasts the entire routing table, including known routes and costs, every 30 seconds. This places a lot of router discovery traffic on the network. When RIP builds its routing table, it does not take into account network congestion or link speed and does not support multiple routes to the same network. A router records the route with the lowest metric to a location and removes the others. RIP is very stable, but convergence is slow. RIP is prone to count-to-infinity loops and does not support many of the new features expected on modern networks such as multicast addressing or VLSMs. RIP has been replaced with RIP version 2 (RIP v2).

Protocol	Description
RIP v2	RIP v2 enhances RIP by supporting the following features: • **Next Hop Addressing:**Includes IP address information in routing tables for every router in a given path to avoid sending packets using additional routers. • **Authentication:**Enables password authentication and the use of a key to authenticate routing information to a router. • **Subnet mask:**Supports additional subnets and hosts on an internetwork by supporting VLSMs and including length information along with the routing information. • **Multicast addressing:**Decreases the workload of non–RIP v2 hosts by communicating only with RIP v2 routers. RIP v2 packets use 224.0.0.9 as their IP multicast address. Most hosts and routers support RIP, so ensure that the RIP v2 mode you configure works with your current RIP configuration.
BGP	*BGP* is a path-vector routing protocol used to establish routing between ISPs. BGP is the routing protocol used to connect Internet backbones. BGP maintains a table of IP networks among autonomous systems. BGP was created as a fully decentralized routing protocol to replace EGP in order to decentralize the Internet. The current version since 1994 is BGP v4. Although BGP was created to replace EGP, BGP is considered an interautonomous routing protocol. When it is used to route information between ASs, it is called External BGP (EBGP), but when EGP is used to route information within an AS, it is referred to as Internal BGP (IBGP).
IGRP	*Interior Gateway Routing Protocol (IGRP)* is a distance-vector routing protocol developed by Cisco® as an improvement over RIP and RIP v2. It was designed to be deployed on interior routers within an AS. IGRP introduced a composite metric, enabling an administrator to manually configure and add to the hop count up to six metric values to give extra value to the metric. Because of this, IGRP can support multiple routes to the same network and can even support load balancing across routes with identical metrics.
EIGRP	*Enhanced Interior Gateway Routing Protocol (EIGRP)* is a proprietary routing protocol by Cisco and considered a hybrid protocol. It includes features that support VLSM and classful and classless subnet masks. Additional updates reduce convergence times and improve network stability during changes. To ensure that EIGRP is a viable solution for interior routing, EIGRP removed routing protocol dependence on the network protocol. This means that routing tables can be built for several different protocols—even protocols that have not been fully deployed yet, such as IPv6.
OSPF	On IP internetworks, link-state routing is usually accomplished by the *OSPF* protocol. Each OSPF router uses the information in its database to build the shortest possible path to destinations on the internetwork. Although OSPF uses less bandwidth than distance-vector protocols, it requires more memory and CPU resources. OSPF uses Dijkstra's algorithm for computing the best path through a network.
IS-IS	*Intermediate System to Intermediate System (IS-IS)* is a link-state routing protocol that is natively an ISO network layer protocol. IS-IS is similar to OSPF (they both use Dijkstra's algorithm) but IS-IS is able to support more routers than OSPF and does not support only a specific type of network address. This made IS-IS easily adaptable to support IPv6.

For more information on RIP v2, see RFC 1387 "RIP Version 2 Protocol Analysis." You might also be interested in RFCs 1388 and 1389 for RIP II information.

RIP vs. OSPF

There are differences in characteristics of RIP and OSPF.

Characteristic	RIP	OSPF
Size of metric	16—This means that a RIP network cannot be larger than 16 hops. This maximum is further reduced when costs other than 1 are used for certain routes.	Limited only by the number of bits in the metric field (64,000). Because OSPF does not suffer from the count-to-infinity problem, it can be the basis for much larger internetworks, and administrators can assign costs to optimize routing without limiting the size of the network.
Maximum number of routers	15—This value is related to the allowable metric size.	65,535. This value is related to the allowable metric size.
Variable-length subnets	Only with RIP v2; RIP treats subnets as part of the internal structure of the network and assumes that all subnets are of equal length. With RIP, all subnets must be contiguous, connected, and hidden from remote networks.	Supported by default; Because OSPF treats the subnet mask as part of the protocol information, the restrictions that affect RIP do not apply.
Convergence	Poison reverse or split horizon must be used to counteract the count-to-infinity problem. RIP must calculate all routes before broadcasting the information.	Link State Acknowledgements (LSAs) provide rapid convergence among tables; no count-to-infinity problem arises. OSPF passes along LSAs as soon as they are received, meaning that nodes can adjust their routing tables at practically the same time.
Broadcast Traffic	The entire routing table is broadcast every 30 seconds.	A partial routing table (Hello packet) is broadcast only to direct connections every 30 minutes.

STP

The *Spanning-Tree Protocol (STP)* is a Layer 2 protocol that is used for routing and prevents network loops by adopting a dynamic routing method. A network loop can occur when you have multiple switches on a network, and connect them to each other using different ports. STP establishes routes on the network by creating virtual circuits. It helps switches achieve a loop-free path by determining the ports that should be forwarding data and the ports that should be blocked to create a single loop-free path. The switch then switches frames from one port to another through the identified path.

In a hierarchical tree network, a root node can communicate with lower level nodes only in a linear path. In case any node fails on the path, the lower level nodes become inaccessible. STP establishes a cross-linked structure between different branches of the hierarchical network thus providing shorter paths and higher link redundancy.

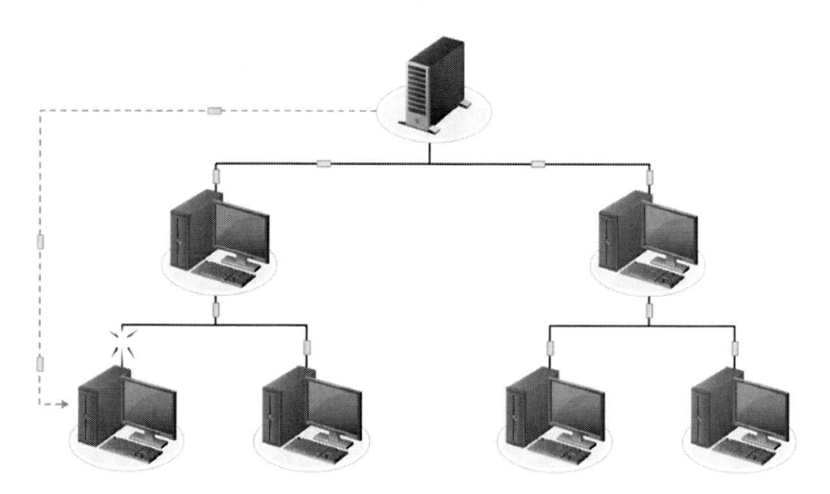

Figure 8-18: *A loop-free path created by STP.*

CARP

Common Address Redundancy Protocol (CARP) allows a number of computers to be grouped together to use a single virtual network interface between them. One of the computers acts as the master and it responds to all packets sent to that virtual interface address. All of the other computers just act as hot spares. If the master computer fails, one of the spares would immediately take over with virtually no downtime. It is also possible to have two different CARP groups using the same IP address. This allows for the load balancing of any traffic destined for that IP. The spreading of the load improves network performance.

ACTIVITY 8-4
Implementing Dynamic IP Routing

There is a simulated version of this activity available on the CD-ROM that shipped with this course. You can run this simulation on any Windows computer to review the activity after class, or as an alternative to performing the activity as a group in class. The activity simulation can be launched either directly from the CD-ROM by clicking the **Interactives** link and navigating to the appropriate one, or from the installed data file location by opening the C:\Data\Simulations\Lesson#\Activity# folder and double-clicking the executable (.exe) file.

Scenario:

Your company has grown and static routing no longer meets the needs of your network. You plan to implement dynamic routing and need to install the routing protocol on your Windows Server 2008 R2 router. Your company DHCP server is running on a Windows Server 2008 R2 system.

---

1. Add RIP v2 as the routing protocol.

a. Choose **Start→Administrative Tools→Routing and Remote Access.**

b. In the Routing and Remote Access window, expand **COMPUTER## (local)**, expand **IPv4** and select **General.**

c. Choose **Action→New Routing Protocol.**

d. In the **New Routing Protocol** dialog box, select **RIP Version 2 for Internet Protocol** and click **OK** to add RIP v2 as the routing protocol.

---

2. Add the RIP interfaces.

a. From the left pane, in the Routing and Remote Access window, under **IPv4**, select **RIP.**

b. Choose **Action→New Interface.**

c. In the **New Interface for RIP Version 2 for Internet Protocol** dialog box, verify that **Local Area Connection** is selected and click **OK.**

d. In the **RIP Properties - Local Area Connection Properties** dialog box, click **OK** to accept the default settings.

e. Choose **Action→New Interface.**

f. Verify the **Loopback Adapter** is selected, and click **OK.**

g. Click **OK** to accept the default settings.

---

3. Examine the dynamic routes.

a. With RIP selected, choose **Action→Show Neighbors.**

b. Observe that you have neighbor routers running the RIP. Close the RIP Neighbors window.

c. Close the Routing and Remote Access window.

TOPIC D

Virtual LANs

In the previous topics in this lesson, you identified the functions of routers and switches in LAN implementations. Once you understand the basic operation of switches and routers, you are ready to start considering implementing some of their more advanced capabilities in a virtual LAN environment. In this topic, you will identify VLANs and their functionalities.

There may be instances where you will have to handle LAN implementations in different locations without modifying or relocating the systems on the network. In such cases, breaking the network into smaller virtual LANs makes them easier to manage. VLANs also contribute to improving the overall network performance by grouping users and network resources that frequently communicate.

VLANs

Definition:

A *virtual LAN (VLAN)* is a LAN in which the network components can be connected even when they are not on the same LAN segment. It is a logical network without the physical characteristics of a LAN. Key hardware in a VLAN includes a configurable managed switch, known as a *VLAN switch,* which can build a logical network in any required configuration, even when computers are on different physical segments.

Configuration management can be done through software and there is no need to relocate the devices physically. Each VLAN is logically a network in itself, and if there are packets that are meant for a node that does not belong to a VLAN, they must be forwarded by a routing device. Unlike the regular LAN that is limited by physical distances, VLANs can network irrespective of the physical distances involved and also can group individual networks that are based on different technologies.

Example:

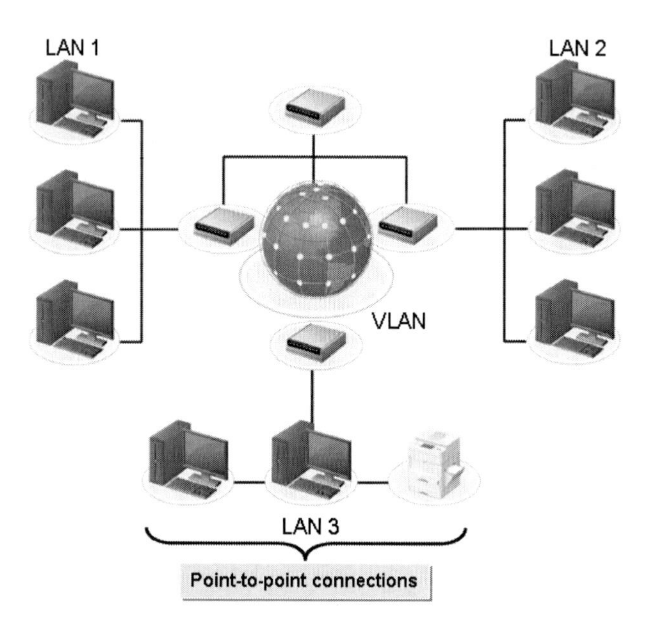

Figure 8-19: *LAN segments forming a VLAN.*

IEEE 802.1q

IEEE 802.1q is a networking standard that supports VLANs in an Ethernet-based network. When a switch assigns the VLAN identification information to a packet, through a process known as tagging. Two popular protocols for tagging are the Inter-Switch Link (ISL) and the IEEE 802.1q protocol. ISL is the Cisco proprietary protocol for tagging packets and associating them with a particular VLAN on legacy switches, while 802.1q is the IEEE standard for VLAN trunking. Newer Cisco and Juniper Networks switches use 802.1q for tagging.

Uses of a VLAN

VLANs can be used to separate groups from the larger network; for example, a group of users that design and test new software. Also, a VLAN can be used to restrict access to network resources from temporary employees or visitors.

Advantages of a VLAN

A VLAN's biggest advantage is that once the physical network is built it is independent of the virtual network, which can be reconfigured for optimal performance by simply changing the VLAN's configuration. The network does not have to be rewired. For example, if a given node sends most of its traffic to an endpoint in a separate subnet, that node can be removed from its current subnet and placed in the endpoint's subnet—all without changing a single cable and without the user's knowledge.

VLANs lend themselves to remote administration because an administrator can telnet into the VLAN device rather than physically visit it, as long as the physical point-to-point configuration does not change. Also, VLAN switches are relatively expensive but the advantages and improvements in network performance outweigh the cost.

Types of VLANs

VLANs can be broadly classified into three types depending upon the characteristics used for its segmentation.

Type	*Computers Are Configured to a VLAN Based On*
Port-based VLANs	The ports that are a part of the VLAN. For example, in a switch with five ports, ports 1, 2, and 3 can be configured to belong to VLAN A and ports 4 and 5 to belong to VLAN B.
MAC address-based VLANs	The MAC address of the computers. Switches are configured to identify the MAC addresses of individual computers connected to it. These MAC addresses are grouped to form the VLAN.
Subnet-based VLANs	The IP subnets that they belong to. The IP addresses are used only as references to identify computers that are to be configured to the VLAN.

VLAN Switch Functions

A VLAN switch is a manageable switch used on VLANs. It enables the network administrator to configure the network in a logical topology. All VLAN segments have equal dedicated connections to all nodes in the segment. The VLAN switch can tie any of its interfaces together into a logical subnet with all the characteristics of a physical subnet. This scheme enables an administrator to control IP addresses, MAC contention domains, and interior routing by using VLAN switch configuration parameters.

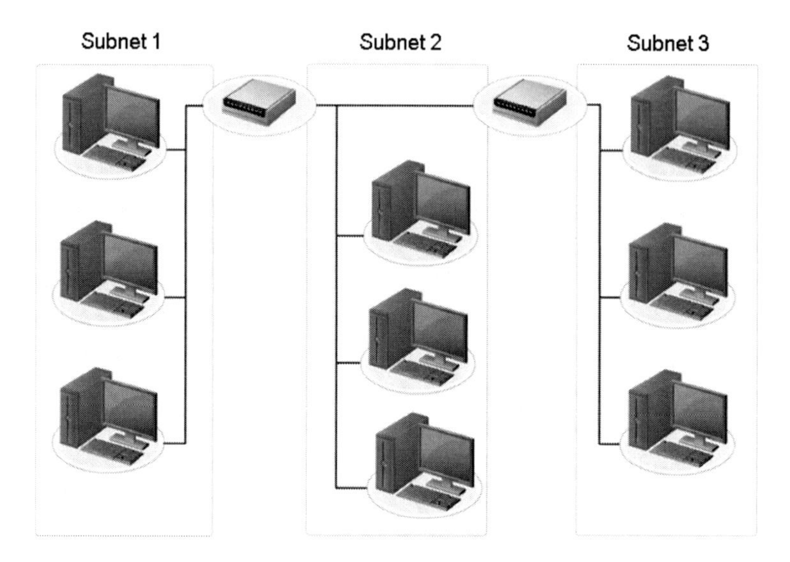

Figure 8-20: *A VLAN switch ties its interfaces into logical subnets.*

VLAN Connections

If it is necessary for users on different VLANs to communicate, you need to connect the VLANs using a Layer 3 network device, such as a router, or by using a higher layer switch.

VLAN Switches vs. Routers

When a VLAN switch receives data, it routes the data based on the destination IP address, just like a router. However, because all the routed subnets are configured in the VLAN, there are no local routes more than two hops away. Exterior routes are handled the same way as they are handled in a regular routed network—they are sent to a default gateway and routed to distant networks.

VTP

The *VLAN Trunking Protocol (VTP)* is a messaging protocol used on VLANs developed by Cisco. All the changes made to a VLAN are documented as VTP configurations. The main function of VTP is to advertise the switching information and configuration changes on a VLAN through all the switches on a network. VTP eliminates the hassles involved in porting the same VLAN to another network, which is managed by different switches. It also allows configuring switches as a group for management in a VLAN.

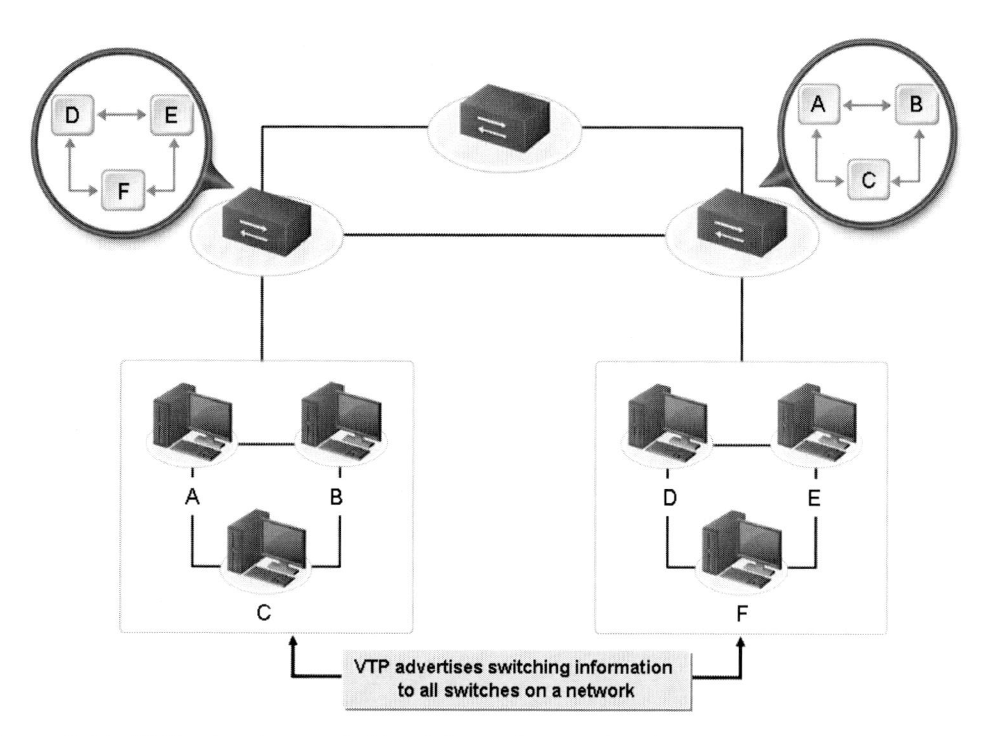

Figure 8-21: *VTP advertises switching information to all switches on a network.*

VTP Modes

There are three VTP modes that a switch can use: server, client, and transparent.

- **Server mode:** This is the default mode for VTP on a switch. In the server mode, a switch can modify VLANs. This information is then transmitted to all the other switches that are configured to the same group using VTP.
- **Client mode:** In the client mode, a switch cannot modify VLANs but will receive configuration information from other switches.
- **Transparent mode:** In the transparent mode, a switch receives configuration messages from other switches but does not process them. Configuration changes to the VLAN are not transmitted to other switches in the group.

ACTIVITY 8-5
Configuring VLANs

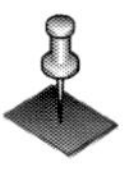

This is a simulated activity available on the CD-ROM that shipped with this course. The activity simulation can be launched either directly from the CD-ROM by clicking the **Interactives** link and navigating to the appropriate one, or from the installed data file location by opening the C:\Data\Simulations\Lesson#\Activity# folder and double-clicking the executable (.exe) file.

Scenario:

You are the network administrator for OGC Technologies. You have been asked to separate the computers used in the R&D department from the computers used in the production environment. As you have a VLAN, you decide to reconfigure the network to separate the computers.

---

1. Configure VLANs.

a. Browse to the C:\Data\Simulations\Lesson8\Activity8-5 folder.

b. Double-click the executable file.

c. In the **Open File - Security Warning** message box, click **Run.**

d. Follow the on-screen steps for the simulation.

e. Close the C:\Data\Simulations\Lesson8\Activity8-5 folder.

TOPIC E

Plan a SOHO Network

In the previous topic, you identified the components of a VLAN implementation. As Network+ certified professionals, you may need to set up a network that is similar to a VLAN but much smaller in magnitude with just a few systems interconnected. In this topic, you will implement a Small Office/Home Office (SOHO) network.

Just as you design a large network, you need to be able to design smaller SOHO networks that suit the physical boundaries of a smaller location. By being aware of the best practices for setting up a small network, you will be able to accurately identify the requirements and resources that match the location.

SOHO Networks

Definition:

A *Small Office/Home Office (SOHO)* network is a small network that can comprise up to 10 nodes. SOHO networks can either be wired or wireless. It is necessary that all the computers in a SOHO network be present at the same physical location. A SOHO can include devices such as switches or routers.

Small Office/Home Office is sometimes referred to as Single Office/Home Office.

Example:

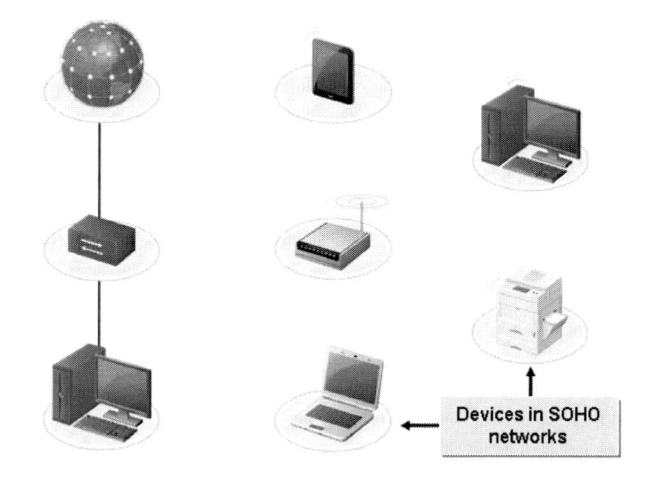

Figure 8-22: *Components of a SOHO network.*

SOHO Network Hardware

The list of device types and other requirements to implement a SOHO network is:

- Computers and laptops: About 1 to 10 computers that are to be connected on the network.
- Specialized connectivity devices - SOHO hubs, switches, and routers.
- Peripheral devices: Printers, fax machines, access points, and biometric devices can also be added to the network.
- Modem: An ADSL modem to connect to the Internet.
- And, Cable length: For a wired SOHO, you need connecting cable lengths of 100 to 200 meters.

Small Office Routers

Routing in a SOHO network does not require routing hardware as large networks and the Internet. There are several popular, relatively inexpensive, and easy to implement router products that are designed to support both wired and wireless SOHO networks, available from D-Link, Linksys, and NETGEAR.

How to Plan a SOHO Network

SOHO networks require meticulous planning to set up. Planning a SOHO network is not the same as planning a regular enterprise network. There are specific requirements that need to be met to successfully set up a SOHO network.

Guidelines

To plan a SOHO network:

- Connect up to 10 computers in the SOHO network.
- Ensure that the access points are distributed strategically to maintain seamless connectivity, if your SOHO network is implemented using the wireless technology.
- Use routers and switches that can scale up, to handle the data transmission requirements of the computers on the network. Personal use routers and switches may not support a SOHO.
- Plan the connectivity and placement of other devices such as printers and fax machines if needed on your network.
- Conceal the cabling to avoid disruption or outages on wired SOHOs.

Example:

Thomas Lee is a network professional who is hired by OGC Technologies to set up a SOHO network for a small unit of staff in a remote location. Before planning the network, Thomas enquires about the number of employees who will be working in the facility. As the new facility will primarily act as a customer support center, it will have no more than 15 employees.

He decides that a wireless SOHO will suit the requirements, and requests that his client procure the required wireless equipment that include laptops for the employees, wireless routers that can handle a small network, access points and a wireless printer. Based on the number of access points required, he determines strategic locations to place them to ensure seamless connectivity. He also determines a suitable location for the printer.

Limitations of a SOHO Network

There are some environment limitations in setting up a SOHO network. All the computers and peripheral devices should be over a short range as long distance networking is not supported.

A SOHO setup has some equipment limitations and is recommended for a maximum of 10 devices that include workstations, printers, and fax machines with one hub, switch, or router. SOHO networks cannot support more devices. Segmentation of the network is also not possible.

Compatibility Requirements

As SOHO is intended for smaller networks or domestic purposes, multiple devices and technologies such as switches, routers, VLANs, VPNs are not recommended. Switches and routers designed for medium-sized or larger networks are expensive to be used in SOHO environments.

ACTIVITY 8-6
Planning a SOHO Network

Scenario:
In this activity, you will plan a SOHO network.

---

1. **What is the maximum number of computers that can be connected in a SOHO network?**

    a) 10

    b) 30

    c) 50

    d) 100

---

2. **True or False? Connectivity devices such as routers and switches meant for domestic purposes can be used on SOHO networks.**

    __ True

    __ False

Lesson 8 Follow-up

In this lesson, you identified the components of a LAN implementation. Since a LAN is the fundamental unit of computer networking, all networking professionals will need a thorough understanding of LAN technologies and their components.

1. **Of the LAN infrastructure technologies discussed in this lesson, which ones do you expect to work with the most? Why?**

2. **What do you see as the pros and cons of implementing static routing over dynamic routing?**

9 WAN Infrastructure

Lesson Time: 2 hour(s), 25 minutes

Lesson Objectives:

In this lesson, you will identify the infrastructure of a WAN implementation.

You will:

- Identify the major transmission technologies used in WANs.
- Identify the major WAN connectivity methods.
- Identify voice over data transmission systems and technologies.

Introduction

In the previous lesson, you identified the components of a LAN implementation. There are other technologies that can be implemented on a WAN. In this lesson, you will identify the components of a WAN implementation.

Many local networks these days have a wide area connection to a distant network. Moreover, virtually every network connects in one way or another to the biggest WAN of them all, the Internet. As a networking professional, you will need to understand the infrastructure of these WAN connections so that you can ensure connectivity in the networks that you support.

This lesson covers all or part of the following CompTIA® Network+® (Exam N10-005) certification objectives:

- Topic A:
  - 1.2 Classify how applications, devices, and protocols relate to the OSI model layers.
  - 3.4 Categorize WAN technology types and properties.
  - 3.5 Describe different network topologies.
  - 3.8 Identify components of wiring distribution.
- Topic B:
  - 1.2 Classify how applications, devices, and protocols relate to the OSI model layers.
  - 3.4 Categorize WAN technology types and properties.
- Topic C:
  - 1.2 Classify how applications, devices, and protocols relate to the OSI model layers.

- 1.6 Explain the function of common networking protocols.
- 2.4 Given a scenario, troubleshoot common wireless problems.
- 4.6 Explain different methods for network performance optimization.

TOPIC A
WAN Transmission Technologies

You have identified the transmission technologies and characteristics of a LAN implementation. When there are multiple LAN implementations that need to communicate, the LANs connect to form the larger framework of a WAN that uses transmission technologies different from a LAN. In this topic, you will identify the transmission technologies used on a WAN implementation.

Present day communications span the globe. A WAN covers a very large geographical area, and can connect multiple smaller networks. The transmission method used on your WAN might affect overall network performance and cost more than any other factor. From the slowest dial-up to the fastest fiber-optic service, you will need to understand the capabilities of and limitations to your network's transmission method to choose the one best-suited for your network.

ATM

Asynchronous Transfer Mode (ATM) is a *cell-switching network* technology that supports high-speed transfer of voice, video, and data in LANs, WANs, and telephone networks. ATM LAN implementations are uncommon because they are expensive and complex. However, ATM WAN implementations have become reasonably popular because of their versatility and high bandwidth availability. Information is transferred in fixed-size packets, called *cells*, each consisting of 53 bytes. ATM networks are made up of switches, which transport data cells among networks.

ATM is a connection-oriented protocol. In other words, if a node is going to send cells to another node, it will first establish a connection. The connection is terminated only after all cells are sent. After connection establishment, ATM routes the cells using identifiers rather than using source and destination addresses. ATM offers reliable Quality of Service (QoS), and is envisioned as the technology for providing broadband *Integrated Services Digital Network (ISDN)* services.

ATM handles broadband applications efficiently, and at the same time, allows users to assign priority to traffic on the network. ATM is used for various applications such as video on demand, high-speed data transfer, teleconferencing, remote sensing, 3-D interactive simulations, and tele-instruction.

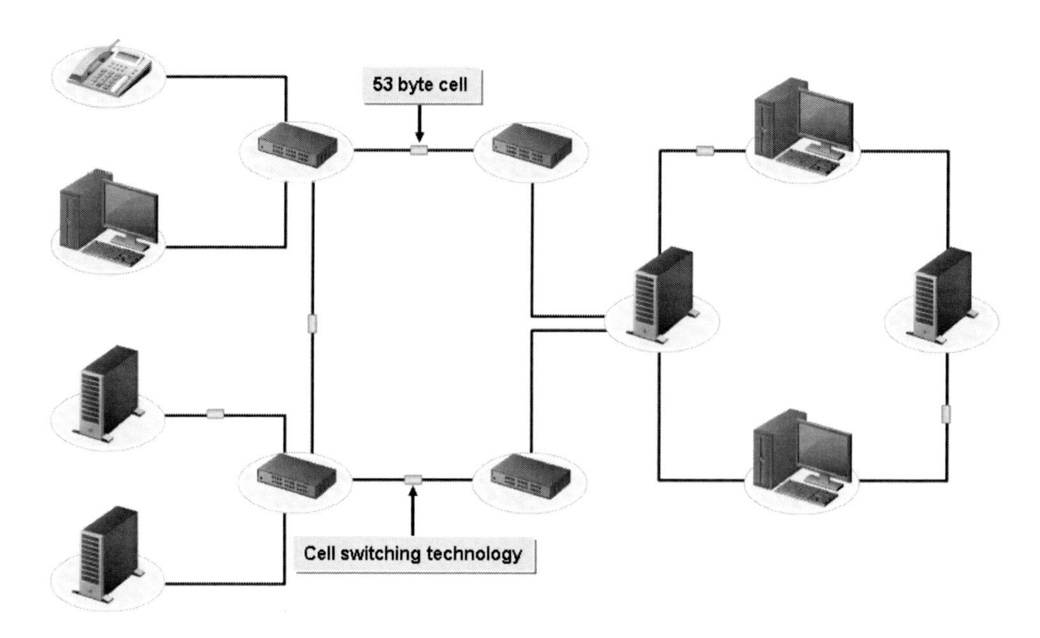

Figure 9-1: *ATM provides high-speed data transfer.*

ATM Features

The versatility of ATM can be attributed to a variety of features.

Feature	Description
Bandwidth options	Provides a wide range of high bandwidth options—155 Mbps to 622 Mbps are commonly deployed, but ATM can support 51.84 Mbps to 2.488 Gbps.
Types of traffic	Allows the capability to carry data, voice, and video simultaneously on the same channel.
Fixed cell size	The fixed 53-byte cell size enables ATM to be implemented in hardware, reducing overhead and drain on resources required to move data on a network.
QoS	Built-in QoS features in the design aid in the flow of data between endpoints of the ATM network.
Traffic contracting and shaping	Traffic contracting assigns a set data rate to an endpoint. When an endpoint connects to an ATM network, it enters into a contract with the network for service quality. The ATM network will not contract more services than it can provide. Traffic shaping optimizes data flow on an ATM network. It includes control of bursts and optimizing bandwidth allocation.
Real-time and non real-time data support	Real-time data support is used for time-sensitive data such as voice or video and travels at a higher priority than non real-time data.

ATM Network Interface Types

ATM network interfaces connect ATM devices and fall into two categories: *User-to-Network Interface (UNI)* and *Network-to-Network Interface (NNI)*. The UNI, as a user device, is an ATM border device that connects one ATM network to another ATM network or a LAN. NNI is a switch that is inside an ATM network. Individual devices can connect to an ATM network, but this is rare.

ATM Connections

ATM is not a channelized service and does not waste channels by assigning them to nodes that are not talking. In a situation when the device is offline, ATM does not hold the channel. It makes that bandwidth available to other nodes, exhibiting traffic contracting to allocate the necessary bandwidth without wasting it by reservation.

An ATM switch makes virtual connections with other switches to provide a data path from endpoint to endpoint. Individual connections are called Virtual Channels (VCs). VCs support the connection-oriented transport between endpoints and are identified by a Virtual Channel Identifier (VCI). VCs with a common path are tied together into Virtual Paths (VPs) and are identified by a Virtual Path Identifier (VPI). You can form a Transmission Path (TP) by combining multiple VPs.

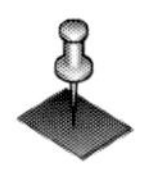

An ATM endpoint (or end system) contains an ATM network interface adapter.

Frame Relay

Frame Relay is a WAN protocol that functions at the Physical and Data Link layers of the OSI model. It is a packet-switched technology that allows transmission of data over a shared network medium and bandwidth using virtual circuits. Frame Relay transmits data using virtual circuits. As virtual circuits consume bandwidth only when they transport data, each device can use more bandwidth and transmit data at higher speeds. Frame Relay provides reliable communication lines and efficient error-handling mechanisms that discard erroneous data frames.

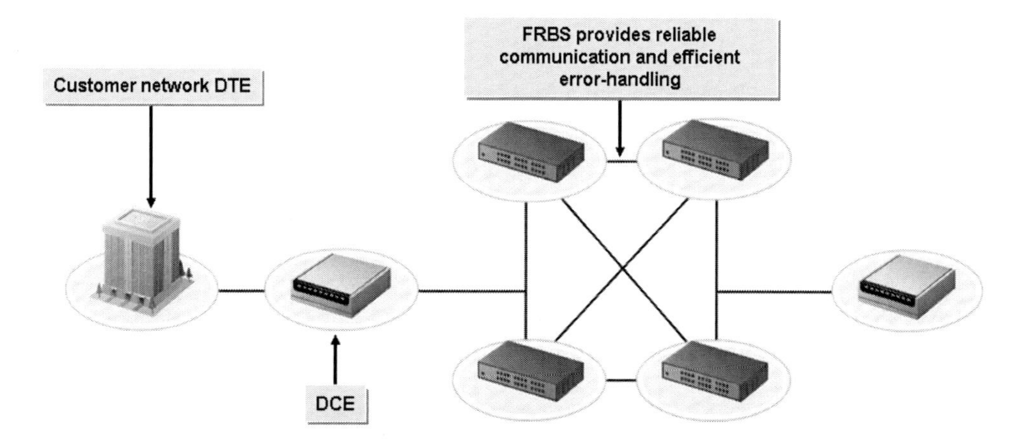

Figure 9-2: *Frame Relay allows stations to share the network medium and bandwidth.*

Frame Relay Network Components

Frame Relay uses *Data Termination Equipment (DTE)* and *Data Communications Equipment (DCE)* to connect to the appropriate Frame Relay network, referred to as the Frame Relay Bearer Service (FRBS). Inside the FRBS—or frame relay network cloud—is a network of switches that makes connections between endpoints. A virtual circuit is established between two DTE devices. DTE equipment can consist of a single network device such as a router. DCE typically is a *Channel Service Unit/Data Service Unit (CSU/DSU)* that sends signals to an *Edge System (ES)*, a switch on the Frame Relay network.

A *CSU/DSU* is a combination of two WAN connectivity devices that work together to connect a digital WAN line with a customer's LAN. The DSU receives the signal from the LAN and passes it to the CSU. The CSU converts the signal format to make it compatible with the Digital Data Service (DDS) on the WAN line.

The virtual circuits used in Frame Relay prevents you from seeing the complexity of communication inside the cloud. Keep in mind that you never see the complexity of communication happening inside the cloud because Frame Relay communicates using virtual circuits. There are two types of virtual circuits: permanent and switched. Permanent Virtual Circuits (PVCs) are created by service providers inside their devices and the circuit is constant. Switched Virtual Circuits (SVCs) are established during data transmission and when the data "conversation" is over, the connection is closed.

Advantages and Disadvantages of Frame Relay

The advantages of Frame Relay are:

- It offers facilities like that of a leased line, but at a significantly lower cost.
- It delivers increased performance with reduced network complexity.
- It can be implemented over the existing technology.
- It can be easily configured to combine traffic from different networking protocols.

The disadvantages of Frame Relay are:

- Data transmission may exceed network capacity as clients use a common network, and this results in the slowing down of the network.
- Since Frame Relay uses variable-length packets, there is difficulty ensuring QoS.

X.25 Switched Networks

Like Frame Relay, *X.25* is a legacy packet switching network technology developed in the 1970s to move data across less-than-reliable long-distance public carriers available at that time. X.25 emphasizes reliable delivery, so it involves a lot of overhead and compromises performance. X.25, like many switched network protocols, is implemented on top of leased lines or other local connection technologies.

In an X.25 network, an endpoint is called Data Terminal Equipment (DTE). DTE can be a card installed in either a PC or a server that interfaces with a router, or it can be a standalone unit. DTE is connected to Data Circuit Equipment (DCE), which connects the customer to the X.25 backbone. The backbone of the network is made up of Packet Switching Equipment (PSE).

MPLS

Multiprotocol Label Switching (MPLS) is a high-performance, multi-service switching technology in use in packet data networks. It is defined by a set of IETF specifications that enable Layer 3 devices, such as routers, to establish and manage network traffic. It ensures faster switching of data as it follows *label switching* that helps save processing time of packets by the label-switching routers.

In an MPLS network, routers add a label to each incoming data packet and forward the packet along a predefined path, based on the label rather than the destination IP address. As a result, routing lookups performed on every router are reduced. MPLS can transport data from different technologies and protocols such as IP, ATM, Frame Relay, *Synchronous Optical Network (SONET),* and Ethernet over a common infrastructure. Therefore, the reference is called multiprotocol.

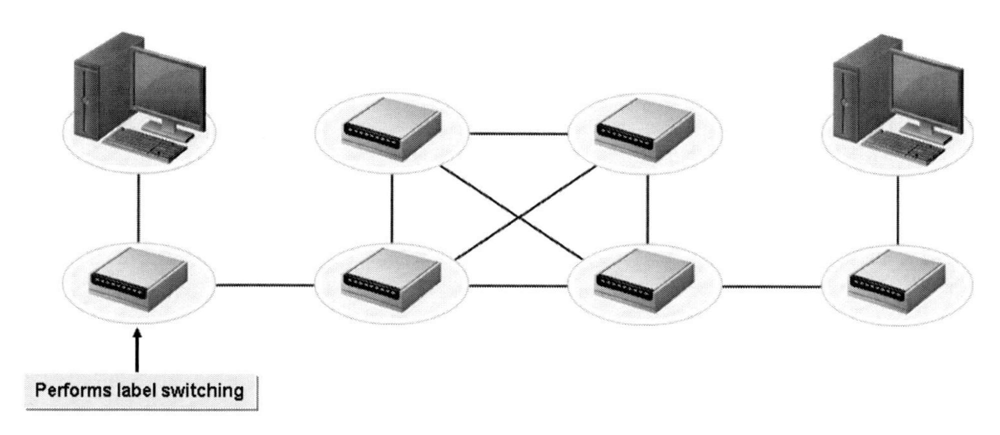

Figure 9-3: *MPLS performs multi-service label switching using Layer 3 routers.*

Benefits of MPLS

With the evolution of converged networks, network developers face major challenges such as increased traffic demands. MPLS enables Class of Service (CoS) tagging and prioritization of network traffic, so network administrators can specify which applications should take priority on a network. This function makes an MPLS network important to applications such as *Voice over IP (VoIP).* MPLS carriers differ on the number of classes of service they offer and the pricing of these CoS tiers.

DSL

A *Digital Subscriber Line (DSL)* is a point-to-point, public network access broadband Internet connection method that transmits digital signals over existing phone lines. Telephone companies use DSL to offer data, video, and voice services over these existing lines. DSL accomplishes this connection by transporting voice as low-frequency signals and data as high-frequency signals. It has become a popular way to connect small businesses and households to the Internet because of its affordability and high download speeds—typically upward of 1.5 Mbps. However, distance and the quality of lines affect the total bandwidth available to a customer.

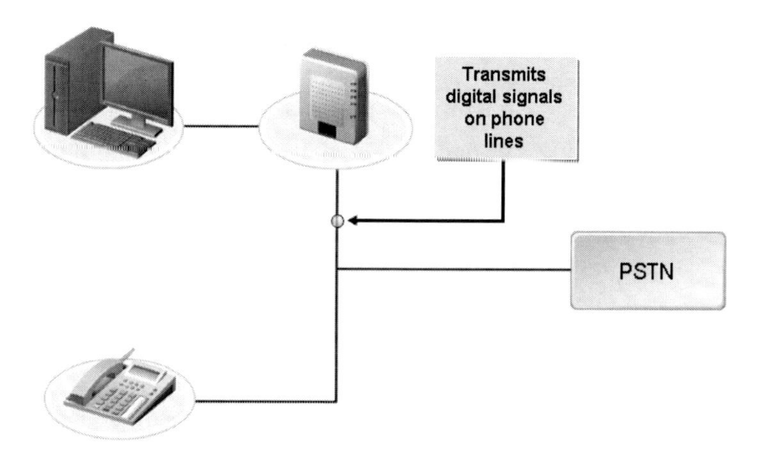

Figure 9-4: *DSL transmits digital signals over phone lines.*

DSL is commonly referred to as xDSL, denoting the different types of DSL technologies.

DSL Technology	Description
Asymmetric DSL	ADSL is the most popular DSL technology. It allows residential customers to access the Internet and receive phone calls simultaneously. Provides high bandwidth, high-speed transmission over regular telephone lines. Called asymmetric as most of the bandwidth is used for information moving downstream. Widely used where users download more information than what they send. Offers speeds of up to 8 Mbps.
Symmetric DSL	Unlike ADSL, SDSL provides symmetric connectivity to users. Although it also uses telephone lines, it offers other services on the same line. It provides the same download and upload speeds. Offers speeds of up to 1.5 Mbps.
High bit rate DSL	HDSL was developed to carry high-speed data over T1 lines. It offers speeds of up to 1.5 Mbps. HDSL2 is a more recent version and offers the same rate over a single pair of copper wires.
Single-pair high-speed DSL	SHDSL improves on both SDSL and HDSL by offering high speed, symmetric DSL over a single copper line. Has speeds of up to 2.3 Mbps.
Rate-adaptive DSL	RADSL adjusts the upstream speed of the connection to maintain higher downstream speeds, i.e., the upstream bandwidth is adjusted to create greater bandwidth for downstream traffic.
Very high-speed DSL	VDSL provides very fast data transmission across short distances over a single pair of copper wires. It offers speeds of up to 55 Mbps for downstream, and 1.6 to 2.3 Mbps in the upstream direction.
ISDN DSL	IDSL is a cross between ISDN and xDSL. Provides data communication channels at a speed of 144 Kbps. Was developed for customers who were not within the reach of DSL service providers.
Voice over DSL	VoDSL adds voice channels to an existing DSL connection. VoDSL digitizes voice signals and transports them as data signals.

Dial-Up and Broadband Connectivity

There are two common methods used to provide Internet connectivity to customers: dial-up and broadband.

Method	**Description**
Dial-up lines	*Dial-up lines* are local loop *PSTN* connections that use modems, existing phone lines, and long-distance carrier services to provide low cost, low bandwidth WAN connectivity, and remote network access. Dial-up lines are generally limited to 56 Kbps, and are sometimes used as backups for higher bandwidth WAN services.
Broadband	Broadband offers high-speed Internet access as it has a higher rate of data transmission. It has speeds of 256 Kbps or higher. It offers much higher speeds than dial-up connections and allows the simultaneous use of a telephone line.

PSTN

PSTN is an international telephone system that carries analog voice data. PSTN offers traditional telephone services to residences and establishments. PSTN includes telephones and fax machines that set up temporary but continuous connections. During a call, a circuit is established between two users and is kept open even during periods of silence. This provides guaranteed QoS but uses bandwidth inefficiently.

ISDN

ISDN is a digital circuit switching technology that carries both voice and data over digital phone lines or PSTN wires. ISDN uses digital channels for data transmission over conventional telephone lines. But unlike telephone signaling, ISDN signals are not converted to analog and are transmitted as digital signals. Similar to a telephone number, ISDN uses identifiers to establish a connection on-demand by dialing another ISDN circuit's telephone number. ISDN uses five identifiers including the telephone number, a Service Profile Identifier (SPID), and three dynamic connection identifiers. ISDN is a channelized service and has two interface modes: Basic Rate Interface (BRI) or Primary Rate Interface (PRI), which includes more data channels to provide higher bandwidth.

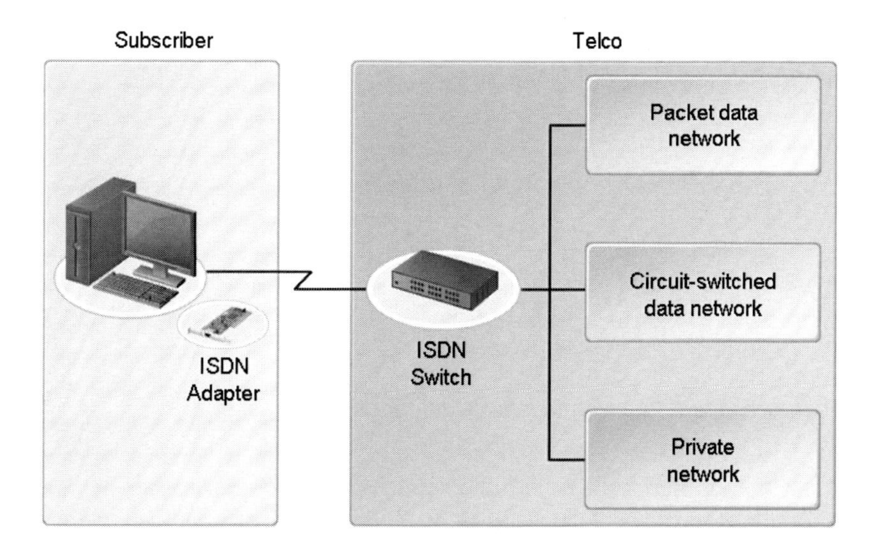

Figure 9-5: *ISDN carries voice and data over digital phone lines or PSTN wires.*

Channels

Channelized services use multiple communication channels, tied logically together within the set bandwidth, to form a single communication path of bandwidth equal to the sum of the individual channels' bandwidth. In other words, they combine all of their individual bandwidths to make one channel with a lot of bandwidth. Channels that carry data are called bearer channels, or B channels, and the channel used to set up, control, and take down the connection is called the delta channel, or D channel.

BRI uses two 64 Kbps B channels and one 16 Kbps D channel for a total bandwidth of 144 Kbps. BRI is a simpler service offering and allows users to use their existing cabling. BRI services have a span of about 3.4 miles from a service provider to the customer's premises. PRI uses twenty-three 64 Kbps B channels and one 64 Kbps D channel for a total bandwidth of 1.5 Mbps. It is used primarily for multi-user WAN connections. As demand for higher bandwidth connections to the Internet grew, BRI-ISDN was deployed at many small businesses and homes. However, ISDN, for the most part, has been replaced by ADSL technology.

ISDN Hardware

ISDN hardware includes *Terminal Equipment (TE)*, *Terminal Adapters (TAs)*, *Network Termination (NT)* devices, Line Termination (LT) and Exchange Termination (ET) equipment. TEs are communications equipment that stations use to accomplish tasks at both ends of a communications link. TAs form the hardware interface between a computer and an ISDN line. NTs are devices that connect the local telephone exchange lines to a customer's telephone or data equipment. ISDN lines terminate at a customer's premises using an RJ-45 connector in a configuration called a U-interface, which usually connects to a *Network Termination Unit (NTU)*. The NTU can directly connect to ISDN-aware equipment, such as phones or ISDN NICs in computers. This type of equipment is called Terminal Equipment type 1 (TE1).

T-Carrier Systems

The *T-carrier system* is a digital and packet-switched system designed to carry multiplexed telephone connections. It makes communications more scalable than analog, circuit-switched systems. T-carrier systems use two twisted pairs of copper wires. The first pair is used for transmission and the second pair for reception. Therefore, T-carrier systems support full-duplex communication. T1 and T3 are the two most common T-service levels. T-services can be used to support a point-to-point WAN where the service provider sets up a dedicated connection between two T-service endpoints.

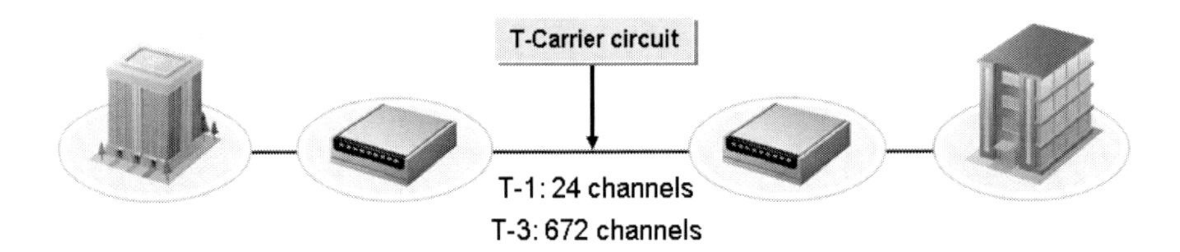

Figure 9-6: *T-carrier systems allow multiplexed telephone connections.*

T-services connect a customer's office with the service provider's network. The internal connection is over Frame Relay. The T-service can also connect an office to the telephone company for remote access. Individual remote clients dial in to a number and the service provider before routing them to the office through the T-service. This way, a server can service multiple dial-in connections without needing many modems.

Digital Signal Services

Digital Signal (DS) services are a hierarchy of different digital signals that transfer data at different rates. The T-carrier system is the most common physical implementation of the ANSI *Digital Signal Hierarchy (DSH)* specifications. DSH is a channelized data transmission standard used to multiplex several single data or voice channels for a greater total bandwidth. It was established in the 1980s, primarily for use with digital voice phones. In T-carrier implementations, DSH systems have become the standard building block of most channelized systems in the United States today.

DSH defines a hierarchy of DSx specifications numbered DS0 to DS5. The basic DS0 level specifies a single voice channel of 64 Kbps. A DS1 signal bundles 24 DS0 channels and uses a T1 carrier line. The different types of DS services vary depending upon their data transmission rates.

- **DS0:** Carries data at the rate of 64 Kbps.
- **DS1:** Carries data at the rate of 1.5 Mbps.
- **DS2:** Carries data at the rate of 6.3 Mbps.
- **DS3:** Carries data at the rate of 44.4 Mbps.
- **DS4:** Carries data at the rate of 274.2 Mbps.

T-Lines

In order to implement a different DS service, telephone companies use T-lines whose carrying capacities match the data rates of DS services.

Type of T-Line	*Service*
T1	DS1
T2	DS2
T3	DS3
T4	DS4

E-Carrier Systems

The E-carrier system is a dedicated digital line that transmits voice or data. It is used in Europe, Mexico, and South America. The different E carriers transmit data at different rates.

Carrier	*Transmission Rate*
E0	64 Kbps
E1	2 Mbps
E2	8.4 Mbps
E3	34.4 Mbps
E4	139.3 Mbps
E5	565 Mbps

Digital Network Hierarchies

Digital networks have two hierarchical structures that define them: the *Plesiochronous Digital Hierarchy (PDH)* and the *Synchronous Digital Hierarchy (SDH)*. PDH networks carry data over fibre optic or microwave radio systems. In this type of network, the different parts are ready, but are not synchronized. They have largely replaced PDH for a synchronized network in which the movement of data is highly synchronized along different parts. In SDH, data moves on an optical fiber using LEDs. Basic data transmission occurs at a rate of 155.5 Mbps.

SONET/SDH

The *Synchronous Optical Network (SONET)* is a standard for synchronous data transport over a fiber optic cable. SONET is the U.S. version of the standard published by ANSI, while SDH is the European version of the standard published by the *International Telecommunications Union (ITU)*.

SONET has two specifications: the OC specification for fiber optic cabling and the STS specification for copper wire, although SONET over copper has severe limitations. SONET is deployed in a self-healing dual-fiber ring topology, similar to FDDI. When one ring works, the other is a standby. Whenever the working ring fails, SONET recognizes the failure and switches over to the second ring.

SONET is most widely used by inside service providers to act as a high-speed backbone for other systems, such as Frame Relay and ATM. SONET/SDH can be used on an ATM network, and connections to the lines can be made using single-mode or multi-mode optical fiber. In such a setup, ATM would be the switching technology, and SONET/SDH would be the transmission technology on the network.

SONET is divided into three areas. Each area is controlled by an integrated management system.

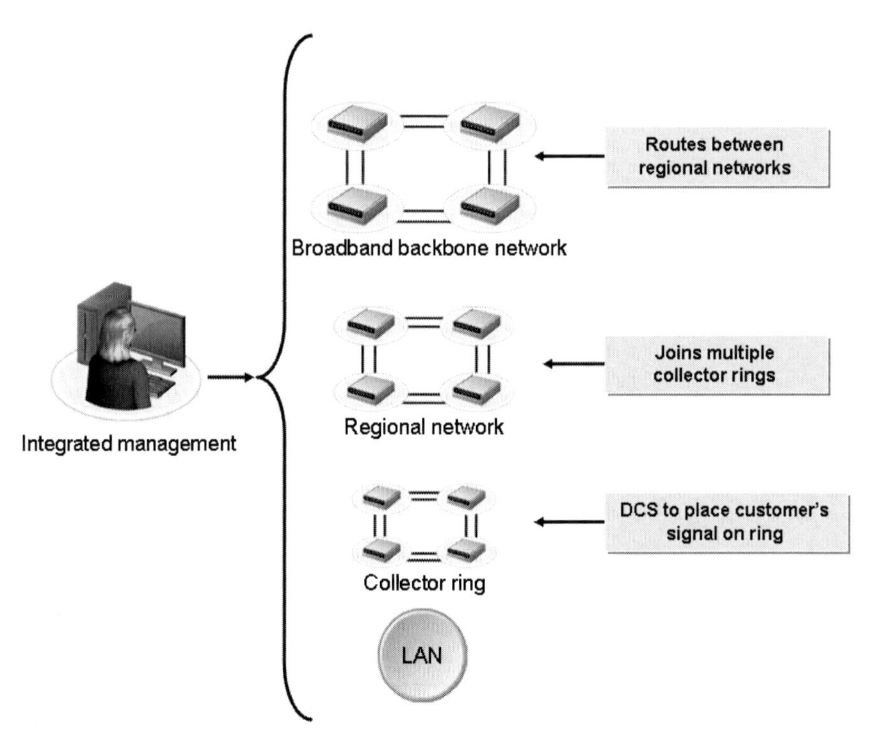

Figure 9-7: *Divisions of a SONET.*

Area	Description
Local collector ring	A local collector ring interfaces with users and comprises Digital Cross-connect Switches (DCSs) at the user's location or connects to the user's location by a T-carrier. The DCS acts as a concentrator to transmit signals from a user to the SONET ring. It supports connections from different technologies and from multiple users. The technologies that can connect to the ring include ATM, T1 or T3 lines, ISDN, or DSL voice.
Regional network	A regional network combines multiple collector rings by using Add/Drop Multiplexers (ADMs). The ADM allows data from collector rings to be added to the regional ring. The data that is not accepted by the service requestor is discarded or sent back to the ADM. By managing bandwidth on the regional network, it becomes more efficient. When data moves between two networks that the same regional network supports, the connection can be through the regional network.
Broadband backbone network	The broadband backbone network routes data between regional networks. It is capable of carrying a large amount of data simultaneously in the ring, and the requestor picks the data as it is transmitted.

Advantages of SONET

The key advantages of SONET are its excellent bandwidth management, built-in fault recovery features, and support for data transfer speeds of up to 2.48 Gbps. A particular advantage to SONET deployments is its interoperability. The technology often is used to aggregate multiple lines (T1, T3 for example).

SONET Transmission Bandwidth

SONET's transmission bandwidth ranges from 51.84 Mbps to 2.48 Gbps. Its hardware actually operates at speeds in the 10 Gbps range, but the SONET standard has not been expanded to include it.

ITU

The *International Telecommunication Union (ITU)* is an international organization within the United Nations that defines global technical standards for telecommunications. ITU also coordinates the widespread use of the radio spectrum, ensuring interference-free wireless communications. ITU also sponsors exhibitions and forums to exchange ideas and discuss issues affecting international telecommunications.

DWDM

Dense Wavelength Division Multiplexing (DWDM) is a multiplexing technology that uses light wavelengths to transmit data. Signals from multiple sources using different technologies are carried simultaneously on separate light wavelengths. DWDM can multiplex up to 80 separate data channels into a lightstream for transmission over an optical fiber. Data from different protocols and technologies such as IP, SONET, and ATM can all travel simultaneously within an optical fiber. SONET is combined with WDM functions by sending SONET data streams out on different colors of light. The sending SONET multiplexer connects light streams to the WDM card. At the receiving end, the fiber demultiplexes the light into a single color stream and sends it to SONET equipment.

The Optical Carrier System

The *Optical Carrier x (OCx)* standard specifies the bandwidth for fiber optic transmissions. It is a channelized technology based on the same 64 Kbps channel as DSH but with a base rate of 810 channels. The OCx standard is open-ended, enabling manufacturers to add specifications as they develop hardware that supports faster transmission speeds.

OCx Specifications

OCx specifications correspond with the data rates of SONET. As one OC channel corresponds to a data rate of 51.84 Mbps, using multiple channels increases the rate by 51.84 Mbps per channel.

OCx Specification	*Description*
OC1	1 OC channel with a data rate of 51.84 Mbps.
OC3	3 OC channels with a data rate of 155.52 Mbps.
OC9	9 OC channels with a data rate of 466.56 Mbps.
OC12	12 OC channels with a data rate of 622.08 Mbps.
OC18	18 OC channels with a data rate of 933.15 Mbps.
OC24	24 OC channels with a data rate of 1.24 Gbps.
OC36	36 OC channels with a data rate of 1.87 Gbps.
OC192	192 OC channels with a data rate of 9.95 Gbps.

PON

The Passive Optical Network (PON) is a point-to-multipoint optical network that is used for broadcast transmissions using optical systems. As the optical transmission requires no power or active electronic parts when the signal passes through the network it is referred to as passive. A PON contains a central office node, known as Optical Line Termination (OLT) and Optical Network Units (ONUs) near end users. An OLT can connect to up to 32 ONUs.

Satellite Transmission Systems

A satellite-based network offers immense geographical coverage, allowing for high-speed connections anywhere in the world to transmit data between endpoints. Satellite transmission systems are used as an alternative to conventional communications, and as a cost-effective method to transmit information to different locations globally. Satellite communications systems use Line-of-Sight (LoS) microwave transmission.

A satellite system consists of two segments: space and ground.

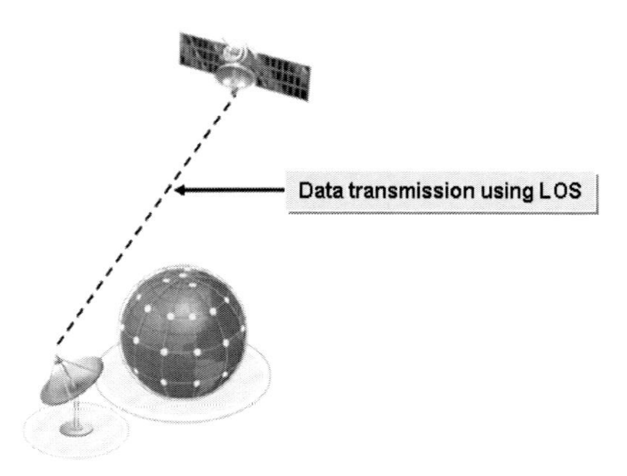

Figure 9-8: *A satellite-based network.*

Segment	***Description***
Space	A space segment contains one or more satellites organized into a constellation and a ground station that provides operational control of the satellites.
Ground	A ground segment provides access from Earth stations to the satellite to meet the communication needs of users. The ground segment contains terminals that utilize the communication capabilities of the space segment. The ground segment contains three basic types of terminals. ● Fixed terminals access satellites while they are stationary. ● Transportable terminals are portable, but remain stationary during transmission. ● Mobile terminals can communicate with satellites even when they are in motion.

Satellite Services

Satellites are used for a variety of purposes and each satellite service has different requirements.

Satellite Service	***Description***
Satellite Internet	The *satellite Internet* is a method of connecting to the Internet using a satellite network. This method can be broadly classified as a one-way or two-way connection, based on how the request for an Internet connection reaches the satellite. In a one-way connection, the request for an Internet connection goes to the ISP via a phone line and is forwarded to the satellite.

Satellite Service	Description
Satellite phone network	A *satellite phone* is a telephone system that relies on the satellite network to provide services, instead of the local telephone switch infrastructure. Satellite phones can be handheld or fixed, usually connected to an antenna at the top of a building. When a call is made from a satellite phone to another satellite phone, the call is routed directly via the satellite. If a call is made to a regular phone, the satellite routes the call to the landline or cellular network via an Earth station known as the gateway. The gateway converts the signals so that the landline or cellular network can read them. Satellite phones work well in open spaces, but they do not have a good reception within buildings and enclosed spaces.
Satellite television	*Satellite television* is a method of relaying video and audio signals directly to a subscriber's television set using satellites. A satellite TV network consists of a programming source that provides the original program. The satellite TV provider, also known as the Direct Broadcast (DB) center, then broadcasts these channels to the satellites, which receive the signals and rebroadcast them to Earth. The subscriber's dish antenna picks up the signals and sends them to the TV via a receiver, also known as the Set-Top Box (STB). The satellite TV technology overcomes the disadvantage of broadcast networks, where an LOS arrangement is necessary.
VSAT	A *Very Small Aperture Terminal (VSAT)* is a telecommunication Earth station that consists of an antenna to transmit and receive signals from satellites. The size of a VSAT ranges from 1.2 to 2.4 meters in diameter. A network of VSATs provides a cost-effective solution to users who need to connect several sites or offices that are dispersed geographically. VSATs support transmission of voice, data, and video. A typical VSAT network consists of an antenna placed on top of a building and connected to a transceiver and modem by a cable. The modem converts the signals from the satellite into data or voice signals, and vice versa. VSAT networks can be connected in a point-to-point, star, or mesh network.
GPS	A *Global Positioning System (GPS)* is a navigational system that consists of a network of 27 satellites: 24 active and 3 in the standby mode. These satellites are arranged in such a pattern that at least four of them are visible from any part of the world. A GPS receiver receives the distance and time information from the four visible satellites and uses that information to calculate its current position. A GPS receiver needs an unobstructed view of the sky.

WWAN

A *Wireless WAN (WWAN)* uses wireless network technology to allow users to check email, surf the web, and connect to corporate resources accessible within wireless network boundaries. Users connect to a WWAN using a WWAN card. WWANs use a number of technologies to transfer data and connect to the Internet. Each of these technologies, however, falls into one of three families: GSM/UMTS, cdmaOne/CDMA2000, and *WiMAX*. The GSM/UMTS and cdmaOne/CDMA2000 protocols started out as cell phone technologies but now support data transmission. WWAN technologies also use the Wireless Application Protocol (WAP), which enables you to access the Internet from your mobile device.

Wireless Application Protocol shares its acronym with Wireless Access Point.

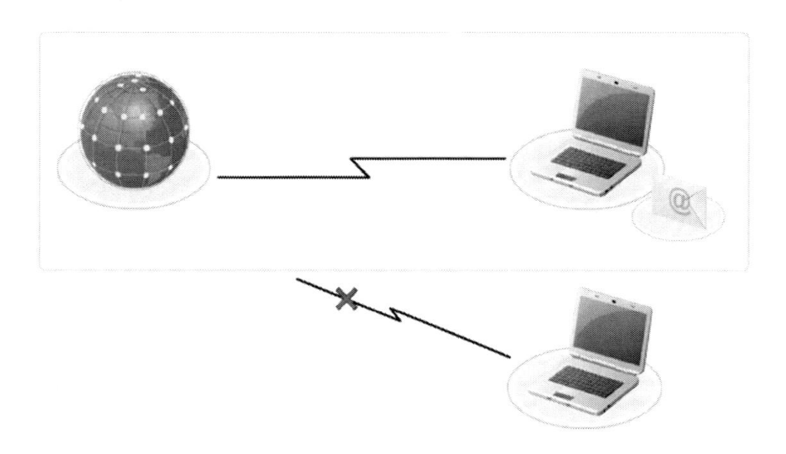

Figure 9-9: *WWAN allows users access within wireless network boundaries.*

Wireless LAN vs. Wireless WAN

The following table compares speeds, security, coverage, and costs of WLANs and WWANs.

Factor	***WLAN***	***WWAN***
Coverage	Used in a single building of an organization, a home, or a hotspot such as a coffee shop. Usually limited to 100 meters.	Used wherever a cellular network provider has coverage—can be regional, national, or even global.
Speed	Typically 1 to 4 Mbps depending on the number of users that share the connection.	Typically 30 to 50 Kbps.
Security	Susceptible to hacking and interoperability issues between WLANs. Operates on a globally allocated frequency that does not require a license.	Tightly regulated frequencies spectrum requiring licenses to operate within the frequency. WWANs incorporate military security technology with a high-level of authentication and encryption.

Factor	WLAN	WWAN
Cost	No cost for the wireless connection within the range but a cost to access the Internet via the WLAN access point.	The subscription fee is similar to a cell phone contract. Can be a monthly fee, per minute or per megabyte charge.

LTE

Long Term Evolution (LTE) is a radio technology for wireless broadband access. It has been introduced in 3GPP Release 8. LTE will be backward compatible with GSM and HSPA. This compatibility will enable users to make voice calls and have access to data networks even when they are in areas without LTE coverage. LTE will offer data rates about 100 times faster than 3G networks, a downlink rate that exceeds 100 Mbps, and an uplink rate of more than 50 Mbps.

HSPA

High Speed Packet Access (HSPA) refers to a family of technologies based on the 3GPP Release 5 specification, which offers high data rate services in mobile networks. HSPA offers a downlink speed of up to 14 Mbps and an uplink speed of up to 5.8 Mbps, making it possible for users to upload or download data at a high speed without having to wait for cellular service providers to upgrade their hardware. The HSPA family includes High Speed Downlink Packet Access (HSDPA), High Speed Uplink Packet Access (HSUPA), and HSPA+.

HSPA+ uses multicarrier technologies in which multiple 5 MHz carriers are aggregated and a bigger data channel is used for data transmission. This large data channel also decreases *latency* and provides an increased capacity for bursty traffic, such as web applications. Evolved HSPA also aims to use an all-IP architecture, where all base stations will be connected to the Internet via the ISP's edge routers.

WiMAX

Wireless Interoperability for Microwave Access (WiMAX) is a packet-based wireless telecommunication technology that provides wireless broadband access over long distances. Based on the *IEEE 802.16* standard, it is intended for wireless MANs. WiMAX provides fixed as well as mobile broadband access. It covers a range of about 30 miles for fixed stations and 3 to 10 miles for mobile stations. WiMAX also provides LoS and NLoS communication, and can provide connection speeds of about 70 Mbps. WiMAX operates in the wireless frequency ranges of between 2 and 11 GHz of the wireless spectrum.

WiMAX was created by an organization known as the WiMAX Forum.

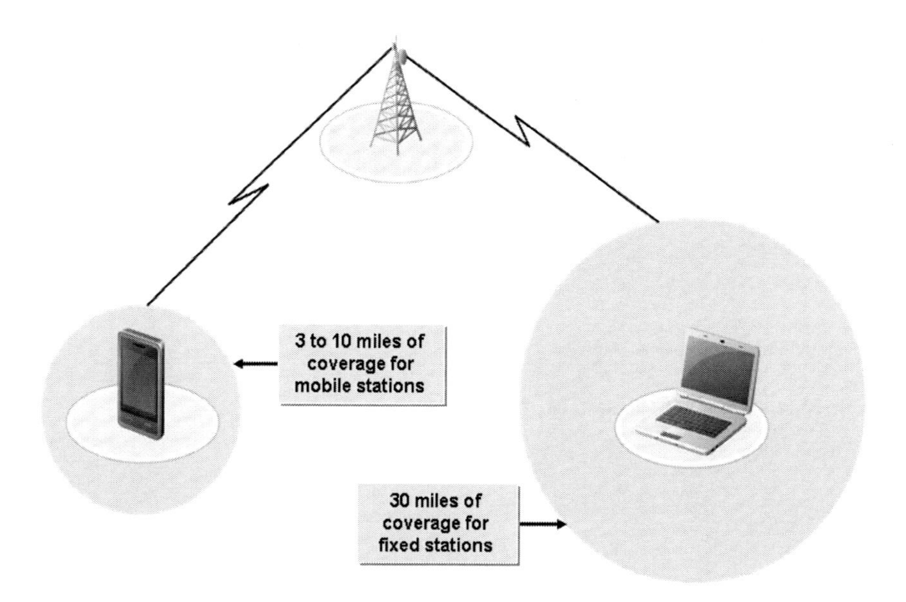

Figure 9-10: *Wireless broadband access using WiMAX.*

WiMAX Services

WiMAX offers two different services: LoS and NLoS.

- **LOS:** Signals travel over a direct path from a transmitter to a receiver.
- **NLOS:** Signals reach a receiver through reflections and diffractions.

Types of WiMAX

WiMAX is of two types: fixed and mobile.

Type	*Description*
Fixed	Is optimized for fixed applications in LOS and NLOS environments. The main disadvantage of fixed WiMAX is its difficulty to compete with established wired technologies such as DSL in places where the wired telecommunication infrastructure is well developed.
Mobile	Is optimized for portable and mobile applications in an NLOS environment. Mobile WiMAX includes additional features such as power management, handoff, frequency reuse, channel bandwidth scalability, and better NLOS performance and indoor penetration.

ACTIVITY 9-1

Discussing WAN Transmission Technologies

Scenario:

In this activity, you will discuss WAN transmission technologies.

---

1. On which type of network is ATM most commonly implemented?

a) LAN

b) MAN

c) WAN

d) PAN

---

2. How many bytes of data can an ATM cell transfer?

a) 56

b) 53

c) 52

d) 58

---

3. Which technologies do OCx specifications match to?

a) ATM

b) SONET

c) Frame Relay

d) SDH

e) T1

---

4. What are the channels used by BRI ISDN?

a) Two D channels and one B channel

b) Two B channels and one D channel

c) Three B channels and one D channel

d) Three B channels and two D channels

---

5. Which of these technologies allows for more downstream traffic than upstream?

a) SDSL

b) SHDSL

c) ADSL

d) VDSL

---

6. Which of these are features of a network with MPLS?

a) Label switching

b) Used with voice traffic

c) Multiprotocol adaptability

d) Not used with Frame Relay

7. Upon which of these OSI layers does Frame Relay operate?

a) Transport

b) Application

c) Network

d) Physical

e) Data Link

TOPIC B
WAN Connectivity Methods

In the previous topic, you identified different WAN transmission technologies. With the transmission technology in place, another important aspect of WANs is their connectivity methods. In this topic, you will identify major WAN connectivity methods.

Once you have decided how you are going to transmit data on a WAN, you still have one last issue to deal with: how do you connect your self-contained LAN to a WAN that uses completely different technologies? Understanding the various WAN connectivity devices and methods will help you implement your WAN connection appropriately.

Cable Internet Access

Cable Internet access uses a cable television connection and a *cable modem* to provide high-speed Internet access to homes and small businesses. Cable access is contention-based, with users arranged in contention groups of nodes that split television and data signals at the cable provider's end. The speed of the network varies depending on the number of nodes in the contention group.

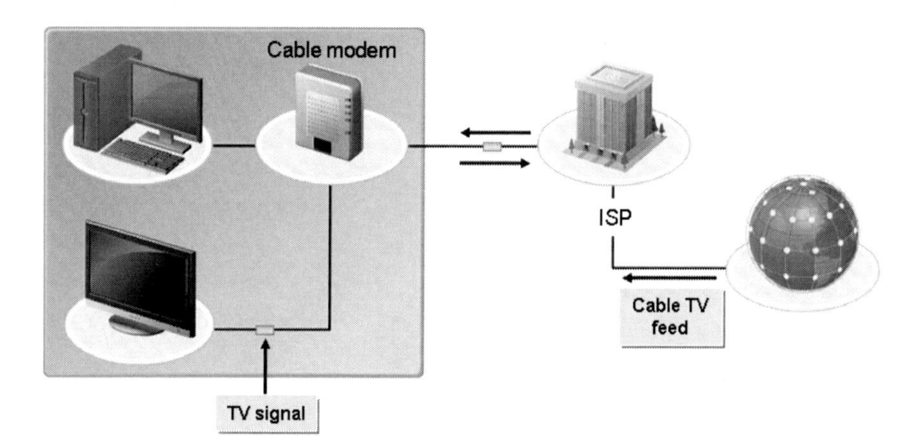

Figure 9-11: *Cable providing high-speed Internet access.*

Cable Modems

Definition:

Cable modems are hardware devices that connect subscribers to the service provider's cable systems. Service providers use a cable modem to connect the subscriber's computer to the Internet using twisted pair cabling and a 10/100 network port or USB connection. On the other end, the cable modem connects to the wall jack using coaxial cabling. Most cable companies provide access up to 10 Mbps and require a 10-MB network adapter. However, a cable modem can function reliably for speeds up to 27 Mbps. Cable modems operate at the Physical and Data Link layers of the OSI model.

Example:

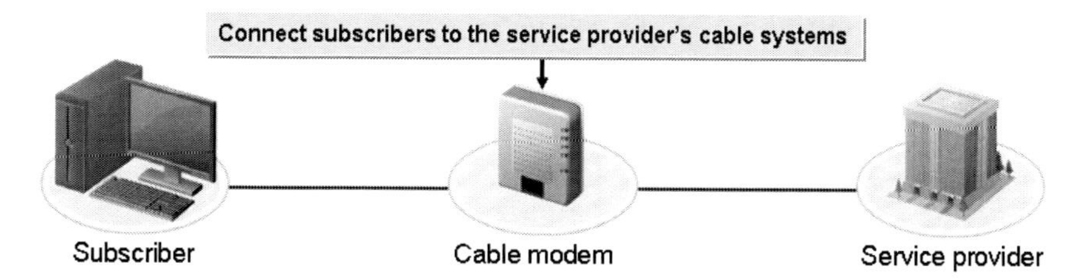

Figure 9-12: *Cable modems provide connectivity to the provider's cable systems.*

Dial-Up Connections

Dial-up lines are PSTN connections that use modems, existing phone lines, and long-distance carrier services to provide low-cost, low-bandwidth WAN connectivity and remote network access. Generally limited to 56 Kbps, dial-up lines are sometimes used as backups for higher-bandwidth WAN services. Dial-up lines have two major drawbacks: they are slow and they can have a considerable connection wait time. Despite these limitations, dial-ups are still used because they provide enough bandwidth for affordable basic Internet connectivity services over the existing telephone infrastructure.

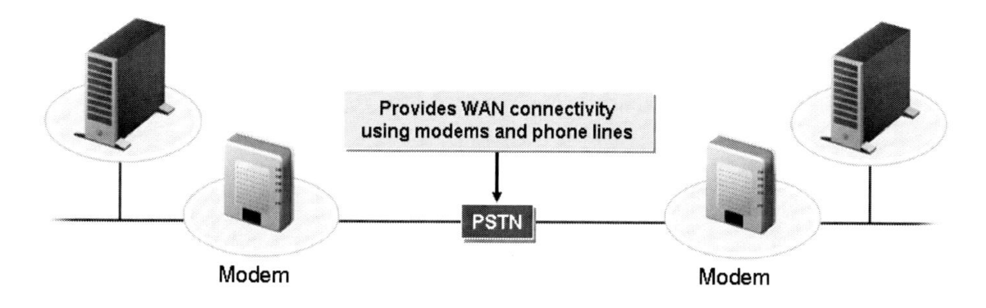

Figure 9-13: *Dial-up connections provide WAN connectivity.*

Dial-Up Modems

Definition:

A *dial-up modem* is a communication device that converts a computer's digital signals into analog signals before transmission over telephone lines. The word, modem, represents *mo*dulation and *dem*odulation because it converts digital signals into analog and analog signals into digital. A dial-up modem can be either internal or external. Internal dial-up modems exist as part of the motherboard and uses the PC's power supply, while external dial-up modems connect via the serial or USB port as separate expansion boxes. Unlike internal dial-up modems, external modems require separate power supply. The disadvantage of a dial-up modem is that it is slow when compared to broadband modems.

Example:

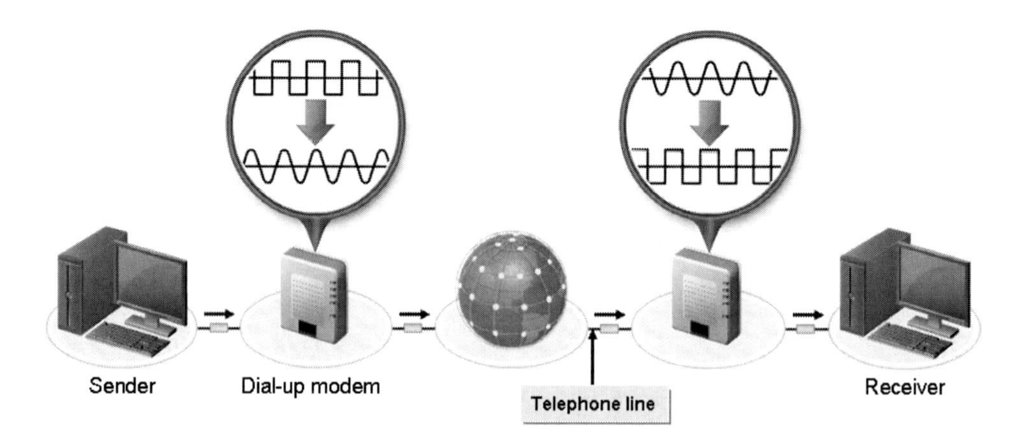

Figure 9-14: *A dial-up modem.*

Leased Data Lines

A *dedicated line* is a telecommunication path that is available 24 hours a day for use by a designated user; dedicated lines and *leased lines* are essentially the same. With dedicated or leased lines, bandwidth availability varies with technology, but is usually between 56 Kbps and 2 Mbps. A company can lease the connection for a fixed fee, typically based on the distance between endpoints. Leasing a line can be advantageous because it guarantees a fixed bandwidth over a dedicated line.

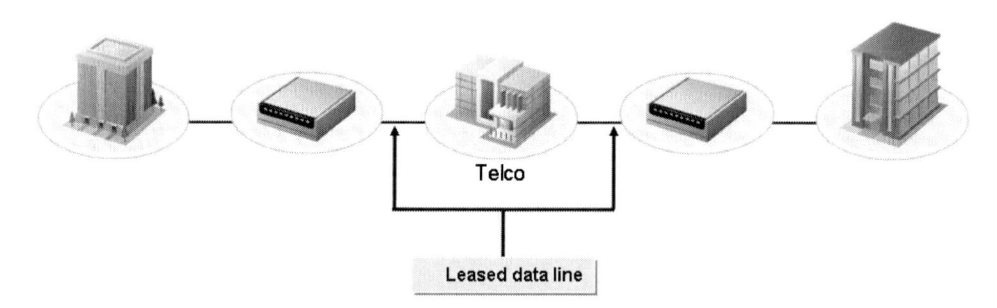

Figure 9-15: *Leased lines for communication.*

ICS

Internet Connection Sharing (ICS) is a connectivity service for computer systems that connects multiple computers to the Internet by using a single Internet connection. The computer that is connected to the Internet is called an ICS host, and the other computers are ICS clients.

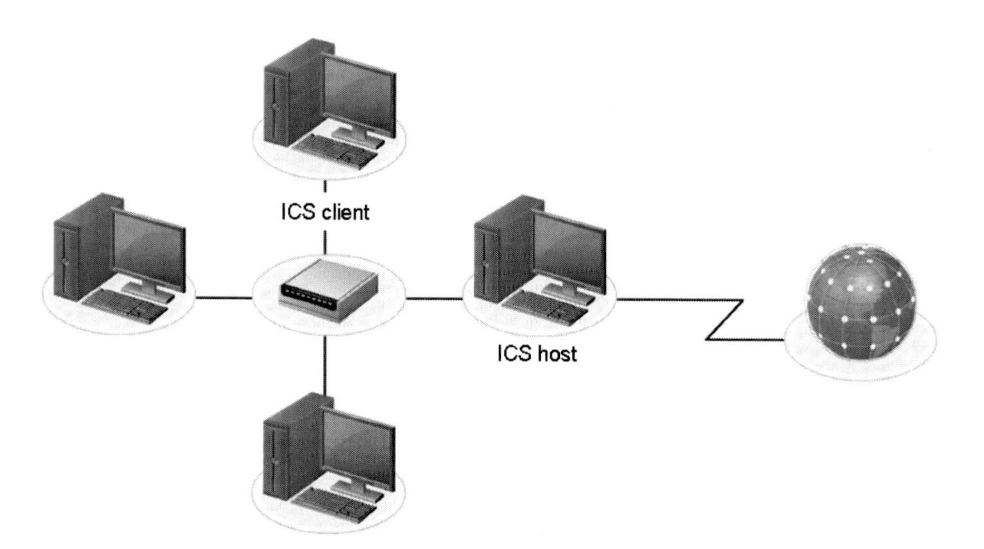

Figure 9-16: *ICS clients connect to the Internet via an ICS host.*

An ICS host must have two network connections:

- A local area connection, which you can create by installing a network adapter that connects computers in your network.
- And, an external connection, which links the home or small-office network and the Internet. ICS is enabled on this connection.

When you enable ICS, the LAN connection to the internal network is given a new static private IP address and configuration. The ICS host then assigns new dynamic private IP addresses to ICS clients.

Additional ICS Implementation Requirements

Other network configuration requirements are available for an ICS connection. Because the ICS host provides dynamic addressing and DNS proxy services to ICS clients, there must not be any other active DNS or DHCP servers on the network, and ICS clients must be configured for dynamic IP addressing. Also, the logon credentials for the Internet connection on the ICS host must be shared for all users.

Satellite Media

Satellite media provide for long-range, global WAN transmissions. A physical link transfers the signal to a satellite link at some point for transmission, and the satellite link then transmits the signal back to a physical link at the other end of the transmission for data delivery. Due to the greater distances the signal must travel, average latency is high, so satellite transmissions do not always work well for real-time applications. Weather conditions also affect the signal. Satellite services provide varying speeds depending on the service agreement.

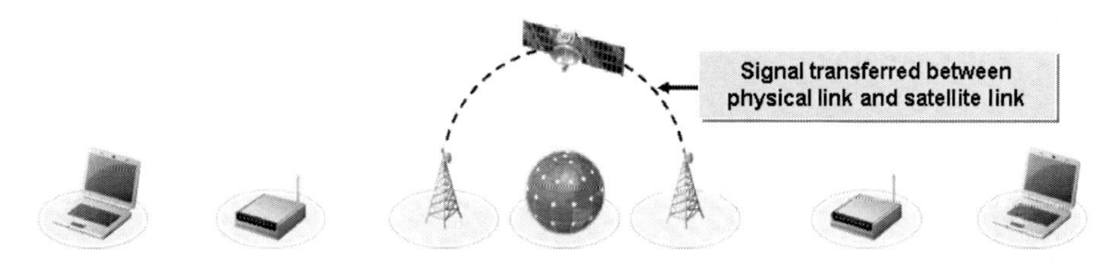

Figure 9-17: *Signal transmission using a satellite.*

Satellite Internet Access

Satellite Internet access is an example of direct, unbounded WAN transmissions. Depending upon the provider, satellite TV customers can choose to receive Internet access through the same satellite dish that receives their TV signals.

ACTIVITY 9-2

Discussing WAN Connectivity Methods

Scenario:

In this activity, you will discuss WAN connectivity methods.

---

1. **Which statement is true of satellite media?**
   a) Used for short-range transmissions
   b) Offers high-speed connections
   c) Has a low latency
   d) Transmits data at the same speed

---

2. **What are the configuration requirements for ICS?**
   a) Clients must have two network connections.
   b) The host must have two network connections.
   c) Clients must be configured for dynamic IP addressing.
   d) The network should not use other methods for dynamic addressing.

---

3. **True or False? The bandwidth availability for a dedicated line is usually between 28 Kbps and 2 Mbps.**

   __ True

   __ False

---

4. **Identify the functionality of each WAN connectivity method.**

___	Dial-up modem	a.	Provides long range global WAN transmissions.
___	Cable modem	b.	Converts a computer's digital signals into analog signals and vice versa.
___	Satellite media	c.	Connects subscribers to the service provider's cable systems.
___	ICS	d.	Connects multiple computers to the Internet using a single Internet connection.

TOPIC C

Voice over Data Transmission

In the previous topics, you identified the data transmission technologies and connectivity methods used in WAN implementations. Another aspect of WAN implementations is the voice transmission technology. In this topic, you will identify major voice over data systems.

A WAN implementation is valuable for moving data efficiently over long distances. But once your WAN is in place, you might find that it is useful for moving other kinds of data as well, including voice that standard telephone systems currently transport. Most networks today implement some form of voice over data technology, so a knowledge of transmitting voice over a WAN is critical to ensure that your network can support this requirement.

Converged Networks

Voice, video, and data are the three types of traffic carried over a network. Initially, there were different networks specifically modeled to carry one type of traffic alone. Converged networks allow all three types of traffic to move over the same network. ATM was the first technology that allowed this convergence over a WAN. More recently, *VoIP* is used in the convergence of data, voice, and video networks.

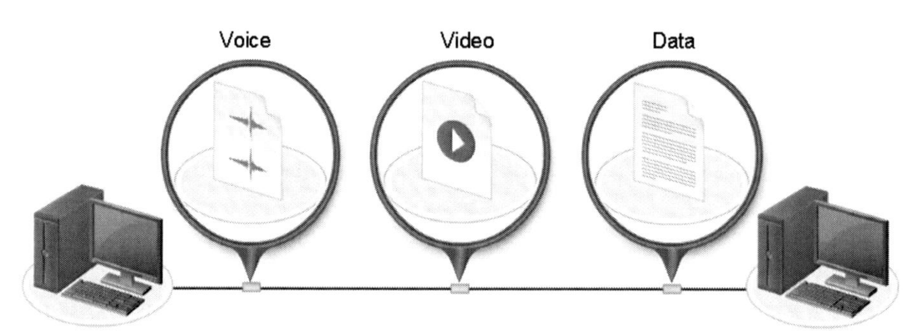

Figure 9-18: *Convergence of networks.*

Voice over Data Systems

Definition:

Voice over data systems are communication systems that replace traditional telephone links by transmitting analog voice communications over digital WAN technologies. Digital WANs provide more bandwidth than analog phone systems, and there is no long-distance service cost involved. Because voice communications are time-sensitive, the voice over data system must ensure that packets arrive complete and in sequence. In a voice over data system, voice software interfaces with an analog voice device, such as a microphone, to convert the analog voice into a data signal and to translate the dialing destination into a network address.

Example:

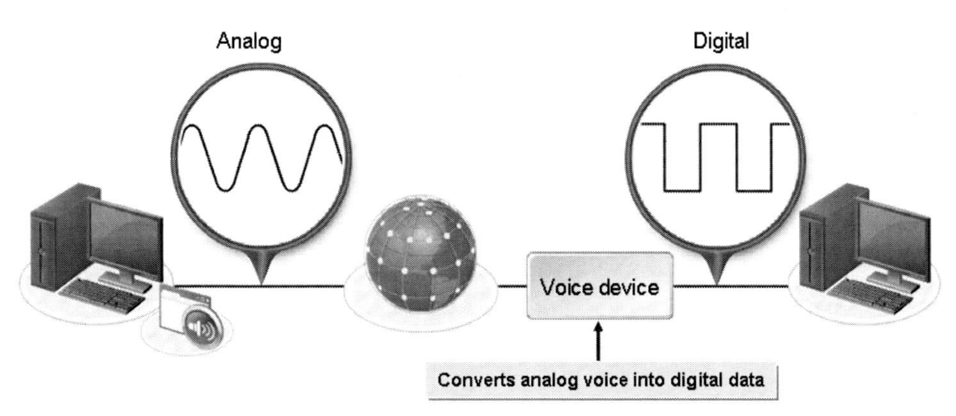

Figure 9-19: *Voice software converts analog voice into digital signals.*

VoIP

Voice over IP (VoIP) is a voice over data implementation in which voice signals are transmitted in real or near-real time over IP networks. In VoIP telephony, analog voice signals are converted into digital signals. As in a typical packet-switched network, digital signals are broken down into packets, to transmit voice as data. After reassembling the packets, the digital signals are reconverted into audio signals.

When you make a telephone call, the network connection transmits signals over data networks, and transfers them to the standard phone system if the called party does not have a VoIP service. Conversely, when you dial a number that maps to a VoIP device, VoIP routes the call to the IP host. VoIP relies on the existing, robust infrastructure of IP networks and the near-universal implementation of IP. It also eliminates per-call costs, especially for long-distance calls, because it uses data channels to transmit voice signals.

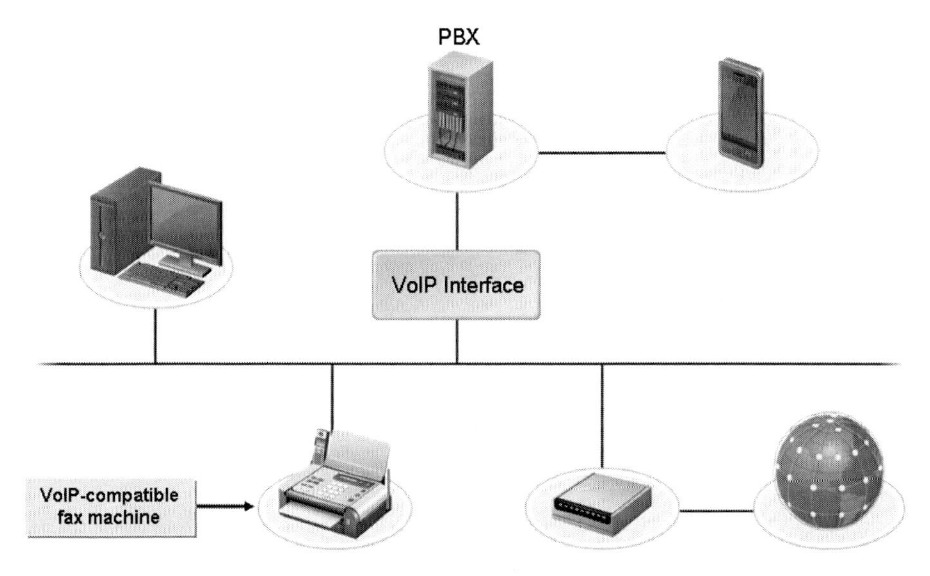

Figure 9-20: *VoIP transmits voice signals over IP networks.*

Benefits of VoIP

Compared to traditional circuit-switched telephony, VoIP telephony provides various benefits for users and is thus gaining popularity.

Benefit	Description
Cost reduction	The most attractive benefit of VoIP telephony is the cost savings it offers. You can make a call to anywhere in the world, yet pay at the rates of downloads. For a business, the savings are especially considerable.
Mobility	Depending on the setup, you can make a VoIP call from anywhere you have Internet access.
Reduced infrastructure	With no need to provide for the cabling for a separate phone system, VoIP telephony reduces infrastructure and its inherent costs.
Integrated communication	As it is based on IP, some VoIP software integrates the transmission of not just voice data, but other forms of data. Thus, in addition to speaking with someone else, you can send image files and exchange video, such as through a webcam.
Complementary features	VoIP service providers usually offer many features for free, such as the caller ID and call forwarding, which are typically charged by fixed line service providers.

Challenges to VoIP

Although VoIP telephony is gaining in popularity, it has many issues that need to be addressed before replacing or even competing with traditional telephony.

Issue	Description
Connectivity	Connections to the Internet are still not completely reliable with most providers, and there are times when you are not able to go online or get disconnected often. An option would be to switch to a more reliable provider.
Voice delivery	As voice is delivered as packets, there may be periods of silence resulting from delays in packet delivery. This can not only be annoying, but also consume online time as a conversation may take longer to complete.
Power outage	During a power outage, you are not able to go online and therefore cannot make a VoIP call. This is usually not a problem with traditional telephony, as phone companies provide for reserve power. An option would be to install a backup system.
Security	With the increasing popularity of VoIP telephony, security vulnerabilities, though not a big concern presently, are bound to increase. Hackers could not only listen to and intercept sensitive data, but even break in to systems and accounts to utilize VoIP services illegitimately.
Emergency 911 calls	An emergency call from a traditional phone, in the event the caller is unable to speak, can be traced. However, it is difficult to trace a VoIP call, as voice packets bear an IP address rather than a location address. The problem gets more complicated if the person is using a portable device.

VoIP Protocols

A VoIP session may use one or more protocols, depending on session parameters.

Protocol	***Description***
Session Initiation Protocol (SIP)	Initiates, modifies, and terminates a session. It is a signaling protocol for multimedia communication sessions. SIP must work with other protocols because it is only responsible for the signaling portion of a communication session.
Session Description Protocol (SDP)	Describes the content of a multimedia communication session.
Real-time Transport Protocol (RTP)	Transmits audio or video content and defines the packet for delivery including the type of content, sequence numbering, time stamping, and delivery monitoring. Has no specific UDP or TCP port number; rather a dynamic range of port numbers, a feature that makes traversing firewalls difficult.
Real-time Transport Control Protocol (RTCP)	Monitors QoS in RTP transmissions. Acts as a partner to RTP to package and deliver data but does not transport data.

QoS on VoIP

The quality of a voice service is affected by latency and *jitter* on a packet network. Therefore, there is a need to ensure QoS for protecting voice from data and to ensure that other critical data applications, which compete with voice, do not lose out on bandwidth. The QoS implementation should also take care of packet loss, delays, and efficient use of bandwidth.

Latency is the time delay for a packet to go from the source to the destination and back to the source. Jitter is the variability of latency over time across a network. Jitter should be minimum for real-time applications using voice and video.

ACTIVITY 9-3

Discussing Voice over Data Systems

Scenario:

In this activity, you will discuss the characteristics of voice over data systems.

---

1. What are the advantages of VoIP as compared to traditional telephone systems?

a) Reduced long-distance call costs

b) Increased bandwidth

c) Portability

d) Power independent

---

2. Match the VoIP protocol with its description.

___	SIP	a.	Transmits audio or video content and defines the packet for delivery.
___	SDP	b.	Monitors QoS in voice over data transmissions.
___	RTP	c.	Initiates, modifies, and terminates a session.
___	RTCP	d.	Describes the content of a multimedia communication session.

---

3. Which statements are valid regarding voice over data systems?

a) Transmits digital signals over WAN technologies.

b) Voice communications are not time-sensitive.

c) Voice software converts digital data to analog voice signals.

d) Voice software translates a dialing destination to a network address.

Lesson 9 Follow-up

In this lesson, you identified the infrastructure and technologies used on a WAN implementation. As almost every LAN uses WAN technologies to connect to other networks, including the Internet, understanding the WAN infrastructure helps you ensure WAN connectivity on the networks you support.

1. **Which WAN technologies do you expect to work with on your home and office networks? Why?**

2. **In your opinion, what is the future for the implementation of voice over data systems on conventional networks?**

10 Remote Networking

Lesson Time: 2 hour(s), 55 minutes

Lesson Objectives:

In this lesson, you will identify the components of a remote network implementation.

You will:

- Identify the architectures used for remote access networking.
- Identify various remote access networking implementations.
- Identify the major components of a VPN implementation.
- Identify various VPN protocols.

Introduction

In the previous lessons, you have described the technologies for implementing networks where users have a computer with a direct connection to the network. Many wide area networks also include remote users, who connect to the network using indirect, remote-networking technologies. In this lesson, you will identify the components of a remote network implementation.

Almost every organization needs to support remote users. Whether it is the employee who is always on the move, works from a home office, or connects to the organization's network from an occasional offsite conference, all your remote users need reliable, secure access to your network from their offsite locations. As a network professional, you will need to understand all components required for remote network implementations so that you can support your remote users effectively.

This lesson covers all or part of the following CompTIA® Network+® (Exam N10-005) certification objectives:

- Topic A, B, and D:
  - 5.2 Explain the methods of network access security.
  - 5.3 Explain methods of user authentication.
- Topic C:
  - 4.1 Explain the purpose and features of various network appliances.
  - 5.2 Explain the methods of network access security.

TOPIC A

Remote Network Architectures

You are familiar with the common network implementations. Many remote network implementations have similar configurations, or architectures. In this topic, you will identify the different remote network architectures.

The needs of remote users are often different than those of other network users. Several common implementation schemes have evolved to meet the most sophisticated remote user requirements. As a network professional, you may need to provide network connectivity to remote users. To provide remote users with the functionality they need, you need to understand the basics of remote networking.

Remote Networking

Definition:

Remote networking is a type of networking that enables users who are not at their physical locations to access network resources. The remote computer uses specific protocols for connectivity and an established connection mechanism to connect to the network. Remote networking can be used to enable a user to connect to a computer for basic access, or it can be a full-service connection with the same functionality that the user would expect to have at the office.

Remote Networking Limitations

The biggest limitations of remote networks are the available bandwidth, link latency, and security.

Example:

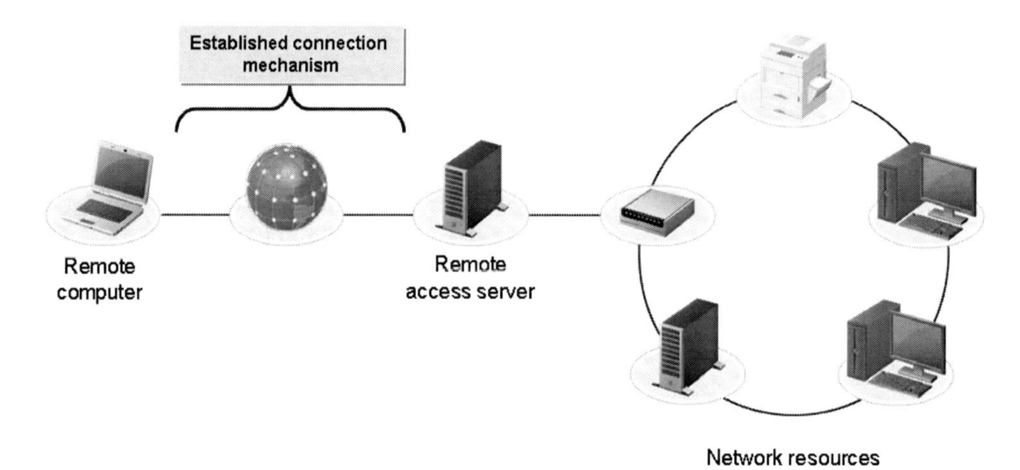

Figure 10-1: *Infrastructure in a remote networking environment.*

Remote Access Networking

In remote access networking, a node uses a remote connection to connect to a network. Once connected, the node can access resources and function as if it is on the same physical network. There is a possibility of the connection being slower due to bandwidth constraints. The server that provides remote access also provides security and authenticates users to access the network. All network traffic to and from the remote node passes through the server.

Remote Desktop Control

A remote desktop is a connection mode that enables users to access any network system from their workstation and perform tasks on the remote system as if they were working locally. Remote desktop control uses a special software package that enables a remote client to control a host computer on the network, or run applications from a server. Once connected, the remote client can send keyboard and mouse inputs and receive the resultant information on-screen.

Remote desktop control can be used on a WAN or on a local network. Remote desktop control can be used for remote server administration and to enable help desk personnel to provide remote assistance. Unless there are sufficient servers to balance the load, remote desktop control requires expensive centralized hardware and software to manage use and maintenance.

Remote Desktop Network Access

Remote desktop control can be used by the host computer as an access point to a remote network. When a host computer is used to access a network, the host should be a dedicated system.

Centralized Computing

Traditional models of centralized computing are based on a central server that has attached terminals. Modern interpretations of centralized computing include remote desktop, hosted and web-based applications, and "thin client" computing, where most of the hardware resources reside on the server side.

Benefits of Remote Desktop Control

Remote desktop control has numerous benefits for both administrators and end users.

Benefit	***Description***
Centralized application deployment and access	Applications are installed on the terminal servers and clients access the applications from their desktops. Applications are not installed on each workstation, and have centralized upgradability and maintenance.
Multiple device support	Servers and clients can run on a wide variety of hardware configurations. These can be different hardware or multiple devices such as low configuration PCs or thin clients.
Server administration and maintenance	Allows an administrator to connect to a server remotely and perform administrative tasks using the GUI of the server.
Enhanced security	Implements basic and advanced *encryption* schemes.

RAS Servers

Remote Access is a feature that allows an administrator to access client systems from any location on the network. *Remote Access Services (RAS)* servers are available from many sources. Microsoft's remote server implementation is called Routing and Remote Access Services (RRAS). On Microsoft networks, using RRAS instead of a third-party remote access server means that the user can dial in and authenticate with the same account as he or she uses at office. With third-party remote access servers, there must be some mechanism in place to synchronize user names and passwords.

RAS Server Vendors

Microsoft, Apple, IBM®, and many other UNIX and Linux vendors offer remote access server implementation either included with their server operating systems, or as separate software. In addition, there are several third-party software vendors that provide remote access solutions, including Cisco, EMC®, Perle®, Citrix®, and Patton®.

RADIUS

Remote Authentication Dial-In User Service (RADIUS) is a protocol that enables a server to provide standardized, centralized *authentication* for remote users. When a network contains several remote access servers, you can configure them to be a RADIUS server and all of the others as RADIUS clients. The RADIUS clients will pass all authentication requests to the RADIUS server for verification. User configuration, remote access policies, and usage logging can be centralized on the RADIUS server. RADIUS is supported by VPN servers, Ethernet switches requiring authentication, WAPs, as well as other types of network devices.

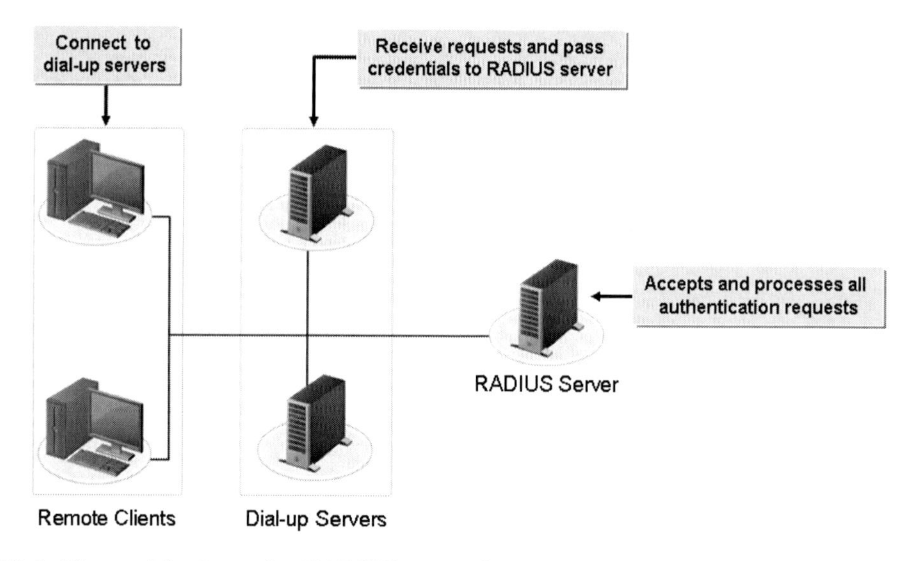

Figure 10-2: *The architecture of a RADIUS network.*

RADIUS Implementation in Windows

In Windows Server 2008 R2, RADIUS implementation is accomplished through the Network Policy server.

Diameter

Diameter is an authentication protocol that is an updated version of RADIUS and improves on some of its features. Diameter is not backward-compatible with RADIUS, but it does provide an upgrade path. Diameter is a stronger protocol that provides more advanced features, but is not as widespread in its implementation due to the lack of compatible products.

The name Diameter is a reference to the mathematical term that indicates that Diameter is twice as good as RADIUS.

AAA

Authorization, Access Control, and Accounting—collectively referred to as AAA can be implemented on a system for authentication as they use RADIUS and TACACS+ to maintain a list of user names and passwords.

ACTIVITY 10-1
Implementing RADIUS for Remote Access

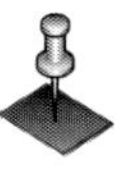

There is a simulated version of this activity available on the CD-ROM that shipped with this course. You can run this simulation on any Windows computer to review the activity after class, or as an alternative to performing the activity as a group in class. The activity simulation can be launched either directly from the CD-ROM by clicking the **Interactives** link and navigating to the appropriate one, or from the installed data file location by opening the C:\Data\Simulations\Lesson#\Activity# folder and double-clicking the executable (.exe) file.

Before You Begin:

Open the Server Manager window.

Scenario:

You are a network administrator for OGC Financial Group, a mid-size company with a growing number of remote connectivity needs. You plan to implement RADIUS for remote authentication, and you want to use it in tandem with wireless authentication for an added layer of security on a wireless network that is mainly accessed by traveling employees. You want to test RADIUS in a lab environment before deploying it in production. On a test RRAS system, you will install a RADIUS server and reconfigure an RRAS server to use RADIUS authentication.

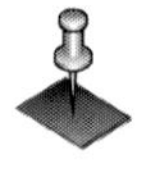

Normally, in organizations, administrators disable/block ports above 1024 as a security measure. They selectively enable ports above 1024 during the installation of the associated services that use the port number.

---

1. View the current remote access authentication methods.

a. In the Server Manager window, expand **Roles,** and then expand **Network Policy and Access Services.** Under**Network Policy and Access Services,** right-click **Routing and Remote Access** and choose **Properties.**

b. In the **Routing and Remote Access Properties** dialog box, select the **Security** tab and in the **Authentication provider** section, click **Authentication Methods.**

c. In the **Authentication Methods** dialog box, observe the options selected by default.

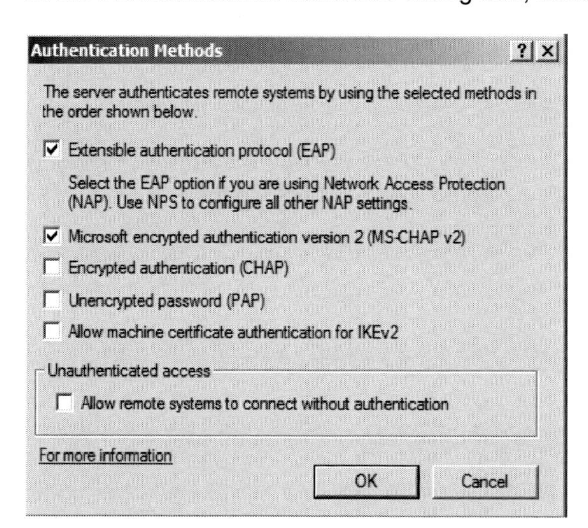

d. Click **Cancel** to close the **Authentication Methods** dialog box.

e. Click **Cancel** to close the **Routing and Remote Access Properties** dialog box.

---

2. Install the Network Policy and Access Services.

a. In the Server Manager window, right-click **Network Policy and Access Services** and choose **Add Role Services** to open the **Add Role Services** wizard.

b. In the **Add Role Services** wizard, on the **Select Role Services** page, in the **Role Services** section, check the **Network Policy Server** check box and click **Next.**

c. Confirm what you are about to install and then click **Install.**

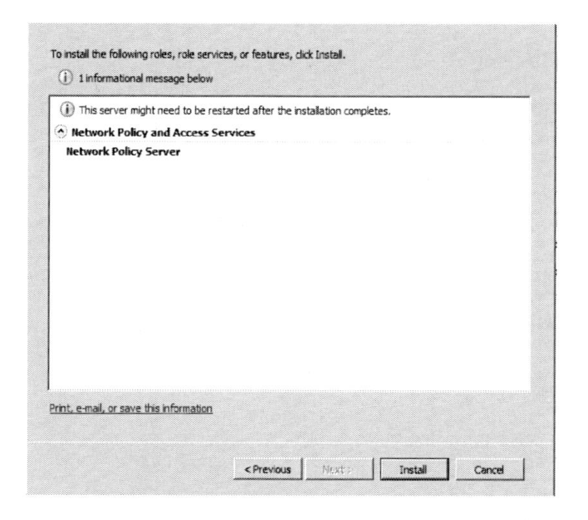

d. Once the installation is complete, click **Close** to close the **Add Role Services** wizard and complete the installation.

---

3. Configure a RADIUS client.

a. In the Server Manager window, expand the **Network Policy and Access Services** and **NPS (Local)** objects.

b. Select the **RADIUS Clients and Servers** folder.

c. In the middle pane, click **Configure RADIUS Clients.**

d. In the **Actions** pane, in the **RADIUS Clients** section, click **New.**

e. In the **New RADIUS Client** dialog box, in the **Name and Address** section, in the **Friendly name** text box, click and type ***My RADIUS Client***

f. In the **Address (IP or DNS)** section, click **Verify.**

g. In the **Verify Address** dialog box, click **Resolve.**

h. In the IP address list, select **192.168.1.*XX*** , where ***XX*** is the IP address of the system, and click **OK.**

i. In the **Shared Secret** section, select the **Generate** option and then click **Generate.**

j. Observe that in the **Shared secret** text box, the key is automatically generated. Click the warning message icon next to the text box.

k. Observe the text displayed as a tool tip and click **OK.**

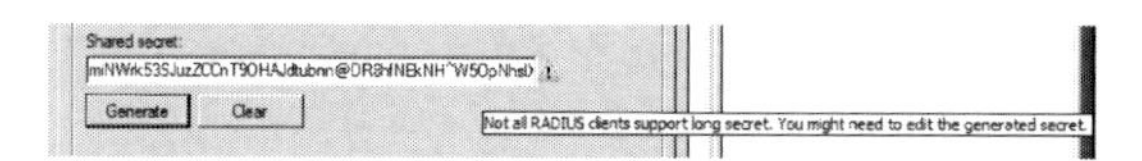

---

4. Reconfigure the RRAS server to use RADIUS authentication.

a. In the Server Manager window, under the **Network Policy and Access Services** object, select the **NPS (Local)** object.

b. In the **Standard Configuration** section, from the drop-down list, select the **RADIUS server for 802.1X Wireless or Wired Connections** option.

c. Read the description and then click the **Configure 802.1X** link.

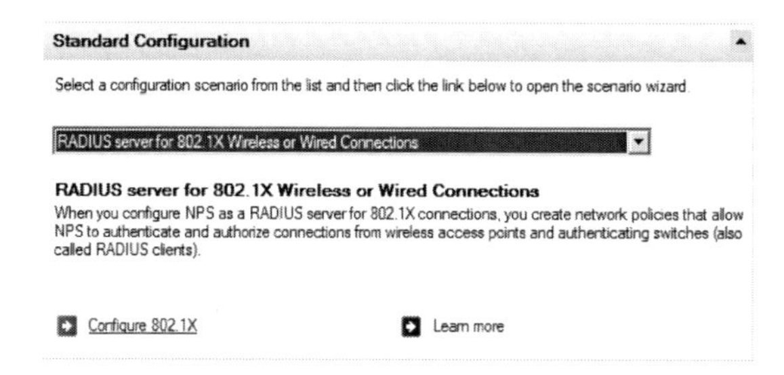

d. In the **Configure 802.1X** dialog box, in the **Type of 802.1X connections** section, select the **Secure Wireless Connections** option and click **Next.**

e. Verify that **My RADIUS Client** appears in the RADIUS clients list, and click **Next.**

f. On the **Configure an Authentication Method** page, from the **Type (based on method of access and network configuration)** drop-down list, select the **Microsoft: Secured password (EAP-MSCHAP v2)** option and click **Next.**

g. On the **Specify User Groups** page, click **Next.**

h. On the **Configure Traffic Controls** page, click **Next** and click **Finish.**

5. Verify the RADIUS port settings.
   a. In the Server Manager window, under the **Network Policy and Access Services** object, right-click the **NPS (Local)** object and choose **Properties.**
   b. In the **Network Policy Server (Local) Properties** dialog box, select the **Ports** tab.
   c. Verify that **1812,** the default port for RADIUS, is listed in the **Authentication** text field. After examining the other port settings, click **Cancel.**
   d. Close the Server Manager window.

Remote Control Protocols

There are several remote control protocols that can be used depending on the remote networking needs.

Remote Control Protocol	***Description***
Remote Desktop Protocol (RDP)	*RDP* is the backbone of Microsoft's Remote Desktop system. Its capabilities include data encryption, remote audio and printing, access to local files, and redirection of the host computer's disk drives and peripheral ports. In client versions 6.1 and later, any application that can be accessed via the normal remote desktop can serve as a standalone remote application. The server component, the terminal server, is available on most Windows operating systems, except for Windows Vista Home Edition, and a desktop client is available for most operating systems. The server listens on port 3389.
Virtual Network Computing (VNC)	*VNC* is a platform-independent desktop sharing system. VNC client and server software is available for almost any operating system (and for Java), so a VNC viewer on a Linux system can connect to a VNC server on a Microsoft system and vice versa. VNC uses the Remote Frame Buffer (RFB) protocol, which allows the client and server to determine the best version of RFB they can support during a session. VNC is not an inherently secure system, but does offer varying levels of password and content encryption, depending on the implementation.
Independent Computing Architecture (ICA)	The Citrix ICA protocol is a remote terminal protocol used by Citrix WinFrame and Citrix Presentation Server software as an add-on to Microsoft Terminal Services. ICA enhances and expands on the core thin-client functionality found in Terminal Services, and provides client support for additional protocols and services.
X Window system	The *X Window system* is a protocol that uses a client-server relationship to provide a GUI and input device management functionality to applications. Current X Window systems are based on the X11 protocol and normally used on UNIX- and Linux-based systems to display local applications. Because X is an open cross-platform protocol and relies on client-server relationships, remote connections are often easy to implement.

Remote Desktop Implementations

Remote control networking solutions include Windows Remote Desktop® and Remote Assistance®, Symantec pcAnywhere®, GoToMyPC®, LogMeIn®, WebEx PCNow®, various VNC clients and servers, Citrix XenApp®, and Apple Remote Desktop®.

Microsoft Windows Terminal Services

The technologies formerly known as Terminal Services were renamed Remote Desktop Services in Windows Server 2008 R2. Terminal Services is a client/server system that enables multiple clients to run applications or manage a server remotely. Terminal Services provides client access to all Windows-compatible applications by opening a user session on the Terminal Server. All application execution, data processing, and data storage is handled by the Terminal Server.

Microsoft's terminal emulation software can be installed on almost any Windows operating system, from Windows NT to Windows 7. Even handheld PCs running Windows CE can connect to a Terminal Server and run applications. Web-based access is also available. The low demands on the client have led a lot of companies to deploy Terminal Services as a way of extending the life of their outdated computers. It is possible for a Terminal Server to support hundreds of sessions simultaneously. Although the upfront investment may be high, organizations spend less money in upgrading equipment.

Citrix ICA Clients

Because of Citrix's digital independence, almost any device can be a Citrix client, including PC desktops, net appliances, web browsers, or mobile devices. Net appliances are dedicated thin clients that have a keyboard, mouse, and video, but no hard drives or CD-ROM drives. The net appliance's OS is embedded in a ROM chip, it has lower CPU power, and its job is to connect to a server. Even though it is a low-power device, it can run any application on the server.

Web browser support is provided through the Citrix NFuse® web server application. Websites that provide the applications are set up, and a client connects to the site with any ActiveX-enabled browser. Like a thin client on a LAN, the applications run on the web server and not on the browser. Mobile devices that use wireless connectivity services can access and run applications from laptops, cell phones, PDAs, or Windows Mobiles.

ACTIVITY 10-2

Enabling Remote Desktop Connections

This is a simulated activity available on the CD-ROM that shipped with this course. The activity simulation can be launched either directly from the CD-ROM by clicking the **Interactives** link and navigating to the appropriate one, or from the installed data file location by opening the C:\Data\Simulations\Lesson#\Activity# folder and double-clicking the executable (.exe) file.

Scenario:

You are a network administrator for OGC Advertising, a growing marketing company. In the past, you used telnet to manage and troubleshoot servers remotely. Since the company has grown, and you now have more dedicated servers, the decision has been made to manage and troubleshoot remotely using Remote Desktop, which is more secure than telnet.

Additionally, since Remote Desktop allows for creating and accessing files on the remote computer, accessing files on the server is more efficient. You now do not need to keep FTP ports open to transfer individual files. In this activity, you will enable Remote Desktop Connections on your workstation to connect to a partner's computer, which is simulating a dedicated file server running Windows Server 2008 R2.

---

1. Enable remote desktop connections.
   a. Browse to the C:\Data\Simulations\Lesson10\Activity10-2 folder.
   b. Double-click the executable file.
   c. In the **Open File - Security Warning** message box, click **Run.**
   d. Follow the on-screen steps for the simulation.
   e. Close the C:\Data\Simulations\Lesson10\Activity10-2 folder.

TOPIC B

Remote Access Networking Implementations

In the previous topic, you identified remote access networking. The different remote network architectures can be used for different implementations of remote networks. In this topic, you will identify various remote access networking implementations.

For many, connecting to a remote network while on the move is a way of life. From telecommuters to traveling sales representatives to a manager attending an annual conference, these remote users need a reliable way to access network services when they are not in an office environment. As a network professional, you need to recognize the components commonly used in remote access networking so that you can support your remote users.

Remote Access Protocols

Definition:

A *remote access protocol* enables a user to access a remote access server and transfer data. Remote access protocols can provide direct dial-in connections via modems, or they can provide connections via ISPs and the Internet. There are various remote access protocols such as PPP, PPPoE, and EAP that provide remote access.

Example:

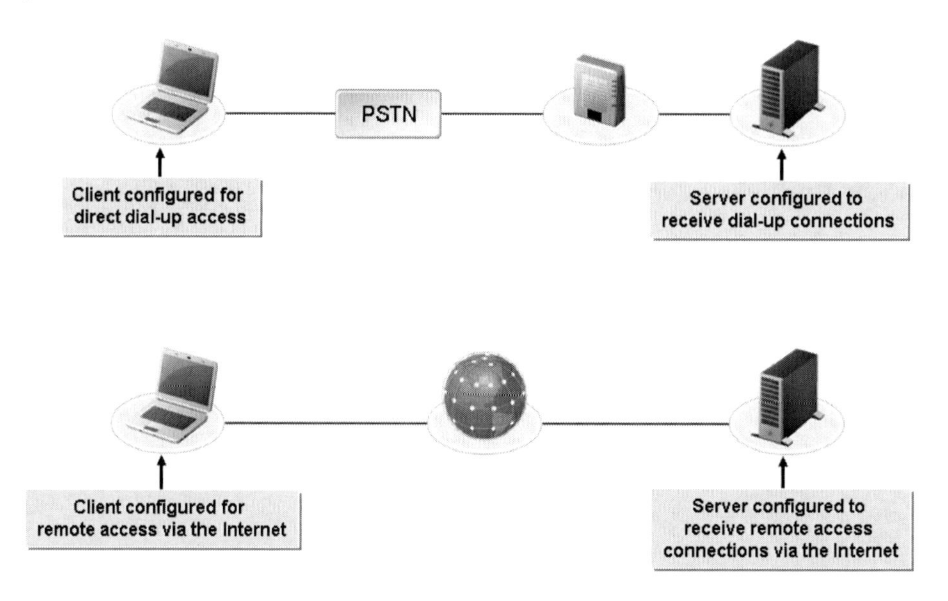

Figure 10-3: *A remote access protocol environment.*

PPP

The *Point-to-Point Protocol (PPP)* is a remote networking protocol that works on the Data Link layer of the TCP/IP protocol suite. It is used to send IP datagrams over serial point-to-point links. It can be used in synchronous and asynchronous connections. PPP can dynamically configure and test remote network connections, and is often used by clients to connect to networks and the Internet. It also provides encryption for passwords, paving the way for secure authentication of remote users. To log on to a remote session via PPP, you need to enable a remote authentication protocol.

The Point-to-Point Protocol over Ethernet (PPPoE) and Point-to-Point Protocol over ATM (PPPoA) are more recent PPP implementations used by many DSL broadband Internet connections.

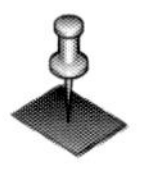

SLIP is a legacy remote access protocol used for sending IP data streams over serial lines such as modem or phone connections. In Windows Server 2008 R2, SLIP is automatically upgraded by the NOS to PPP.

PPP Variants

There are three commonly used variants of PPP: the PPPoE, Extensible Authentication Protocol (EAP), and Protected Extensible Authentication Protocol (PEAP).

Variant	*Description*
PPPoE	A standard that provides the features and functionality of PPP to DSL connections that use Ethernet to transfer signals from a carrier to a client. In addition, it contains a discovery process that determines a client's Ethernet MAC address prior to establishing a connection.
EAP	A protocol which is an extension of PPP and provides support for additional authentication methods, such as tokens, smart cards, and certificates.
PEAP	A protocol that secures EAP by creating an encrypted channel between a remote client and a server. PEAP can also be used with *Microsoft Challenge Handshake Authentication Protocol v2 (MS-CHAPv2)* to strengthen the protocol's password authentication.

Remote Access Authentication

To authenticate a remote session connection, you need to perform several steps.

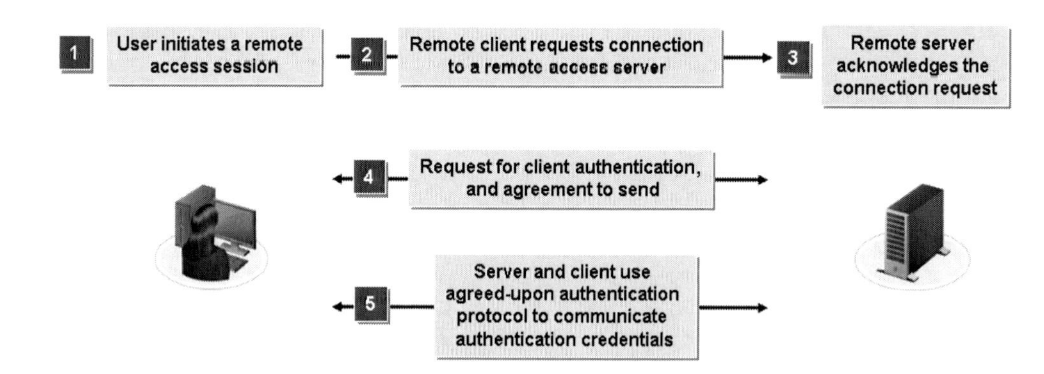

Figure 10-4: *Steps in the remote access authentication process.*

Step	***Description***
Step 1: Session initiation	A user initiates a session using a remote computer.
Step 2: Connection request	The remote computer requests a connection to a remote access server so that it can connect to another computer.
Step 3: Link establishment	The remote access server acknowledges the connection request, and establishes the physical link between the two computers.
Step 4: Client authentication	The remote access server requires the client to authenticate itself by using a remote authentication protocol. If the client does not agree to provide the requested authentication data, the server refuses to create a connection and the physical link is dropped. If the client agrees to send the authentication data, the server establishes a connection and authenticates the client.
Step 5: Authentication credentials communications	The server and client use the agreed-upon authentication protocol to communicate authentication credentials. If the server does not accept the authentication credentials provided by the client, the server closes the connection and drops the physical link. If the server accepts the authentication credentials provided by the client, the server allows the client to access resources.

Web-Based Remote Access

Web-based remote access implementations provide access to services and data via web browsers. A well-deployed web-based service allows clients to access web-based applications and data without any additional software installed on their system. However, proper security mechanisms should be in place when you use these implementations. Web-based remote access also allows administrators to manage application servers from remote locations. Web-based remote access applications require a higher configuration of web servers when clients access the server.

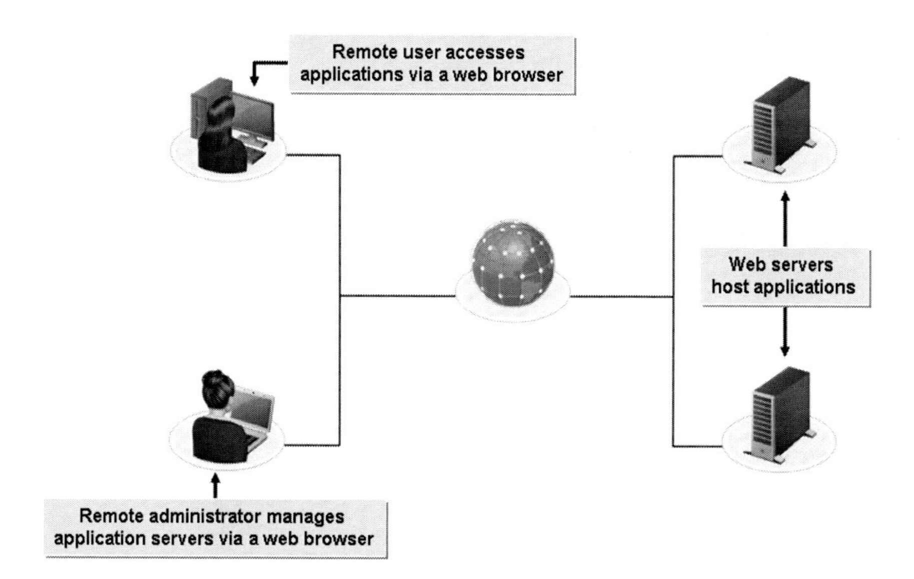

Figure 10-5: *Web-based remote access using a web browser.*

Web-Based Access in Windows

In Windows Server 2008 R2, Windows XP Professional, and Windows 7, web-based remote access is available through the Remote Desktop Web Connection (RDWC). The remote machine requires Internet Explorer 7 or higher, while the web server requires RDWC to be installed and running. RDWC is a component of IIS and is included with Windows Server and XP Professional, but must be downloaded separately for Windows 7.

Another web-based access feature in Windows Server 2008 R2 is called Web Interface For Remote Administration. Designed for remote management of application servers, it enables administrators to access a server from any computer running Internet Explorer 7 or higher. On the application server, which cannot be a domain controller, Web Interface For Remote Administration must be installed. Windows Server 2008 R2 can make use of the Remote Server Administration tools available for Windows 7.

ACTIVITY 10-3

Identifying Remote Access Networking Implementations

Scenario:

In this activity, you will identify various remote access networking implementations.

---

1. **EAP is an extension of:**
   a) PEAP
   b) CHAP
   c) PAP
   d) PPP

---

2. **Which of these statements about PPP are true?**
   a) Sends IP datagrams over serial point-to-point links.
   b) Works on the Physical layer of the TCP/IP protocol suite.
   c) Used for both asynchronous and synchronous connections.
   d) Provides secure authentication for remote users.

---

3. **What is the correct sequence of steps in the Remote Access Authentication Process?**

   Authentication credentials communication

   Client authentication

   Link establishment

   Connection request

   Session initiation

---

4. **Which remote access protocol is used with DSL connections?**
   a) PEAP
   b) PPP
   c) PPPoE
   d) EAP

TOPIC C
Virtual Private Networking

In the previous topic, you identified remote access networking protocols and implementations. In some organizations, the sheer number of remote users makes the implementation of traditional remote access networking cost-prohibitive. This is where a *Virtual Private Network (VPN)* comes into the picture. In this topic, you will identify the major components of VPN implementations.

Although standard dial-up implementations can still be found in some network environments, other considerations, such as security and the number of remote users to be supported, require additional measures to provide remote connections. When organizations opt to take advantage of public networks such as the Internet, the issue of securing data transmissions becomes critical. To counter the security risks associated with public networks, organizations implement a VPN within the public network to ensure secure communications. As a network professional, you need to recognize the components of VPN implementations to support remote users.

VPNs

Definition:

A *Virtual Private Network (VPN)* is a private network that is configured by *tunneling* through a public network such as the Internet. Because tunneling is used to encapsulate and encrypt data, VPNs ensure that connections between endpoints, such as routers, clients, and servers are secure. To provide VPN tunneling, security, and data encryption services, special *VPN protocols* are required.

Example:

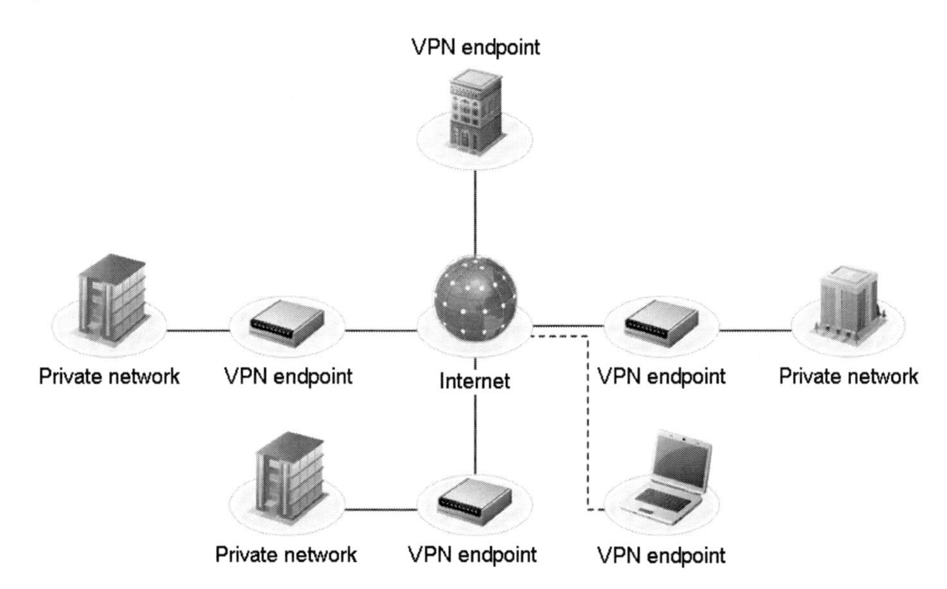

Figure 10-6: *VPN infrastructure makes a private network secure.*

Example:

Secure Socket Layer VPNs

A *Secure Socket Layer VPN (SSL VPN)* is a VPN format that works with a web browser—without needing the installation of a separate client. SSL ensures that the connection can be made only by using HTTPS instead of HTTP. This format works well in schools and libraries where easy access is required but security it still a concern.

Tunneling

Definition:

A *tunnel* is a logical path through the network that appears like a point-to-point connection. *Tunneling* is a data transport technique in which a data packet from one protocol, called the passenger protocol, is transferred inside the frame or packet of another protocol, called the carrier protocol. Tunneling enables data from one network to pass from one endpoint of a tunnel to the other through the infrastructure of another network. The carrier protocol can encapsulate and route nonroutable passenger protocols, or it can provide additional security by hiding passenger data from the carrier network.

Example:

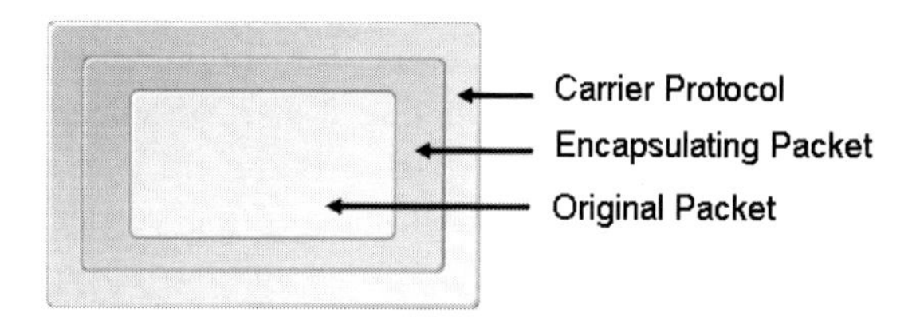

Figure 10-7: *Tunneling through a network.*

Tunnel Types

Essentially, there are two tunnel types: voluntary and compulsory.

- *Voluntary tunnels* are created between endpoints at the request of a client. When a user runs a software application that supports encrypted data communications, the client establishes an encrypted tunnel to the other end of the communication session, whether it is on a local network or the Internet.
- *Compulsory tunnels* are established by a WAN carrier with no involvement with client endpoints. Clients send data between endpoints, and all data is tunneled without affecting the client. Compulsory tunnels can be in place permanently (static), or they can be put in place based on the data or client type (dynamic).

VPN Types

VPNs can be one of three types depending on the network: Access, Intranet, and Extranet.

VPN Type	Description
Access VPNs	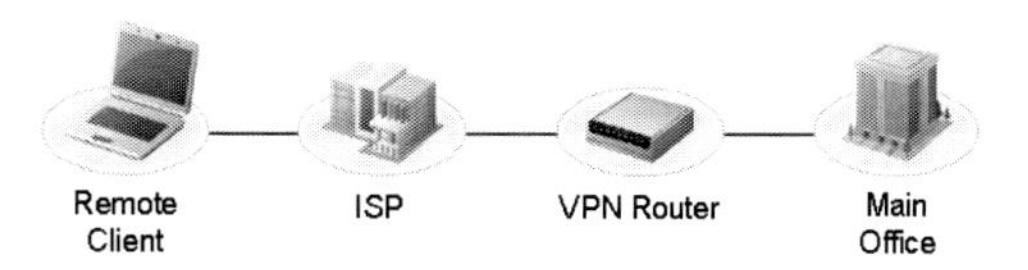 Provides remote access to single users via dial-up, ISDN, xDSL, or cable modem connections.
Intranet VPNs	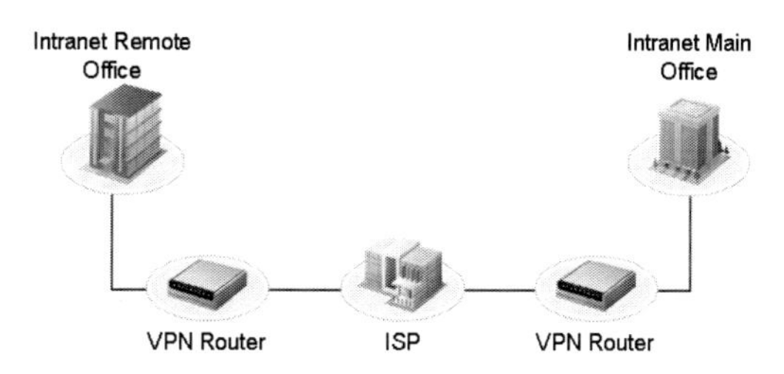 Connects sections of a network, such as remote offices tying into a corporate headquarters.
Extranet VPNs	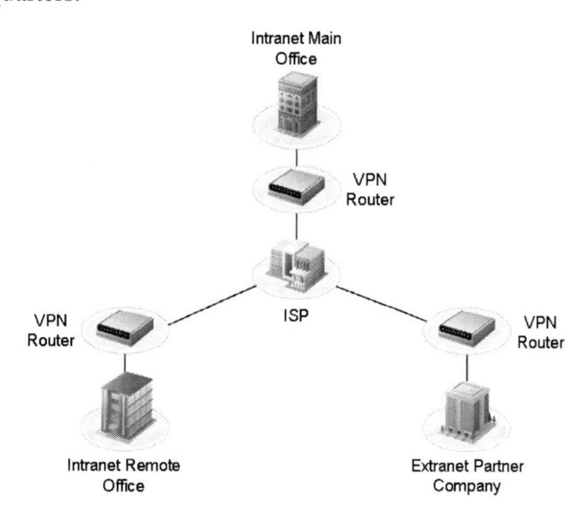 Connects networks belonging to different companies for the purposes of sharing resources.

VPNs can also be classified by their implementations.

Implementation	Description
Hardware-based	Uses hardware such as encrypting routers.
Firewall-based	Uses a firewall's security mechanisms.
Software-based	Uses software when VPN endpoints are not controlled by the same organization.

Advantages of VPNs

The two biggest reasons that most organizations implement VPNs are cost savings and data confidentiality. The cost of maintaining a VPN is generally lower than other remote access technologies. For instance, if a remote access technology depends on long-distance or toll-free calls, an organization's communication expenditure can become very high. Another reason for implementing VPNs is its versatility. One VPN endpoint connected to a T1 or T3 line through the service provider can accommodate hundreds of simultaneous connections from any type of client using any type of connection.

VPN Data Encryption

In most VPNs, data encryption is accomplished by either MPPE or IPSec.

Encryption Method	Description
MPPE	*Microsoft Point-to-Point Encryption (MPPE)* is often used with *Point-to-Point Tunneling Protocol (PPTP)*. It provides both strong (128-bit key) and standard (40- or 56-bit key) data encryptions. MPPE requires the use of MS-CHAP, MS-CHAPv2, or EAP remote authentication, because the keys used for MPPE encryption are derived from the authentication method.
IPSec	IPSec in Tunnel mode is often used with *Layer Two Tunneling Protocol (L2TP)*. Data encryption is accomplished by IPSec, which uses Data Encryption Standard (DES) or Triple DES (3DES) encryption to provide data confidentiality. IPSec can also be used on its own to provide both tunneling and encryption of data.

VPN Concentrators

Definition:

A *VPN concentrator* is a device that incorporates advanced encryption and authentication methods to handle a large number of VPN tunnels. It is geared specifically towards secure remote access or site-to-site VPNs. VPN concentrators provide high performance, high availability, and impressive scalability.

Example:

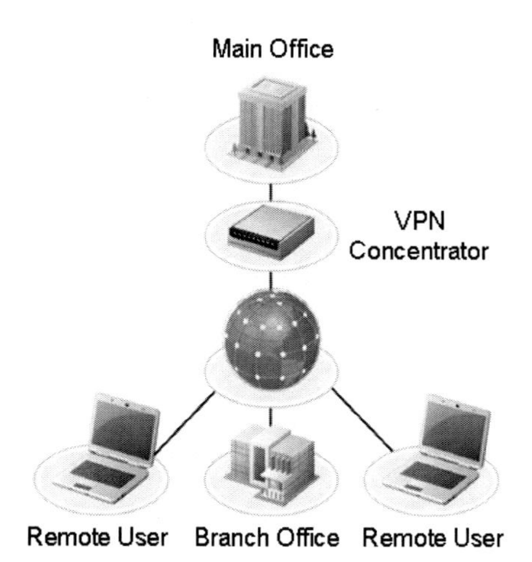

Figure 10-8: *A VPN concentrator used in a corporate environment.*

VPN Connection Models

VPNs can be connected in one of two VPN connection models: site-to-site or client-to-site.

Connection Model	*Description*
Site-to-site	In the site-to-site VPN connection model, each node on the network is connected to a remote network that may be separated by public or other unsecured networks. Site-to-site VPNs may be either open or closed. In case of an open site-to-site VPN connection, the exchange of data among nodes can be unsecured. In case of a closed site-to-site VPN connection, data can be communicated only using the VPN in a secure mode. In both types of VPNs, IPSec is implemented to ensure secure data transactions.
Client-to-site	In the client-to-site VPN connection model also, there are two types of networks—open and closed. In the case of an open VPN, the path between the end node and the IPSec gateway is not secured. In the case of a closed VPN, the path between the end node and the IPSec gateway is secured.

Onsite vs. Offsite

VPNs can also connect offsite to the virtual network components of VLANs or to other virtual networks that are onsite. The offsite components can also include proxy or reverse proxy servers.

ACTIVITY 10-4

Verifying VPN Configuration on RRAS

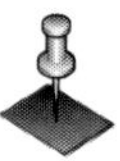

There is a simulated version of this activity available on the CD-ROM that shipped with this course. You can run this simulation on any Windows computer to review the activity after class, or as an alternative to performing the activity as a group in class. The activity simulation can be launched either directly from the CD-ROM by clicking the **Interactives** link and navigating to the appropriate one, or from the installed data file location by opening the C:\Data\Simulations\Lesson#\Activity# folder and double-clicking the executable (.exe) file.

Before You Begin:

1. Open the Server Manager window.
2. Verify that RRAS is running.

Scenario:

In this activity, you will verify VPN configuration on RRAS.

---

1. Verify that VPN support is enabled on the WAN Miniport that uses PPTP.

   a. In the Server Manager window, in the left pane, expand **Roles,** expand the **Network Policy and Access Services** object, expand the **Routing and Remote Access** object, and select the **Ports** object.

   b. In the **Actions** pane, click **More Actions** and then choose **Properties.**

   c. In the **Ports Properties** dialog box, select the WAN miniport that uses PPTP and click **Configure.**

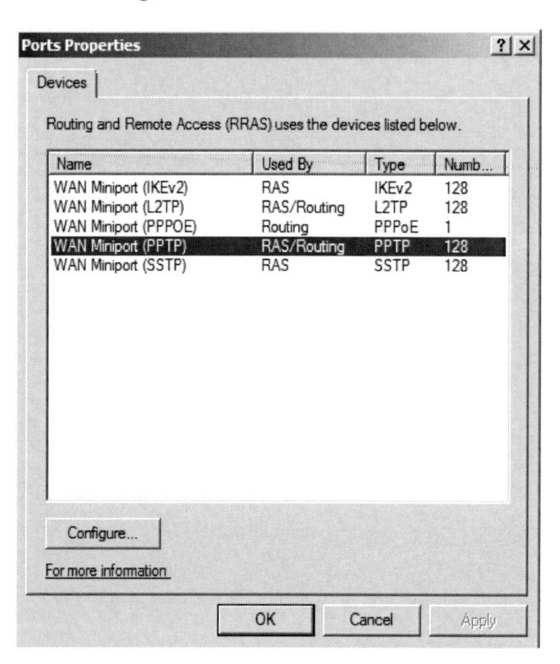

d. In the **Configure Device - WAN Miniport (PPTP)** dialog box, verify that the **Remote access connections (inbound only)** and **Demand-dial routing connections (inbound and outbound)** check boxes are checked and click **OK.**

2. Verify that VPN support is enabled on the WAN Miniport that uses L2TP.

   a. Select the WAN miniport that uses L2TP and click **Configure.**

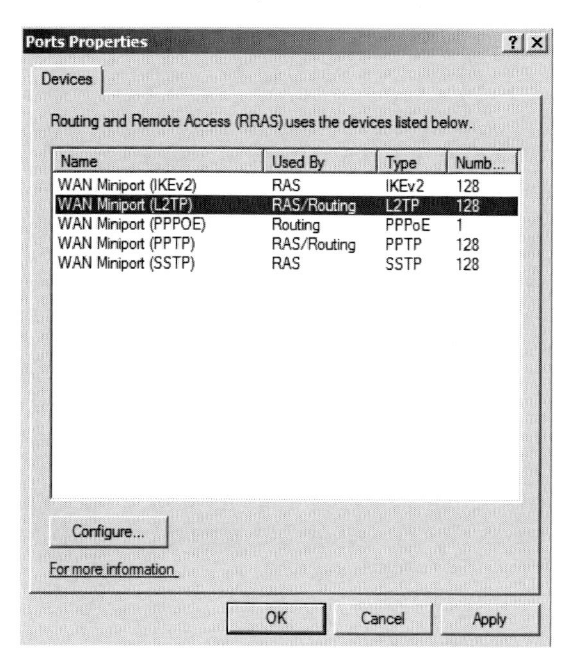

   b. In the **Configure Device - WAN Miniport (L2TP)** dialog box, verify that **Remote Access Connections (inbound only)** and **Demand-dial routing connections (inbound and outbound)** check boxes are checked and click **OK.**

   c. Verify that the **Used By** column for the two ports displays **RAS/Routing.**

   d. In the **Ports Properties** dialog box, click **OK.**

   e. Close the Server Manager window.

TOPIC D

VPN Protocols

In the previous topic, you identified the basic characteristics of VPNs. VPNs have additional data packet formatting and security requirements for which it uses specific protocols. In this topic, you will identify the protocols that are used on VPNs.

When using the public network as a channel for communication, organizations need to deploy additional layers of security to mitigate threats and attacks. VPNs have in-built protocols to address this security risk because one of the key benefits to implementing a VPN is the security provided by the protocols that it uses. As a network professional, you should be aware of VPN protocols and their characteristics. This background information will ensure that you will be able to implement VPNs successfully.

PAP

The *Password Authentication Protocol (PAP)* is a remote-access authentication method that sends client IDs and passwords as cleartext. It is generally used when a remote client is connecting to a non-Windows PPP server that does not support password encryption. When the server receives a client ID and password, it compares them to its local list of credentials. If a match is found, the server accepts the credentials and allows the remote client to access resources. If no match is found, the connection is terminated.

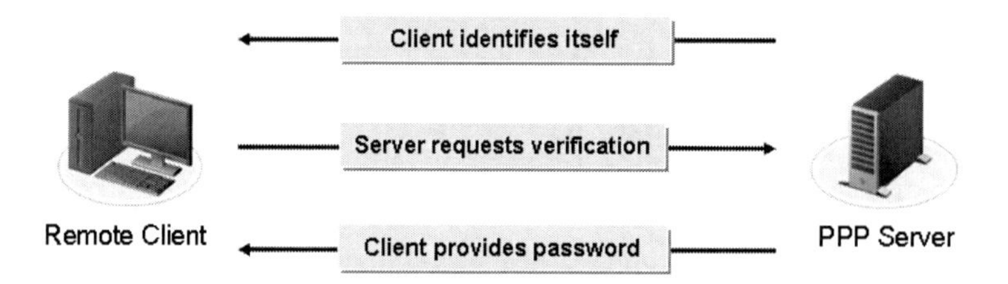

Figure 10-9: *PAP authentication of a client by a server.*

CHAP

The *Challenge Handshake Authentication Protocol (CHAP)* is a RAS protocol that uses an encryption method to transmit authentication information. Generally used to connect to non-Microsoft servers, CHAP was developed so that passwords would not have to be sent in plaintext. CHAP uses a combination of Message Digest 5 (MD5) hashing and a challenge-response mechanism, and authenticates without sending passwords as plaintext over the network.

MS-CHAP is a Microsoft extension of CHAP that is specifically designed for authenticating remote Windows workstations. MS-CHAPv2 provides all the functionality of MS-CHAP, and in addition provides security features such as two-way authentication and stronger encryption keys.

CHAP does not support PAP or Secure PAP unencrypted authentication.

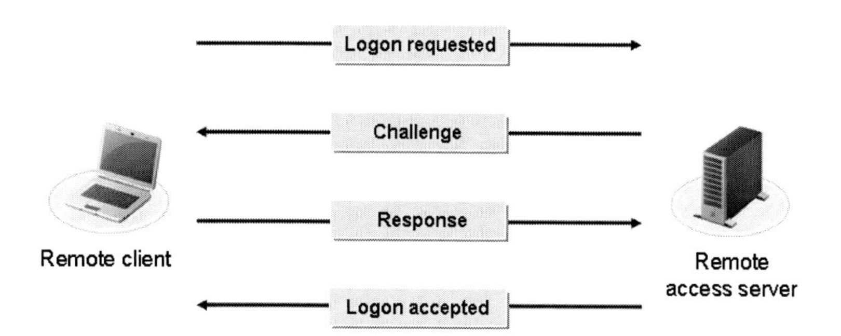

***Figure 10-10:** CHAP between a remote client and server.*

The Challenge-Response Authentication Process

In the challenge-response authentication process used in CHAP, the password is never sent across the network. The challenges that are tokens are encrypted.

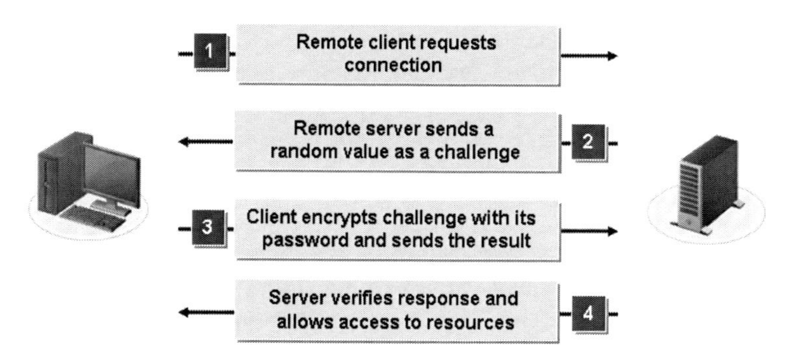

***Figure 10-11:** Steps in the CHAP process.*

Step	Description
Step 1: Client requests a connection	A remote client requests a connection to a RAS.
Step 2: Server sends the challenge sequence	The remote server sends a challenge sequence, which is usually a random value. This is to receive an acknowledgment from the client.
Step 3: Client encrypts the challenge sequence	The remote client uses its password as an encryption key to encrypt the challenge sequence and sends the modified sequence to the server.
Step 4: Server encrypts the challenge sequence and compares the results	The server encrypts the original challenge sequence with the password stored in its local credentials list and compares the results with the modified sequence received from the client. • If the two sequences do not match, the server closes the connection. • If the two sequences match, the server allows the client to access resources.

TACACS+

Terminal Access Controller Access Control System (TACACS) and *TACACS Plus (TACACS+)* protocols provide centralized authentication and authorization services for remote users. TACACS includes process-wide encryption for authentication while RADIUS encrypts only passwords. TACACS utilizes TCP rather than UDP and supports multiple protocols. Extensions to the TACACS protocols exist, such as Cisco's TACACS+ and XTACACS.

Features of TACACS+

TACACS+, which is Cisco's proprietary product, uses TCP port 49 and also supports multifactor authentication. TACACS+ is considered more secure and more scalable than RADIUS because it accepts login requests and authenticates the access credentials of the user. TACACS+ is not compatible with TACACS because it uses an advanced version of the TACACS algorithm.

PPTP

The *Point-to-Point Tunneling Protocol (PPTP)* is a layer 2 Microsoft VPN protocol that increases the security of PPP by providing tunneling and data encryption for PPP packets. It uses the same authentication methods as PPP, and is the most widely supported VPN protocol among older Windows clients. Deployed over public, unsecured networks such as the Internet, PPTP encapsulates and transports multiprotocol data traffic over IP networks.

L2TP

The *Layer Two Tunneling Protocol (L2TP)* is a protocol that works on the Internet and combines the capabilities of PPTP and Layer 2 Forwarding (L2F) to enable the tunneling of PPP sessions across a variety of network protocols, such as IP, Frame Relay, or ATM. L2TP was specifically designed to provide tunneling and security interoperability for client-to-gateway and gateway-to-gateway connections. L2TP does not provide any encryption on its own and L2TP packets appear as IP packets because, like IP packets, they also have a header, footer, and CRC. As a result, L2TP employs IPSec as the transport mode for authentication, integrity, and confidentiality.

L2TP has wide vendor support because it addresses the IPSec shortcomings of client-to-gateway and gateway-to-gateway connections.

SSTP

Windows Server 2008, Windows Server 2008 R2, Windows XP SP3, and Windows 7 support a new tunneling protocol, Secure Socket Tunneling Protocol (SSTP). SSTP uses the HTTP over SSL protocol. It encapsulates a data packet from IP with an SSTP header. The IP packet and SSTP header are encrypted by SSL. An IP header containing the destination addresses is then added to the packet.

ACTIVITY 10-5

Identifying VPN Protocols

Scenario:

In this activity, you will identify the characteristics of VPN protocols.

---

1. **Which statements are true of PAP?**

   a) Encrypts user credentials.

   b) Connects a remote client to a non-Windows PPP server.

   c) Updates its local list of credentials when it receives a new set of credentials on the server.

   d) Compares credentials from a remote client with local credentials to allow access to resources.

---

2. **Which of these is an encrypted authentication protocol that is used to connect to non-Microsoft servers?**

   a) MS-CHAP

   b) PPTP

   c) CHAP

   d) PAP

---

3. **Which statements are true of CHAP?**

   a) Sends passwords as plaintext.

   b) Used to connect to non-Microsoft servers.

   c) Does not send passwords as plaintext.

   d) Uses MD5 hashing.

---

4. **Match the protocol with its description.**

___	PPTP	a. Uses a challenge response mechanism.
___	TACACS+	b. Encapsulates and transports multiprotocol data traffic.
___	TACACS	c. Performs process-wide encryption using TCP.
___	CHAP	d. Combines the capabilities of PPTP and L2F.
___	L2TP	e. Supports multifactor authentication.

5. **Arrange the steps in the CHAP process in sequence.**

The remote client requests a connection to RAS.

The remote client uses its password as encryption key and sends the modified challenge sequence to the server.

The remote server sends a challenge response.

RAS encrypts the challenge sequence with the password stored in its local credential list.

Lesson 10 Follow-up

In this lesson, you identified the components of a remote network implementation. As a network professional, you will need to understand the technologies involved in remote network implementations so that you can implement them on your network to effectively support remote users.

1. **What are the solutions that you can use for remote networking?**

2. **Which of the remote networking protocols are you most likely to encounter in your network?**

085708 S3PB rev 1.1
ISBN-13 978-1-4246-1890-3
ISBN-10 1-4246-1890-8